SHAKESPEARE AND CHILDHOOD

This collection offers the first definitive study of a surprisingly underdeveloped area of scholarly investigation, namely the relationship between Shakespeare, children and childhood, from Shakespeare's time to the present. It offers a thorough, multi-perspectival mapping of the domain in which Shakespearean childhoods need to be studied, in order to show how studying Shakespearean childhoods makes significant contributions both to Shakespearean scholarship, and to the history of childhood and its representations. The book is divided into two sections, each with a substantial introduction outlining relevant critical debates and contextualizing the rich combination of new research and re-readings of familiar Shakespearean texts that characterize the individual essays. The first part of the book examines the complex significance of the figure of the child in the Shakespearean canon and within early modern theatrical and literary culture. The second part traces the rich histories of negotiation, exchange and appropriation that have characterized Shakespeare's subsequent relations to the cultures of childhood in the literary, educational, theatrical and cinematic realms.

KATE CHEDGZOY is Professor of Renaissance Literature at the University of Newcastle.

SUSANNE GREENHALGH is Principal Lecturer at the School of Arts, Roehampton University.

ROBERT SHAUGHNESSY is Professor of Theatre in the School of Drama, Film and Visual Arts at the University of Kent.

SHAKESPEARE AND CHILDHOOD

EDITED BY

KATE CHEDGZOY, SUSANNE GREENHALGH
AND ROBERT SHAUGHNESSY

CAMBRIDGE UNIVERSITY PRESS
Cambridge, New York, Melbourne, Madrid, Cape Town, Singapore, São Paulo

Cambridge University Press
The Edinburgh Building, Cambridge CB2 8RU, UK

Published in the United States of America by Cambridge University Press, New York

www.cambridge.org
Information on this title: www.cambridge.org/9780521871259

First published 2007

Printed in the United Kingdom at the University Press, Cambridge

A catalogue record for this publication is available from the British Library

ISBN 978-0-521-87125-9 hardback

Contents

Acknowledgements

We would like to thank the many people whose help has been material in the making of this book.

Participants in the 'Shakespearean Childhoods' seminar convened by Kate at the British Shakespeare Association conference in 2003, and in the conference organized by Susanne and Robert at Roehampton University in October of that year, 'Shakespeare's Children/Children's Shakespeares', played a key role in shaping the book's initial agenda and directions. The anonymous readers for Cambridge University Press subsequently helped us enormously in clarifying and developing what we thought the book was about. At the press, we appreciate everything Sarah Stanton has done to help us to make this the best book it could be. At the beginning and end of the project, we have benefited from Kim Reynolds's expert understanding of the relations between children and literature. Throughout the process, Kate Thorpe and Edel Lamb have been energetic, diligent and astute research assistants.

Kate would like to thank the participants in the 'Liminal Subjects: Children and Early Modern Drama' seminar, convened by Gina Bloom and Michael Witmore at the 2005 meeting of the Shakespeare Association of America, for helping her to think about children in early modern culture; she is grateful to Carol Rutter and Gina Bloom for reading and commenting on drafts of her contributions. Susanne is grateful to Victor Watson for help with her chapter.

Thanks are due to the British Academy, the School of Arts Research Committee, Roehampton University, and the Arts and Humanities Research Fund of Newcastle University for financial assistance.

Thanks to the Minack theatre for permission to use the cover image.

Finally, special thanks to our families, who have perhaps found childhood to be more Shakespearean than they might have anticipated or wished: Di Paton, Alistair Chisholm, Geof Ellingham, and Polly and Miriam Paton Chedgzoy; Alex Greenhalgh; and Nicola, Caitlin, Nathaniel, Gabriel and Erina Shaughnessy.

Notes on contributors

PASCALE AEBISCHER is Lecturer in Renaissance Studies at the University of Exeter. She is the author of *Shakespeare's Violated Bodies: Stage and Screen Performances* (2004) and principal editor of *Remaking Shakespeare: Performance Across Media, Genres and Cultures* (2003). She has written a number of articles on Shakespeare, performance, drama theory, nineteenth-century theatrical memoirs and Henry Green. She is currently writing a book on Jacobean drama (forthcoming, 2009) and researching the role played by Shakespeare in Victorian theatrical memoirs.

CATHERINE BELSEY is Research Professor in the English Department at the University of Wales, Swansea. Her books include *Critical Practice* (1980), *The Subject of Tragedy: Identity and Difference in Renaissance Drama* (1985), *Shakespeare and the Loss of Eden* (1999), and *Why Shakespeare?* (2007).

RICHARD BURT is Professor of English and Film and Media Studies at the University of Florida. He is the author of *Unspeakable ShaXXXspeares: Queer Theory and American Kiddie Culture* (1998) and co-author of *Movie Medievalism: Projecting the Past in Film and Media* (2007). Burt is also the editor of *Shakespeare After Mass Media* (2001) and *Shakespeares After Shakespeare: An Encyclopedia of the Bard in Mass Culture and Popular Culture* (2006) and co-editor of *Shakespeare, the Movie, II* (2003). He is presently finishing a book entitled *Alluding to Shakespeare: the Remains of the Play in Transnational Cinema and Television.*

KATE CHEDGZOY is Professor of Renaissance Literature at the University of Newcastle. She is the author of *Shakespeare's Queer Children: Sexual Politics and Contemporary Culture* (1996), and co-editor with Susanne Greenhalgh of a special issue of the journal *Shakespeare* on Shakespeare's incorporation into the cultures of childhood (2006). Her book *Women's Writing in the British Atlantic World: Memory, Place and History, 1550–1700* will be published by Cambridge University Press in 2007.

HATTIE FLETCHER is a freelance writer and the managing editor of the literary journal *Creative Nonfiction.* Formerly a middle-school Latin and English teacher, she is working on a manuscript about teaching and is pursuing an MFA in creative writing from the University of Pittsburgh.

SUSANNE GREENHALGH is Principal Lecturer in Drama, Theatre and Performance Studies at Roehampton University, London, where she also teaches Film and Media Studies. She has published many articles, on topics including children's literature in the media, children's drama, and Shakespeare on radio and television. She is currently researching a book, *At Home with Shakespeare*, on the experience and reception of Shakespeare in the domestic setting.

MARK LAWHORN is Assistant Professor of English in the Department of Languages, Linguistics, and Literature at the University of Hawaii-Kapiolani. He is the author of several articles on children and early modern English drama and is Vice-President of Children's Literature Hawaii.

NAOMI J. MILLER is Professor of English and Women's Studies at Smith College, Northampton, Massachusetts. In addition to books and articles on women writers in the Renaissance, her research and creative interests include Shakespeare for children. Her recent volume of essays, *Reimagining Shakespeare for Children* (2003), includes essays by children's book authors, Shakespeare scholars, and teachers of Shakespeare at all levels. She is currently working on a novel adapting Shakespeare's *The Tempest* for a young adult audience.

LUCY MUNRO is Lecturer in English at Keele University. Her publications include *Children of the Queen's Revels: A Jacobean Theatre Repertory* (Cambridge, 2005), an edition of Edward Sharpham's *The Fleer* (2006), and various essays on early modern drama. She is a contributing editor to the *RSC Complete Works of Shakespeare* and to forthcoming major editions of the works of James Shirley and Richard Brome.

MARIANNE NOVY is a professor of English and Women's Studies at the University of Pittsburgh. Her most recent books are *Imagining Adoption: Essays on Literature and Culture* (2001), an edited collection, and *Reading Adoption: Family and Difference in Fiction and Drama* (2005). She has also written *Love's Argument: Gender Relations in Shakespeare* (1984) and *Engaging with Shakespeare: Responses of George Eliot and Other Women Novelists* (1994), and edited three collections of essays on women's revisions of Shakespeare. Her current work is on Shakespeare's representations of outsiders.

PATRICIA PHILLIPPY is Professor of English at Texas A&M University. Her most recent publications are *Women, Death and Literature in Post-Reformation England* (Cambridge, 2002) and *Painting Women: Cosmetics, Canvases and Early Modern Culture* (2005). She is currently at work on an interdisciplinary study of the place of gender in the creation of funerary monuments and epitaphs in early modern England.

A. J. PIESSE is Senior Lecturer at Trinity College Dublin, where she works in the areas of Renaissance drama and children's literature. She has published articles variously on moral interludes, morality plays, the language of the Reformation, and Shakespeare; in the area of children's literature, she has written mostly on twentieth-century Irish writing and has a special interest in older people in books for children.

KATHRYN PRINCE is a Social Science and Humanities Research Council of Canada postdoctoral research fellow at Birkbeck, University of London. Her work on Shakespeare reception before the twentieth century has already yielded a PhD thesis and several forthcoming articles, and is the focus of her current research for a book entitled *England, France, and the Shakespeare Controversy from the French Revolution to World War I.* She is also writing the *Much Ado About Nothing* volume for Manchester University Press's *Shakespeare in Performance* series.

ROBERT SHAUGHNESSY is Professor of Theatre at the University of Kent. His publications include *Representing Shakespeare: England, History and the RSC* (1994), *The Shakespeare Effect: A History of Twentieth-Century Performance* (2002), and, as editor, *The Cambridge Companion to Shakespeare and Popular Culture* (2007).

Note on the text

Throughout this volume, unless otherwise specified, all references to Shakespeare's plays cite *The Norton Shakespeare, Based on the Oxford Edition*, ed. Stephen Greenblatt, Walter Cohen, Jean E. Howard and Katharine Eisaman Maus (New York: W. W. Norton, 1997).

1

Introduction

Robert Shaughnessy

On the front cover of this book is a detail from a photograph, taken in 1930, of a group of some thirty children in an amateur performance of *A Midsummer Night's Dream*, designed and directed by Rowena Cade for the open-air theatre at Minack in Cornwall.[1] Standing, crouching and kneeling before a woodland backdrop, some with arms draped over others' shoulders, others clutching garlands and long wands (excepting one figure towards the extreme left of the picture, who scowls at the camera, arms defiantly folded), these young persons range in age from preschool to teenage. Clad in home-sewn tights, tunics, acorn-cup headgear and (for Oberon and Titania) cloaks and ruffs, the members of this motley assembly of elves, sprites and pixies squint uncomfortably into the glare of an English sun that strips the sylvan scene of any vestige of nocturnal mystery or magic. Still, the broad provenance of this memento of Shakespearean performance is readily identifiable, even if the nature of the children's investment in the event it commemorates is not; it images a relationship between Shakespeare, childhood and performance that is liable to provoke a variety of reactions, ranging from indulgent amusement to faint nausea. On the one hand, the conjunction of the child, the fairy, performance and Shakespeare may evoke a lost time and space of naïve pleasure and innocent make-believe, a prospect to be contemplated with deep nostalgia, as befitting the *Dream*'s special status as the scene of many Shakespeare-lovers' first encounter with the Bard.[2] On the other hand, the stern faces of this particular cast of juveniles, which suggest that few of them are actually having much fun, may also remind us that the ideal of childhood performance to which the image alludes is a retrospective adult fantasy, one shaped not only by a careful monitoring and censorship of the less than child-friendly dimensions of Shakespeare's play, but also by a partial and selective understanding of the nature of childhood itself, of what it is and of what it is made to signify.

For those who believe that *A Midsummer Night's Dream*, and Shakespeare more generally, is for grown-ups, there is something faintly embarrassing about this vision of a performance vocabulary that is still current at the turn of the twenty-first century; while for those whose business it is to make the writer and his works available and attractive to the young, there is little in it to suggest that Shakespeare might be in any way cool. Stationed at the boundary of a dark forest which they are best off not to enter just yet, the children can be seen to occupy a threshold, or liminal, space more thoroughly overdetermined than either they or their photographer probably realized: costumed for the play but not yet engaged in performance of it, and thus inhabiting the realm between theatre and the everyday, between nature and nurturing culture, and between reality, desire and dreams, the child-as-fairy poses as an awkward, makeshift hybrid, epitomizing adult ambivalences about what to make of, and how to deal with, his or her beguiling and disquieting otherness.

One would not want to read too much into what is, after all, only a snapshot taken on the margins of Shakespearean performance history. But the mixed emotions that it involves may provide one kind of clue as to why, despite the complex and varied significances of the figure of the child in the Shakespearean canon and within early modern culture, and despite the rich histories of negotiation, exchange and appropriation that have characterized the works' subsequent relations to the cultures of childhood in the literary, educational, theatrical and cinematic realms, the subject matter of this volume has, until relatively recently, been a surprisingly underdeveloped area of scholarly investigation. As far as the first three centuries of Shakespearean criticism were concerned, the children in, behind or implied by Shakespeare's plays were intermittently seen but rarely heard about (and certainly not heard). Initially, the references to children and childhood were anecdotal, incidental or pejorative: Shakespeare's own boyhood and youth is briefly mentioned in Nicholas Rowe's biographical sketch of 1709, in the shape of the mythical episode of juvenile delinquency (deer poaching) that resulted in his departure from Warwickshire. For Alexander Pope, Shakespeare's youthful exuberance and inexperience accounts for the 'irregularity' of his drama, 'more like an ancient majestick piece of *Gothic* Architecture' than 'a neat Modern building', in which 'many of the parts are childish, ill-plac'd, and unequal to its grandeur'.[3]

The emergence of a conception of Shakespeare as a 'child of nature' towards the end of the eighteenth century, the formation of a new market of juvenile readers of Shakespeare, and the increasing importance of children and childhood more generally within the cultural imaginary, shifted the terms of reference to a certain extent, but even the Romantic critics demonstrated little sustained interest in the topic: Samuel Taylor Coleridge's musings on Shakespeare's 'fondness for children', for example, went no further than a brief manuscript note listing 'his Arthur; the sweet scene in the *Winter's Tale* between Hermione and the little prince; nay, even Evans's examination of Mrs Page's school-boy'.[4] Edmund Dowden's widely read and influential manual of Victorian Shakespearean interpretation, *Shakspere: A Critical Study of His Mind and Art* (1875), adopted an evolutionary approach to the author's development 'from youth to full maturity' but passed over his formative years fairly speedily, and refers to children in the plays themselves only once, in the form of a fatherly pat on the heads of the 'exquisite girlish figures' of the last plays, 'children who have known no sorrow, over whom is shed a magical beauty, an ideal light, while above them Shakspere is seen, as it were, bowing tenderly'.[5]

The high Victorian sentiment of this picture of idealized girlhood as the locus of embodiment of innocence, purity and grace hardly needs elaborating upon (and might be usefully contrasted with the appropriation of Shakespeare's girlhoods by earlier nineteenth-century writers such as Mary Cowden Clarke and Anna Jameson), but its legacy is still evident at the beginning of the twentieth century in the more restrained, though still pretty idealized, perception of the Shakespearean child that is offered in the criticism of Dowden's major immediate successor, A. C. Bradley. Pausing for a moment in his analysis of *Macbeth* in *Shakespearean Tragedy* (1904), Bradley remarks on the 'somewhat curious' appearance of 'Shakespeare's boys' in 'tragic or semi-tragic dramas', citing Arthur and Mamillius as examples of Shakespeare's 'power of pathos'; as a group, the boys are 'affectionate, frank, brave, high-spirited ... amusing and charming as well as pathetic; comical in their mingled acuteness and *naïveté*, charming in their confidence in themselves and the world, and in the seriousness with which they receive the jocosity of their elders'.[6] As far as Bradley and his contemporary readers were concerned, this was all that needed to be said on the topic of Shakespeare's children, but this did not stop him being taken to task in the early 1930s by L. C. Knights, who notoriously posed in rhetorical form the question that Bradley didn't ask ('How Many Children had Lady Macbeth?') in order to discredit what he saw as the kind of irresponsibly speculative, character-based criticism in which 'the detective interest supersedes the critical'.[7] The question is not worth debating, or even considering, because it is irrelevant to the task of working out how the Shakespearean text 'communicates a rich and controlled experience by means of words – words used in a way to which, without some training, we are no longer accustomed to respond';[8] the last thing the serious critic wants to be bothered by in this context is a group of pesky hypothetical kids. Even so, but not really surprisingly, the child also serves another rhetorical purpose in Knights's discourse, which is to act as a marker of the difference between naïve and sophisticated responses to the text: 'in school children are taught to think that they have "appreciated" the poet if they are able to talk about the characters'.[9]

Knights's polemical formalism is representative of a major strand of mid-twentieth-century criticism in terms of a preoccupation with dehumanized textuality seemingly at odds with the historical and cultural concerns that underpin this collection; though, as Carol Chillington Rutter observes, it is somewhat ironic that the critical text which is widely regarded as brilliantly exemplary of the New Critical method advocated by Knights (Cleanth Brooks's 'The Naked Babe and the Cloak of Manliness' (1947)) comprehensively demonstrates the centrality of infancy, children and childhood to the image structure of *Macbeth*.[10] In the past few decades, there has been a small but steady stream of articles and essays dealing with aspects of the relationship between Shakespeare, children and childhood, and early modern children have, from the early part of the twentieth century onwards, featured as historical subjects rather than metaphors in a number of works investigating the linked phenomena of the boy player and the chorister companies.[11] By and large, however, the critical and imaginative tradition which has engaged most directly and fully with the broadest spectrum of Shakespearean childhoods has been primarily addressed to young readers themselves, from the Lambs' *Tales from Shakespear* (1807) through to the school editions and related educational materials currently in widespread use. It is, I suggest, not coincidental that this pattern of critical production and consumption has historically tended to reflect a gender divide as well as a generational one. As Ann Thompson and Sasha Roberts point out in their introduction to an anthology of female-authored Shakespearean scholarship and commentary that spans the period from the late seventeenth to the nineteenth century, 'both in England and America, women were to play a large part in the growing "youth market" for Shakespeare in the nineteenth century, preparing juvenile editions and numerous adaptations of Shakespeare's "tales", with the aim of introducing and popularising Shakespeare's plays'. While this may partly reflect a traditionally patriarchal division of scholarly labour so that the production of child-centred or child-related materials falls within the purview of the woman's primary responsibility for homemaking and childrearing, female scholars also found opportunities to 'use their writing on Shakespeare to raise issues of particular concern to women', addressing 'subjects such as women's education, women's role in public life, and power relations between the sexes in society and in marriage'.[12] Viewed in this context, even Clarke's now notorious narrative elaborations in *The Girlhood of Shakespeare's Heroines* (1850) – which in their own time were critically well received – deserve to be read not only as naïvely novelistic concoctions of a nonexistent subtext but as attempts to engage constructively a Shakespeare who, as she put it, 'has seen most deeply into the female heart . . . has most vividly depicted it in its strength, and in its weakness'.[13]

In this respect, then, the convergence of intellectual enquiry, pedagogic intervention, creative appropriation, and social and political activism, which in the work of nineteenth-century women Shakespearean scholars manifests itself in materials both concerned with childhood and produced for children, provides an important (and only recently acknowledged) precursor of the project of late twentieth-century feminism, which is itself one of the shaping theoretical, critical and political contexts of this collection. Childhood, and its developmental relation to the construction of adult gender and sexual identities, has been an implicit concern of modern feminist scholarship since its moment of emergence in the early 1980s, in a variety of forms: in psychoanalytic criticism, which has anatomized and interrogated Shakespearean representations of masculinity and femininity by means of a Freudianism reread in the light of Jacques Lacan, Julia Kristeva and others;[14] in studies which have scrutinized the sexual ambiguity of the 'boy actress';[15] and, more recently, in a developing body of work which, as Catherine Belsey puts it, seeks 'to historicize and thus denaturalize family values' by investigating 'the story of the nuclear family . . . from romance through marital conflict to parenthood and the relations between the children'.[16] The chapters in this collection build upon these areas of investigation, elaborating their established emphases on ideology, power and sexuality, through a focus on children and childhoods, both actual and imaginary, early modern and more recent. They respond to recent scholarship which reassesses performance by the young in Renaissance culture, and in royal and aristocratic households as well as the boy and adult companies. There is an equal attention to the current strong interest in manifestations of Shakespeare in popular, visual and media culture, from the eighteenth century to the present day, and in a range of genres, from children's books and magazines, to theatrical memoirs, documentary and animated films, and tie-in Shakespeare products.

The volume's dual concern with the historical origins and contexts of Shakespearean childhoods and their continuing history of cultural reinvention is reflected in its two-part structure. The chapters in the first part, 'Shakespeare's children', all address, from various angles, the questions of what being a child might have meant, both to children, and to adult others, during this period, and of how these meanings were reflected, constructed and negotiated by children both as the subjects and the agents of fictional, theatrical and poetic representation. As Kate Chedgzoy points out in her introduction to part 1, the marginality – bordering on invisibility – of early modern children in many existing accounts of Shakespeare's England and its drama needs to be drastically rethought in the light of 'evidence for early modern children's cultural presence and agency', including both the material artefacts they made and used and the work they performed, which is 'richer and more extensive' than has previously been thought (p. 28); the chapters that follow utilize that evidence, as well as the evidence of plays, poems and other literary and visual texts, to begin to recover the hidden history they trace. Reading the conventions for theatrically invoking childhood alongside the evolving techniques of children's portraiture during the early seventeenth century, Catherine Belsey examines the particularity of Shakespeare's own contribution to the emergence of a recognizably modern conception of the loving nuclear family, wherein childhood incrementally acquires 'a life of its own', having previously been 'barely visible ... as a distinctive state of being' (p. 33).

The idea that boundaries between childhood and adulthood are both porous and ambiguous in Shakespeare's works is also explored, from the standpoint of affective relations within the family, and between fathers and daughters in particular, in Hattie Fletcher and Marianne Novy's chapter, which identifies a recurrent trope of paternal loss that is both biographically and culturally resonant, in the context of a drama in which, 'for parents ... the relationship to their children is dramatized as crucial to their identity' (p. 49). In A. J. Piesse's chapter, which addresses the subject of Renaissance education, Shakespeare's children are discussed as textual constructs whose identities, and roles within both the historical narratives and the dramas they inhabit, are fashioned within the discourses of early modern pedagogy, in an examination of 'the dramatic significance of the relationship between school texts, texts of formation, the process of history and the child figure' (p. 64). Drawing upon the evidence of the performance practices of the late sixteenth and early seventeenth century children's companies, in relation to the complex dynamics of the juvenile impersonation of adult masculinity, Lucy Munro offers a reading of *Coriolanus* as a play in which Shakespeare 'attempts to overwrite children's performance', especially those recently seen at the Blackfriars playhouse for which it was written, 'picking up and reworking certain aspects of children's performance, specifically their tradition of satiric detachment and their exploitation of the distance between actor and role' (p. 84). The section concludes with Patricia Phillippy's investigation of the significance, both literal and metaphorical, of images of procreation, infant mortality and mourning in two contrasting sonnet sequences: Shakespeare's, and Anne de Vere's 'Foure Epytaphes'. In both, Phillippy argues, gender identity is specifically 'predicated upon procreation and child-loss', and in this respect the sequences are deeply indicative not only of 'early modern formulations of gender in relation to absent children' (p. 97) but also of the struggle between the competing conceptions of masculine and feminine reproductive and textual creativity, parenthood and authorship that they encode.

The essays in the second part of the volume, 'Children's Shakespeares', selectively address the cultural history of the relationship between Shakespeare(s) and childhood(s) from a period spanning the eighteenth century to the present. In her introduction to this section, Susanne Greenhalgh contextualizes the case studies that follow by outlining the ways in which Shakespeare and the cultural construction of childhood have been interlinked since the early modern period, with a particular emphasis on the ideological purposes to which these relationships have been put, as the place of children in society has changed. As Naomi J. Miller demonstrates in her survey of two centuries of Shakespearean adaptations for children, which charts a shift from a pedagogy of moral improvement to more recent 'child-centred' notions of play, changing expectations of the nature and limits of children's agency during this period have been vividly reflected through the tactics of textual abridgement and adaptation, and illustration and exposition, adopted by authors, artists and educators. One of the key instruments for disseminating Shakespeare's works throughout popular culture, and to child readers in particular, during the Victorian period was the children's periodical, and in her essay on this publishing tradition Kathryn Prince traces the strategies through which they not only made Shakespeare available in a popular and accessible form, but also contributed to his, and its, role in 'the formation of English national identity', whereby a 'growing sense of Shakespeare's centrality and importance was transmitted in the nineteenth century beyond the purview of gentlemen, scholars and poets to members of society who might never choose to read poetry or literary criticism' (p. 153). The cultural heritage of Victorian Shakespeare also informs Pascale Aebischer's chapter, which examines the iconic centrality of Shakespeare within the autobiographical self-fashionings of two members of Edwardian England's leading theatrical dynasties, Ellen Terry and Edward Gordon Craig, and, by extension, 'Shakespeare's role in shaping the narratives of the childhood and adolescence of these nineteenth-century theatre practitioners', which is seen to constitute 'the very way personal experience is conceptualized and the experience of growing up is understood' (p. 169).

The final three chapters in the volume focus upon more recent examples of, and current concerns about, the relations between Shakespearean childhoods, media and cultural forms. Situating Shakespeare within children's literature, Kate Chedgzoy examines how his iconic presence has functioned within a number of recent novels to explore the performance of boyhood, in a context of considerable cultural and social anxiety about it. In a reading of Susan Cooper's *King of Shadows* (1999), which, as one of the most intriguing recent examples of the genre of Shakespeare-related fictions, attempts to bridge the gap between the modern and the early modern through the device of time travel, Chedgzoy shows how a Shakespearean reframing of contemporary boyhood can enable more open and diverse ways of thinking about this contested and contentious phase of childhood. Susanne Greenhalgh's chapter, which locates the screen history of *A Midsummer Night's Dream* within the modern traditions – and conceptualizations – of child performance, demonstrates how 'attending to child actors of Shakespeare, as well as to their roles, reveals how the shifting constructions of childhood current in different eras have been refracted, and perhaps reformulated, through Shakespearean performance' (p. 201).

Shakespeare's exhaustingly constant (re)mediatization in ever-more unexpected cultural forms and contexts, including cartoons and sitcoms aimed at young viewers whose acquaintance with the works of Shakespeare is, at best, partial and fragmentary and, more typically, defined by incomprehension, indifference or derision, is the subject of Richard Burt's chapter, which investigates Shakespeare's position 'between ('tween) media markets' as well as describing the 'new space that Shakespeare inhabits between childhood and adolescence, namely the tween (no apostrophe), a space that marks the fluidity of both terms that flank it'. Citing a variety of media texts in which Shakespeare remains – sometimes bafflingly – present as a cultural marker and reference point, Burt suggests that 'tween' culture 'has increasingly destabilized and even collapsed the distinction between child and adult'. Thus 'what emerges in the tween market is less the disappearance of childhood than the disappearance of adulthood: the tripartite distinction between child, teenager and adult is displaced by a new tripartite distinction between child, tween and teenager' (p. 219). Finally, in Appendix 1, Mark Lawhorn provides a detailed and comprehensive listing and categorization of the children in Shakespeare's plays, a taxonomy which, as Lawhorn proposes, 'is meant to suggest a generous range of performance possibilities' (p. 233).

There is, it seems, a world of difference between the iconic naïvety of the photographic image of Shakespearean childhood performance with which I began this introduction and the hypermediatized world of media cool invoked in Burt's chapter; whether this is to be judged a matter for mourning or for celebration is perhaps a matter of both personal taste and generational positioning. Looking again at the monochrome image of the 1920s English children's *A Midsummer Night's Dream*, I am struck by its inadvertent pathos, a sadness that proceeds in part, from what Susan Sontag once defined as any photograph's status 'as a message from time past', irrefutably redolent of 'another person's (or thing's) mortality, vulnerability, mutability',[17] and is compounded by the awareness that three-quarters of a century on from the moment it captures, even the youngest of its participants is more likely than not to have achieved an immateriality far more enduring, than that of a stage fairy. In its own way the photograph quite precisely encapsulates some of the dynamics of the different ways of researching Shakespearean childhoods that are explored in this book. It is enormously rich and resonant as a screen for adult projections; but one could also, if so inclined and given time, try to excavate the historical child subjects posed in it, what they thought of the whole thing, what became of them subsequently, what cultural and pedagogic role amateur performance played in the lives of early twentieth-century middle-class English white children, and so on. I am also aware, or hope I am aware, of a sense of optimism, born out of the conviction not only that the collective act of performance, like the makeshift and temporary experience of being magically, Shakespeareanly, other, is a significant marker in a young life that is worthy of fond record, but also that it participates in an unofficial history of make-believe in which the relationships between play, role-play and a play are rather more fluent and flexible than an allegedly more mature and sophisticated understanding of Shakespearean theatre would seem to demand. In this respect, as in others, the spectacle of the performing, and not-quite-performing, Shakespearean child may well prompt us to think again about the adult theatres, and cultures, that he or she both does, and does not, mimic, and may or may not eventually inhabit. If, as the essays in this collection richly demonstrate, there is much in the topic of Shakespeare and childhood to be discovered and revisited, its capacity to make us take another look at the meanings of adulthood, Shakespearean and otherwise, is by no means the least of it. But it is the agency of Shakespeare's children, and of the children who have continued to engage Shakespeare in performance, in reading and conversation, and through the arts of the imagination, that are the focus of this book.

NOTES

1 For an account of the work at Minack, see Michael Dobson, 'Shakespeare Exposed: Outdoor Performance and Ideology, 1880–1940', in Peter Holland, ed., *Shakespeare, Memory and Performance* (Cambridge: Cambridge University Press, 2006), pp. 256–77. Many thanks to Michael Dobson for bringing this picture to our attention.

2 To take a pair of examples immediately to hand, the Arden 2 and Oxford editions of this play, which are otherwise scrupulously adults-only, both anchor their introductions in childhood reminiscence: thus Harold Brooks records his 'first experience of theatre: a matinee of Granville Barker's famous production, to which at the age of seven I was taken by my aunts' (The Arden Shakespeare, *A Midsummer Night's Dream* (London: Methuen, 1979), p. ix); while Peter Holland, similarly, recalls it as 'the first Shakespeare play that I can remember seeing ... Peter Hall's production in Stratford in 1959 when I was eight' (The Oxford Shakespeare, *A Midsummer Night's Dream* (Oxford: Oxford University Press, 1994), p. v). Rarely is the boyhood of Shakespeare's editors and critics, a Barrie-esque world of aunts and special theatre trips, so directly – and longingly – evoked.

3 Alexander Pope, 'Preface to *The Works of Shakespeare*' (1725), in D. Nichol Smith, ed., *Eighteenth Century Essays on Shakespeare* (Oxford: Clarendon Press, 1963), p. 58.

4 Samuel Taylor Coleridge, 'Shakespeare's Children: The Correct Master', in Terence Hawkes, ed., *Coleridge on Shakespeare* (Harmondsworth: Penguin, 1969), p. 274.

5 Edmund Dowden, *Shakspere: A Critical Study of His Mind and Art* (1875; London: Routledge and Kegan Paul, 1967), pp. xiii, 93.

6 A. C. Bradley, *Shakespearean Tragedy*, 4th edn, ed. Robert Shaughnessy (Basingstoke: Palgrave, 2006), pp. 302–3. In a footnote to this passage, Bradley – who is usually strenuously averse to biographical speculation – invokes the spectre of Shakespeare's son Hamnet, a dead child who has continued to exercise a remarkable grip on the modern critical imagination.

7 L. C. Knights, 'How Many Children had Lady Macbeth?', in Knights, *Explorations* (1946; Harmondsworth: Peregrine Books, 1964), p. 15.

8 *Ibid.*, p. 16.

9 *Ibid.*

10 See Cleanth Brooks, 'The Naked Babe and the Cloak of Manliness', in Brooks, *The Well Wrought Urn* (New York: Harcourt Ltd., 1947), pp. 22–49, and Carol Chillington Rutter, 'Remind Me: How Many Children had Lady Macbeth?', *Shakespeare Survey* 57 (2004), 38–53.

11 See, for example, H. N. Hillebrand, *The Child Actors: A Chapter in Elizabethan Stage History* (Urbana: University of Illinois Press, 1926).

12 Ann Thompson and Sasha Roberts, 'Introduction', *Women Reading Shakespeare 1660–1900: An Anthology of Criticism* (Manchester: Manchester University Press, 1997), pp. 3, 5.

13 Mary Cowden Clarke, 'Shakespeare – Studies of Women', *The Ladies Companion* (1849–54), p. 25, quoted in *ibid.*, p. 82.

14 See, for example, Coppélia Kahn, *Man's Estate: Masculine Identity in Shakespeare* (Berkeley: University of California Press, 1981); Marianne Novy, *Love's Argument: Gender Relations in Shakespeare* (Chapel Hill: University of North Carolina Press, 1984); and Janet Adelman, '"Born of Woman": Fantasies of Maternal Power in *Macbeth*', in Shirley Nelson Garner and Madelon Sprengnether, eds., *Shakespearean Tragedy and Gender* (Bloomington: Indiana University Press, 1996).

15 See Phyllis Rackin, 'Androgyny, Mimesis, and the Marriage of the Boy Heroine on the English Renaissance Stage', *PMLA* 102 (1987), 29–41; Stephen Orgel, *Impersonations: The Performance of Gender in Shakespeare's England* (Cambridge: Cambridge University Press, 1996); and Michael Shapiro, *Gender in Play on the Shakespearean Stage: Boy Heroines and Female Pages* (Ann Arbor: University of Michigan, 1996).

16 Catherine Belsey, *Shakespeare and the Loss of Eden: The Construction of Family Values in Early Modern Culture* (Basingstoke: Palgrave, 1999), pp. xiv, xv.

17 Susan Sontag, *On Photography* (Harmondsworth: Penguin, 1977), pp. 9, 16.

PART I

Shakespeare's children

2

Introduction: 'What, are they children?'

Kate Chedgzoy

I

I begin with a child at the margin of childhood: Miranda, Prospero's daughter, barely fifteen years old, newly embarked on the transition from childhood to adulthood that for many girls in Shakespeare's works and world was enacted and marked by the ritual of marriage. Awaiting the formal solemnization of her marriage to Ferdinand, Miranda watches a wedding masque that uses music, poetry and dance to celebrate the life-changing event ahead of her (*The Tempest* 4.1.60–138). Her father enjoins her (and Ferdinand) to watch the masque in silence (4.1.59), and she obeys; but tongue-tied submissiveness is not her customary mode. We already know that she can use words to give a vivid and dramatic account of an event she witnessed (1.2.1–13), to conjure up an emotional evocation of the personal past (1.2.44–7), and to express desire (3.1.53–7). She has enabled her quasi-sibling Caliban to acquire eloquent speech (1.2.354–65), and she has challenged her father's expressions of hostility to Ferdinand (1.2.477, 485–7). Declaring to Ferdinand, 'I am your wife, if you will marry me' (3.1.83), she has already revealed herself to be confident and subversive enough to take control of the event that initiates her formally into adulthood, embarking on an exchange that could be considered to constitute a marriage ceremony mutually and legitimately undertaken by husband and wife. As far as Miranda knows, she is committing herself to her adult future in a space outside of patriarchal control; yet the audience is aware of Prospero as a concealed onlooker onstage, confirming the father's continuing presence in the daughter's life.[1]

Now let us imagine Miranda putting all those qualities to work in writing and staging her own dramatic spectacles. This Miranda will be a figure not unlike Lady Rachel Fane, who in her early teens scripted and staged domestic performances at her Northamptonshire home, Apethorpe, with youthful casts drawn from her siblings and servants in the household. Inscribing traces of many children's voices, the texts which document these performances include a May masque, probably staged in 1627 when Rachel was fourteen, which has some attributes of the wedding masque genre.[2] It is not known whether Rachel Fane had any direct familiarity with Shakespeare's works, but her masque features many evocatively Shakespearean elements: the use of a clown figure (the jester) who mediates between performance and audience (recalling *King Lear* and *Twelfth Night*); a pastoral/woodland setting (*As You Like It*, *A Midsummer Night's Dream*, *The Winter's Tale*); seasonal festive performance (*Dream*, *The Winter's Tale*); liminal begging of the audience's favour and appreciation (*As You Like It*, *Dream*, *The Tempest*); Virgilian allusion (*The Tempest*, among others). Equally Shakespearean is the inclusion of metatheatrical elements, dance and music. Shakespeare's representation in *The Tempest* of a girl whose departure from childhood is marked by a wedding masque resonates with Rachel's masque, composed by another aristocratic daughter poised, like Miranda, at this liminal stage of life, hesitating on the margins between childhood and adulthood.[3]

As performance event and text, Rachel's May masque uniquely documents crucial elements of early modern childhood and adolescence as stages of life and ways of being in the world. It touches on many important themes in the history of childhood and its representations, themes that recur throughout this book. These include the family and household; relations with other children and with adults, within and beyond the family; work, which played an enormously significant role in the lives of early modern children, in the home and in formal workplaces, as part of a family economy or as waged labour; play, seen as of crucial significance to childhood (Montaigne remarked that 'children's playes are not sports and should be deemed as their most serious actions');[4] formal education, largely directed at the children of the elite in this period; the boundaries of childhood, and transitions to other life-stages; the tensions between children's sense of themselves as subjects and adult perceptions of them, associated with the fundamental questions of what constitutes childhood and what it means to be a child; and the gendering of childhood.

Providing a youthful view of these powerful aspects of childhood experience, Rachel's masque both speaks to the representation and construction of childhood, and offers rare insights into how early modern children might have understood themselves as agents and subjects in a world made primarily by and for adults. As a female-authored document emerging from the social world of childhood, it valuably counterpoints this book's central concern with representations of girls and boys produced by an adult man. Playfully evoking the possibility of children's cultural agency, the May masque offers a rare child-authored perspective on the early modern world. It thus serves as an apt point of departure for an essay which seeks to situate the discussions of Shakespearean childhoods that follow in the first part of this book in relation to the developing body of knowledge and methodological strategies that can enable us to make sense of the lives and representations of children in the world Shakespeare inhabited, and the plays and poems he wrote about it.

II

'Childhood as an analytical term . . . is too familiar,' reflects the social historian Anna Davin.[5] She argues that it is hard to establish the critical distance that would make it possible to analyse childhood effectively, because '[w]e have all been children; we all know children; some of us have had children, brought them up or taught them'. But this apparent familiarity is deceptive, as the controversial and contested status of childhood in contemporary debate makes plain.[6] Varying across time and place, childhoods are multiple and contingent, and they elude easy scrutiny and interpretation.

Hamlet's question about the boy actors, 'What, are they children?' (*Hamlet* 2.2.331), has a productively defamiliarizing effect in drawing attention to the fundamental difficulty of making sense both of children as subjects, and of childhood as a cultural concept and social formation. Addressing Hamlet's question, and meditating on the implications for children and the cultures they inhabit of the many possible answers to it, is the province of the multidisciplinary field of childhood studies, which 'concerns itself with the nature of childhood experience and with ways cultures construct and have constructed childhood'.[7] But where this field has so far tended to concentrate on studying childhood in the modern world, early modern literary studies has the capacity to extend its insights and analytical scope in new directions. Focusing on Shakespeare, whose figurations of childhood have had such enduring resonance, this book suggests some of the directions such research might take.

Of fundamental importance for childhood studies are the closely connected questions of how childhood is to be defined and how children are to be known, perceived and enabled to articulate their own kinds of knowledge. Equally critical is the question of the nature, availability and overdeterminations of the sources and resources for studying childhood. This chapter has already highlighted the value of examining literary representations and children's own writings. Previous work on early modern children and childhood has made use of diverse forms of evidence in addition to these, including visual materials, drawn from both popular and elite culture; material culture – the artefacts of childhood, especially toys; life-writings in which adults recollect their own childhood or report on their offspring; didactic works, such as medical and educational texts; and more public and formal kinds of sources, such as legal and welfare records. Central to the selection and interpretation of these and other kinds of sources is a constant awareness of the dual responsibility to consider how we can access both the cultural significance of the representation of children by adults, and children's own perspectives on their world. This book focuses primarily on the first of these concerns, of course; yet in reexamining Shakespeare's figurations of childhood, we may find clues to the kinds of questions we need to ask of these and other sources in order to enrich our understanding of a child's view of the early modern world.

The sources and debates pertinent to the study of Shakespearean childhoods are framed by the fields of Shakespeare criticism and the history of childhood. Robert Shaughnessy's introduction to this volume summarized the first of these; here I offer some waymarkers in relation to the second. Inaugurated by Philippe Ariès's truly agenda-setting *Centuries of Childhood* (1960), for many years the history of early modern childhood was dominated by contention arising from that book's concern with what constituted recognizably modern notions of childhood, and when they emerged.[8] In this extended debate the object of study was in fact not childhood so much as parenthood, for the question of childhood was reduced to one of adult perceptions of children, the family was privileged as the most important frame for interpreting children's lives, and children's perspectives were largely ignored. The family was undoubtedly uniquely important as a place where early modern childhood was lived out and its meanings negotiated.[9] But those experiences and meanings need to be considered from the point of view of children, as well as parents, in a context which does not seek to circumscribe the domain of childhood within the family, but which attends to the wider cultural, political and social structures that also shaped it.

The historian Paul Griffiths has moved beyond the familial context privileged by Ariès and many of his successors to highlight some of the other factors that shaped early modern childhoods, noting that the 'many different ways of growing up in early modern society . . . were affected by social class, gender, the state of labour markets, customary access to the land, and, above all, the responses of the young'.[10] There were many childhoods, Griffiths reminds us; many different ways of being a child, and of perceiving children. He counters the privileging of adult prescriptions and perceptions by tackling the difficult but essential task of considering how it might be possible to reinsert the agency of the young person into the construction of childhood. This book suggests, perhaps counterintuitively, that studying dramatic fictions of childhood can be helpful in this task. All the children who appear in Shakespeare's plays are, of course, fictional characters created by an adult – though not, perhaps, without some indirect input from the boy actors who first played those roles. Yet through the multivocal, multiperspectival experience of theatre, they can offer us ways of glimpsing situations from a child's point of view, and of seeing children in many places and settings beyond the family, and in relationships with adults who are not their kin. Macduff's son, whose close proximity to his mother suggests that he may, like Mamillius, be an as yet unbreeched inhabitant of the feminized, domestic world of early childhood, is nevertheless capable of uttering a remarkably lucid and pragmatic critique from a child's point of view of the national power politics in which his family is caught up (*Macbeth* 4.3). The shocking, violent death of this 'egg' – an epithet also used of Mamillius (*The Winter's Tale* 1.2.132), emphasizing the unfinished, potential quality these boys share – contributes to the play's closely woven and frequently deeply ambivalent symbolism of childhood as evocative of vulnerability, innocence and peril.

Macduff's son has a poignant counterpart in the anonymous Boy in *Henry V*, whose appearances constitute one of the more sustained and complex child roles in the Shakespeare canon. A working child separated from his family, the Boy rejects the model of adult masculinity offered him by the men he serves (Nim, Bardolph and Pistol), resolving to take responsibility for his future by 'seek[ing] some better service' (*Henry V* 3.2.47–8). He reveals an ethical capacity and maturity exceeding anything his employers can muster when he determines to 'stay with the lackeys with the luggage of our camp', vulnerable because 'there is none to guard it but boys' (4.4.66–8). As with some of Shakespeare's other precociously insightful boys, the combination of child status with adult aspiration will prove fatal, as the child is caught up in the retreating French army's slaughter of the boys (4.7). At the same time as offering a touching and funny glimpse of a child's view of the adult world, this role shows the endless vulnerability of children to adult appropriation and manipulation, not least when the child's limp corpse is employed to stage an iconic moment of national and personal loss and heroism in Kenneth Branagh's 1989 film of *Henry V*.

Even where they are positioned in a more comic frame, the fundamental disempowerment of young people in relation to adults is often foregrounded in Shakespeare's plays, when children are involved in encounters with adults that take place in public spaces and beyond the familial context. The boy actors of Shakespeare's company, hard-worked and marginal figures in its social economy, may have winced in recognition of Hal's relentless taunting for his own amusement of the 'puny drawer' Francis (*1 Henry IV* 2.5), a hapless apprentice about thirteen years old whose youth and lowly status are representative of the many boys in servant roles who pass through Shakespeare's dramatic worlds. The spectacle of the small bundle that represents the infant Perdita, abandoned to the Bohemian storm and 'exposed / To loss and what may follow' (*The Winter's Tale* 3.3.49–50) makes shockingly visible both the utter dependence of human infants on adult care, and their lack of recourse when that care is withheld. Yet babies, in Renaissance literature as elsewhere in culture, often symbolize hope and potential, and a future is secured for Perdita when the kindness of strangers counteracts the harshness of the aristocratic family.[11]

All these encounters and relationships between adults and children have one thing in common: they are asymmetrical and hierarchical. They thus confirm Davin's politicized definition of children as people who are different from adults, and who exist in an unequal power relationship with them.[12] By highlighting power, Davin foregrounds a crucial aspect of child-adult interrelations which depictions of children and childhood frequently mystify and misrepresent. The occlusion of power relations in discussions of children has been challenged by scholars who liken the history of childhood to the revisionary histories that have recently been written of other oppressed groups such as women, black people, the working class, or lesbians and gay men.[13] Childhood is itself inflected by factors such as race, gender and social status, of course; and it should be noted that like those other groups, children do not constitute a united, homogeneous group – infancy is very different from adolescence, and the next section of this chapter considers the dramatic implications of this internal diversity. Yet children differ from other oppressed groups in ways that crucially limit their capacity to write their own histories, a process which has been vital in feminist, postcolonial and queer scholarship. Children lack public agency and a political voice, because in most times and places adult status is precisely what is required in order to access such agency. Because of this, as Anna Mae Duane shows, the metaphor of childhood has long been used to characterize the condition of those who, because of class, gender, disability or race, are excluded from full membership of civil society. Consequently, Duane argues, even though not produced by children themselves, childhood studies resembles 'other modes of minority scholarship' in its capacity to 'illuminate how notions of power, strength and rationality are created by projecting the qualities of subservience, weakness and emotionality onto others, in this case, children'.[14]

In many areas of childhood studies primarily concerned with the contemporary world, the priority is rightly to engage with questions of power and seek to create academic and other spaces where children's voices can be heard and children can advance their own interpretations and analyses of the world and their place in it. But this is harder to manage for children who have been dead for four hundred years, or who were never more than fictions, not least because the power dynamics highlighted by Davin and Duane affect the production and preservation of evidence for the study of children and childhood. Mapping the political and epistemological complexities of studying children, Andrea Immel and Michael Witmore insist that scholars should rise to these challenges by undertaking primary research that enriches and extends the available data on children and childhood across as many domains as possible – an effort exemplified by the diversity of the chapters in their book, *Childhood and Children's Books in Early Modern Europe, 1550–1800* (2005).[15]

Alongside this commitment to fresh archival research, the study of early modern children and their representations draws on new methodological directions in the interdisciplinary analysis of contemporary childhood, expanding the range of ways in which we attend to children and consider the meanings of childhood. In this growing body of work, which frequently takes its cues from the historicist and constructionist bias of much recent scholarship on other marginalized groups in early modern culture, Ariès's 'underlying assumption – that childhood and its subcultures are always, in some sense, made, and not found' continues to exert a powerful influence.[16] Drawing sources and methods from literature, history, the visual arts, archaeology, educational theory and anthropology, among other disciplines, a new generation of scholars is greatly enriching our understanding of Shakespearean and other early modern childhoods.[17] The chapters in this book benefit from sharing in this new and growing set of conversations, and seek to point out some directions in which scholarship may continue to develop fruitfully.

III

If childhood is, then, a highly significant category of cultural and ideological meaning, it is also susceptible to a more pragmatic chronological definition, as a stage of development occurring in the early years of a human life. Early modern didactic texts including medical, parenting, educational and courtesy manuals defined childhood in this way, though many of them subdivided and interpreted it according to a variety of principles.[18] For some authors, it is a developmental phase in which adulthood is formed; for others, it is a discrete and self-contained stage. Some texts split childhood itself into three distinct phases of infancy, childhood and youth; others see youth as distinct from and subsequent to childhood, and the age at which either stage ends is debatable.

The experience and representation of each of these stages of childhood was inflected by numerous social and cultural factors: Jaques's 'infant / Mewling and puking in the nurse's arms' (*As You Like It* 2.7.142–3) is not Everychild, but an elite baby nurtured by a paid carer.[19] Yet an important part of the theatrical power of infancy lies in its capacity to elude such social specificity, so that representations of tiny babies often serve as screens on to which adults may project their own fears and longings. Shakespearean infants – unusual, among child characters, in being represented by stage props rather than actors – are often born into politically and emotionally fraught or contested situations, and are frequently at risk of violence. As Mark Lawhorn suggests in Appendix 1, they have little dramatic significance as individual characters, functioning rather as sites for the symbolic exploration of cultural anxieties about concerns such as legitimacy, inheritance, political crisis and personal vulnerability. Aaron's baby in *Titus Andronicus*, a 'black slave' like his father (4.2.119) whose visible racial identity adds a further layer of significance to his mute presence, powerfully illustrates this dynamic. Where Shakespeare's script leaves his fate somewhat ambiguous, recent stage and film versions have used the infant to symbolize and evoke the anxieties about violence, social order and the relations between past, present and future that are caught up in the discourse of childhood throughout the play. In each version the staged infant is a site where we can read shifting adult investments in fantasies of childhood.

The next phase of development, as the child emerges from infancy and becomes mobile and articulate, is the one most often celebrated by people commenting affectionately on their own children in diaries and autobiographies.[20] It is rarely depicted theatrically, however, and the majority of child characters represented by Shakespeare and other dramatists are somewhat older. They tend to be boys nearing the age of breeching (about seven years old) or older – like Mamillius, Macduff's son, and the Boy in *Henry V*, discussed above, and young Martius, considered below – or girls approaching the end of childhood. Many of the older child characters in Shakespeare's plays – Juliet, for example, Marina, or Fleance – might be considered adolescents as much as children. Indeed, the line between the two stages of life is very blurred: according to Hugh Cunningham, 'in nearly all societies people have differed quite substantially in their thinking on the age at which childhood ends'.[21] Should we, then, complement or complicate the category of childhood by also invoking that of adolescence in studying young people in early modern culture? To do so, we would need to take up key questions posed by Christopher Corley: 'If a transitional period between childhood and adulthood existed in pre-modern Europe, what categories defined it, how did people create their identities within it, and did these boundaries change over time?'[22] Considering adolescence as a liminal period between childhood and adulthood brings into question both the nature of those two adjacent categories and the boundaries between them, foregrounding the need to ask how this transitional period might have been represented, and what cultural work it may have done as a concept. Ilana Krausman Ben-Amos's study of the meanings of early modern adolescence suggests that this was as complex and contested a life-stage as childhood.[23]

Adolescence is a site where the gendering of childhood comes into particularly clear focus, revealing that not only the experience of childhood but the stages of life themselves may be different for boys and girls. While adult women and young children of both genders shared a social space in early modern households, older boys were required to move out of it. Lingering around women's skirts is, as we have seen, problematic for several Shakespearean boys, signalling the precariousness of the child reluctant to take up his allotted place in the gendered world of adulthood. Although girls remained within that familiar domestic realm, change came to them, too, as service or courtship might take them into a different household, requiring them to forge new relationships with other children and adults, as Viola does in *Twelfth Night*, albeit in highly untypical circumstances. During the years when they moved from childhood towards adulthood, boys spent a good deal of their time in nonfamilial settings and institutions such as schools, workplaces and under apprenticeship, situations which allowed for a certain amount of licence and permitted inversion of the normal hierarchies of adult-child relationships. For boys, then, adolescence was not so much a chronological, developmental stage, as a socially produced time of temporary destabilization of the normal structures of dependence and autonomy that regulate the lives of children and adults. In contrast, girls moved between a series of dependent, submissive positions as daughters, servants and wives, in a sequence of patriarchal households. As a result, Jennifer Higginbotham argues, adolescent girlhood was potentially contradictory and multifaceted, at once 'a time of danger and exposure, and, consequently, of potential freedom and resistance', and, conversely, 'a time when ideological forces work to inculcate femininity and produce mature women'.[24]

The two adolescent girls with whom I began this chapter, Shakespeare's Miranda and her real-life peer Rachel Fane, foreground these fundamental questions about what exactly constitutes a child. Positioned at the boundaries of childhood as a chronological stage, these daughters occupy a role of continuing dependence on and socially exacted subordination to their familial superiors, highlighting that childhood is not merely a developmental phase, but also a relational condition that does not end with accession to adulthood. As Hattie Fletcher and Marianne Novy demonstrate in chapter 4, it is when parents and adult children – King Lear and his daughters, Brabanzio and Desdemona – fail to take full measure of the complex interactions of age, gender, power and status in their relations with each other that the Shakespearean family becomes a site of conflict and danger. It is no haven for boys, either. Shakespeare's plays are often painfully aware that boys' accession to adulthood in a world where they may be caught up in power plays or required to shoulder military responsibilities at an early age can issue in the brutal termination of the possibilities for growth and potential that childhood symbolizes. Witness the offscene death of Mamillius (*The Winter's Tale*), the spectacle of Arthur's fatal leap (*King John*), and the carnage inflicted on the sons of Titus and Tamora in *Titus Andronicus*.

IV

I began this chapter by asking how our understanding of Shakespearean childhoods could be enhanced by reading Rachel Fane's May masque; in closing, I return to that text and its ability to prompt us to attempt to see the early modern world through the eyes of real-life peers of Shakespeare's child characters. Fane's masque is a record of aristocratic children's play as recreation, performance and imitation of the adult world. And taking play seriously is arguably crucial to any attempt to understand children's cultures and agency. In an informative and stimulating essay on children's lives in early modern England, Keith Thomas suggests that play was central to an early modern 'children's subculture which has yet to be reconstructed'.[25] How might we access this culture, and how would doing so enrich our understanding of Shakespeare's theatrical children?

One starting point is education, which is unique as a site of cultural activity developed expressly for children. Although its formal structures reflect adult priorities, children have always shown themselves to be assiduous and inventive in appropriating educational settings for their own purposes. It was because she received an exceptionally advanced education for an early modern girl that Rachel was able not only to orchestrate such a sophisticated and complex form of play for herself and her siblings, but to document it in a way that enables us to reconstruct the activities of the Fane children. As the chapters by Catherine Belsey and A. J. Piesse in this volume show, children in Shakespeare's plays are frequently found putting their education to work for themselves, by reading, writing, telling stories or performing – communicating, in some way, an account of the world to readers or audiences that may include adults as well as other children. Their real-life counterparts also found ways to express themselves, in the margins of commonplace books and around the edges of writing tasks set as part of their formal education, through the playing of linguistic games, and in the composition of original writings. Jan Mark's novel for young readers, *Stratford Boys* (2003), imagines the teenage Shakespeare's youthful adventures in playwriting. Studying the literary and dramatic efforts of real-life counterparts such as Rachel would enable us to learn much about the cultures of early modern childhood.

Introducing the masque that Rachel scripted, I focused on her authorship as an adolescent girl apparently employing the genre to articulate her own concerns. But masquing is of course a collective performance activity, and the involvement of her siblings, friends and youthful household servants as actors, dancers and singers means that as an event the May masque was a multifaceted site where children could join in playing at performance, at imagining themselves in adult roles, and at commenting on the adult world that surrounded them. As actors, singers and dancers, both boys and girls could at different times take part in educational, domestic and commercial performances. Many of these child performers were in paid employment – what was play for Rachel and her siblings was work for them, though the apprentices of the London theatres were generally rather older (aged from about twelve upwards) than Fane's troupe, of whom she was the oldest at fourteen. The commercial theatre was a distinctive early modern cultural institution where children (boys, at any rate) were exceptionally visible because they were in demand as performers. Some plays by Shakespeare and his contemporaries may have involved as many as eight child performers, giving youthful bodies a prominent place on the Renaissance stage: *As You Like It* involves two singing pageboys and four acting roles probably taken by boys, none of which could have been doubled; even with doubling, *A Midsummer Night's Dream* would have called for eight.[26]

Although children were clearly able to create, in the interstices of their adult-directed experiences of work and education, spaces in which they could challenge, critique or invert adult concerns, perhaps the most important site where they could express their own values and desires was in their own self-directed play. Thomas's insight into its central significance in the lives of early modern children has been corroborated by theorists of childhood in other times and places, who suggest that the 'games of children' may constitute a distinctive 'collective culture, enduring and separated off from the adult world', but nonetheless characteristically reflecting and commenting on that world and children's positioning in relation to it.[27] Crucially important to any attempt to excavate the culture of childhood and the agency of children, play is a particularly difficult aspect of the history of childhood and its representations to research because it is inherently evanescent. Happening in the moment and in the body, children's play is a matter of process and action, rather than outcome.

As with childhood more broadly, though, scholars have made some headway in retrieving traces of different kinds of play, and in suggesting how they can illuminate our understanding of children as subjects, and as they are represented by adults. Play with toys is most easily reconstructed through material culture, for 'toys and children-specific artefacts are a constant and recognisable component of the historical record' which historical archaeologists have become adept at recovering and analysing.[28] Yet toys – even those that we know to have been in use in early modern England, such as hobbyhorses, puppets, bats and balls, whipping tops, kites and dolls – are rarely mentioned in Shakespeare as artefacts to be played with by children. The word 'toys' and references to specific toys in fact are almost invariably used to denote adult interest in trivial, thus implicitly childish, objects and concerns, as when Hotspur constructs a feminized, infantilized domain in opposition to a man's world of war, declaring to his wife 'this is no world / To play with maumets [dolls] . . . / We must have bloody noses and crack'd crowns' (*1 Henry IV* 2.3.82–4). Nor do any stage directions name toys as properties to be employed by any of the performers playing child characters. Yet such characters are frequently to be found on stage for long periods, as silent bystanders or witnesses to action in which they are not directly involved, and modern directors often foreground their child status at such moments by having them play with toys. In the Propeller theatre company's all-male production of *The Winter's Tale*, which toured the UK in 2005, Mamillius began the performance by playing presciently with a toy ship, while in Derek Jarman's 1979 film of *The Tempest*, Miranda's position as a girl not yet emerged from childhood is signalled by the doll she plays with.

Imaginary and imitative play are more readily accessed through textual accounts, observational and fictional. In 1583 John Dee told how his son Arthur and Mary Herbert 'being but three years old ... did make as it wer a shew of childish marriage, of calling ech other husband and wife'.[29] There is a tinge of paternal pride here, and early modern commentators sometimes assume that play imitative of adult behaviour in this way is aspirational, but it might also be mocking, subversive or contestatory. When Nehemiah Wallington relates how shortly before her death, his three-year-old daughter Elizabeth, 'being merry went unto her mother and said unto her, "what do you here, my wife?"' he clearly expresses parental pride, grief and nostalgia.[30] Yet the irresistibly comic scenario evoked also has the potential to deflate paternal authority by imitating it playfully. Similarly, Valeria's celebration of young Martius's childlike mimicking of his father's military dedication when he persistently chases a 'gilded butterfly' (*Coriolanus* 1.3.54–61) conjures up a spectacle that ironizes Roman martial masculinity as well as applauding it. Moreover, the boy's later promise, 'I'll run away till I am bigger, but then I'll fight' (5.3.129) gives his youthful play an ominously anticipatory edge. Children's play comments on the world that adults make for children to live in.

Early modern Britain was a youthful society, where 'a good 70 per cent of all English pre-industrial households contained children ... and there were between two-and-a-half and three children to every household with them'.[31] These bald demographic facts led the historian Peter Laslett to meditate, in a much-cited passage, on what it must have been like to inhabit, as Shakespeare did, a world where 'there were children everywhere':

> playing in the village street and fields when they were very small, hanging round the farmyards and getting in the way, until they had grown enough to be given

child-sized jobs to do; thronging the churches; forever clinging to the skirts of women in the house and wherever they went . . . The perpetual distraction of childish noise and talk must have affected everyone almost all of the time.[32]

Laslett's depiction of children as ubiquitous noisy nuisances perhaps says more about modern culture's anxious desire to confine children to demarcated social spaces that enforce their difference from adults than it does about the reality of their place in the early modern social world. Nevertheless, his account does offer a glimpse of a world in which children were publicly present, vocal and active. This is not a world we have lost, but one which continues to exist and is remade by every generation of children.

As the examples drawn from child-authored manuscripts, material culture and rereadings of familiar representations cited in this essay and throughout part I demonstrate, the evidence for early modern children's cultural presence and agency is richer and more extensive than has sometimes been thought. It is important to read such evidence with a view to grasping that, as Laurie Wilkie says, 'Children peopled the past, not just as passive recipients of their communities' and families' standards, but as individual social actors who negotiated opportunities and identities for themselves within their cultures'.[33] Critical perspectives and methodologies drawn from fields such as childhood studies can enable us to develop a more complex understanding of an early modern world that was full of children, enabling us to grasp both how children inhabited that world, and how representing them and thinking about them enabled adults to make sense of their own journeys away from childhood. Hamlet's question, 'What, are they children?', then, is both susceptible to many answers, and needs to be nuanced and specified with reference to individual children, and particular childhoods, lived, represented and remembered. Children are best understood not as an undifferentiated 'they', but rather as diverse and multiple 'Is' and 'yous', as the Shakespearean and other children whose voices echo through the plays and through these chapters insistently remind the adults who think and write about them.

NOTES

1 Prospero, looking on, declares himself to be manipulating these events, and later insistently redescribes the marriage in terms of his gifting of Miranda to Ferdinand (4.1.2–3, 7–8, 13–14); but as far as Miranda knows here, she is acting autonomously.

2 MS Kent Archives Office U269/F38/3 is a collection of dramatic and poetic texts which Rachel composed for the entertainment of the Fane household at times of festivity. For a partial edition of this MS, see Marion O'Connor, 'Rachel Fane's May Masque at Apethorpe, 1627', *English Literary Renaissance* 36:1 (2006), 90–113. See also Caroline Bowden, 'The Notebooks of Rachael Fane: Education for Authorship?', in Victoria E. Burke and Jonathan Gibson, eds., *Early Modern Women's Manuscript Writing: Selected Papers from the Trinity/Trent Colloquium* (Burlington, VT: Ashgate, 2004), pp. 157–80.

3 For a fuller discussion of Fane's masque in relation to Shakespeare, see my essay, 'Playing with Cupid: Gender, Sexuality, and Adolescence', in Diana Henderson, ed., *Alternative Shakespeares 3* (London: Routledge, forthcoming 2007).

4 Cited in Keith Thomas, 'Children in Early Modern England', in Gillian Avery and Julia Briggs, eds., *Children and Their Books: A Celebration of the Work of Iona and Peter Opie* (Oxford: Clarendon Press, 1989), pp. 45–77 (p. 58).

5 Anna Davin, 'What is a Child?', in Anthony Fletcher and Stephen Hussey, eds., *Childhood in Question* (Manchester: Manchester University Press, 1999), pp. 15–36 (p. 15).

6 For an insightful and accessible overview of such debates, see Libby Brooks, *The Story of Childhood: Growing Up in Modern Britain* (London: Bloomsbury, 2006).

7 Thomas Travisano, 'Of Dialectic and Divided Consciousness: Intersections between Children's Literature and Childhood Studies', *Children's Literature* 28 (2000), 22–9 (22).

8 Philippe Ariès, *L'enfant et la vie familiale sous l'ancien régime* (literally, *The child and family life under the former régime*) (1960), translated as *Centuries of Childhood: A Social History of Family Life* (New York: Vintage, 1962). The original French title foregrounds the interdependence of the family and childhood in Ariès's thesis more frankly than the English version. Although the specifics of their analyses are very different, later studies have often aligned Ariès with Lawrence Stone, as representatives of the argument that the emotional texture of childhood and parental relations in the early modern period was extremely thin: see Stone, *The Family, Sex and Marriage in England, 1500–1800* (Harmondsworth: Penguin, 1977).

This view has been challenged by Linda Pollock, *Forgotten Children: Parent–Child Relations from 1500–1800* (Cambridge: Cambridge University Press, 1983), and *A Lasting Relationship: Parents and Children Over Three Centuries* (Cambridge: Cambridge University Press, 1987); and by Ralph Houlbrooke, *The English Family 1450–1700* (Harlow: Longman, 1984), and *English Family Life, 1576–1716: An Anthology from Diaries* (Oxford: Oxford University Press, 1988). For a summary of these debates, see Hugh Cunningham, *Children and Childhood in Western Society since 1500* (London: Longman, 1995).

9 Catherine Belsey, *Shakespeare and the Loss of Eden: The Construction of Family Values in Early Modern Culture* (Basingstoke: Palgrave, 1998).

10 Paul Griffiths, *Youth and Authority: Formative Experiences in England 1560–1640* (Oxford: Clarendon Press, 1996), p. 6.

11 John Boswell, *The Kindness of Strangers: The Abandonment of Children in Western Europe from Late Antiquity to the Renaissance* (Chicago: University of Chicago Press, 1989). In differing forms, fosterage and adoption, such as Perdita experienced, were common aspects of early modern childhoods. See Marianne Novy, *Reading Adoption: Family and Difference in Fiction and Drama* (Ann Arbor: University of Michigan Press, 2005).

12 Davin, 'What is a Child?', p. 32. In particular instances this power differential may of course be inflected by other factors such as status and gender, potentially equalizing or rebalancing the relationship. Such exceptions do not contradict the basic structure of inequality.

13 Harry Hendrick, *Children, Childhood and English Society 1880–1990* (Cambridge: Cambridge University Press, 1997), p. 3.

14 Anna Mae Duane, 'An Infant Nation: Childhood Studies and Early America', *Literature Compass* 2 (2005), 1–9 (1). The notion that adults project their feelings on to children is central to the controversial work of the psychohistorian Lloyd De Mause, in his *The History of Childhood* (New York: The Psychohistory Press, 1974).

15 Andrea Immel and Michael Witmore, eds., 'Introduction', *Childhood and Children's Books in Early Modern Europe, 1550–1800* (New York: Routledge, 2005), pp. 1–18 (p. 6).

16 *Ibid.*, p. 13.

17 Significant new research is contained in recent doctoral dissertations, many of which can be expected to issue in publications. See, for example, Edel Lamb, *The Children's Playing Companies of Early Modern London: Childhood, Theatre and Identity, 1599–1613*, Queen's University of Belfast, 2005; Jennifer Higginbotham, *Fair Maids and Golden Girls: Early Modern Girlhood and the Production of Femininity*, University of Pennsylvania, 2006; Stephen Kavanagh, *Shakespeare and the Politics of Childhood*, Trinity College Dublin, 2006; and Marie Rutkoski, *The Mouths of Babes: Children and Knowledge in English Renaissance Drama*, Harvard University, 2006.

18 My discussion of the early modern sense of the stages of childhood is indebted to Lamb, *Children's Playing Companies*, pp. 13–14.

19 Patricia Crawford, *Blood, Bodies and Families in Early Modern England* (Harlow: Pearson Education, 2004), pp. 89, 148.

20 For examples, see Houlbrooke, *English Family Life, 1576–1716*.

21 Cunningham, *Children and Childhood*, p. 17.

22 Christopher Corley, 'Review of *The Premodern Teenager: Youth in Society, 1150–1650*, ed. Konrad Eisenbichler', *Sixteenth Century Journal: The Journal of Early Modern Studies* 35 (2004), 219–20 (219).

23 Ilana Krausman Ben-Amos, *Adolescence and Youth in Early Modern England* (New Haven: Yale University Press, 1994).

24 Jennifer Higginbotham, 'Shakespearean Girlhoods: Gender and Childhood in Shakespeare's England', unpublished paper presented to the 'Shakespeare's Children/Children's Shakespeare' conference, Roehampton University, 2003.
25 Thomas, 'Children in Early Modern England', p. 51.
26 Catherine Belsey, 'Shakespeare's Little Boys: Theatrical Apprenticeship and the Construction of Childhood', in Bryan Reynolds and William West, eds., *Rematerializing Shakespeare: Authority and Representation on the Early Modern English Stage* (Basingstoke: Palgrave Macmillan, 2005), pp. 53–72 (pp. 54–6).
27 Allison James, Chris Jenks and Alan Prout, *Theorising Childhood* (Cambridge: Polity, 1998), p. 99.
28 Laurie Wilkie, 'Not Merely Child's Play: Creating a Historical Archaeology of Children and Childhood', in Joanna Sofaer Derevenski, ed., *Children and Material Culture* (London: Routledge, 2000), pp. 100–111 (p. 101). See also Karin Calvert, *Children in the House: The Material Culture of Early Childhood, 1600–1900* (Boston: Northeastern University Press, 1992).
29 *The Private Diary of John Dee*, ed. J. O. Halliwell, Camden Society 19 (1842), p. 14.
30 Paul S. Seaver, *Wallington's World: A Puritan Artisan in Seventeenth-Century London* (London: Methuen, 1985), p. 87.
31 Peter Laslett, *The World We Have Lost – Further Explored* (London: Methuen, 1971), p. 119.
32 *Ibid.*, p. 119.
33 Wilkie, 'Not Merely Child's Play', p. 111.

3

Little princes: Shakespeare's royal children

Catherine Belsey

CHILDHOOD

Five children appear in Shakespeare's *Richard III*, including, unusually, a little girl. One boy appears briefly as a page. The primary role of the others is evidently to throw into relief the tyranny of Richard, as he remorselessly clears them out of his path to the throne. Even now, the princes he murders in the Tower of London remain a legendary instance of childhood helplessness in the face of adult cruelty. While all Richard's child victims are repeatedly identified, whatever their ages, as 'babes', the play credits them not only with the vulnerability they all share but also with varying degrees of autonomy. If, on the one hand, Clarence's orphans are presented as naïve in their ignorance of the world and incapable of intervention on their own behalf, the princes, on the other, are seen as more knowing and more independent. In its depiction of the encounter between the princes and Richard, this play of perhaps as early as 1591 begins ascribing to childhood a life of its own.

The representation of the princes themselves, however, is not without its attendant questions from a twenty-first-century perspective. In detail, the scene does not seem to charm the audience in quite the ways we might now expect.[1] Can the early modern understanding of childhood illuminate the play's presentation of the princes? Can the princes in turn tell us something about the cultural history of childhood? Early modern children were conventionally vulnerable, but little princes had special responsibilities that detracted from their innocence. At the same time, it was only gradually in the course of the period when Shakespeare was writing that a reprehensible mischief was to redefine itself as a charming and playful childishness in our sense of the term.

More than forty years after *Richard III* was first performed, Anthony Van Dyck, then salaried painter to the royal household, depicted, at the Queen's behest, the three eldest children of Charles I. His enchanting portrait of 1635 shows childhood triumphant. Standing before a doorway that opens on to a red rosebush, and with more red roses at their feet, the three children are subtly differentiated. The heir apparent, then five years old, faces the viewer with a look of lively expectation. His hand rests lightly on the head of an obedient spaniel. Prince Charles wears a little boy's bonnet and a richly decorated scarlet satin 'coat' with floor-length skirts, the mode of dress appropriate to aristocratic boys in the period until, at the age of seven or so, they were 'breeched' and taken from their mother's care to be taught by men. James, Duke of York, not yet two, wears blue satin petticoats and holds an apple. Princess Mary, nearly four years old, stands between them in white, with red roses in her perfectly curled and dressed hair. In each case the painting precisely captures the contours of childhood. These children, with their rounded cheeks, could never be mistaken for grown-ups. Children's heads are larger in proportion to their bodies than adults'; their legs are shorter.[2] Posed though it evidently is, the painting shows childhood as we still recognize it, or perhaps idealize it: natural, vulnerable, disarming.[3]

This image could not be taken for granted. In 1605 their father, also Prince Charles, had himself been depicted at the age of five. In the earlier portrait the contours are much more austere: the painting shows a boy, certainly, but a solemn one, with a much thinner face and longer legs.[4] The emphasis here is not on his childishness. Three years before, when Sir Walter Raleigh had made over his Sherborne estate to his eldest son, the boy was eight or nine. In a portrait of Raleigh and his heir painted at that time, the son's outline and stance perfectly replicate his father's. This child is a miniature adult, only, perhaps, less muscular than his father and, of course, beardless.[5] Although there is a delightful Hans Holbein portrait of the one-year-old Prince Edward, heir apparent to Henry VIII, depicted in 1538 with the face of a baby,[6] Holbein's realism was not imitated in England for many years after his death. By the time he was eight, the Prince of Wales was beginning to be portrayed with the codpiece and the wide shoulders, as well as indications of the swaggering stance, that his father had made famous.[7]

Childhood, in other words, was barely visible until well into the seventeenth century as a distinctive state of being. This is not, of course, to say that children were not children. We shall probably never know quite how the young perceived themselves. But cultural history gives us access to the way childhood was understood, and a characteristic sixteenth-century image of childhood, in so far as children feature in painting at all, can be seen in the stiff little figures who sit solemnly round the dining table of William Brooke, Lord Cobham, in 1567.[8] There were no young princes in England in this epoch, of course: the Virgin Queen disappointed her subjects by resolutely refusing to give them an heir. But a portrait of James VI of Scotland, aged eight, in 1574 shows the young King gravely facing the viewer with a hawk on his wrist. Although he wears breeches, something about the proportions of the body, the beardless face and the tight waist oddly suggests a young woman rather than a little boy.[9]

Art historians would point out that the absence in the sixteenth century of recognizably childlike children was to a high degree a matter of fashion. The manner of English art at this time was iconic, emblematic, medievalist in inclination. Even where, as was often the case, pictures of children were painted or influenced by foreign artists, especially from the Low Countries, English tastes played their part. Painting followed the manner preferred by the Queen, and the last thing Elizabeth wanted, as the century wore on, was realism. Her own official image, undimmed by time, contributed significantly to the iconography of royal power. At the same time, however, from the point of view of cultural history, paintings tend to depict what a culture considers important, and the *difference* of childhood was evidently not considered worth a great deal of attention. In the portraits children feature mainly as evidence of parental fecundity, or to guarantee the continuity of the dynasty.

VULNERABILITY

Children were also represented in fiction, and especially on the stage. Probably the nearest analogue in the drama for the Van Dyck painting of the royal children is Shakespeare's depiction of Mamillius in *The Winter's Tale*. This little prince is explicitly 'unbreech'd' (1.2.157); he belongs in the company of his mother and her ladies, where he offers to recount a fairy tale 'Of sprites and goblins' (2.1.28); and his guileless chatter succeeds momentarily in distracting his father from the anguish of jealousy. Childhood features in this play of perhaps 1611 as a time of innocence, and of unselfconscious play, in the belief that 'there was no more behind, / But such a day to-morrow as to-day, / And to be boy eternal' (1.2.64–6). His innocent world destroyed by his father's suspicion and his mother's trial, Mamillius eventually dies of grief.

If such playful children are still rare at this time, their vulnerability, by contrast, has a longer heritage. The pathos of Tyrrel's account of the dead princes in the Tower must have contributed to their iconic status

(*King Richard III* 4.3.1–22). After the onstage death of Clarence, the murder of the princes is not shown, but the story itself is both dramatized and authenticated by its ascription to the murderers. 'Flesh'd villains', like hounds that have already tasted game (6), Dighton and Forrest, Tyrrel recounts, nevertheless wept like children themselves as they told him of it:

> 'O thus', quoth Dighton, 'lay the gentle babes';
> 'Thus, thus', quoth Forrest, 'girdling one another
> Within their alabaster innocent arms;
> Their lips were four red roses on a stalk,
> And in their summer beauty kiss'd each other.' (9–13)

The element of formality in this description detaches it slightly from reality, but at the same time monumentalizes the image of the children, whose 'alabaster' arms evoke both their whiteness and the effigy that is their due. The same red roses that Van Dyck depicts to celebrate the freshness of childhood and its naturalness here serve to emphasize its transience and the unnaturalness of the crime. Their mother's reaction confirms the association: 'Ah, my poor Princes! Ah, my tender babes, / My unblow'd flowers, new-appearing sweets' (4.4.9–10). Tyrrel, who arranged the whole event, calls it 'tyrannous and bloody', 'The most arch deed of piteous massacre / That ever yet this land was guilty of' (4.3.1–3).

Richard's murder of the princes is not his last act of violence, but it represents the climactic confirmation of his tyranny. The slaughter of innocent children was the traditional mark of the tyrant. His projected murder of Prince Arthur establishes the rapacity of Shakespeare's King John.[10] Thomas Preston's *Cambises*, printed in 1569, shows the despotic king shoot an arrow into the heart of a child to prove that he is not incapacitated by drink. At the beginning of *The Battle of Alcazar* (1588–9) the bloodthirsty usurper, Muly Mahamet, smothers his two young brothers in their bed. And the mounting violence of Macbeth's reign is demonstrated by his butchery of Macduff's wife and children, including the engaging little 'prattler' who teases his mother (*Macbeth* 4.2.64). These tyrants are descended ultimately from Herod, who gave orders for the extermination of all boys under two when the Wise Men brought him news of the birth of the new king he perceived as a rival (Matt. 2.1–18). Shakespeare evidently assumed that he could count on his audience to know the story, since Henry V threatens the citizens of Harfleur with appalling brutalities, including

> Your naked infants spitted upon pikes,
> Whiles the mad mothers with their howls confused

Do break the clouds, as did the wives of Jewry
At Herod's bloody-hunting slaughtermen. (*Henry V* 3.3.115–18)

Herod owed some of his familiarity to the mystery play cycles. Shakespeare might possibly have seen the pageant of the Shearmen and Tailors, which was performed in Coventry into the 1580s. There the mothers cling desperately to their babies, and when the soldiers carry out their orders nonetheless, the women lament bitterly.[11]

The princes are not the only vulnerable children in *Richard III*. Clarence's death leaves two helpless orphans, a boy and a girl, who are wise enough to see through the efforts of their grandmother to shelter them from the knowledge of their father's death, but not yet astute enough to believe the extent of Richard's villainy. He had, after all, promised to love them:

Boy. Think you my uncle did dissemble, grannam?
Duch. Ay, boy.
Boy. I cannot think it. (2.2.31–3)

Their lamentations echo those of the Queen, now also unprotected after the death of Edward IV, and are echoed in turn by their grandmother, who has lost two sons:

Eliz. Ah, for my husband, for my dear Lord Edward!
Children. Ah, for our father, for our dear Lord Clarence!
Duch. Alas for both, both mine, Edward and Clarence!
Eliz. What stay had I but Edward, and he's gone?
Children. What stay had we but Clarence, and he's gone?
Duch. What stays had I but they, and they are gone? (2.2.71–6)

The alignment of the children with these women perhaps suggests that the little boy is still in petticoats. It also associates tyranny with manhood.

Richard's rise to power represents the culmination of the Wars of the Roses. Memories of other butchered children haunt the margins of the play, throwing into relief the brutality of that long period of civil strife. Richard himself cannot forgive the torment inflicted on his dying father, the Duke of York, by Margaret, widow of Henry VI, when she offered to dry his tears with a napkin soaked in the blood of his child and Richard's brother, 'pretty Rutland' (1.3.175). Margaret's hostility to them all is the only consideration that can unite Richard with the Queen and her brothers. Margaret's sufferings now are a proper punishment for the murder of little Rutland, the Queen piously affirms: 'So just is God, to right the innocent' (178). Hastings comments, 'O, 'twas the foulest deed to slay that babe, / And the most merciless that e'er was heard of.' And Rivers, Richard's enemy in the rest of the play, adds, 'Tyrants themselves wept when it was reported' (179–81). Rutland's murder is dramatized in *3 Henry VI*. This defenceless schoolboy is killed simply because his father killed Clifford's father. The child pleads in vain for his life: 'sweet Clifford, pity me'; 'I never did thee harm – why wilt thou slay me?' (1.3.37, 39). Even his murderer seems to concede the pathos that ought to move him: 'In vain thou speak'st, poor boy. My father's blood / Hath stopped the passage where thy words should enter' (21–2).

These little victims are not much differentiated from one another, except, perhaps, in terms of age. On the contrary, their main role in the plays is to put on display the oppressive nature of ambition, war and the revenge ethic. They constitute primarily, in other words, a screen on which butchery is projected and made visible. Yet, as a group, they are distinguishable from adults by the artless innocence registered in their diction. Like Clarence's children, Rutland tends to speak in a relatively elementary vocabulary, and in uncomplicated sentences with the minimum of subordinate clauses. This, too, is traditional. The contrast between simplicity and rhetorical elaboration is very striking in *Cambises*, where the protagonist was to become a byword for bombast. Thirty years after the play's first printing, Falstaff threatens to impersonate Hal's autocratic father 'in King Cambyses's vein'; and he suits the rhetoric to the word when he tries to stop Mistress Quickly from laughing till she cries, with 'For God's sake, lords, convey my tristful Queen, / For tears do stop the floodgates of her eyes' (*1 Henry IV* 2.5.359–60). But when in *Cambises* itself the Young Child pleads for his life, the contrast between his diction and the King's emphasizes his childishness and the corresponding pathos of his plight: 'Good Master King, do not shoot at me, my mother loves me best of all' (553).[12]

Rutland's death reverberates throughout *3 Henry VI*. Ironically, Richard himself calls Clifford a 'cruel child-killer' (2.2.112). Coming, as it does, at the beginning of the play, this episode is symmetrically paired with the death of the Prince of Wales at the end. Prince Edward's murder, in the presence of his mother, Margaret, is just as shameful as Rutland's: he is defeated, guarded, no threat to his captors. But when he taunts them, the Yorkists stab him, first Edward, now king, then Richard, and then Clarence.[13] Margaret compares the moment with the assassination of Caesar, but then adds, 'He was a man – this, in respect, a child, / And men ne'er spend their fury on a child' (5.5.55–6). When Richard comes to kill him, too, Henry VI calls it 'murdering innocents' (5.6.32).

3 Henry VI and *Richard III* are conceived as continuous. The crime of Prince Edward's murder resonates through the succeeding play in Richard's wooing of his widow (*King Richard III* 1.2.91–110), at Clarence's death (1.4.197–219) and in Margaret's reproaches (4.4). History is rewritten to implicate Rivers and Grey as bystanders (3.3.14–15), so that their deaths are also seen as punishments for the crime. In this play another kind of symmetry is adumbrated by Margaret, as she curses the Queen: 'Edward thy son, that now is Prince of Wales, / For Edward my son, that was Prince of Wales, / Die in his youth by like untimely violence' (1.3.196–8). The murder of the princes in the Tower thus takes its place in a cycle of child deaths which represents the brutal evidence of adult tyranny. Margaret reacts to their death with a grim satisfaction that throws into relief for the audience the familial violence, and perhaps the absurdity, of civil war itself: 'Plantagenet doth quit Plantagenet; / Edward for Edward pays a dying debt' (4.4.20–21).[14]

AUTHORITY

In the case of little princes, the vulnerability of childhood may come into conflict with royal authority. Charles I did not like Van Dyck's painting of his three children in 1635. There is some uncertainty about why this was, but it seems probable that the King did not approve of the representation of the heir to the throne in skirts. The painting had been commissioned by Queen Henrietta Maria as an image of her children for her sister Christina, Duchess of Savoy. In return she received portraits of her sister's children. This sisterly display of maternal pride shows how childhood was beginning to be valued. Later in 1635, Van Dyck was asked to paint the three children again. The result is a picture in the Royal Collection, much copied at the time, and displayed in a number of aristocratic houses as a badge of loyalty. The heir apparent is now shown in gold satin breeches with a matching jacket. He leans nonchalantly against a pillar, perhaps an emblem of the stability of the monarchy. Charles's left hand supports the little Duke of York, still in petticoats. The distinction between the expectations of the two boys is thus sharpened. Charles gazes into the distance, perhaps slightly abstracted, contemplating his destiny. This time it is Princess Mary, her hands folded demurely in front of her, who meets the viewer's gaze.

Ironically, Charles I had himself been portrayed in a long 'coat' in the painting of 1605. But he was not at that time the heir apparent. His brother, Prince Henry, was never, as far as I know, depicted in this childish garb.[15] The future Charles II had been shown in voluminous white petticoats at the age of four months, and again in one of Van Dyck's portraits of his parents when he was two,[16] but evidently by 1635 the heir to the throne no longer seemed to his father an infant. At this age he was already entrusted with minor ceremonial duties, such as ushering ambassadors into the royal presence.[17]

Royal childhood could involve other solemn responsibilities in the period. When she was eleven the future Elizabeth I translated *The Mirror of the Sinful Soul* into English. She sent the translation to Queen Katharine Parr, explaining that she has devoted her 'simple wit' to this grave task on the grounds that 'pusillanimity and idleness are most repugnant unto a reasonable creature'.[18] At this stage no one can have expected Elizabeth to become queen, but all children knew that they were born to die, and should live their lives in the light of that knowledge.[19] First-born princes, however, were also born to rule. In 1599, when James VI completed *Basilikon Doron* to instruct his heir in the proprieties of kingship, Prince Henry was only five. But then this little boy had had the labours of Hercules embroidered on the blanket covering his cradle.[20] James himself has left letters from his own childhood that show the preoccupations of a youthful early modern king. In the earliest of these, undated, he writes a polite thank-you letter to Annabel, Countess of Mar for the fruit she has evidently sent him, and indicates that he is ready for more as soon as she is willing to send it. But by 1575, when he was only nine, James was already involved in politics, writing in his own hand to thank one of his supporters in the war, and promising to remember his loyalty in due course. He concludes authoritatively: 'In the meanwhile, be of good comfort, and reserve you to that time with patience, being assured of my favour. Farewell.'[21]

One of the most striking instances of a similar disjunction in the drama between the innocent child and the authoritative king must be the Prince Edward who succeeds his father in Christopher Marlowe's *Edward II.* When the boy first appears in the play in the company of his mother, the King sends them to her native France to seek reconciliation between himself and the French King. The little Prince, instructed to bear himself 'bravely' on this mission, urges his father not to ask of him more than his youth will bear, but then stoutly assures the King that 'heaven's great beams / On Atlas' shoulder shall not lie more safe / Than shall your charge committed to my trust' (3.1.72–8).[22] The Queen comments on this 'towardness' (79). In much of Act 4, as the war against Edward II develops, the Prince is a near-silent presence. His occasional interventions show no doubt about his loyalty to his father, but some uncertainty about whether he understands what is going on. He naïvely supposes that he can win his father round: ''A loves me better than a thousand Spencers' (4.2.7). The play repeatedly insists that he is young (5.2.72 S.D., 74), 'too young to reign' (92), 'childish' (75). At the same time, he consistently stands up to Mortimer, whom he very properly distrusts from the beginning. Even when he becomes king, however, the boy has no effective power, until he learns to enlist the Council on his behalf. But with the support of the Lords in the final scene of the play, he wields complete authority, brings the rebels to justice and orders his father's funeral. Yet he remains a child. His tears, he says, are witness to his grief 'and innocency' (5.6.101).

There is general agreement that *Edward II* is likely to have been written in 1591–2, in the light of *3 Henry VI* and *Richard III*. Certainly, some of the same ambiguities surround the figure of Prince Edward in *3 Henry VI*. This child first appears in the company of his mother, Queen Margaret, and throughout the play his future promise is contrasted with the ineffectual present of his peace-loving father. Henry VI is prepared to go to any lengths to put an end to the contention between the house of York and his own house of Lancaster. When these include bequeathing the realm to his brother, Richard, Duke of York, thereby disinheriting his own son, the Prince speaks up with the irresistible logic of childhood and a corresponding ignorance of political complexity: 'Father, you cannot disinherit me. / If you be king, why should not I succeed?' (1.1.227–8). The boy's words augur well: 'When I return with victory from the field, / I'll see your Grace' (1.1.262–3). But it is not until Act 5, when years have elapsed, that we find him actively engaged in armed conflict. Although he accompanies his mother in her campaigns earlier in the play, it is clear that she is in command of the army, not the Prince, who is too young.

When Prince Edward seconds Margaret's battle speech in Act 5, Oxford comments, 'O brave young Prince, thy famous grandfather / Doth live again in thee' (5.4.52–3). His famous grandfather was Henry V, whose rhetorical example the Prince has already echoed in little (2.2.80). In between the first and last acts, Prince Edward is highly visible, but mostly silent. He is there as an example to his saintly, bookish father (2.2.39–42), 'forward' (58), 'toward' (66). The implication seems to be that with his death the realm loses the hope of an authoritative monarch, who would have established law and order, avoiding the remorseless violence of Richard III's regime. But Prince Edward's authority remains unrealized in the play itself.

MISCHIEF

There was, of course, another side to childhood in the period, and this, too, might come into collision with the responsibilities of little princes. In Van Dyck's first painting, Princess Mary and the Duke of York wear smocks or aprons to keep their clothes clean, presumably on the eminently sensible grounds that such young children could not be relied on to keep out of mischief. (Although these garments are so filmy as to be almost invisible, it was thought at the time that this was one basis of Charles I's objection to the portrait.[23] There are no aprons in the second version.) Like the artist, the Protestant reformers in particular also knew all too well that children did not always live up to the high expectations they generated.

Even though 'pretty Rutland' died quoting Ovid in Latin (*3 Henry VI* 1.3.48), as Jaques recognized, ordinary children, however scrubbed clean, might be less than enthusiastic about their lessons: 'Then the whining schoolboy with his satchel / And shining morning face, creeping like snail / Unwillingly to school' (*As You Like It* 2.7.144–6). A moral play from much earlier in the sixteenth century borrows the medieval tradition of the distinct ages of man to anticipate Jaques's division into seven stages. *The World and the Child*, printed in 1522, shows its protagonist changing his name and his identity at roughly seven-year intervals. The World first confirms the infant's name as 'Dalliance' for the duration of the period during which he needs to be fed and clothed, then subsequently renames him Wanton, an appellation he is to bear until he is fourteen. This schoolboy is distinctly naughty:

> When I to school shall take the way,
> Some good man's garden I will assay,
> Pears and plums to pluck.
> I can spy a sparrow's nest,
> I will not go to school but when me lest. (108–12)

While this might seem harmless enough, Wanton's mischief also has less attractive manifestations:

> If brother or sister do me chide
> I will scratch and also bite,
> I can cry and also kick,
> And mock them all berew.
> If father or mother will me smite
> I will wring with my lip
> And lightly from him make a skip
> And call my dame shrew. (84–91)[24]

According to the theology of the play, the child is recalcitrant because he is subject to the values of the World, whose care he needs while his immortal soul is joined to a material body. Later Protestant moral plays will be much harsher in their depiction of disobedient children, and will be very ready to show them coming to a bad end. At the end of *The World and the Child*, the hero repents and is saved, but in the Protestant *Nice Wanton*, for example, performed during the reign of Edward VI, the naughty little girl eventually dies of the pox, while her unrepentant brother is finally hanged.

John Lyly's pert pages are not wicked, only cheeky. But they display a precocious knowingness and an ability to outwit the adults. Lyly's delicate courtly entertainments have no direct repercussions for Shakespeare's history plays, perhaps, though their influence can be seen in the presentation of Moth in *Love's Labour's Lost*. But the mischief of these little boys constitutes part of the framework within which Shakespeare's princes contribute to the emerging understanding of childhood.

Is it heroic loyalty, then, or mischief that impels Prince Edward to correct the Earl of Warwick when he calls his mother 'Injurious Margaret'? The Prince intervenes sharply: 'And why not "Queen"?' (*3 Henry VI* 3.3.78). In the same spirit, he puts the King of France straight when the monarch declares that his daughter will be married to Edward IV, 'the English King'. 'To Edward, but not to the English King', the Prince observes (139–40). When he is finally captured by the Yorkists, he still refuses to acknowledge the kingship of Edward IV. At first, this seems only to confirm his authority as the rightful heir, but the derision that provokes his uncles to stab him is heard uneasily in the twenty-first century:

> I know my duty – you are all undutiful.
> Lascivious Edward, and thou, perjur'd George,
> And thou, misshapen Dick, – I tell ye all
> I am your better, traitors as ye are. (5.5.33–6)

With incidental variants, the octavo of 1595 stops here. The Folio adds, 'And thou usurp'st my father's right and mine', which slightly softens the effect by reverting to the legitimacy of his claim.

Are our current sensibilities here anachronistic? The Prince's taunts are justified by the play. They are nothing compared with the verbal abuse that Margaret will deliver to all and sundry in *Richard III*. Moreover, he is no longer the little boy of the early scenes. What is more, nothing here justifies the death he at once incurs, and this fact distracts attention from the barbs. Yet something in the nature of his words seems unappealing now. It is impossible to say how contemporary audiences would have reacted to Prince Edward's defiance. My own best guess is that this was a culture that had yet to associate precocity with charm, at least in such a context. It was only gradually that mischief was able to recast itself as the playfulness demonstrated by Mamillius and the young Macduff, soliciting adult indulgence and, in consequence, intensifying the pathos of their deaths.

Richard III

By providing two little princes for Richard to murder in the Tower, history offered a way of resolving the problem of the collision between innocence and authority, as well as between authority and mischief. In Shakespeare's play the new Prince of Wales shows the same promise as his namesake in *3 Henry VI* and, indeed, his predecessor in the anonymous *True Tragedy of Richard the Third*: 'if I live until I be a man, / I'll win our ancient right in France again, / Or die a soldier, as I lived a king' (3.1.91–3). But he knows there is some doubt about whether he will survive so long, and the older brother shows himself capable of caution. The mischief, meanwhile, is mainly ascribed to the younger Duke of York. Both show a well-founded suspicion of Richard, but where York's words are provocative, Edward's are more circumspect. In consequence, while there is nothing but the traditional pathos in Tyrrel's account of their deaths, the scene where they encounter their uncle both differentiates the princes from one another and invests them with an autonomy more secure than Prince Edward's in the earlier play.

How old are the princes? Historically, they were eleven and twelve. But history is not reliable as a guide to the plays themselves: Shakespeare happily extends or telescopes chronology to suit the interests of theatre.[25] It would be consistent with those interests and with the text to dress York in petticoats.[26] The ages of Shakespeare's children are very rarely specified precisely. Perhaps this was practical, a matter of the sizes of the boy actors available at the time. But my impression is that the tendency was to think in terms of distinct stages. *The World and the Child* transforms its protagonist every seven years: first the infant, called Dalliance, then the schoolboy, Wanton. When he reaches fourteen the World reappears to name him Lust-and-Liking, the lover, 'fresh as flowers in May' (132), and at twenty-one he becomes Manhood. This is exactly the development that

Jaques charts: 'At first the infant .... Then the whining schoolboy .... And then the lover .... Then a soldier ... bearded' (*As You Like It* 2.7.142–9). The allocation of seven years to each phase makes sense in relation to the social practices of the period. Breeching at about seven marked a significant stage in the lives of aristocratic boys, transferring them to the care of men for education and instruction in manly pastimes. Henry VIII's heir began his classical education shortly before his seventh birthday; it ended when he was fourteen. A grammar school education generally lasted six or seven years from the age of seven. Meanwhile, fourteen was the legal age of marriage for boys, and the textbook age of puberty, though in practice there is reason to suppose that this was considerably higher.[27] Fourteen was also the minimum legal age of apprenticeship. The age of majority was twenty-one.

The stage of life reached by Shakespeare's princes would have been immediately apparent from their costume. Mamillius, we know, is 'unbreech'd', and we see him still in the care of Hermione and her ladies. The young Macduff and Clarence's orphans are also seen only with women. In *Richard III* the Prince of Wales is old enough to be separated from his mother. He has his own household at Ludlow in the care of his uncle, Lord Rivers. This was consistent with early modern practice for princes of about seven and above.[28] Moreover, Edward talks like a schoolboy. He knows about Julius Caesar, and is able to assess the relation between his life and his writing in a series of neat rhetorical turns:

> With what his valour did t'enrich his wit,
> His wit set down to make his valour live.
> Death makes no conquest of this conqueror,
> For yet he lives in fame though not in life. (3.1.85–8)[29]

As he suggests here, the Prince is much concerned with the question of historical memory. The truth ought to survive, he believes, even if it escapes the written record (75–8). These words would carry considerable irony for the audience: the princes' deaths were not attributed to their uncle in writing until long after the event; they had no tomb and thus no epitaph (4.3.29–30). To judge by Richard's reaction, he suspects that the irony is available to the Prince as well: 'So wise so young, they say, do never live long' (3.1.79).

York, however, is still in the care of his mother and his grandmother. His size and his growth are recurring issues (2.4.6–15; 3.1.102–4, 120–22, 130). It is not clear how small the actor would have been. I have suggested elsewhere that the inclusion of so many young children in Shakespeare's plays gave apprentice actors the opportunity to practise their skills by playing relatively small parts in preparation for the demands of major roles. There seems no good reason to apply the principle of thrift that governs the doubling of adult roles: these were not necessarily the same boys who reappeared as grown women. The youngest recorded theatrical apprentices were eleven or twelve when they started, and this, allowing for a later age of puberty and a degree of dramatic skill, would enable them to impersonate relatively young children.[30] An exchange between York's anxious mother and his indulgent grandmother indirectly treats him as very young. He has heard the old wives' tale that Richard was born with teeth and the Queen feels his interest in this issue should not be encouraged:

Eliz. A parlous boy! Go to, you are too shrewd.
Duch. Good madam, be not angry with the child.
Eliz. Pitchers have ears. (2.4.35–7)

'Parlous' means clever, mischievous; it also means perilous. This little boy's precocious curiosity is dangerous: the Duke of York is too clever for his own good.

His older brother also recognizes this. When York engages in a contest of wit with his uncle, the Prince of Wales prudently intervenes: 'My lord of York will still be cross in talk / – Uncle, your grace knows how to bear with him' (3.1.126–7). It is Richard, he implicitly acknowledges, who makes the jokes here. York's overture may have concealed an insult. He asks for Richard's dagger, calling it a 'toy' (114). Is this childish innocence, or is he drawing attention to the nervous mannerism recorded in the sources, which made Richard repeatedly finger his dagger? Or is he linking Richard with the traditional stage Vice and his dagger of lath, embodiment of every kind of evil in the moral plays?[31] Whatever we conclude on this issue, the offence is more explicit when York tells Richard, 'Because that I am little like an ape, / . . . you should bear me on your shoulders!' (130–1). There was a tradition that fools carried monkeys; moreover, the shoulder-saddle made them look deformed. However, the insult is also oblique, as Buckingham notices:

With what a sharp, prodigal wit he reasons:
To mitigate the scorn he gives his uncle,
He prettily and aptly taunts himself.
So cunning and so young is wonderful. (132–5)

When Buckingham draws Richard's attention to the offence, this time it is the Duke of Gloucester who calls him 'parlous' (153).

Meanwhile, the Prince of Wales is more alert to their danger, if less ready to intensify it. When York alludes to the murdered Clarence, he insists that he is not afraid of ghosts. Richard is unctuousness itself, but the Prince is not fooled:

Prince. I fear no uncles dead.
Rich. Nor none that live, I hope?
Prince. An if they live, I hope I need not fear. (146–8)

In this battle of wits, Richard does not always have the last word. For all Margaret's railing, it is the little princes who represent his most effective verbal opponents – until a grown man with an army comes to defeat him.

More than just a screen on which Richard's tyranny is projected, the princes defy the usurping Duke with ingenuity, if not yet charm. The disarming playfulness would come later. At this moment, in the early 1590s, the culture does not seem to have perceived what we have come to think of as the distinctive appeal of childishness. But the princes represent a stage on the way to the autonomy of children. While their diction remains fairly simple, differentiating them from adults, their interventions are ironic, layered, ambiguous. Even though most of the audience would have known the outcome, a certain tension informs their struggle against Richard, not least thanks to the difference the play sets up between the princes. In the process it also invests the children with an independent role in the conflict, and childhood itself with concerns, capacities and responsibilities of its own.

NOTES

1 The play's most recent editor calls the princes 'a pair of pert adolescent youths', 'gangly' and confrontational (William Shakespeare, *The Tragedy of King Richard III*, ed. John Jowett (Oxford: Oxford University Press, 2000), pp. 39, 53).

2 A baby's head is generally about 22 per cent of the length of the total skeleton from crown to heel, while an adult's might be about 14 per cent. Charles's head takes up roughly 19 per cent of his height.

3 Galleria Sabauda, Turin.

4 City of Bristol Museum and Art Gallery. Attributed to Robert Peake.

5 National Portrait Gallery, London. Artist unknown.

6 National Gallery of Art, Washington, DC.

7 Royal Collection. Artist unknown.

8 Longleat House, Wiltshire. Attributed to Hans Eworth.

9 National Portrait Gallery, London. Attributed to Rowland Lockey after Arnold van Brounckhorst.

10 See also Catherine Belsey, 'Shakespeare's Little Boys: Theatrical Apprenticeship and the Construction of Childhood', in Bryan Reynolds and William West, eds., *Rematerializing Shakespeare: Authority and Representation on the Early Modern English Stage* (Basingstoke: Palgrave Macmillan, 2005), pp. 53–72 (pp. 57–9).

11 *Two Coventry Corpus Christi Plays*, ed. Hardin Craig (London: Oxford University Press, 1957), pp. 1–32, lines 830–76.

12 Thomas Preston, *Cambises*, ed. Robert Carl Johnson (Salzburg: Institut für Englische Sprache, 1975). I have modernized the quotation.

13 The octavo text of 1595 is slightly less explicit on this point than the Folio of 1623, but the impression here, too, is that all three stab him.

14 The tragedy of civil war for the family is emblematically dramatized by the nameless figures of a son and a father in *3 Henry VI* (2.5.55–122): '*Exit* [at one door] *with* [the body of] *his father*' (113 S.D.); '*Exit* [at another door] *with* [the body of] *his son*' (122 S.D.).

15 In a painting by Marcus Gheeraerts of about 1608, he wears the Garter robes, but by then he was fourteen (National Portrait Gallery, London).

16 National Portrait Gallery, London; Royal Collection.

17 Christopher Brown and Hans Vlieghe, eds., *Van Dyck 1599–1641*, Catalogue of the Exhibition (London: Royal Academy; Antwerp: Antwerpen Open, 1999), p. 296.

18 G. B. Harrison, ed., *The Letters of Queen Elizabeth I* (London: Cassell, 1968), pp. 5–6. For an account of Elizabeth's rigorous education, see T. W. Baldwin, *William Shakspere's Small Latin and Lesse Greeke*, 2 vols. (Urbana: University of Illinois Press, 1944), vol. 1, pp. 257–84.

19 The infant protagonist of *The World and the Child* announces, 'Now to seek death I must begin' (l. 36). *The Worlde and the Chylde*, ed. Clifford Davidson and Peter Happé (Kalamazoo: Western Michigan University, 1999). I have modernized the quotations.

20 J. W. Williamson, *The Myth of the Conqueror. Prince Henry Stuart: A Study of Seventeenth-Century Personation* (New York: AMS Press, 1978), pp. 1–2.

21 G. P. V. Akrigg, ed., *Letters of King James I* (Berkeley: University of California Press, 1984), pp. 41–3.

22 References are to Christopher Marlowe, *Edward the Second*, ed. Charles R. Forker (Manchester: Manchester University Press, 1994).

23 Brown and Vlieghe, eds., *Van Dyck*, p. 296.

24 For medieval analogues, visual as well as written, of the ages of man, see *The Worlde and the Chylde* pp. 6–8, 16–19.

25 In one notable instance, Richard himself is presented as the military hero of *3 Henry VI*, 1.1. Historically, at this time he would have been eight years old, while the young Earl of Rutland was his elder brother.

26 This distinction might also have been made in *The True Tragedy*, where the young King is aware of their danger, while York innocently asks Forest to tell them 'a merry story' to cheer his brother (Barron Field, ed., *The True Tragedy of Richard the Third* (London: Shakespeare Society, 1844), p. 42).

27 Richard Rastall assesses the likely age of male puberty as seventeen to eighteen in the late Middle Ages (Rastall, 'Female Roles in All-Male Casts', *Medieval Drama in English* 7 (1985), 25–50).

28 Henry VIII packed his heir, Prince Edward, off to Hampton Court with an all-male retinue just before his seventh birthday; from 1603, when he was nine, Prince Henry had his own house at Oatlands, governed by Sir Thomas Chaloner, with Adam Newton as his tutor. Three years after the Van Dyck portrait, Prince Charles was installed as Prince of Wales and given his own all-male household.

29 The main figure here is antimetabole, the repetition of the same words in inverted order.

30 Belsey, 'Shakespeare's Little Boys'.

31 Alan C. Dessen, *Shakespeare and the Late Moral Plays* (Lincoln: University of Nebraska Press, 1986), pp. 41–4.

4

Father-child identification, loss and gender in Shakespeare's plays

Hattie Fletcher and Marianne Novy

'Shakespeare's art', wrote the critic C. L. Barber, 'is distinguished by the intensity of its investment in the human family, and especially in the continuity of the family across generations.'[1] But in the theatre, as historically, such continuity is fragile, for parents cannot always ensure their children's survival or control their choices. Still, for parents in Shakespeare, the relationship to their children is dramatized as crucial to their own identity. Throughout Shakespeare's career, one of the most recurrent constellations of themes is a father's identification with a child, particularly with a daughter, followed by some kind of loss of that child, whether to death or to marriage. This father-child relation often contributes to a central conflict of the play, as well as to its greatest emotional intensity. The plays suggest that emotions related both to having children and to having memories of childhood are central to the identities of many of the characters.

While childhood in most of the chapters in this volume is a matter of age, the word 'child' is ambiguous; it can also apply to persons of all ages in relation to their parents. In many cultures parents' experiences of young children as their dependants and even possessions may continue to affect parental perceptions of offspring even after the children have become adults. Such dynamics also influence some adult children's attitudes toward their parents. Elizabethan conduct manuals' emphasis on the duty of obedience to parents no doubt encouraged this expectancy of continued control by parents, especially by fathers. In particular, it was hard to see daughters as ever becoming adults, because in a basic typology women were always linked with boys and subordinate to men. That 'child' might even be used synonymously with 'girl' as opposed to 'boy' is suggested by the Old Shepherd's question in *The Winter's Tale* about the foundling Perdita: 'A boy or a child, I wonder?' (3.3.68). This infantilization of daughters was heightened when, as so often in Shakespeare, the relation at issue was that of fathers and unmarried daughters.[2] At especially emotional moments, as many lines quoted here will show, fathers very often refer to or address even married daughters as 'my child', rather than 'my daughter'.

Shakespeare's deliberate emphasis on the youth of even older children – for example, with Juliet, Marina, Perdita and Miranda, whose ages are specified in the mid-teens – further blurs the boundary between childhood and adulthood, particularly in the case of daughters. In fact, each of these daughters marries significantly earlier than the average woman, even the average aristocratic woman, in Shakespeare's society, a device that on stage might serve to heighten the dramatic tension in an already emotionally fraught situation. The youth of the daughters might also intensify the perception of the fathers' loss.

This emphasis on the youth of the younger generation is particularly striking at the beginning and the end of Shakespeare's career; the plays in these periods feature the losses not only of daughters of barely marriageable age, but also of babies and very young children. The death rate of young children was high enough that the deaths of characters such as Arthur and Mamillius clearly resonated with Shakespeare's audience. At the beginning of the seventeenth century, life expectancy in London was only 22.3 years,[3] and across early modern Europe 'an infant in the first four months of life had in general a 20 to 40 percent chance of dying before his or her first birthday'.[4] Furthermore, temporary losses of children were part of familial routine. Upper-class children were frequently sent out to wet nurses in the country, and from about ten years of age on, upper-class children might be sent to other families to learn manners and to bond dynasties, middle-class children to learn trades and professions, and lower-class children to become servants.[5]

In spite of the circulation and frequent death of children, and contrary to the view of Lawrence Stone, historians such as Keith Wrightson have found much evidence of affection between parents and children in Elizabethan England.[6] Nor are moments of such affection absent in the plays; Prospero's recollection of little Miranda's smile, for example, may have prompted his audience to fond recollections of their own.

However common and desirable, affection was not the only crucial ingredient in the parent-child relationship. As in most patriarchal societies, in Elizabethan England parents' identification with their children was important. Physical resemblance (a concern more for fathers than for mothers, because the maternal genetic connection was less open to doubt) reinforced the father's belief that he had begotten the child, that his line would be perpetuated, and that his inheritance would go where it should. Similarity heightened the sense of family solidarity. Advice books sometimes used this physical connection as a rationale for children's obligation to their parents. William Gouge, for example, wrote that 'children have received their very substance from the substance of their parents'.[7] The implication was that children began with a debt to their parents that they could never repay. In the second of his procreation sonnets, Shakespeare summarizes the advantage of parenthood as 'to be new made when thou art old, / And see thy blood warm when thou feel'st it cold' (Sonnet 2, ll. 13–14). Identification could permit parents to enjoy their children's youth as a kind of second youth of their own, and to take credit for their children's accomplishments; conversely, of course, they might also suffer from this identification, whether because of the child's death or sufferings, frustration and shame at not being able to control the child, and/or guilt in believing that their children were being punished for their own conduct. Indeed, certain kinds of identification with one's children, especially if frustrated, may lead parents to words and behaviour that suggest anger sufficient to override any affection.

Perhaps, just as physical similarity was more of a concern for fathers than for mothers, control may also have been more of a concern for fathers because of their status as head of the family. Whatever the reason, it is almost always fathers in Shakespeare's plays who speak of identification with their children, whether in enjoyment, in grief, or as an attempt to control. But family resemblance is such a frequent concern in Shakespeare that other characters sometimes note it as well; in fact, he frequently adds it to his sources. Elinor's declaration that her son has 'a trick of Cordelion's face' (*King John* 1.1.85), and Paulina's list of Perdita's resemblances to Leontes (*The Winter's Tale* 2.3.98–103) are two of Shakespeare's many inventions of this kind. His use of similar language in the sonnets shows that this concern with physical resemblance is more than simply an attempt to guide audience response to different-looking actors in the theatre.[8]

Perhaps Shakespeare's earliest play to emphasize parent-child identification, *Titus Andronicus*, his first tragedy, introduces four themes that recur elsewhere: physical similarity, parental authority, moral identification and (less repeated until the late romances) revivifying power, sometimes associated with a child's smile. Parental authority and moral identification, both more relevant to a child in adolescence or older than to an infant, are associated particularly with Titus himself. Significantly, Titus is the character most linked with the values of ancient Rome, in which fathers had literal power of life and death over their children. In the first scene

Titus, having lost twenty of his twenty-five sons in battle, kills Mutius, the youngest, because he goes against Titus's choice of husband for Lavinia. Later, he also kills his daughter Lavinia after she is raped and mutilated, saying, 'Die, die, Lavinia, and thy shame with thee / And with thy shame thy father's sorrow die' (5.3.45–6). The Emperor Saturninus and the other bystanders are shocked by Titus's behaviour, and it is tempting to see *Titus* as in part a critique of the patriarchal Roman family. But the play also shows fatherly affection: Titus at first speaks of Lavinia as 'cordial of mine age to glad mine heart' (1.1.166), a phrase that King Lear might have used of Cordelia, whose name it suggests – 'cordial', like 'Cordelia', being derived from the Latin word for 'heart'. After Titus's death, his sons Lucius and Marcus remember his love of his grandson: Marcus says to the boy, 'How many thousand times hath [Titus's] poor lips, / When they were living, warmed themselves on thine!' (5.3.166–7). Nevertheless, a spectator thinking of Titus's killing of two of his children might see in this image a self-serving quality in his affection.

Aaron the Moor, the character most visually marked as an outsider to Roman society, shows for his child (conceived outside a legal Roman family) the affection most recognizable as ordinary parental love.[9] His identification with his child is also more vivid than Titus's with any of his children. Aaron is delighted with the similarity of his infant to himself – the seal 'stamped in his face' (4.2.126) – and with the suggestion of youthful energy which at the same time pays tribute to his own potency: 'My mistress is my mistress, this myself, / The [vigour] and the picture of my youth' (4.2.106–7).[10] While Tamora's other sons despise the child because his blackness proves their mother's adultery, Aaron glories in the colour as a sign of his paternity: 'Look, how the black slave smiles upon the father, / As who should say, "Old lad, I am thine own"' (119–20). Aaron may lose whatever audience sympathy he gains from this love when he suddenly kills the midwife; yet his care for his child continues. After he is betrayed, he negotiates a promise from Titus's son Lucius to 'nurse and bring . . . up' his baby (5.1.84). Ultimately, however, the baby's fate is uncertain; Aaron is sentenced to die a painful death, and in the last scene, although the baby appears as testimony to Tamora's affair with Aaron, no one mentions what will happen to him. Even Aaron not only ignores him in his last speech but also, in a sense, disavows his identification when, in refusing to repent, he says, 'I am no baby, I' (5.3.184). In the final scene of some recent productions, the baby appears dead; on the other hand, Julie Taymor's 1999 film puts much emphasis on his final survival and his fostering by Lucius's young son.

More than Aaron's relationship with his son, Titus's relationship with Lavinia anticipates what is to follow in Shakespeare: fathers' identification with young and marriageable daughters dominates many plays of the subsequent career. Shakespeare knew Roman comedies, which were a text in Elizabethan grade schools; some of his plays, such as *The Comedy of Errors*, have clear sources in Plautus, and some critics have related Shakespeare's blocking fathers to the *senex iratus*.[11] But Roman comedies put more emphasis on father-son than father-daughter relationships, and they lack much of the poetically extended dialogue in which Shakespeare shows the ambivalence and pain that accompany angry paternal identification. Why, then, is Shakespeare more concerned with the father-daughter relationship, and why is it such a site of painful ambivalence?

Typically, in the early plays, conflict arises between father and daughter over the issue of betrothal or marriage. Wrightson argues that marriage practices in seventeenth-century England were varied, but that in general 'the likelihood of parents initiating or proposing a match was not uniform even at the highest social levels, while even when they did so, children usually seem to have enjoyed a right of refusal'.[12] But there were notorious cases of conflict, and it is on situations like these that most of Shakespeare's comedies and tragedies build.

In two early comedies and one early tragedy, *A Midsummer Night's Dream*, *Much Ado About Nothing* and *Romeo and Juliet*, the father's language about a daughter whose behaviour at the point of marriage displeases him suggests issues which figure in many of the later plays. In both *A Midsummer Night's Dream* and *Romeo and Juliet*, the father becomes angry because of his daughter's refusal to marry the suitor of his choice, and in *Much Ado About Nothing* the father expresses shame and sorrow at what he thinks is his daughter's lack of chastity. In every case the father's identification with his daughter heightens his emotion.

A Midsummer Night's Dream begins in the same type of patriarchal Greco-Roman society as *Titus*. Egeus clearly views fatherhood as almost a legal contract: in response to Hermia's choice of Lysander, he counters, 'As she is mine, I may dispose of her, / Which shall be either to this gentleman [Demetrius] / or to her death, according to our law' (I.I.42–4). As in *Titus*, the law is on his side; Theseus supports the angry father, and his justification for this harsh sentence makes the classic connection between father-child physical similarity and paternal authority, developing further the 'stamp' image used by Aaron. He tells Hermia that to her father she is 'but as a form in wax, / By him imprinted, and within his power / To leave the figure or disfigure it' (1.1.49–51). Hermia is to be a reproduction of her father, a copy not only of his image but also of his character.

In *Much Ado About Nothing*, Leonato's reaction is similar when he believes that Hero has shamed him before Don Pedro and Claudio. Again, grief stems from the father's identification with his daughter. Early in the play, the men remark on the physical – and, apparently, moral – resemblance between father and daughter. 'Truly the lady fathers herself,' exclaims Don Pedro. 'Be happy, lady, for you are like an honourable father' (1.1.90–1). When Leonato thinks that she is unchaste, he hopes that Hero will die instantly, rather than live to reflect badly upon him, in another classic statement where the repetition of the word 'mine' suggests the egotism and possessiveness in such parent-child identification:

> Do not live, Hero, do not ope thine eyes . . .
> . . .
> . . . Grieved I I had but one?
> Chid I for that at frugal nature's frame?
> O one too much by thee! Why had I one?
> Why wast thou ever lovely in my eyes?
> Why had I not with charitable hand
> Took up a beggar's issue at my gates,
> Who smirched thus and mired with infamy,
> I might have said, 'No part of it is mine,
> This shame derives itself from unknown loins.'
> But mine, and mine I loved, and mine I praised,
> And mine that I was proud on, mine so much
> That I myself was to myself not mine,
> Valuing of her – (4.1.122–37)

Hero's shame does not belong to her alone; because of her father's identification with her, any misdeed on her part belongs also to him. Indeed, to hear him tell it, he seems almost to have no identity of his own. The darker potential of his identification becomes clear now, and Leonato regrets having become a father only to receive such treatment at the hands of his daughter. He even wishes for death himself; 'Hath no man's dagger here a point for me?' he demands (4.1.107). If his daughter should die, so should he.

Capulet echoes this sentiment upon the discovery of Juliet's 'death'. He tells Paris, 'Death is my son-in-law, death is my heir. / My daughter he hath wedded. I will die, / and leave him all' (4.4.65–7). He emphasizes the connection between himself and Juliet even more strongly a few lines later: 'O child, O child, my soul and not my child! / Dead art thou, alack, my child is dead, / And with my child my joys are buried' (4.4.89–91).

All these crises begin with the issue of losing a daughter in marriage. The fathers of dutiful Hero and more daring Juliet and Hermia are at the same life-stage, and different as Hero and Juliet are, each of them performs a fictive death, though in *Romeo and Juliet* the death initially only feigned will soon become real. Of the three plays, the tragedy most emphasizes the daughter's youth; the word 'child' appears in the play fifteen times (more than in any other Shakespeare play except *King John*), and on twelve of those times it refers to Juliet.[13] In one other use she compares herself, waiting for her night with Romeo, to 'an impatient child that hath new robes / And may not wear them' (3.2.30–31).

Surprisingly, despite overt father-daughter conflicts, most of the daughters in the comedies and the early tragedies do not really discuss their attitudes towards their fathers. Rosalind's flippant remark to Celia in *As You Life It*, 'What talk we of fathers when there is such a man as Orlando?' (3.4.33–4) might as easily apply to the others: why reflect on even a problematic relationship with the old man, when there is Lysander or Romeo or Claudio to think about? *The Merchant of Venice* is an exception. Both Portia and Jessica reflect on their relationships to their fathers, and both chafe against their father's control, though only Jessica rebels openly. Portia comments that 'the will of a live daughter [is] curbed by the will of a dead father' (1.2.21–2); Jessica makes a point of acknowledging the limits of the father-daughter connection:

> Alack, what heinous sin is it in me
> To be ashamed to be my father's child!
> But though I am a daughter to his blood,
> I am not to his manners. (2.3.15–18)

Perhaps Shylock's status as a religious outsider made this criticism more palatable to the original audience. For his part, Shylock seems equally upset by the loss of his daughter and his money, a reaction which undercuts to some degree the audience's sympathy for his grief. But clear partisanship with Jessica is also difficult; she has not only taken his money, she has sold his turquoise, the memento of her mother Leah. The repeated shifting of sympathies anticipates the ambivalent effect of the major tragedies, where the daughters, like Jessica, speak more about the limits of their relationship with their fathers.

In *Othello* Desdemona, for example, explains to Brabanzio in the court room:

> To you I am bound for life and education.
> My life and education both do learn me
> How to respect you. You are the lord of duty;
> I am hitherto your daughter. But here's my husband. (1.3.181–4)

When Brabanzio confronts the reality of his daughter's elopement, he echoes Capulet and Leonato. Note again the reference to Desdemona specifically as a child rather than a daughter, a word without quite as much explicit suggestion of youth, and, as with Leonato, the suggestion that he identifies with her more because she has no sister or brother.

> I had rather adopt a child than get it.
> . . . For your sake, jewel,
> I am glad at soul I have no other child,
> For thy escape would teach me tyranny,
> To hang clogs on 'em. (1.3.190, 194–7)

Like Leonato, he wishes that Desdemona had been adopted rather than his child by birth. He thinks that he might then have identified with her less and the loss would have been less painful. Later, he fulfils the threats made by Capulet and Leonato; his grief at Desdemona's marriage to Othello, we eventually learn, kills him.

While Desdemona can be performed as older and/or more mature than the daughters previously discussed, when she sees Othello's violent anger she also compares herself to a child in age, though for different reasons than Juliet:

> Those that do teach young babes
> Do it with gentle means and easy tasks.
> He might ha' chid me so; for, in good faith,
> I am a child to chiding. (4.2.114–17)

This passage contributes to the tendency to see Desdemona as losing her strength under Othello's attack.

In *King Lear*, unlike the previous cases, the daughter offends the father not by a real or apparent sexual choice, but by emphasizing her autonomy and the potential limits of their relationship. Cordelia tells Lear: 'You have begot me, bred me, loved me. I / Return those duties back as are right fit / Obey you, love you, and most honour you' (1.1.95–7). Lear responds by denying any kinship with her, though critics over the years have seen father and daughter as similar in stubbornness. Having to lose his fantasy of control over her, he brings about what at first seems a destruction of their relationship, and ultimately becomes the destruction of both their lives.

Unlike Leonato and Brabantio in having several daughters, Lear tries to conquer their love by dividing them. After rejecting Cordelia, he plays Goneril and Regan off against each other. Then, even in rage and grief as he recognizes the depth of his daughters' betrayal, he finds it harder to dissociate from them than he had thought. He tells Goneril:

> I will not trouble thee, my child; farewell.
> We'll no more meet, no more see one another.
> But yet thou art my flesh, my blood, my daughter;
> Or rather a disease that's in my flesh,
> Which I must needs call mine. (2.4.214–18)

When Cordelia finally returns and Lear realizes that she has forgiven him, he puts all his hope in her. He fantasizes about being alone in prison with her, and the relationship he describes in 5.3 demands precisely the all-encompassing love that Cordelia explains at the beginning that she cannot give him. Perhaps Lear has not learnt from his experience at all. Without Cordelia, there is nothing left for him in the world, and so he dies.

After *King Lear*, Shakespeare develops the father-daughter relationship in another key: the romances begin with the separation of parents and children and end with family reunion and harmony. *Pericles*, *The Winter's Tale* and *The Tempest* also give a more vivid picture than most of the other plays of the daughter as an infant. And in these plays the theme of children renewing parental life, not treated explicitly since *Titus Andronicus*, returns. In the first of the romances, *Pericles*, father and daughter are separated for most of the play. Rather than finding in the infant Marina a renewal of his life, Pericles, who thinks that his wife is dead, gives her to substitute parents.[14] Their eventual reunion, however, makes Pericles welcome her as 'Thou that begett'st him that did thee beget' and speak of her as giving him 'another life' (21.182, 194). He is interested not in her similarity to him, but in the fact that 'My dearest wife was like this maid' (21.95). There is no problem for father or daughter when Lord Lysimachus asks for her hand in marriage; indeed, because of their long separation there has been little opportunity for Marina's tractability to her father to become a point of contention.

In *The Winter's Tale* Leontes's separation from his daughter in her infancy is more obviously blameworthy. Hermione's friend Paulina tries to convince him that his daughter looks just like him, but he refuses to believe her, either about this or about his wife's faithfulness, and commands that

Perdita be exposed. But, like Pericles, he gets a second chance, and similarly, when reunited, he is interested in Perdita's resemblance not to him, but to her mother. He no longer doubts Hermione's faithfulness. Again, after such a long absence the daughter's tractability is not an issue. It is enough that she is found again. And her marriage is not simply nonconflictual, as in *Pericles*, but the means of confirming his restored relationship with his best friend.

Unlike the other romances, *The Tempest* does not show a father's separation from and reunion with his daughter, though it concludes with his relinquishment of her in marriage. This play splits the theme of father-child identification away from the theme of affection, loss, control and recovery, thus differentiating two aspects of fatherhood that we first saw combined in Aaron. Caliban imagines parent-child identification when he wishes that he had been able to have sex with Miranda and '[people] this isle with Calibans' (1.2.354), a desire that parallels Aaron's delight in his child's similarity to his appearance. Prospero, on the other hand, never mentions Miranda's physical resemblance to him. Like Aaron commenting on his baby, he recalls her smile when she, as a young child, escaped Milan with him, but he attributes it to 'fortitude from heaven' (54) which gave him strength as well. Unlike other fathers in Shakespeare, Prospero knows that losing his daughter to marriage and even more to her own independence is inevitable, but he acts out his emotional resistance to that independence at the same time as he counts on it. Appearing to give up control can be seen as the way that he can control her, though he understands that this more circuitous control will not last. Like Pericles, he says that his daughter has renewed his life, but more than the other fathers of the romances he acknowledges that his life, as well as his power, has a limit.

Although the father-daughter relationship is the dominant familial relationship in the romances, the theme of a young son renewing his father's life, emphasized in language used about Aaron's son in *Titus Andronicus*, also reappears in *The Winter's Tale*. Even as Leontes begins to doubt his wife, he calls his son Mamillius 'My collop' (1.2.139), meaning a piece of his own flesh, and believes that Mamillius looks just like him in his youth:

> I did recoil
> Twenty-three years, and saw myself unbreeched . . .
> How like, methought, I then was to this kernel,
> This squash, this gentleman. (1.2.156–7, 61–2)

He concurs when Polixenes says that his son is 'all my exercise, my mirth, my matter' (167). As his jealousy increases, however, he expresses it partly in terms of his hostility to Hermione's part in Mamillius: 'though he does bear some signs of me, yet you / Have too much blood in him' (2.1.59–60). After he separates son and mother, his identification continues in his interpretation of his son's illness; he assumes that Mamillius sees Hermione in the same way that he does, and is without sleep, as he is, for the same reason: 'Conceiving the dishonour of his mother, / He straight declined, drooped, took it deeply, / Fastened, and fixed the shame on't in himself' (2.3.13–15). The news of his son's death makes Leontes repent his injustice to his queen, but it is too late. His wife and daughter will be restored at the end, but Mamillius returns only in so far as looking at Florizel brings him to Leontes's mind: 'I lost a couple that 'twixt heaven and earth, / Might thus have stood begetting wonder as / You, gracious couple, do' (5.1.131–3).

There are a few Shakespearean plays in which fathers lose or think they lose older sons than Mamillius; in none of these cases, however, are the sons referred to as 'children' in the way daughters of comparable ages might be, and the emotional weight seems generally less. In *The Tempest*, for example, father-son loss occurs as a subordinate theme; part of the happy ending is the reunion of Alonso with his apparently lost son Ferdinand, though the loss is only an illusion created by Prospero. When Alonso speaks of the loss of Ferdinand as irreparable, Prospero self-centredly claims that his loss of a daughter leaves him with weaker means of comfort.

Given the patriarchal structure of Shakespeare's society, it is rather surprising that the plays dramatize a father's loss of a son – whether to death or to autonomy – so much less often than the loss of a daughter, and also that Prospero suggests that losing a daughter is worse. With the tradition of filial inheritance of the throne, we might expect to find more instances of fathers grieving sons in the history plays, and in *1 Henry IV* we do find a father distressed by his son's behaviour in a way we might compare to Lear's or Brabantio's attitude towards their daughters. Just as Lear considers Goneril a punishment and a disease in his blood, Henry believes that God is punishing him through his son: 'Out of my blood / He'll breed revengement and a scourge for me' (3.2.6–7). He never speaks of any similarity between himself and Hal, but a parody of the motif appears. Falstaff, playing King Henry, speaks of a resemblance between father and son in 'a villainous trick of thine eye and a foolish hanging of thy nether lip' (2.5.369–70) as evidence of Hal's parentage. In *2 Henry IV*, after the two Henrys have been reconciled, they are more clearly identified with each other. For example, Hal speaks of his wildness as having died with his father: 'In his tomb lie my affections' (5.2.124). In *Henry V* Hal even worries that his father's sins will be punished in him: he prays, 'Not today, O Lord, / O not today, think not upon the fault / My father made in compassing the crown' (4.1.274–6). These are among the few lines in Shakespeare in which we see expressed a child's identification with his father, rather than the reverse. (Before she recognizes her father, Marina says to him that she 'hath endured a grief / Might equal yours' (*Pericles* 5.1.90–1), and Cordelia and Desdemona both offer their fathers reciprocity, but these examples do not suggest as full an identification as Hal experiences here.) Hal's full identification, in spite of its ambivalence, shows that he successfully takes the place of the adult male as few other 'children' discussed in this chapter are able to. Indeed, the word 'child' is not applied to him, and in becoming king he refuses to be Falstaff's 'sweet boy' (*2 Henry IV* 5.5.41).

Another father enraged at a son's behaviour appears in the same act of *Richard II* in which we first hear Henry IV's discontent with his 'unthrifty son' (5.3.1), when the Duke of York denounces his son for joining a conspiracy against Henry. The motif of father-son similarity appears, though, in the mouth of York's Duchess, who thinks that York suspects his son of having a different father. She pleads: 'Sweet York, sweet husband, be not of that mind! / He is as like thee as a man [not a boy or a child] may be' (5.2.107–8). The theme of moral identification appears here when Henry says that he could forgive Rutland because of York's virtues: 'Thy overflow of good converts to bad, / And thy abundant goodness shall excuse / This deadly blot in thy digressing son' (5.3.62–4). But York, perhaps feeling the identification more strongly, does not want his son forgiven: he responds, 'Mine honor lives when his dishonor dies, / Or my shamed life in his dishonor lies' (5.3.68–9). While the Duchess pleads for mercy and Henry is willing to give it, York denounces his son.

This, like many scenes of parent-child mourning, exemplifies the idea that women generally feel, or express, the loss of their children more than men.[15] The Duchess of York says to her husband, 'Hadst thou groan'd for him / As I have done thou wouldst be more pitiful' (5.2.102–3). The father who has killed his son in *3 Henry VI* fears his wife's grief. And Macduff – although he says when his children are killed, 'Sinful Macduff, / They were all struck for thee' (4.3.226–7) – refuses to 'play the woman with mine eyes' (4.3.232). Yet identification rarely seems to be in play, even where women mourn their children at length. The mourning mothers of *Richard III* turn their grief into cursing the King; their children's similarity to them, or lack of it, or being punished for their sins, is not an issue. Because the question of cuckoldry does not enter into a mother-child relation, physical similarity may not be as important; or perhaps the plays suggest that maternal identification is of a different kind.

In *King John*, the play that uses the word 'child' most often and the one that might have been written closest to the death of Shakespeare's young son Hamnet, Constance's speeches of grief for her endangered son Arthur are even longer than Capulet's similar speeches about Juliet, but his resemblance to her never comes into the picture, though she calls him 'My life, my joy, my food, my all the world, / My widow-comfort, and my sorrow's cure' (3.4.104–5). Unlike Capulet, however, Constance is rebuked for her show of emotion: 'You are as fond of grief as of your child' (3.4.92), implying that her grief is selfish. Perhaps maternal grief was more likely to be rebuked as excessive because of a general devaluation of women.

The Shakespearean mother whose identification with her son is the most obvious is a tragic one, Volumnia, who says to Coriolanus, 'Thy valiantness was mine, thou suck'st it from me, / But owe thy pride thyself' (3.2.129–30). Arguably, Volumnia is the mother in Shakespeare who comes nearest to filling a 'patriarchal' authoritarian role, and like the tragic Shakespearean fathers she is threatened by her child's desire for autonomy – though in this play the only way he knows to seek autonomy is to take his mother's military values to the extreme of rejecting Rome because the Romans value military worth insufficiently. As Lucy Munro writes in chapter 6, the play repeatedly characterizes Coriolanus as a boy, and even the presence of his own son emphasizes rather than mitigates Coriolanus's childishness.

Shakespeare wrote for a male-dominated theatre in a male-dominated society. But he wrote many plays that show the limitation of the father's power. In most of the comedies, and in the Henriad, where children act in ways where the fathers lose control of them, the losses are resolved when children take an appropriate social place, in most cases in a new family. But in the tragedies the loss of children is more absolute.

The predominant gendering of paternal loss in Shakespeare's plays can be seen in biographical terms; like his own dead Hamnet, the named young children who die in the plays are all boys. Most of the children whom parents lose because they act against their parents' wishes, on the other hand, are female; Shakespeare's daughters, unlike Hamnet, survived, and presumably he had many opportunities to learn that they had wills of their own. Although the term 'child' is used of Lavinia, Cordelia, Juliet and Desdemona, their deaths come at a somewhat older age and in every case except Lavinia's it is associated with their exercise of autonomy – and for Desdemona and Juliet with a choice in marriage that links this loss closely with the kind seen in the comedies.

The echoes of Shakespeare's life in his plays, to a large extent, resonate with the values of his culture. As a patriarchal society, it was, because of the cuckoldry issue, more concerned about a father's similarity to his son than a mother's, and more apt to valorize a father's desire for control than a mother's. Similarly, it would have been officially more concerned about the death of the male child, the presumptive heir, than the death of a daughter, and since obedience was such an ideal for women, more shocked at the rebellion of a daughter than that of a son. A father was expected to feel and express some grief at his son's death.[16] But what is not so predictable is the persistence of the father-daughter identification and loss theme in Shakespeare's plays, which are unusual in how often a daughter, instead, evokes the depth of paternal loss, as well as the height of the consolation attendant on her return.

NOTES

1 C. L. Barber, 'The Family in Shakespeare's Development: Tragedy and Sacredness', in Coppélia Kahn and Murray Schwartz, eds., *Representing Shakespeare: New Psychoanalytic Essays* (Baltimore: Johns Hopkins University Press, 1980), pp. 188–202 (p. 188).

2 For a pioneering feminist discussion of father-daughter relations in Shakespeare using ritual theory and psychoanalysis, see Lynda Boose, 'The Father and the Bride in Shakespeare', *PMLA* 97 (1982), 325–47. For a contrasting poststructuralist approach, see Alan Sinfield, *Faultlines: Cultural Materialism and the Politics of Dissident Reading* (Oxford: Oxford University Press, 1992), pp. 29–51.

3 Heather Dubrow, *Shakespeare and Domestic Loss: Forms of Deprivation, Mourning, and Recuperation* (Cambridge: Cambridge University Press, 1999), p. 162.

4 Beatrice Gottlieb, *The Family in the Western World from the Black Death to the Industrial Age* (New York: Oxford University Press, 1993), p. 133.

5 *Ibid.*, p. 160.

6 Lawrence Stone, *The Family, Sex and Marriage in England, 1500–1800* (New York: Harper & Row, 1977), pp. 105–14, and Keith Wrightson, *English Society, 1580–1680* (London: Routledge, 2002), pp. 108–18.

7 William Gouge, *Of Domesticall Duties: Eight Treatises* (London, 1622), p. 431. We owe this reference to Claire Busse.

8 See, for example, Phyllis Rackin's discussion of King John in *Stages of History: Shakespeare's English Chronicles* (Ithaca: Cornell University Press, 1990), p. 187, p. 190. For Shakespeare's addition of the language of resemblance in *The Winter's Tale* to Robert Greene's *Pandosto* (1588), see Geoffrey Bullough, *Narrative and Dramatic Sources of Shakespeare*, 8 vols. (New York: Columbia University Press, 1966), vol. 8, p. 175. On the complicated effect of using the language of resemblance in the theatre, see Marianne Novy, *Reading Adoption: Family and Difference in Fiction and Drama* (Ann Arbor: University of Michigan Press, 2005), pp. 71–2.

9 See Meredith Skura, 'Discourse and the Individual: The Case of Colonialism in *The Tempest*', *Shakespeare Quarterly* 40 (1989), 42–69.

10 Q reads 'vigour'; the Norton has 'figure'. Whichever reading dominates, a pun on the other might be in the background.

11 See Leo Salingar, *Shakespeare and the Traditions of Comedy* (Cambridge: Cambridge University Press, 1974).

12 Wrightson, *English Society*, p. 79.

13 See Marvin Spevack, *A Complete and Systematic Concordance to the Works of Shakespeare*, 8 vols. (Hildesheim: Georg Olms, 1968–75).

14 *Pericles* is discussed in connection with contemporary fostering customs in Novy, *Reading Adoption*, pp. 75–8.

15 See Patricia Phillippy, *Women, Death, and Literature in Post-Reformation England* (Cambridge: Cambridge University Press, 2002), p. 1, for the general view of feminine sorrow as 'excessive, violent, and immoderate,' and 'men's grief' as 'stoic and short-lived'.

16 William Fulwood's letter-writing manual *The Enemie of idlenesse* (1598) and Robert Burton's *Anatomy of Melancholy* (1621) use the death of a son, not a daughter, as an example of a situation in which fathers might grieve. See Lynne Bruckner, '"Let Grief Convert to Anger": Authority and Affect in *Macbeth*', in Nicholas Moschovakis, ed., *Macbeth: New Critical Essays* (New York: Routledge, 2007).

5

Character building: Shakespeare's children in context

A. J. Piesse

> If we broadly define culture in terms of what is learnt and shared, then children as carriers of culture, and childhood where so much learning occurs, must be seen as crucial to the reproduction of culture.[1]

When Shakespeare examines the experience of children and childhood in his plays, he aligns his child and his young adult characters specifically and deliberately with ideas about textuality and history, showing them engaging directly with certain significant books and with ideas about the processes of history. The idea that formation of character and induction into an understanding of society is as much a product of text, of story, of history, as it is of experience is thereby made explicit. The fact that all the Shakespearean characters treated in this way are boys, and that only boys were formally educated in the Tudor system, where girls were not, lends further weight to this approach. What is the dramatic significance of the relationship between school texts, texts of formation, the process of history and the child figure in Shakespeare? How does this Shakespearean pedagogy construct masculine childhood as the site for the making of the early modern performative textual self?[2]

I want, in this chapter, to suggest two ways of reading the dramatic function of these child characters. The first is to acknowledge the explicit connection made between text, history and character: the Luciuses of *Julius Caesar* and *Titus Andronicus*, William in *The Merry Wives of Windsor* and Mamillius in *The Winter's Tale* are connected to specific texts or kinds of texts; Arthur and his female counterpart, Blanche, in *King John*, the two princes and the young Clarence children in *Richard III* and young Martius in *Coriolanus* are connected to an interrogation of the process of constructing history. In these roles there is a clear indication of the child's induction into society, the moment at which he or she becomes aware of society as political, being deliberately connected to social record, whether that be through myth, history, school texts or letters, which are records of social exchange.

These child figures are shown to be in possession of a knowledge of culture obtained not only from other people, but from books, letters or inscriptions, and the possession of this knowledge is generally shown to be a good thing. They are shown to be self-consciously aware that the historical moment in which they exist might be written down, represented, altered, preserved; and to be aware of this because they know that the history they already know is not monolithic. Speaking directly about a particular text, or kind of text, or the subject of history, they draw attention to their own function as carriers of literary and historical culture within the texts they inhabit. I will argue that in creating the characters in such a way, Shakespeare makes them resist already existing educational, historical or societal practice.

There is, however, a second way of reading dramatic function, and that is to see these moments as epitomizing the fundamental matter of each of the plays, so that the child's moment of political/social self-consciousness stands as an icon onstage for the audience's sudden recognition of what the play is fundamentally about. That is to say, the child character can also be seen to be functioning as a metatheatrical icon of the relation between text (albeit a performed text) and social understanding, to be performing the role of receiver and transmitter of information between page/stage and audience just as it does between generations within the confines of the play. In this way, too, the child character might be said to be fulfilling an ideological function, in so far as it is depicted in a way that draws attention to the gaps between how society is perceived to function by its dominant participants, and how it actually does function.[3] From time to time, then, I will suggest that particular moments of heightened sensitivity towards the relationships among the child, text and society are moments concerned with the ideological significance of the specific moment in the play, but also that these moments of focus gesture towards the wider ideological concerns of the text.

In *The Merry Wives of Windsor*, for example, the characters of William the grammar-school boy and Robin the page show children with differing social statuses being crucial to the construction of social expectation in the play. William's verbatim repetition of an instantly recognizable standard grammar lesson from William Lilly and John Colet draws audience attention to the functions of textuality and metatextuality in the play, while Robin's negotiations of role show Shakespeare's willingness to construct a child character investigating the socially constructed self, a motif ideologically at the centre of the play. Similarly, the exchanges between Richard and the two young princes in *Richard III* examine the power struggle between chronological, intellectual and hereditary seniority through a discussion of the relationship between myth, formally recorded history and history as the princes have been taught it. Shakespeare draws a clear distinction between the diction and preoccupation of each, however, and in this way the play uses the formation of the youthful character of the princes to draw attention to matters of historiography in direct parallel to the way it uses the figure of Richard to draw attention to construction of character.

Arthur, in *King John*, shows a similarly precocious awareness of ideas of historiography. He insists on setting a personal history against a publicly inscribed one – what Phyllis Rackin might see as a feminized (because domestic) rather than masculinized (because public) view of history – in order to change his would-be murderer's point of view in a way that fits perfectly into the play's wider historiographical concerns.[4] But Shakespeare holds up the unfixed, coming-into-being nature of the child for examination again in this moment, because precisely as Arthur's childishness is aligned with a feminized rather than masculinized account of history, aligning the child with the marginalized rather than the centralized view, so, too, his ability to see things from more than one point of view runs ideologically in parallel with an adult character, this time the Bastard. In the construction of these child characters, with their unrelenting, self-conscious interrogation of text in social context, Shakespeare repeatedly asks how ideas of self are built, in a form that draws attention to and investigates the concerns fundamental to each genre.

Mamillius in *The Winter's Tale* is at one level a conventional character, the princely son of a princely family. But he also typifies this questioning child, full of ideas and interrogations of his own about his position in domestic and political society. His proposal to tell a 'sad tale' of sprites and goblins shows him to be absolutely on that borderline between late infancy and growing into a more individualized status as a young boy, and his continued presence around the skirts of the women of the court to be therefore inappropriate and dangerous to his moral health as regularly suggested in texts on the rearing of children.[5] It is obvious that Mamillius's retreat into fantasy when confronted with sexuality in this scene stands in clear relation to his father's behaviour; given the agency to create his own narrative, he, like his father, chooses a sad tale.

This choice sets up in little the examination of the romance genre that is at the ideological centre of the play. The play as a whole, with its theme of jealousy and redemption through the journey to the pastoral and back again, is an examination of the relationship between what is real and what is imagined, and, metatextually, how the fundamental tenets of generic exposition come to influence such an examination. Thus Mamillius's choice of tale and the attention drawn to the moment causes the audience to reflect on what the telling of tales in the theatre means, and therefore to consider the romance genre within the confines of which the play is unfolding. Mamillius has a dual function within the family, being a physical outward and visible sign of a consummated and stable union for his mother but a politically unstable phantasmagoria for his father, since Leontes convinces himself that the boy is a travesty of the legitimate line. The tale Mamillius tells mimics this parallel, being for him simply a story of sprites and goblins but, for the audience, a vastly more significant indicator, epitomizing the wider vacillation of the play and the genre between literal and symbolic meaning. What kinds of stories about ourselves and our societies can we trust to be true?

In *Titus Andronicus* the audience is made doubly aware of the significance of the child in unfolding the relationship between the social and the private being. Young Lucius, pursued by his mutilated aunt with a copy of Ovid's *Metamorphoses* clutched between her bloody stumps, is the medium by which the Ovidian archetype for Lavinia's rape is made plain, and serves to draw attention to a number of intertextual and metatextual moments in the play. At the same time, the relationship between Young Lucius and his father throws into sharp relief Titus's dawning recognition that relationships between children and parents have a private as well as a civic aspect. Lucius is also instrumental in the firing of messages on arrows and in the delivery of extracts from Horace to Tamora's sons. Like his namesake in *Julius Caesar*, the explicit dramatic function of the child as bearer of text is held up as a gesture towards the symbolic function of the child as bearer of knowledge.[6]

As all these examples demonstrate, one function of the child figure in these plays is to stand as a symbol of growing into knowledge of self through the media of the text studied and the life lived. At the same time, the scenes in which the children appear can be seen to stand in epitome to the broader ideologies of the plays, so that the part of the text informed by the presence of the children draws attention to the meaning of the text as a whole. The idea of the character of the child being formed both by the text it inhabits and also by the texts its presence introduces creates an interesting interrogation of the child as subject both within and outside of the confines of the play. Does the child character have a separate agency in its own right, within history and within the plays? Or does it have agency only within a particular paradigm, standing in little for the experience of adult characters and modelled as an epitome? Does placing the child within the context of stories, histories and school texts reduce it to a symbol of a particular form of representation, or does it provoke so many different ways of thinking about the function of character that it actually has an enriching effect on the representational value of the child figure?[7]

If we are to accept this alignment, both metaphorical and literal, of the child with the text as a means to exploring agency, a fundamental question needs to be asked: what kind of books informed the intellects and imaginations of early modern children? There is no shortage of information on the prescribed reading for schoolchildren in early modern England. A whole range of documents survives, and while considerable work has been done on gathering and examining the material, there has been little focus on how such knowledge might be applied to the social realities of childhood in the period, and still less on the relationship between the realities of the education of children and how this is constructed and represented for the staging of childhood.[8] Among the documents that might give some idea of the kind of child that might emerge from a Tudor upbringing are specific and detailed curriculums, like Cardinal Thomas Wolsey's for Ipswich grammar school and Colet's for St Paul's, Cambridge records of book purchases for tutees (relevant to my discussion since undergraduates regularly went up to University at twelve and were finished by the time they were fifteen), and broad accounts by grammar-school masters such as William Kempe and Dudley Fenner of methods of education and recommended authors for the sons of merchants.[9] On the evidence of these curriculums, the young person whom books built in the sixteenth century would learn grammatical substance and style, the value of variety in expression, and a strong sense of social identity and self-representation, and would be inculcated with a firm classical and Christian sense of moral behaviour.[10] A sense of human frailty would be derived from texts conveying mutability and the inherent comedy of the human condition, while an awareness of paradigmatic approaches to learning would admit the possibility of a variety of subjectivities. Notions of history and of historiography would vie for attention with essays on proper familial and social conduct.

What we see here, then, is an education in alertness to style, to form, to self-expression, and in alertness not only to how those things can be made to work for the writer but also how those things can be made to work on the writer. Rhetorical adeptness comes from understanding what it is to be human well enough to be able to express what it is to be human in such a variety of ways that all varieties of the human will be persuaded. What emerges is precisely that practice of competing interpretations that is actively urged by the child characters within the plays under examination here and by the rhetorical effect of those characters on the audience's response to the play as a whole.

Plenty of writing survives on the kind of young person that Renaissance educators hoped to produce from such a programme.[11] William in *The Merry Wives of Windsor* is a parody of one such child. About to be escorted to school by his mother, he is caught in the happy circumstance of meeting the master coming from the school and being told that it is a holiday; less happily, his mother insists on him being put through his grammatical paces. He acquits himself reasonably well, though the answers he gives have clearly been learnt verbatim rather than derived from any real understanding.[12] His propensity for the literal, however

Eva. What is *lapis*, William?
Will. A stone.
Eva. And what is *a stone*, William?
Will. A pebble. (4.1.26–9)

seems a paradigm of clarity in juxtaposition with the master's pedantry and Mistress Quickly's apparent ability to see sexual innuendo in everything:

Will. *Genitive horum, harum, horum.*
Quick. Vengeance of Jenny's case! Fie on her! Never name her, child, if she be a whore. (4.1.52–4)

In a previous scene another child has been seen to conform exactly to what is expected of him. The exchange between Robin and Mistress Page at 3.3 has Robin as dutiful communicator but also has the child led to consider a role he might grow into:

Mrs Page. Here comes little Robin.
Mrs Ford. How now, my eyas-musket, what news with you?
Rob. My master, Sir John, is come in at your back door, Mistress Ford, and requests your company.
Mrs Page. You little Jack-a-Lent, have you been true to us?

Rob. Ay, I'll be sworn. My master knows not of your being here, and hath threatened to put me into everlasting liberty if I tell you of it; for he swears he'll turn me away.

Mrs Page. Thou'rt a good boy. This secrecy of thine shall be a tailor to thee, and shall make thee a new doublet and hose. (3.3.18–27)

The role of the child as bearer of information to the older generation is clear; his reward, befitting his station, is to be 'a new doublet and hose', but at the same time his social insignificance as both servant and child allows him to play the role of go-between without attracting undue attention to himself. Robin's willingness to forswear loyalty to his master and choose rather to honour those closer to his own class who honour him for what he is and what he can do, for his willingness to embrace their morals rather than those of the court, align the child firmly with the wider moral project of the play, which valorizes the commonsense, small-town, female, middle-class morals of the eponymous merry wives over the corrupt and cynical attitudes of sleazy, borderline upper-class male city morals as epitomized in Falstaff. At its very centre is the freedom of Ann Page and Fenton to achieve their union in the face of her father's morally questionable social aspirations. The ideological trajectory of the play, then, is epitomized in Robin's quiet moral choice in the scene just addressed, and the child's delivery of the note is a clear example of how a character might choose to be the carrier of its own inscribed culture.

The formation of William, as demonstrated in the grammar lesson, carries with it equal significance. As Giorgio Melchiori has pointed out, the 'comedy of languages' at the centre of the grammar scene is a central motif in the play, and 'word-play, mostly with marked sexual innuendos, on the terminology of grammar and on (mis)translation . . . runs through the play like a hidden linguistic thread that links together all or most of the characters'. Melchiori notes further that this particular scene is 'absent from earlier versions of the play and irrelevant to the action' but provides 'the essential clue to its inner meaning'.[13] Just as grammatical structure provides a fundamental, transferable framework for understanding, then, so this scene, with its examination of understanding and misunderstanding of the fundamental tools of communication, is essential to determining where meaning really lies in the play. That William answers quite literally by the book reinforces the idea that the scene lies in epitome to the play, where playing fast and loose with social rules, choosing to ignore them or deliberately misinterpret them, leads to a lesson being forcibly applied to Falstaff in the climactic 'baiting' scene at Herne's Wood. By showing the children obedient to the expectation of bourgeois social formation at the heart of the play's social structures, Shakespeare uses them to reflect a degree of stability in its mores. And, as Edward Berry observes, it is not accidental that 'Falstaff is subjected to symbolic punishment and public humiliation at the hands of the entire community, children included'.[14]

Clarence's children in *Richard III* at 2.2 similarly set up a crucial pattern which will be repeated more forcibly in relation to the two princes moments later. As the family meet to discuss the reasons for and possible consequences of their father's arrest (known to the audience, but not to them, to be the first of Richard's moves to clear his path to the throne) the children cut through prevarication from the Duchess of York, and their words seem to resist her imposition of a certain pattern of childhood on them. Despite their precocious questioning of her actions, she calls them 'Incapable and shallow innocents' (2.2.18); moments later, however, as the boy tells how Uncle Richard wept 'And pitied me, and kindly kissed my cheek, / Bade me rely on him as on my father, / And he would love me dearly as a child' (2.2.23–6), the notion of the child 'impressionable as wax' is brought to the fore.[15] The boy's male self-assurance is clear when he asks 'Think you mine uncle did dissemble, grannam?' (31) and, receiving the reply 'Ay, boy' (32), dismisses it with what can only be a moment when gender supersedes seniority: 'I cannot think it' (33). Richard's influence has reached into the younger generation and the authority of the older woman has been dismissed, just as Anne's acceptance of Richard's wooing of her even as she weeps over her father-in-law's murdered corpse has involved her dismissing the proprieties of imposed social constructs.

The scene sets up what will happen when Richard greets young Prince Edward, heir to the throne, at 3.1, and the parallel is intensified when initially Hastings and Buckingham join forces to drown out the younger voice, trying to assert seniority over precocity just as the Duchess of York did in the earlier scene. But Edward's subsequent interrogation of Buckingham shows that a solid grounding in early modern disputation, as well as a clear consciousness of his role as king-in-waiting, has put him in a position to hold his own in such a debate.

Prince. I do not like the Tower of any place. –
Did Julius Caesar build that place, my lord?
Buck. He did, my gracious lord, begin that place,
Which since succeeding ages have re-edified.
Prince. Is it upon record, or else reported
Successively from age to age, he built it?

Buck. Upon record, my gracious liege.
Prince. But say, my lord, it were not registered,
Methinks the truth should live from age to age,
As 'twere retailed to all posterity
Even to the general all-ending day.
Glo. (*Aside*) So wise so young, they say, do never live long.
Prince. What say you, uncle?
Glo. I say, 'Without characters fame lives long'.
(*Aside*) Thus like the formal Vice, Iniquity,
I moralize two meanings in one word. (3.1.68–83)

In questioning the veracity of the history surrounding the building of the Tower of London, and using a thoroughly appropriate rhetoric in doing so, Edward draws attention to the liminality of the histories that will attach to him, and prompts a significant act of 'self-speaking' from Richard.[16]

It is worth reiterating that Julius Caesar's *Histories* is one of the texts that occurs repeatedly on the school curriculum, and that there is a significant pun within the speech here on 're-edified'. The immediate meaning is to do with literal building, but the notion of learning, of personal edification, is implied, too, and the audience perhaps reminded of its own education in kinds of history and logical investigation into ways of knowing the truth. At the centre of the exchange is Richard's declaration of duplicity, and we see here again how a scene whose detail is largely irrelevant to the unfolding of the plot is actually pivotal in revealing fundamental notions about the play and draws attention to itself by the politically dangerous precocity of its child speaker.

Later in the same scene, young York's lesser gravity, as he jokes competently with Richard about the giving of a sword as a gift, befits the younger son, upon whom the burden of kingship is not expected to rest. But York's rhetorical ability is as well grounded as his brother's interrogation of history has been and perhaps more of a threat to Richard, playing him at his own game. Nor is he afraid to refer to a private domestic history, being the younger child still more closely aligned to the female household. York tells his grandmother, too, that the fantastic stories he has heard about Richard's being born with teeth ('he could gnaw a crust at two hours old', 2.4.28) were told to him by Richard's nurse – another moment that links him with being just out of the nursery, since he still trusts old wives' tales as a form of truth. As in *The Winter's Tale*, the younger boy's attachment to feminine behaviours – including faith in fairy stories and ghost stories – makes the alignment of domestic history with national history clear.

York. I shall not sleep in quiet at the Tower.
Glo. Why, what should you fear there?
York. Marry, my uncle Clarence' angry ghost.
My grannam told me he was murdered there.
Prince. I fear no uncles dead.
Glo. Nor none that live, I hope.
Prince. An if they live, I hope I need not fear.
(*To York*) But come, my lord, and with a heavy heart,
Thinking on them, go we unto the Tower. (3.1.142–9)

Interestingly, York's characteristics are put down to the direct influence of his mother:

Buck. Think you, my lord, this little prating York
Was not incensed by his subtle mother
To taunt and scorn you thus opprobriously?
Glo. No doubt, no doubt; O, 'tis a parlous boy,
Bold, quick, ingenious, forward, capable;
He is all the mother's from the top to the toe. (3.1.150–5)

York's views are dismissed, considered to be too closely informed by proximity to feminine and domestic company. Nevertheless, the scene shows how different kinds of training in different kinds of disputation can be equally effective and equally disruptive. The princes pose a real threat to Richard because they know their histories, both public and private, and are well equipped with the means of expressing them.

Thinking about history, and how it is communicated, is part of the proper process of growing into authority for these two young princes. In a play which investigates its own terms, not least through the self-interrogating character of Richard, the role of the young in identifying the idea of historiography (weighing up written against oral public history, male against female familial history, history set in stone as opposed to history in the making, history in edifice and history in edification) and realizing their own inscription within the history in which they participate, connects the formulation of these characters to the textuality of history. When all those slaughtered by Richard reappear as ghosts to unnerve him on the night before his fatal battle with Richmond at Bosworth Field, the princes are univocal in their condemnation, emblematic rather than individualized. Richard has lost his facility with manipulation of history and with presenting the many-faceted, self-created Vice figure necessary to his control of the dramatic process within the play. The indiscriminate dispatching of children has undone any remaining vestige of sympathy for Richard; history will be univocal in its condemnation of him for centuries to come.

The notion of the precocious and rhetorically able prince is allowed a more central and detailed treatment in the figure of Arthur in *King John*. That his role stands in important relation to the central preoccupation of the play – to what degree one's private history validates one's right to rule – is made clear by Eleanor and Constance bickering first over his father's legitimacy and then Arthur's own choice between the two sides who are competing for his fidelity. The opening of the play sees Eleanor deeply involved in her son John's governance of the kingdom, particularly over issues of legitimacy, and she means to have the same authority over her grandson Arthur. She has reckoned, however, without the equally determined maternal authority of Arthur's mother Constance. Stichomythic exchange between the competing women points up the intractability of the stand-off: 'There's a good mother, boy, that blots thy father,' points out grandmother Eleanor at 2.1.133–4; 'There's a good grandam, boy, that would blot thee,' retorts Constance, at once asserting Arthur's individuality and agency without letting him get a word in edgeways for himself. Twenty-five lines later, they are still at it, with Eleanor entreating directly and appealing to family feeling, 'Come to thy grandam, child', her tone immediately mimicked and undermined by Constance's 'Do, child, go to it grandam, child, . . . and it grandam will/ Give it a plum, a cherry and a fig' (2.1.159–62). In this way a particular notion of the mother's child (whether independent adult son or dependent minor) is made clear before the child (in Arthur's case) speaks for itself. Arthur's only interjection initially is to beg his mother and grandmother to be at peace; and I think it not accidental that the destructive argument here prefigures a later moment when a daughter, Blanche, symbolizing the contested site of France, complains that she will be rent asunder by familial dispute:

> Which is the side that I must go withal?
> I am with both; each army hath a hand;
> And in their rage, I having hold of both,
> They whirl asunder and dismember me. (3.1.253–6)

Arthur sees his personal predicament as epitomizing the political one, and it is his ability to consider both simultaneously that proves his momentary salvation at 4.1, where the invocation of a personal history springs from a consciousness of the value of different kinds of history. Rather than invoking his public social significance, Arthur appeals to the intimate, personal history he shares with the man who is about to act not in terms consistent with their hitherto close friendship but rather as a public servant on the King's orders. As Hubert moves to blind Arthur at the King's command, Arthur stops him in his tracks, not with physical resistance, or with mute appeal, or by invocation of his princely status, but rather with

> Have you the heart? When your head did but ache,
> I knot my handkerchief about your brows
> The best I had – a princess wrought it me,
> And I did never ask it you again –
> And with my hand at midnight held your head;
> And like the watchful minutes to the hour,
> Still and anon cheered up the heavy time,
> Saying, 'What lack you?' and 'Where lies your grief?' (4.1.41–8)

Arthur is able to manipulate different kinds of history, can usefully invoke a personal history, and can prompt a recasting of the present by insisting on the recall of that past. And it is clear that he does this quite consciously, because at the end of the scene he explicitly announces that he has reconciled the briefly lost Hubert to the personally true historical version of self: 'O now you look like Hubert. All this while / You were disguised' (4.1.125–6). In the perceptions of Arthur, a momentarily possible saviour of the kingdom, there is a temporary rapprochement between personal history and the broader notion of seeming and proper integrity. There is a brief glimpse that the problematic elements of the play as a whole might potentially be resolved in this figure, because he momentarily recasts historiography, in a way similar to the figure of the Bastard, whose character drives the play precisely because he is able to manipulate versions of history. Here the child figure is aligned with what Rackin has identified as an alternative, subordinate but subversive form of historicizing the self: the private history of the self held up in competition with the history of a nation. It is interesting, too, that even the rumour of Arthur's death provokes 'old men and beldames in the street' to 'prophesy upon it dangerously' (4.2.185–6) and 'another lean unwash'd artificer' to '[cut] off his tale and [talk] of Arthur's death' (4.2.203). The history of Arthur's death moves immediately into the order of prophecy and folk tale, the romancing of an unnatural act.

Striking in the formation of Arthur's character is his care for private relationships and his position in the family as well as in the state, the two things being inextricably linked. The scene where he pleads with Hubert is vital in drawing attention to the larger preoccupation of the play with the construction of history and ideas of historiography. In Arthur's case his self-historicization is immediate and individual. In the young princes' it is the product of the tension between a primary education and the intuitive knowledge that what one is taught with words by those in authority is not necessarily the only true rendition of the material. Within the context of each play, the young *précoces* also work in counterpoint to the construction of those to whom they are a threat. John sees himself as helpless, fatally inscribed in a certain way into history, and Arthur works against this by means of a self-constructed, self-saving verbal account of self. The young princes fear that what they know of history will mean that the truth of their sojourn in London is unlikely to be monosemous: Richard, turning at precisely that moment to reaffirm the Morality-villain version of self announced in his opening soliloquy, confirms those fears.

In terms of the relationship between the child, the texts that inform the formation of the child, and the construction of the dramatic text, the single most interesting figure in Shakespeare's plays is Young Lucius in *Titus Andronicus*. The play is full of quotation, intertextual reference and references to the creation or possession of texts. Lucius is frequently present at the point at which the informing of one text by another becomes plain, indicating that he will be the medium by which the textually unresolved future of the next generation becomes clear.

Shakespeare's play repeatedly recalls *Metamorphoses*, along with other standard Tudor school texts, and holds up to scrutiny not only the content of the texts but their process of signification by aligning them with the figure of the schoolboy. Most explicit is the scene where Young Lucius is the figure by which Lavinia's ravishment is made plain. References to Philomel and Tereus have peppered the text already, and Marcus has described Lavinia's plight by analogy, without, apparently, recognizing the direct relevance of the conjunction. Young Lucius's bundle of schoolbooks seems not dissimilar from those of a Tudor schoolboy, and Tamora's sons are marked out as able to recollect a similar education easily through their ready recognition of the text that Titus sends them. In a play that is so clearly pushing the mesh of analogous revelation to the limit, why is Young Lucius made the mechanism of explicit announcement, and why is his status as receptor of standard schoolboy stories revisited in the closing moments of the play? By repeatedly invoking the Ovidian telling of the Procne and Philomel myth, the play continually reasserts the need to think analogously, and invites the audience to arrive at the terrible denouement ahead of the action of the play itself. Is it not obvious to everyone except Lucius why it is that his aunt is pursuing him and his bundle of books so gruesomely? Is this perhaps why the stage direction, 'Enter Lucius' son and Lavinia running after him, and the boy flies from her with his books under his arm', is emphatic almost to the point of dreadful comedy? The wild anachronism that superimposes the Tudor schoolboy's knowledge on a classical child figure is a palimpsest that mimics the notion of characters and texts of quotation, a movement that draws attention to the relationship between the particular and the universal, the essential nature of things and its diluted manifestation, in terms of both text and dramatic performance.

In finding some kind of impossible moral pathway through the bloodbath that is *Titus Andronicus*, an audience must hold tight to its communal sense of justice. Is it possible to read these Ovidian texts, to be young, and to hold fast to any kind of hope for the future? To be Young Lucius, and to be able to confront the atrocity that is his ruined aunt by virtue of knowing that this is the replay of an ancient story; to be able to redeem the telling of such stories by affirming that the act of telling them – of being blessed with such a dubious wisdom – is an act of love on the part of the teller: that is the metatextual thread to this play. And to recognize that sometimes the abstract notion, the archetype and the particular agent/actor are one and the same thing, as Titus does at 5.2, is to understand the broadest parameters of metatextuality within the theatre.

In Shakespeare's dramatizations of childhood, the process of character-building is addressed in a number of ways – social, familial, textual, intertextual, metatextual. The way in which the character of the child is formulated regularly interrogates the ideological formation of the text as a whole, and the child character frequently stands, in its figurative role, as an epitome of the metatextual function of character in the play. The relation of the child to the culture in which it is being formed echoes the play's relationship to the genre into which it is inscribed. Just as an education in particular forms of self-representation produces a particular kind of questioning child, so the placing of the child character as an interrogatory voice in a particular genre causes the reproduction of that genre to be interrogated and reinformed. The idea that the drama is informed by the culture of textuality, and that the child stands in epitome both to that notion and to dramatic genre, is made explicit. Interrogating or inscribing its own process of growth into character, and drawing attention to the way in which the play itself is inscribed into a particular ideological way of thinking through genre, the Shakespearean child figure is a carrier of culture between the generations.

NOTES

I should like to record a debt of thanks to the present editors for their assistance in bringing this chapter to its final form, and also to Stephen Kavanagh, currently in the throes of a PhD thesis on children in Shakespeare, for his invaluable assistance with the final draft.

1 Chris Curtin and Anthony Varley, 'Children and Childhood in Rural Ireland: A Consideration of the Ethnographic Structure', in Chris Curtin, Mary Kelly and Liam O'Dowd, eds., *Culture and Ideology in Ireland* (Galway: Galway University Press, 1984), pp. 30–46 (p. 30).
2 Richard Lanham, *The Motives of Eloquence: Literary Rhetoric in the Renaissance* (New Haven and London: Yale University Press, 1976), p. 3.
3 See Louis Althusser, 'Ideology and Ideological State Apparatuses (Notes Toward an Investigation)', in Althusser, *Lenin and Philosophy and Other Essays*, trans. Ben Brewster (London: New Left Books, 1977), pp. 153, 149.
4 Phyllis Rackin, *Stages of History: Shakespeare's English Chronicles* (Ithaca: Cornell University Press, 1990). See also Eugene Waith, '*King John* and the Drama of History', *Shakespeare Quarterly* 29 (1978), 192–211, and Marsha Robinson, 'The Historiographic Method of *King John*', in Deborah T. Curren-Aquino, ed., *King John: New Perspectives* (Newark/London and Toronto: University of Delaware Press/Associated University Presses, 1989), pp. 29–39.
5 'After that a child is come to seven years of age, I hold it expedient that he be taken from the company of women, saving that he may have one year, or two at the most, an ancient and sad matron attending on him in his chamber, which shall not have any young woman in her company' (Thomas Elyot, *The Book Named the Governor* (1531; London: Dent, 1962), p. 19).
6 The moment when Young Lucius brings the message to Brutus with details of what is to happen to Caesar – the text which is to change history absolutely – is highlighted in Leon Garfield's *Animated Tales* version for children, which rehearses a version of the play only thirty minutes long.
7 These, of course, are the same sorts of questions that prompted feminist approaches to Shakespeare's tragedies and histories. See, for example, Catherine Belsey, *The Subject of Tragedy: Identity and Difference in Renaissance Drama* (London: Methuen, 1985), and Rackin, *Stages of History*.
8 See, for example, David Cressy, *Literacy and the Social Order: Reading and Writing in Tudor and Stuart England* (Cambridge: Cambridge University Press, 1980); Anthony Grafton and Lisa Jardine, *From Humanism to the Humanities: Education and the Liberal Arts in Fifteenth- and Sixteenth-Century Europe* (Cambridge: Cambridge University Press, 1986); and Rebecca W. Bushnell, *A Culture of Teaching: Early Modern Humanism in Theory and Practice* (Ithaca and London: Cornell University Press, 1996). No such study could be undertaken without reference to T. W. Baldwin, *William Shakspere's Small Latin and Lesse Greeke*, 2 vols. (Urbana: University of Illinois Press, 1944).

9 Foster Watson, *The Old Grammar Schools* (London: Cass and Company, 1968), p. 16; Joseph H. Lupton, *A Life of John Colet, D.D.* (London, 1887), pp. 281–2, cited in John B. Gleason, *John Colet* (Los Angeles and London: University of California Press, 1989), p. 219 n. 14; Philip Gaskell, 'Books Bought by Whitgift's Pupils in the 1570s', *Transactions, Cambridge Bibliographical Society, 1970–1980* 7 (1981), 284–93; Lisa Jardine, 'The Place of Dialectic Teaching in Sixteenth-Century Cambridge', *Studies in the Renaissance* 21 (1974), 46–7; Dudley Fenner, *The Artes of Logike and Rethorike* (Middleburg, 1584); and William Kempe, *The Education of Children in Learning* (London, 1558).

10 Francis Spufford, *The Child That Books Built* (London: Faber and Faber, 2002).

11 See Elyot, Clement, Fenner and Kempe in Robert D. Pepper, *Four Tudor Books on Education* (Gainesville: Scholars' Facsimiles and Reprints, 1966); other obvious works are Thomas Elyot, *The Boke named the Governour* (1531), Roger Ascham, *The Scholemaster* (1570), and Richard Mulcaster, *Positions* (1581) and *The First Part of the Elementarie* (1582). Four significant translations of Plutarch's essay on the formation of the child, translated into Latin as *De Liberis Educandis*, on which Elyot draws heavily for his 1533 text *The Education or Bringing up of Children translated out of Plutarche*, are printed in the period 1571–1603, and the placing of the essay on education first in Xylander's complete Latin Plutarch (1560–1570) draws attention to it. See Pepper, *Four Tudor Books*, pp. x–xiii.

12 'William's speech is a nearly verbatim quotation from Lilly and Colet, which he has learnt by heart' (William Shakespeare, *The Merry Wives of Windsor*, ed. Giorgio Melchiori, Arden Third Series (London: Thomas Nelson and Sons, 2000), note to 4.1.356).

13 *Ibid.*

14 Edward Berry, *Patterns of Decay: Shakespeare's Early Histories* (Charlottesville: University Press of Virginia, 1975), p. 15.

15 'For youth is impressionable and plastic, and while such minds are still tender lessons are infused deeply into them . . . just as seals leave their impressions in soft wax, so are lessons impressed upon the minds of children while they are young' (Plutarch, 'De Liberis Educandis', *Moralia*, 15 vols., trans. Frank Cole Babbitt, Loeb Classical Library (London: Heinemann, 1927–69), vol. 1, p. 17.

16 Richard Hillman, *Self-speaking in Medieval and Early Modern English Drama: Subjectivity, Discourse and the Stage* (Basingstoke: Macmillan, 1997).

6

Coriolanus *and the little eyases: the boyhood of Shakespeare's hero*

Lucy Munro

> *Ros.* Where have you *been*?
> *Player.* Roundabout. A nest of children carries the custom of the town. Juvenile companies, they are the fashion. But they cannot match our repertoire . . . we'll stoop to anything if that's your bent . . . (*He regards* ROS *meaningfully, but* ROS *returns the stare blankly.*)
> *Ros.* They'll grow up.[1]

This chapter explores an important context for Shakespeare's engagement with childhood: the performances of professional and semi-professional children's companies in the late sixteenth and early seventeenth century. Rather than focusing solely on the influence of specific plays, I examine the impact of children's performance on Shakespeare's dramaturgy in his late tragedy *Coriolanus*. Child characters are relatively rare in children's company plays; instead, boy actors are required to perform adult roles and to mimic adult status and authority. Their plays, in particular their tragedies, demonstrate a complex interconnection of issues relating to age and masculinity, anxieties about the respective authority of adult and child performance, and concerns about political agency. These preoccupations are reflected in *Coriolanus*, at the 'psychological and political heart' of which is, as R. B. Parker notes, the term 'boy'.[2] Shakespeare draws on children's company tragedies such as Samuel Daniel's *Philotas* (1604) and George Chapman's *Bussy D'Ambois* (*c.*1604) and *The Conspiracy and Tragedy of Charles, Duke of Byron* (1608) to create a military hero who is repeatedly reduced to the status of a boy or youth. Unlike the boy actors, Caius Martius will not 'grow up', and his childishness is the foundation on which Shakespeare constructs his tragedy.

THE HUMOUR OF CHILDREN

For much of the sixteenth century, children's performance was firmly positioned in the mainstream of theatrical culture. Groups of children performed in choir schools and grammar schools, in civic pageants and, increasingly, before paying audiences. One of the earliest of their commercial or semi-commercial theatres, the first Blackfriars, was converted into a theatre from buildings on former monastery lands in 1576, the same year in which James Burbage built the Theatre. For much of the sixteenth century, children's companies kept pace with the adults in performances at court; indeed, in the 1560s and early 1570s they actually surpassed them.[3] The adults finally overtook the children decisively only in the early 1590s, the most prominent of the children's companies having been dissolved in the wake of the Martin Marprelate controversy; the adults' dominance at court between 1591 and 1599 was unprecedented.[4]

The children's companies of the sixteenth century also exercised a shaping influence on the dramaturgy of the adult companies. In plays such as *Damon and Pithias* (Children of the Chapel, *c.*1564–5) and the lost *Palamon and Arcite* (1566), Richard Edwards set a pattern for sophisticated vernacular drama. His lead was followed by John Lyly, whose plays were performed by various children's companies in the 1580s; by George Peele, whose *Arraignment of Paris* (*c.*1582) was performed by the Children of the Chapel; and by Christopher Marlowe and Thomas Nashe, whose *Dido Queen of Carthage* (*c.*1588–92) was also performed by the Children of the Chapel. Shakespeare's romantic comedies of the 1590s are heavily indebted to Lyly, their style much closer to that of the children's companies than to the comedies of the other adult companies.[5] The page Moth in *Love's Labour's Lost* is an obvious descendant of the insolent pages of Lyly's plays, and heroines such as Rosalind and Portia, with their determined agency and linguistic dexterity, are patterned on those of the older dramatist. On a narrative level the romantic comedies also mimic plays such as Lyly's *Gallathea* (1592) in their frequent recourse to plots in which girls disguise themselves as boys. As G. K. Hunter points out, these plays were written in the years immediately following the closure of the children's theatres, during which 'their audiences [were] footloose and open to bids for their favor'.[6] This is the period during which Burbage attempted to install the Chamberlain's Men in their own indoor theatre, the second Blackfriars, suggesting a strategic attempt on the part of the Chamberlain's Men to attract the neglected audiences of the children's companies. It was only in the face of a hostile reaction from local residents that this scheme was abandoned and the Globe theatre built.[7]

The turn of the seventeenth century saw the revival of the children's companies, first the Children of Paul's, who in 1599 resumed performances in a tiny theatre attached to St Paul's Cathedral. They were followed by the Children of the Chapel Royal, to whom Richard Burbage, James's son, leased the second Blackfriars in 1600. On the accession of James I, the Children of the Chapel Royal were taken under the patronage of Anne of Denmark, becoming the Children of the Queen's Revels; another company, the Children of the King's Revels, briefly performed in a theatre in Whitefriars in 1607–8. The Children of the Queen's Revels' performance of politically contentious material led to the loss of the Queen's patronage and, eventually, the dissolution of the company in 1608, whereupon Burbage was finally able to install the King's Men (as the Chamberlain's Men had become) in the second Blackfriars theatre. A reconstituted Children of the Queen's Revels began performing in the Whitefriars theatre in late 1609 or early 1610, and they continued to perform there until early 1613, when they were merged with the adult Lady Elizabeth's Men.[8]

Shakespeare and Thomas Heywood were among the few major dramatists never to have written for the children's companies, probably as a result of their positions as resident dramatists for the Chamberlain's/King's Men and Worcester's/Queen's Men respectively. This does not mean, however, that Shakespeare ignored the revived children's companies' activities or the plays they produced. While the children's companies of the 1580s influenced Shakespeare's work in the 1590s, the early seventeenth-century companies affected Shakespeare and his company more directly. Something of this contested relationship can be seen in *Hamlet*, in which the adult players arrive in Elsinore having lost their audiences in the city to a group of children. The famous comment in the Folio text, in which Rosencrantz describes 'an eyrie of children, little eyases, that cry out on the top of question and are most tyrannically clapped for't' (2.2.339–41) may also betray the anxiety caused to the adult companies by the political disruption of many plays performed by the children between 1604 and 1608.[9] Writing around 1608, Heywood was at pains to attack 'The liberty, which some arrogate to themselves, committing their bitternesse, and liberall invectives against all estates, to the mouthes of Children, supposing their juniority to be a priviledge for any rayling, be it never so violent.'[10] The adult companies were, it seems, worried by the risky tactics being adopted by the managers of the children's companies; it is striking to find these ambivalent views of the children's companies expressed by Shakespeare and Heywood, attached playwrights with leading adult companies.

The Chamberlain's/King's Men seem to have been particularly conscious of the activities of the children's companies, perhaps as a consequence of Richard Burbage's status as the owner of the Blackfriars theatre. In the first years of the seventeenth century, they acquired two plays also produced by children's companies, Thomas Dekker's *Satiromastix* (1601), also performed by the Children of Paul's, and John Marston's *The Malcontent* (1603), also performed by the Children of the Chapel/Queen's Revels. They claimed that the appropriation of the latter play was a reprisal for the theft of one of their own plays, demonstrating another possible area of interaction between adult and child companies. In appropriating *The Malcontent*, the Chamberlain's/King's Men were forced to negotiate not only the requirements of roles such as Malevole but also the audiences' memories of the boy actors who originally performed the roles.

The children's companies of the early seventeenth century also exercised a direct influence on Shakespeare's dramaturgy and generic experimentation. The relationship between *Hamlet* and Marston's contemporaneous *Antonio's Revenge* (1600), performed by the Children of Paul's, has been long debated, most scholars either acknowledging Marston's play as a source for Shakespeare's or arguing that Marston drew on Shakespeare.[11] It is more certain that Marston's *The Malcontent*, performed by the Children of the Chapel/Queen's Revels around 1603, was recast by Shakespeare in *Measure for Measure*; the 'disguised ruler' play was, Shakespeare aside, a mode developed and sustained by the children's companies.[12] As R. A. Foakes demonstrates, children's company tragedies such as *Antonio's Revenge*, *Philotas*, *Bussy D'Ambois*, *The Conspiracy and Tragedy of Charles, Duke of Byron* and Marston's *Sophonisba* (1606) were to exercise a shaping influence on those of the adult companies, challenging them and forcing them to innovate in turn.[13] When the King's Men began to perform at the Blackfriars theatre, probably in late 1609 or early 1610, they employed John Fletcher and Francis Beaumont, dramatists who had previously worked with the Children of the Queen's Revels at the Blackfriars. It is again difficult to establish precedence, but King's Men plays of this period such as Shakespeare's *Cymbeline* and Beaumont and Fletcher's *Philaster* (*c.*1609) are closely related both to each other and to the innovations of the Queen's Revels dramatists.

'RATHER SAY I PLAY THE MAN I AM'

In the rest of this chapter I examine the interaction between Shakespeare and the children's companies more closely, focusing on the children's reconstitution of the tragic hero and its impact on *Coriolanus*. In *Coriolanus*, which seems to have been among the first plays written with the second Blackfriars theatre in mind,[14] Shakespeare attempts to overwrite children's performance and, in particular, the recent performances of tragedies by the Children of the Queen's Revels on that same Blackfriars stage. He does so by picking up and reworking certain aspects of children's performance, specifically their tradition of satiric detachment and their exploitation of the distance between actor and role. In children's company tragedies, boy actors play aspiring protagonists who never quite live up to their heroic roles, an alienating technique that Shakespeare develops and extends. Although Plutarch suggests that the historical Caius Martius was thirty-two at the time of the events depicted in the play, and the role was probably performed by the forty-year-old Richard Burbage, he is presented as a 'boy of tears', in Aufidius's resonant term, repeatedly reduced to the status of a boy or youth.

Children's company plays foreground the discontinuous relationship between age and adult male status through their very constitution. As Will Fisher suggests, 'when boy actors donned beards in order to play the parts of men, they would have been as much "in drag" as when they played the parts of women'.[15] This implicit critique evolved throughout the careers of the early seventeenth-century companies. Plays performed around the turn of the century, such as Marston's *Antonio and Mellida* (Paul's, 1599) and Ben Jonson's *Cynthia's Revels* (Chapel, 1600), foreground the physical condition of the youthful performers, who seem to have been aged between nine and fourteen, drawing attention to their impersonation of adult male status. In the induction to *Cynthia's Revels*, the Third Child (an actor with a breaking voice who probably played Anaides in the play itself) is required to perform an impromptu impersonation of a stereotypical gallant, complete with a modish tobacco habit. Swearing liberally and puffing on his pipe, he damns the performance of the boy actors ('*They doe act like so manie* Wrens, *or* Pismires – *not the fift part of a good Face amongst them all*'), criticizes their famous music and condemns their '*pittifull*' poets.[16] Pretending to a status he does not possess, the Third Child creates a distance between himself and the other boy actors, disparaging them as insignificant 'Tits', 'Wrens' and 'Pismires'. The speech creates a swaggering bravado and an ironic illusion of age in its repetition of blasphemous oaths such as '*By Gods so*' and '*By Gods lid*' and in the swirl of smoke that surrounds the boy actor; it is a clear example of what Fisher calls 'prosthetic masculinity',[17] in which props and mannerisms might create an illusion of adult male status.

In his impersonation of masculinity, the boy actor also points ironically towards the performances of adult actors in the public theatres; this critique is made explicit in the induction to *Antonio and Mellida*, in which the performers swap hints on acting technique. The boy who will play Alberto tells the boy who is to play the villainous Piero to 'grow big in thought, / As swoll'n with glory of successful arms', and Piero responds by asking, 'Who cannot be proud, stroke up the hair and strut[?]'[18] Alberto comments further:

> such rank custom is grown popular;
> And now the vulgar fashion strides as wide,
> And stalks as proud, upon the weakest stilts
> Of the slight'st fortunes, as if Hercules
> Or burly Atlas shoulder'd up their state. (Induction, 15–19)

The induction targets a different kind of masculinity than that caricatured in *Cynthia's Revels*: the conventionally heroic performance of adult actors such as Edward Alleyn. That Marston has Alleyn in mind is suggested by the juxtaposition of Alberto's advice with clear references to two of the actor's most famous roles, Hieronimo in Thomas Kyd's *The Spanish Tragedy* (first published 1592) and the title role in Marlowe's *Tamburlaine* (first published 1590). Marston creates miniature Herculean Alleyns, proudly strutting around the tiny Paul's stage and presenting an exaggeratedly heroic masculinity.

Anxiety about the performance of masculinity and, in particular, heroic masculinity was to be central to tragedies performed by the Children of the Queen's Revels such as Daniel's *Philotas*, Chapman's *Bussy D'Ambois* and his *Byron* plays. The protagonists of these plays are proud, wilful and politically naïve men who are eventually seen as liabilities and/or traitors. Bussy D'Ambois is described by the Monsieur as 'young and haughty, apt to take / Fire at advancement'; he rises in status through the favour first of Monsieur and then of King Henry, but finally meets an unheroic death when his affair with another courtier's wife is discovered.[19] Having fought a duel with Montsurry, the cuckolded husband, Bussy is shot from a pistol offstage; his heroic status is only partially recouped in a stunning dying speech in which he constructs himself as his own monument: 'Here like a Roman statue I will stand /

Till death hath made me marble' (5.3.144–5). The childish caprice of Philotas, who is first seen reading a letter of advice from his father, is summed up neatly by his friend Chalisthenes: 'He that will fret at Lords and at the raine / Is but a foole, and grieves himself in vaine.'[20] Philotas repeatedly, and ironically, denigrates Alexander by referring to him as the 'young man', a detail which Daniel picks up from Plutarch's *Lives* and exploits in his characterization of the hero as child.[21] Like Philotas, the title character in Chapman's *Byron* plays is progressively entangled in a conspiracy with which he initially seems to have little involvement. Byron's pride makes him vulnerable to manipulation; as the wily Savoy comments, 'great men' take compliments 'as their state potatoes, / High cullises, and potions to excite / The lust of their ambition'.[22] Alexander Leggatt observes of Byron, that 'He knows neither himself nor the world around him; he is as demanding, and (in a curious way) as artless and innocent, as a child'.[23] This comment holds true of the heroes of all of these tragedies: like the miniature Alleyns of *Antonio and Mellida*, they seem to be boys playing at being heroes.

As this comparison suggests, and as Leggatt notes in relation to *Byron*, such an effect would be given additional emphasis by the fact that these roles were performed by boy actors. It is important to recall, however, that the average age of the actors in children's companies does not seem to have remained static. The oldest of the boy actors of 1599–1600 seem to have been aged around fourteen, meaning that the incongruity of their performances of age and masculine status would have been accentuated. But actors stayed with the companies, leading to a higher average age as the century progressed; references to breaking voices in *Cynthia's Revels* and *Antonio and Mellida* suggest that in 1599–1600 their status as 'children' was already becoming less certain. Nathan Field, who according to a prologue to *Bussy D'Ambois* printed in 1641 was the first performer to act Bussy, was aged sixteen or seventeen in 1604, and other actors were of a similar age.[24] The lead roles in *Philotas*, *Bussy D'Ambois* and *Byron* seem, therefore, to have been performed by actors who would have been considered 'youths' by their contemporaries, a phase often associated with recklessness and unstable behaviour. In a 1612 conduct book aimed at youths, Anthony Stafford argues that 'A yong man is like a wilde horse; who, if hee want a course, will runne himselfe to death'.[25] Some of this quality in the performance of *Bussy D'Ambois* is suggested in the 1641 prologue's comment on the second actor to play Bussy, who is now '*denide / By his gray beard to shew the height and pride / Of* D'Ambois *youth and braverie*'.[26]

The social insurgency of youth may also have heightened the political critique offered by children's company plays. The performances of both *Philotas* and the *Byron* plays by the Children of the Queen's Revels were politically contentious. Daniel was called before the Privy Council in early 1605 to explain *Philotas*, which was thought to comment on the Essex rebellion; he vigorously denied this charge, but his denials have been viewed sceptically by scholars.[27] In March 1608 the Queen's Revels' performances of *Byron* offended the French ambassador; the company compounded their offence by performing a play on the subject of King James's Scottish silver mine which satirized his hunting and portrayed him as 'drunk at least once a day'.[28] Boy players might be protected by their status as children – though this does not seem to have deterred James from declaring that the Queen's Revels actors 'should never play more, but should first begg their bred'[29] – but they would have been close enough to adulthood to prevent their performance being mere caricature. The boy player, who adopts an adult persona and authority which is at odds with his own status as a juvenile and an actor, calls into question the assumptions on which dramatic character and political authority are based. In children's company tragedies the young actors are not used merely to burlesque the pretensions of adult characters and actors; their performance instead critiques tragic heroism itself.

It is this critique that Shakespeare was to adopt in *Coriolanus*. This last tragedy looks back to the children's experiments with tragedy and, in particular, the *Byron* plays, which were partly responsible for the Queen's Revels' loss of the Blackfriars theatre. As Lee Bliss suggests, 'Shakespeare's own interest in heroic individualism would have nicely coincided with an opportunity to take on Chapman on his home ground while also providing the Blackfriars audience with a play in a genre for which it had a known taste'.[30] While much criticism has focused on the play's characterization of Caius Martius as son, my interest here lies in the way in which it simultaneously 'belittles' him, rhetorically placing him in the position of a boy or youth. In the children's tragedies a boy plays out the role of a hero; in *Coriolanus* the hero is repeatedly reduced to the status of a boy. In both cases incongruity undercuts the pretensions of the hero and unmasks the uncertain foundations on which his confidence is based. As Janet Adelman points out, Martius initially seems to be the invulnerable 'man-child' of Macbeth's exhortation to Lady Macbeth, 'the child who sucks only valiantness from the mettle/metal of his mother's breast',[31] but the play systematically undermines this initial presentation. I suggest that the play's problematization of heroic masculinity lies in the ironic gap between actor and role – a separation common in the children's company plays, in which adolescent boys played tragic heroes, but one which takes on new force in *Coriolanus*. To quote Bliss, Martius's protest to Volumnia, 'Rather say I play / The man I am' (3.2.14–15) highlights the extent to which he 'has been "playing" the super-masculine patrician warrior since his youth'.[32] Like the boy actor playing Bussy or Byron, Martius both is and is not the role he plays.

The first reference to Martius in *Coriolanus* puts him in the position of a child, the first Citizen commenting scornfully that although 'soft-conscienced men' attribute Martius's deeds to his patriotism, 'he did it to please his mother, and to be partly proud' (1.1.35, 36–7). The depiction of Martius's relationship with his mother is part of a wider blurring of the boundaries between adult and child. Volumnia celebrates her son's victories by telling Virgilia about his childhood, and the play creates insistent parallels between Martius and his son, also called Martius. For instance, the elder Martius's military activities are mirrored in a distorting and reductive fashion by the younger's unendearing habit of pulling the wings from butterflies. That this activity is praised by Volumnia suggests the extent to which, as R. B. Parker notes, Young Martius 'replicates both his father's education and the element of "boy" that Coriolanus has been unable to outgrow'.[33] The mirroring of Martius and Young Martius has been emphasized in production: in Trevor Nunn's 1977 Royal Shakespeare Company production of *Coriolanus*, on her triumphant entry into Rome Volumnia threw off Young Martius's cloak 'to show him, hands crossed over a sword, black leather armour and defiant chin, the young image of his father'.[34]

Volumnia's blurring of the distinction between Martius as child and as adult is developed in an important speech in the second act. Cominius extols Martius's valour to the Senate by recounting the origins of his military career:

> At sixteen years,
> When Tarquin made a head for Rome, he fought
> Beyond the mark of others. Our then dictator,
> Whom with all praise I point at, saw him fight
> When with his Amazonian chin he drove
> The bristled lips before him. He bestrid
> An o'erpressed Roman, and, i'th' consul's view,
> Slew three opposers. Tarquin's self he met,
> And struck him on his knee. In that day's feats,
> When he might act the woman in the scene,

He proved best man i'th' field, and for his meed
Was brow-bound with the oak. (2.2.87–98)

The description of the epicene adolescent Martius, a beardless boy driving grizzled veterans before him, suggests something of the quality of Bussy or Byron in performance: a boy young enough to play a female role with an adult company nonetheless performs with consummate skill the role of the hero and warrior. Intriguingly, the speech has a direct parallel in one of the children's tragedies. In the first speech of the *Tragedy of Byron*, King Henry recounts Byron's military career, recalling that 'At fourteen years of age he was made Colonel / To all the Suisses serving then in Flanders'(1.1.7–8).[35] Both Shakespeare and Chapman recall the martial boyhood of their hero, tracing his masculine identity to his activities during the pivotal period of youth. In *Coriolanus* the description also recalls the intensity of the bond between Martius and Volumnia, the effeminate young man acting out the military career his masculine mother could never have. As the play will demonstrate, although Martius is now a man who has borne 'the brunt of seventeen battles since' (2.2.100), his mother nonetheless outmans him.

References to childishness cluster at one of the play's climactic moments, when Volumnia tries to persuade Martius to submit to the plebeians. A discontented Martius finally says:

Well, I must do't.
Away, my disposition; and possess me
Some harlot's spirit! My throat of war be turned,
Which choired with my drum, into a pipe
Small as an eunuch or the virgin voice
That babies lull asleep! The smiles of knaves
Tent in my cheeks, and schoolboys' tears take up
The glasses of my sight! A beggar's tongue
Make motion through my lips, and my armed knees,
Who bowed but in my stirrup, bend like his
That hath received an alms! I will not do't,
Least I surcease to honour mine own truth,
And by my body's action teach my mind
A most inherent baseness. (3.2.110–23)

As Adelman suggests, Martius imagines that asking for the populace's favour would 'undo the process by which he was transformed on the battlefield from boy or woman to man'; his image of the reversed voice change 'suggests the extent to which his phallic aggressive pose is a defence against collapse into the dependent oral mode of the small boy'.[36]

But also notable here is the fact Martius sees both his gender *and* class identities as being disrupted by his submission to the plebeians: his vocal change is to be accompanied by the invasion of the 'smiles of knaves', 'schoolboys' tears' and a 'beggar's tongue'. It is no coincidence that gender and class are intermingled, since a regression to childhood could also bring with it ambiguity in social status. A boy's status could be fluid, given that it was linked to that of his parents; that of a boy actor was all the more indeterminate, since he was separated from his parents by impressment or apprenticeship.

The image of 'schoolboys' tears' returns in the moments before Martius's death, in the potent jibes aimed at him by Aufidius. Aufidius tells the Volscian Senate that Martius has betrayed them to Rome for the sake of 'certain drops of salt', the tears of his wife and, especially, his mother. Seeing 'his nurse's tears', Martius 'whined and roared away your victory, / That pages blushed at him, and men of heart / Looked wond'ring each at others' (5.6.95, 99, 100–2). The description of Martius whining and roaring recalls the fretful Philotas, and it is significant that Martius's rejection of heroic masculinity makes him the object of scorn among pages, that is, boys or youths. Developing his theme, Aufidius counters Martius's appeal to the martial god Mars with a precisely calculated insult:

Aufid. Name not the god, thou boy of tears.
Corio. Ha?
Aufid. No more.
Corio. Measureless liar, thou hast made my heart
Too great for what contains it. 'Boy'? Oh slave! –
Pardon me, lords, 'tis the first time that ever
I was forced to scold. Your judgements, my grave lords,
Must give this cur the lie, and his own notion –
Who wears my stripes impressed upon him, that
Must bear my beating to his grave – shall join
To thrust the lie unto him.
1 *Lord.* Peace both, and hear me speak.
Corio. Cut me to pieces, Volsces. Men and lads,
Stain all your edges on me. 'Boy'! False hound,
If you have writ your annals true, 'tis there
That, like an eagle in a dove-cote, I
Fluttered your Volscians in Corioles.
Alone I did it. 'Boy'! (5.6.103–17)

The astute Aufidius has chosen precisely the right provocation for the immature and class-conscious Martius, and his comment 'No more' suggests that he is fully aware of its power. As Paul Griffiths notes, 'In adult discourse terms like "boy" or "lad" belonged to a vocabulary of insult, and their potential to trim reputations turned on their more usual application to people in pre-adult years, and their association with immorality and inadequacy.'[37] Griffiths cites an exchange which reads like a condensed version of the dialogue between Aufidius and Martius; Thomas Mesaunte, an Essex churchwarden, insulted William Gassock by telling him, 'Sirrah boy, I will use you like a boy', to which Gassock responded, 'Boy, boy on your face for I am as good a man as you.'[38] Like Gassock, Martius picks at the term 'boy', finally turning it back on Aufidius.

Michael Long astutely observes that this 'keyword' levels a 'fearfully accurate charge that all this man-child strength and predatory virility has nothing to do with real adulthood'.[39] In addition, the term 'boy' carried potent imputations of low class status (emphasized by the way in which Martius responds to Aufidius's 'boy' with 'slave' and 'cur') and of sodomitic behaviour; the latter associations are surely invoked in the homosocial intensity of the relationship between Aufidius and Coriolanus.[40] In attempting to refute the insult, Martius recapitulates his victories against the Volscians. However, Martius's military victories are too intimately bound up with his immaturity for this strategy to convince: in bragging of his victories, Martius is 'forced to scold', that is, to indulge in extravagant linguistic display and thus to behave in an inappropriately effeminate manner.

Martius's attempt to deny that he is 'a boy of tears' leads to his death at the hands of the Volscian conspirators. The full political importance of Martius's 'belittling' is revealed, however, in his earlier treatment of the Roman plebeians, whose perceived political illegitimacy he sums up in his reference to the 'children's voices' (3.1.32). As Cathy Shrank points out, Martius's insult foreshadows Thomas Hobbes's political analysis in *Leviathan* (1651), in which children and the insane are barred from the commonwealth because they are unable to understand 'the will of him that commandeth, by voice, writing, or some other sufficient argument of the same' and 'had never power to make any covenant, or to understand the consequences thereof . . . as they must do that make to themselves a commonwealth'.[41] While Martius attempts to brand the plebeians as childishly incapable, his own political childishness is evident throughout the play. His final miscalculated assertion of his heroic, adult and masculine persona is another attempt to overcome those who consistently place him in the position of a boy, but paradoxically it also reveals the truth of those accusations. Like a boy's performance as Byron, Martius's performance of masculinity in *Coriolanus* reveals the uncertain foundations upon which adult status and political agency are based.

In a recent essay, Judith Kegan Gardiner asks, 'What does it mean to act your age – or to act your gender?'[42] Her question highlights the extent to which age is not just a biological imperative, conditioned by social and cultural assumptions about age categories. It can also be performative, as I have explored in relation to the presentation of age and authority in the inductions to children's company plays such as *Antonio and Mellida* and *Cynthia's Revels*. Moreover, the performance of age and adult masculinity is crucial to the effect of the children's tragedies and of *Coriolanus*. Plays such as *Philotas*, *Bussy* and *Byron* feature heroes whose childishness and political immaturity are reinforced by their performance by adolescent youths. Because his hero was played by an adult actor, the children's companies' radical discontinuity between actor and role was not available to Shakespeare. He instead amplifies and intensifies the earlier tragedies' explicit references to the childishness of their heroes, creating a play in which an adult actor plays a grown man who is psychologically an immature 'boy'.

Gardiner points out that 'dissonance between biological age and self-perception is considered normal, though often comic, in comparison with dissonance between biological sex and self-defined gender, which is often considered tragic'.[43] In the plays discussed here, dissonance between biological age and an assumed or performed age can be both comic and tragic. The boy actors in comedies such as *Antonio and Mellida* and *Cynthia's Revels* impersonate mature masculinity to comic effect; in tragedies such as *Byron* and *Coriolanus*, the clash between a character's adult status and his childishness is altogether more serious. Like the Queen's Revels' boy actors, Martius is 'in drag', playing out the role of the hypermasculine military hero. In a comedy this might be funny; in the political arena of *Coriolanus*, it is the stuff of tragedy.

NOTES

I am very grateful to the editors, especially Kate Chedgzoy and Susanne Greenhalgh, for their helpful comments on the first draft of this chapter.

1 Tom Stoppard, *Rosencrantz and Guildenstern are Dead* (London: Faber and Faber, 1967), p. 18.

2 William Shakespeare, *Coriolanus*, ed. R. B. Parker (Oxford: Oxford University Press, 1994), p. 48.

3 See John H. Astington, *English Court Theatre 1558–1642* (Cambridge: Cambridge University Press, 1999), Appendix (pp. 221–67).
4 For background, see H. N. Hillebrand, *The Child Actors: A Chapter in Elizabethan Stage History* (Urbana: University of Illinois Press, 1926), and Michael Shapiro, *Children of the Revels: The Boy Companies of Shakespeare's Time and Their Plays* (New York: Columbia University Press, 1977).
5 See G. K. Hunter, 'Theatrical Politics and Shakespeare's Comedies, 1590–1600', in R. B. Parker and S. P. Zitner, eds., *Elizabethan Theater: Essays in Honour of S. Schoenbaum* (London: Associated University Presses, 1996), pp. 241–51.
6 *Ibid.*, p. 242.
7 See E. K. Chambers, *The Elizabethan Stage*, 4 vols. (Oxford: Clarendon Press, 1923), vol. 2, p. 508.
8 For accounts of the Jacobean children's companies, see W. Reavley Gair, *The Children of Paul's: The Story of a Theatre Company* (Cambridge: Cambridge University Press, 1982); Mary Bly, *Queer Virgins and Virgin Queans on the Early Modern Stage* (Oxford: Oxford University Press, 2000) and Lucy Munro, *Children of the Queen's Revels: A Jacobean Theatre Repertory* (Cambridge: Cambridge University Press, 2005).
9 See Roslyn Lander Knutson, 'Falconer to the Little Eyases: A New Date and Commercial Agenda for the "Little Eyases" Passage in *Hamlet*', *Shakespeare Quarterly* 46 (1995), 1–31.
10 Thomas Heywood, *An Apology for Actors* (London, 1612), G3v.
11 For summaries, see G. K. Hunter, ed., *Antonio's Revenge* (London: Edward Arnold, 1966), pp. xviii–xxi, and Charles Cathcart, '*Hamlet*: Date and Early Afterlife', *Review of English Studies* 52 (2001), 341–59.
12 Other 'disguised ruler' plays include Thomas Middleton's *The Phoenix* (Paul's, *c.*1603), John Day's *Law Tricks* (Queen's Revels, *c.*1604), John Marston's *The Fawn* (Queen's Revels, *c.*1604–5, Paul's, 1606) and Edward Sharpham's *The Fleer* (1606).
13 R. A. Foakes, 'Tragedy at the Children's Theatres After 1600: A Challenge to the Adult Stage', in David Galloway, ed., *The Elizabethan Theatre II* (London: Macmillan, 1970), pp. 37–59.
14 See Parker, ed., *Coriolanus*, pp. 2–7, and Lee Bliss, ed., *Coriolanus* (Cambridge: Cambridge University Press, 2000), pp. 1–5.
15 Will Fisher, 'The Renaissance Beard: Masculinity in Early Modern England', *Renaissance Quarterly* 54 (2001), 155–87 (180).
16 Ben Jonson, *The Fountaine of Self-Love. Or Cynthias Revels* (London, 1601), A3v. See Matthew Steggle, 'Casting the Prelude in *Cynthia's Revels*', *Notes & Queries* 50 (2003), 62–3.
17 Fisher, 'The Renaissance Beard', 184.
18 John Marston, *Antonio and Mellida*, ed. G. K. Hunter (London: Edward Arnold, 1965), Induction.

19 George Chapman, *Bussy D'Ambois*, ed. Nicholas Brooke (London: Methuen, 1965), 1.1.49–50.
20 Samuel Daniel, *Philotas*, in *Certaine Small Poems with the Tragedie of Philotas* (London, 1605), 2B3v.
21 Plutarch, *The Lives of the Noble Grecians and Romanes*, trans. Thomas North (London, 1595), p. 743.
22 George Chapman, *The Conspiracy and Tragedy of Charles, Duke of Byron*, ed. John Margeson (Manchester: Manchester University Press, 1988), 3.2.16–18.
23 Alexander Leggatt, 'Tone and Structure in Chapman's *Byron* Plays', *Studies in English Literature* 24 (1984), 307–26 (312–13).
24 See David Kathman, 'How Old Were Shakespeare's Boy Actors?', *Shakespeare Survey* 58 (2005), 220–46 (222–3).
25 Anthony Stafford, *Meditations and Resolutions, Moral, Divine, Political . . . Written for the Instruction and Bettering of Youth* (London, 1612), F7r-v.
26 George Chapman, *Bussy D'Ambois* (London, 1641), A2r-v.
27 For recent reassessment, see Hugh Gazzard, '"Those Graue Presentments of Antiquitie": Samuel Daniel's *Philotas* and the Earl of Essex', *Review of English Studies* 51 (2000), 423–50.
28 Report by the French ambassador Antoine Lefèvre de la Boderie (Bibliothèque Nationale MS Fr. 15984), translated in Margeson, ed., *The Conspiracy and Tragedy of Charles, Duke of Byron*, p. 276.
29 National Archives, SP 14/31/73, reprinted in Chambers, *Elizabethan Stage*, vol. 2, pp. 53–4.
30 Bliss, ed., *Coriolanus*, p. 5.
31 Janet Adelman, *Suffocating Mothers: Fantasies of Maternal Origin in Shakespeare's Plays: Hamlet to The Tempest* (London and New York: Routledge, 1992), p. 147.
32 Bliss, ed., *Coriolanus*, p. 54.
33 Parker, ed., *Coriolanus*, p. 23.
34 David Daniell, *Coriolanus in Europe* (London: Athlone, 1980), p. 40. This image was repeated in Terry Hands's 1989 RSC production (Bliss, ed., *Coriolanus*, p. 58).
35 Although Shakespeare derives the display of Coriolanus's wounds from Plutarch, it is notable that the 'five and thirty' wounds received by Byron in his service of France are repeatedly invoked in the *Conspiracy* and *Tragedy*.
36 Adelman, *Suffocating Mothers*, p. 151.
37 Paul Griffiths, *Youth and Authority: Formative Experiences in England 1560–1640* (Oxford: Clarendon Press, 1996), p. 102.
38 *Ibid.*, citing F. G. Emmison, *Elizabethan Life: Morals and the Church Courts* (Chelmsford: Essex Record Office Publications, 1973), pp. 114, 137.
39 Michael Long, *The Unnatural Scene: A Study in Shakespearean Tragedy* (London: Methuen, 1976), p. 67.
40 See Bruce R. Smith, *Homosexual Desire in Shakespeare's England: A Cultural Poetics* (Chicago: University of Chicago Press, 1991), pp. 194–7.

41 Cathy Shrank, 'Civility and the City in *Coriolanus*', *Shakespeare Quarterly* 54 (2003), 406–23 (415–16), quoting Thomas Hobbes, *Leviathan* (1651), ed. Michael Oakeshott (Oxford: Basil Blackwell, 1962), pp. 176–7.
42 Judith Kegan Gardiner, 'Theorizing Age and Gender: Bly's Boys, Feminism, and Maturity Masculinity', in Gardiner, ed., *Masculinity Studies and Feminist Theory: New Directions* (New York: Columbia University Press, 2002), pp. 90–118 (p. 95).
43 *Ibid.*, p. 95.

7

Procreation, child-loss and the gendering of the sonnet

Patricia Phillippy

When Anne Cecil de Vere, Countess of Oxford, died at the age of thirty-one two weeks after the birth of her fifth child in June 1588, Wilfred Samonde presented an elegy to her grieving parents. Their daughter was 'for modesty a chaste Penelope', he assured William Cecil, Lord Burghley and Mildred, Lady Burghley, and 'another Grissel for her patience'.[1] Samonde's conventional praise gains poignancy when considered in the light of Anne's difficult marriage to Edward de Vere, the seventeenth Earl of Oxford.[2] The union, which began auspiciously in 1571, erupted notoriously after the birth of the couple's first child, Elizabeth. As rumour had it, Oxford had maintained before his departure for an extended tour of Europe in January 1575 'that if she [Anne] were with child it was not his'.[3] He wrote to his father-in-law on his return to England in April 1576, approving of Burghley's suggestion that Anne return to the Cecil home, 'for there as yowre doughter or her mothers more then my wife yow may take comfort of her and I rid of the comber therby, shall remaine well eased of many griefes'.[4] The couple remained separated for six years. Anne gave birth to a son in 1583 – the promising product of his parents' reconciliation and the earl's first male heir – but hopes were quickly dashed when the infant died within three weeks of his birth.[5] The burial is recorded in the parish register of St Nicholas's Church at Castle Hedingham, '1583: May 9th. The Earl of Oxenford's first son'.[6] The death is also painfully memorialized in the brief sonnet sequence 'Foure Epytaphes, made by the Countes of Oxenford, after the death of her young Sonne, the Lord Bulbecke, &c.', attributed to Anne de Vere by John Soowthern and published in his *Pandora* in 1584.[7] Samonde's elegy, then, continues even after Anne's death the all-too-public campaign waged by the Cecils for more than a decade to vindicate their daughter and repair her damaged reputation.

The most remarkable artefact of this campaign is the tomb erected by Burghley in Westminster Abbey, originally planned to commemorate Anne alone but reconceived as a joint tomb when Lady Burghley died less than a year after her daughter. A lengthy Latin inscription in Burghley's first-person voice recalls that 'mea filia dilectissima . . . vixit . . . semper Pudica & casta, Uxor erga Virum in amando mire constans, Filia in Parentes per omnia obsequens' (my most darling daughter . . . lived . . . always modest and chaste, a constant and loving wife to her husband, to her parents a daughter obedient in all things).[8] If Oxford had questioned who retained ownership of Anne in her adulthood with his derisive 'as yowre doughter or her mothers more then my wife', the tomb insists that Anne admirably fulfilled the duties of her various roles. At the same time, it enfolds her permanently in the bosom of her family: Anne's effigy rests eternally alongside her mother's, the kneeling figure of her father surmounts the tomb, and those of her three surviving daughters and her brother attend her head and feet. Rescued from ignominy and reinserted into the paternal household, Anne and her children, as depicted on the tomb, offer an extraordinary commentary on the cultural and affective value of *daughters* in a society usually cited as primarily concerned with the rights of primogeniture and the overwhelming worth of sons.

The competing claims to the possession and importance of sons and daughters are the subject of this chapter, which undertakes a comparison of the 'Foure Epytaphes' and Shakespeare's 'procreation sonnets'. In early modern texts and culture, as the Burghley tomb suggests, childbirth and child-loss could serve to anchor free-floating notions of masculine and feminine identity in relation to offspring, whether actual or figurative. The two sonnet sequences construct gender as predicated upon procreation and child-loss, both exploiting early modern formulations of gender in relation to absent children. As each work strives to grant immortality to its subject, it engages in and records gendered interplays between poetry and 'breed' (Sonnet 12, l.14), to borrow Shakespeare's terms. Shakespeare's procreation sonnets replace the unproductive voice of maternal mourning, depicted in the epitaphs, with the poet's paternal voice, figuring the imagined (but ultimately absent) maternal body as an emblem of the bankruptcy of the poetics of procreation: 'breed' thus gives way to an ideal of textual reproduction that elides maternity. If Shakespeare incorporates and subsumes maternal grief within his work, the *Pandora* epitaphs imagine the melancholic incorporation of the absent child into the maternal body.[9] Mobilizing a naturalized concept of maternity, essentially tied to the female body, the poems conflate the mother's womb, the child's tomb and the sonnet form to construct a memorial to insuperable loss. In the former work ownership of the child passes from mother to father; in the latter the grieving mother strives to retain possession of her child and herself, even as she resists the irresistible encroachment of death. Thus the 'Foure Epytaphes' offers a performance of maternity that counters and illuminates Shakespeare's deployment of parenthood in the sonnets. These different estimations of the symbolic value of children respond and contribute to the period's castings of men's and women's roles and emotions, as parents and as authors.[10]

I

Edward de Vere's son is known to history only as 'Lord Bulbecke', his father's title which he inherited at birth. No Christian name survives.[11] In his title for the four sonnets and two fragments memorializing the infant in *Pandora*, Soowthern underscores his dedication of the book to 'Edward Dever, Earle of Oxenford &c' (A1) by recalling his son's title. The poems themselves, however, replace the concerns of primogeniture with profound, excessive maternal mourning. Throughout the sonnets, moreover, the speaker repeatedly refers to the infant as 'my Sonne', refusing to acknowledge joint parenthood or ownership of the child. The sequence begins:

> Had with the moorning the Gods left their willes undone
> They had not so soone herited such a soule:
> Or if the mouth, tyme did not glotton up all.
> Nor I, nor the world, were depriv'd of my Sonne. (Sonnet 1, ll. 1–4; C3v)

The notion of inheritance alludes here not to rights of property passed from father to son, but to the death of the child – himself the inheritance of the gods – felt most deeply, the speaker insists, by his mother. Again, in Sonnet 2, the speaker complains, 'With my Sone, my Gold, my Nightingale, and Rose, / Is gone' (ll. 5–6; C3v). Sonnet 3 begins, 'The hevens, death, and life? have conjured my yll: / For death hath take away the breath of my sonne' (ll. 1–2; C4), and continues in the *volta*, 'And as for life, let it doo me all despite: / For if it leave me, I shall goe to my childe' (ll. 9–10; C4). The first of two fragmentary poems that conclude the sequence laments, 'My Sonne is gone? and with it, death end my sorrow' (l. 11; C4v), and the final fragment closes the sequence:

> *Amphion's* wife was turned to a rocke.
> How well I had beene, had I had such adventure,

> For then I might againe have been the Sepulcure,
> Of him that I bare in mee, so long ago. (ll. 11–14; C4v)

As the poems assert the speaker's unique and primary relationship with the child, they also imagine a community of women, including Venus, Niobe, the Destinies (Clotho, Lachesis and Atropos), Thetis, Cybele, the Muses, the 'Charits' or Graces (Sonnet 4, l. 9), and 'the *Nymphes* of the Cave' (Sonnet 4, l. 10), who either accompany the speaker in mourning her son's death or appear as her rivals for possession of the child. Together, the poems create a feminine universe where the infant's definition and value within the system of primogeniture is displaced by his affective worth to his devastated mother and her female attendants.

Throughout the sequence, the implications of female ownership of the lost son – her sole possession of the child, bestowed upon her by childbirth and child-loss – are explored. Rooted in the maternal body itself, the speaker's rights of ownership are expressed in the poems' many conflated images of the womb and the tomb. The speaker's final wish to become a second Niobe so that she might physically enclose the infant's body within her petrified womb figures the maternal body as a tomb. Elsewhere, too, the speaker struggles from being possessed to possessing, and works towards a dream of autonomous feminine creation, procreation and re-creation. When Niobe appears earlier in the sequence, in Sonnet 2, she participates in a series of images, resonant throughout the poems, of living rock, the womb of stone and the tomb of flesh:

> And well though mine eies run downe like fountaines here
> The stone wil not speak yet, that doth it inclose.
> . . .
> And of this world what shall I hope, since I knoe,
> That in his respect, it can yeeld but mosse: (ll. 8–9, 11–12; C3v–C4)

Similarly, in Sonnet 1 the 'golden tears' of Venus, washing Lord Bulbecke's tomb, 'makes almost alive, the Marble, of my Childe' (ll. 4, 6; C3v). In the sequence's most powerful rendering of the imagery of feminine creation, the speaker casts herself as a second Prometheus, and imagines that her tears can, literally, raise the dead:

> But if our life be caus'de with moisture and heate,
> I care neither for the death, the life, nor skyes:
> For I'll sigh him warmth, and weat him with my eies:
> (And thus I shall be thought a second *Promëtt*) (Sonnet 3, ll. 5–8; C4)

Here the speaker's attempted evasion of patriarchal ownership is also an escape from the constraints of religious orthodoxy. Far from gesturing towards consolation, the sonnet revises the idea of Resurrection, on which early modern consolation is based, in the figure of a feminine Prometheus who autonomously restores life to the lifeless, repairing a wound that can be eased by nothing short of physical rebirth.

The image of Niobe which ends the sequence, however, also signals a retreat from autonomy to acquiescence: the speaker herself, as '*Amphion's* wife', is the property of her husband. In invoking Amphion as well as Niobe, the sonnet alludes to Oxford's poetic prowess in the figure of the poet-musician, and gestures towards inconsolable *paternal* grief, since, as Ovid reports, Amphion killed himself after the death of his sons.[12] Oxford's desire for a son is well documented: he wrote to Burghley upon hearing of Anne's first pregnancy, 'if it be a boij I shall lekwise be the partaker withe yow in a greater contentation', and 'now it hathe pleased god to giue me a sune of myne owne (as I hope it is)'.[13] Although his disappointment at Lord Bulbecke's death must have been devastating, his response did no violence to himself but to his wife and daughters. Burghley confided to Sir Francis Walsingham in May 1587:

> I was so vexed yesternight very late by some grievous sight of my poor daughter's affliction whom her husband had in the afternoon so troubled her with words of reproach of me to her . . . I did as much as I could to comfort her with hope; yet she, being as she is great with child, and continually afflicted to behold the misery of her husband and of his children, to whom he will not be leaving a farthing of land.[14]

In recalling Oxford's reputation as a poet, the closing fragment casts parental rivalry for the ownership of the son as a contest between rival poets. The speaker's offspring – the sonnets as well as the child they memorialize – are thus set against Oxford's 'sune of myne owne'. Here, the speaker argues, she alone is author and owner of her work. Yet the sequence's final line, 'Of him that I bare in mee, so long ago', conflates son and father. With the connotation of the speaker's sexual possession by her husband (the 'him' that she bore so long ago), the procreative autonomy she claims can no longer be sustained. The lines reinsert her into the marital and textual structures containing and creating her.

The ephemeral quality of the speaker's productive feminine power is determined by the child's death, which challenges even as it defines maternity. This is a loss that remains beyond repair as the sequence closes, and is attended in the epitaphs by violent images of the speaker's self-consumption in inconsolable grief. The first sonnet displaces the speaker's first-person lamentation to the child's surrogate mother, Venus, who 'invey[s] the skies / . . . with a voice inflamed / (Feeling therewith her venime, to be more bitter)' (ll. 6, 11–12; C3v). The 'mouth, tyme' which 'glotton[s] up all' in the opening lines of the sequence threatens, finally, to consume the speaker in an empathetic dissolution approximating her son's death. Thus Sonnet 2 begins with the image of self-feeding, 'In dolefull wayes I spend the wealth of my time: / Feeding on my heart, that ever comes agen' (ll. 1–2; C3v) and ends by recognizing that the speaker's sorrow has exhausted not only herself but also the world: 'Or what should I consume any more in woe, / When Destins, Gods, and worlds, are all in my losse' (ll. 13–14; C4). In the first fragmentary poem, Death personified ironically consoles the speaker, since her sorrow has effectively placed her beyond the world of 'blood and bones': 'But death makes mee aunswere? Madame, cease these mones: / My force is but on bodies of blood and bones: / And that of yours, is no more now, but a shadow' (Sonnet 1, ll. 12–14; C4v). Finally, in the closing fragment, the speaker can aspire only to reincarnation in and as the material tomb of her child, an aspiration cast as illusory in the same moment that her attempt to achieve an autonomous creative power falters and she becomes, once again, '*Amphion's* wife'.

The contested authorship of the 'Foure Epytaphes' invites speculation on the text's motives even as it frustrates firm conclusions as to its ultimate meaning.[15] If we imagine the poems to be Soowthern's compositions alone, their appearance in a work dedicated to Oxford must be construed as a compliment to Anne and a gesture of consolation on the loss of the couple's son. Thus the poems' portrait of the speaker's extreme grief, created by mobilizing recognizable features of early modern maternal lament, would prove Anne's commitment to maternity and her virtues as mother, while congratulating Oxford on his possession of such a wife. Yet the defiant emotion voiced by the maternal mourner in the epitaphs seems to qualify consolation and undermine their complimentary character. Profiting from the powerful affective licence granted by his culture to maternal grief, Soowthern's poems nonetheless err in their specificity: when assigned to Anne de Vere, this obdurate sorrow too easily indicts her husband's cruelty, passing beyond orthodox mourning for the death of an heir to unorthodox and unrestrained lamentation for the misery in which she languished throughout her marriage. Indeed, the scarcity of extant copies of *Pandora* and the troubled subject matter of the poems may suggest that the text was suppressed, while an allusion to Anne as 'Pandora' in an epitaph by Robert Bibens may reflect contemporary readers' identification of the 'Foure Epytaphes' and its stubborn sorrow with Anne an identification that surely would not have been welcomed.[16] Soowthern's ventriloquism, then, would amount to a violation.

Imagined as manuscript works written by Anne and pirated into print, the epitaphs connote, visually and symbolically, their author's dissolution in empathetic death. It is this dissolution that Soowthern approximates in the presentation of his printed text, regardless of the provenance of the poems. If the poems offer a textual monument to the lost son – a monument constructed and inscribed, as their imagery would have it, with the flesh and blood of the maternal mourner – their visual structure and fragmentary character seem to reflect the self-consuming passion perceived as proper to maternal grief. They are solid blocks of dense text, textual tombs as it were, that dissolve into fragments. Soowthern's marginal enumeration of the fragmentary lines to represent incomplete sonnets by Anne seems engineered to imply that the despondent maternal author composed from end to beginning: she is a resident in death more than in life. In this fiction of maternal authorship, the unproductive, excessive grief articulated in the poems finds its visual equivalent in an unproductive text: one that can be brought to press only surreptitiously, one so unstable that it seems on the verge of collapse. Considered in these terms, the poems' wavering between life and death takes material form as the body of maternal grief is both crafted and undone in the living tomb of the text; the sepulchre of the child and his defiant mother.

II

'What thinge is so agreeynge with Nature as Matrimonye?' asks Erasmus in his 'Epistle to perswade a young gentleman to Mariage', included in Thomas Wilson's *Arte of Rhetorique* in 1553. 'For there is no thinge so naturall not onelye unto mankinde, but also unto all other livinge creatures as it is for everye one of them to kepe their owne kinde from decaye, and through encrease of issue, to make the whole kinde immortall.'[17] Echoing the wisdom of his source, Shakespeare's speaker advises his young male addressee, 'From fairest creatures we desire increase, / That thereby beauty's rose might never die' (Sonnet 1, ll. 1–2). Erasmus's epistle argues that 'wedlocke is a manly thinge, suche as is mete for man',[18] and asserts that 'suche a one as hathe no minde of Mariage, semeth to be no manne, but rather a Stone, an enemye to Nature, a rebel to God him selfe, seking thrrough his owne folye, his last ende and destruction'.[19] Accordingly, Shakespeare's Sonnet 11 reasons, in procreation 'lives wisdom, beauty, and increase, / Without this, folly, age, and cold decay' (ll. 5–6). The counsel gleaned from Erasmus's epistle in the procreation sonnets seeks (unsuccessfully, in the end) to correct and redirect the young man's unnatural self-love.

If the procreation sonnets exploit a naturalization of paternity derived from Erasmus's epistle, they also engage a naturalization of maternity like that governing the 'Foure Epytaphes', with its attendant imagery of self-consumption and dissolution now transferred from the speaker to his addressee. Childlessness and child-loss thus share a common language. Shakespeare's first sonnet recalls the epitaphs' image of Time's gluttony as the speaker counsels the young man, 'Pity the world or else this glutton be: / To eat the world's due, by the grave and thee' (ll. 13–14). While the *Pandora* epitaphs complain of the barrenness of the petrified womb, Shakespeare follows Erasmus in describing the young man's decision 'to lyve syngle' as 'barren, and smally agreeyng with the state of mannes nature' (l. 22). 'Die single', Sonnet 3 warns, 'and thine image dies with thee' (l. 14), while Sonnet 11 urges, 'Let those whom nature hath not made for store, / Harsh, featurelesse, and rude, barrenly perish' (ll. 9–10). The procreation sonnets deal not with emotional excess and prodigality but with the pragmatic concerns of the household. The maternal mourner's profligate emotional expense in the 'Foure Epytaphes' parallels that of Shakespeare's 'Unthrifty lovelinesse' (Sonnet 4, l. 1) – 'contracted to [his] own bright eyes' (Sonnet 1, l. 5) and 'consum[ing him]self in single life' (Sonnet 9, l. 2) – in whom self-consumption is a symptom of self-love. As the procreation sonnets regender the commonplaces of maternal mourning, applying them not to the grieving mother but to the narcissistic young man, Shakespeare deconstructs the notion of feminine essence on which they proceed.[20] By invoking the restraining power of patriarchy in the theme of the early modern household, the procreation sonnets initially promise to subsume the maternal voice within the voice of the father. As they proceed, however, the speaker comes to approximate the maternal mourner's position exemplified in the 'Foure Epytaphes'. Shakespeare both deploys and *denaturalizes* the assumptions of Erasmus's epistle to reproduce and gain possession of his speaker and the young man. He does so, on the one hand, by associating procreation with the debased practices of usury and print, and, on the other, by containing and appropriating the power and threat of, in Margreta De Grazia's words, 'the promiscuous womb'.[21]

Self-feeding in the procreation sonnets is not, as it is in the 'Foure Epytaphes', an empathetic dissolution of the self in sorrow, but a deferral of the responsibility to reproduce which would transform a boy into a father. Accordingly, the poems are permeated with the language of primogeniture, and dwell specifically on the value of producing a son. Sonnet 7 simply states, 'thou . . . / Unlooked on diest unless thou get a sonne' (ll. 13–14). Sonnet 2 merges the speaker's preoccupations with the family value of thrift with his interest in primogeniture as he states, 'If thou couldst answer "This fair child of mine / Shall sum my count, and make my old excuse", / Proving his beautie by succession thine' (ll. 10–12). These concerns culminate in Sonnet 13's extended meditation on the duties of fathers and sons:

> O, that you were yourself! But love you are
> No longer yours than you your selfe here live.
> Against this coming end you should prepare,
> And your sweet semblance to some other give.
> So should that beauty which you hold in lease
> Find no determination; then you were
> Yourself again after your self's decrease
> When your sweet issue your sweet forme should beare.
> Who lets so faire a house fall to decay,
> Which husbandry in honour might uphold,
> Against the stormy gusts of winter's day
> And barren rage of death's eternal cold?
> O none but unthrifts, dear my love you know,
> You had a father, let your son say so.

In this exhortation to good husbandry, the image of the 'faire house' merges nature and culture by referring simultaneously to the young man's physical form and his dynastic line, both threatened by prodigality (sexual as well as financial) and repaired through a fiscally responsible and sexually orthodox act of reproduction.[22] Procreation thus assures the young man of an 'executor' of his beauty's legacy which, 'unused . . . must be tombed with [him]' (Sonnet 4, ll. 13–14). Urging the young man, 'Be not thee self-willed, for thou art much too fair / To be death's conquest and make wormes thine heir' (Sonnet 6, ll. 13–14), the speaker conflates his addressee's state of mind (his stubbornness) with his estate (he is willed only to himself) to characterize him as an embodiment of Erasmus's 'enemye to Nature . . . [seking] his last ende and destruction'.[23] This conflation of nature and culture permeates the procreation sonnets' treatment of primogeniture, estimating the value of the young man and his imagined offspring in legal and social, rather than natural or biological, terms. When Sonnet 13 assures the young man, 'then you were / Your selfe again after your selfes decrease / When your sweet issue your sweet forme should beare', Shakespeare employs a heraldic metaphor which understands the young man's physical form in and as his arms, borne by his successor. Sonnet 1 echoes the metaphor when the speaker assures the young man that 'His tender heir might bear his memory' (l. 4), displaying to posterity a physical resemblance to his father which is also the visible emblem of his family's identity.[24] Procreation is thus imagined as heraldry.

This interpretation of nature as culture, conducted through Shakespeare's denaturalization of the language and imagery of primogeniture, is elaborated in his adoption of economic figures to characterize reproduction throughout the procreation sonnets. The fourth sonnet's invocation of 'unus'd beauty' suggests that procreation is use, while sexual hoarding leads to death. Sonnet 6 makes this suggestion explicit in advising the young man:

> That use is not forbidden usury
> Which happies those that pay the willing lone.
> That's for thyself to breed another thee,
> Or ten times happier; be it ten for one; (ll. 5–8)

Yet if breed is a form of usury, by means of which, the young man is told, 'To give away yourself keeps yourself still' (Sonnet 16, l. 13), the refusal to beget an heir is figured as use as well; as unprofitable expense rather than profitable investment.[25] Sonnet 4 complains:

> Then, beauteous niggard, why doost thou abuse
> The bountious largesse given thee to give?
> Profitles usurer, why dost thou use
> So great a sum of sums yet can'st not live? (ll. 5–8)

As both niggard and usurer, the young man wastes himself in an illicit sexual economy, his self-consumption robbing him of immortality through breed. By complicating the terms with which sexual activity is legitimized in his source, Shakespeare reimagines and reveals the foundation of the early modern household, procreation itself, as economic and social rather than natural. The results of this denaturalization of reproduction are to establish and 'privilege male over female generation',[26] and to subordinate the womb to 'beauty's use' (Sonnet 2, l. 9). Thus Shakespeare contains and appropriates women's procreative power within a 'reproductive economy' involving only the poet and the young man.[27]

Read alongside the claims of maternal essence advanced by the 'Foure Epytaphes', the stakes of Shakespeare's denaturalized poetics, and the language it shares with the poetics of maternal mourning, become clear. As the procreation sonnets refigure the maternal mourner's petrified womb as the 'uneared wombe' (Sonnet 3, l. 5) that would bear the young man's son, Shakespeare marginalizes the maternal body and appropriates its enunciative power. Sonnet 6 advises the young man, 'Make sweet some vial, treasure thou some place / With beauty's treasure ere it be self-killed' (ll. 3–4), casting the womb as an inanimate container, a vial which is also vile, and discounting the woman's part in procreation.[28] The invitation of Sonnet 10, 'Make thee another self for love of me' (l. 13), implies both the young man's self-authorship and the singularity of his child in embodying his second self. While Erasmus's epistle celebrates the heir who is the goal and the product of married sex as 'a pretie litle boye, runnyng up and doune your house, such a wone as shall expresse your looke, and your wives looke',[29] the procreation sonnets represent him solely as the mirror of his father's face, retaining neither the features nor the memory of his mother: 'Look in thy glass, and tell the face thou viewest,' the speaker urges, 'Now is the time that face should form another' (Sonnet 3, ll. 1–2). When the poem concludes, 'But if thou live remembered not to be, / Die single and thine Image dies with thee', it is the young man's image alone that is remembered (that is, both recalled to posterity through his heir, and physically reassembled) in the form of his offspring.[30]

Like the 'Foure Epytaphes', Shakespeare's sonnets imagine self-consumption as feeding the *poet's* desire, and as providing the means by which the sonnet form becomes both the womb and the tomb containing the body of the beloved. This formula is most clearly articulated in Sonnet 86, which pits the poet against his rival for possession of the young man, a dramatic situation shared by Shakespeare's sequence and the *Pandora* sonnets, as they share the conflated imagery of the womb-as-tomb attending it:[31]

> Was it the proud full sail of his great verse,
> Bound for the prize of all-too-precious you
> That did my ripe thoughts in my braine inhearse,
> Making their tomb the womb wherein they grew? (ll. 1–4)

In the procreation sonnets the juxtaposition of the womb and the tomb serves alternatively to remind the young man of the need to procreate, and to exert the poet's rights of ownership over his subject. Shakespeare's Sonnet 3 asks:

> For where is she so faire whose uneared womb
> Disdains the tillage of thy husbandry?

Or who is he so fond will be the tomb
Of his self-love to stop posterity? (ll. 5–8)

Although ostensibly offering a *memento mori* to prompt the addressee to produce an heir, one repeated in the warning, 'Thy unused beauty must be tombed with thee' (Sonnet 4, l. 13), the equivalence between 'wombe' and 'tombe' established by their rhyme qualifies the Erasmian counsel to procreate. The qualification permits Shakespeare to augment the womb's reproductive capacity with his own poetic powers of reproduction, and to exert his ownership over the young man's legacy and his memory.[32] Accordingly, Shakespeare's appropriation of procreative power casts his verse as the womb recreating the young man, but also as the tomb in which he is 'inhearsed'. As Sonnet 17 states it:

Who will believe my verse in time to come
If it were filled with your most high deserts? –
Though yet, heaven knows, it is but as a tomb
Which hides your life, and shows not half your parts. (ll. 1–4)

Read in the light of the imagery of the monumental womb in the 'Foure Epytaphes', Shakespeare's appropriation at once manipulates the figure of childlessness to celebrate reproduction within his offspring poems, and bears the traces of the maternal mourning which it redirects and subsumes. As in the 'Foure Epytaphes', the procreation sonnets affirm the poet's right to reproduce and possess the beloved within the textual monument. Thus Shakespeare learns from the monumental body of maternal mourning how the sonnet can be imagined as a living, reproductive tomb.

If the *Pandora* sequence ends with the realization of the limits of that project, as the speaker is herself repossessed by the social bonds that lay claim to her child, the procreation sonnets conclude with a similar investigation of the rival claims of nature and culture – that is, of poetry and breed – on the young man, the poet and the poetic work. Sonnet 15 concludes with an equivocating promise of the poet's powers to reproduce and immortalize the young man in the face of 'wasteful time' (l. 11): 'And all in war with Time for love of you / As he takes from you, I engraft you new' (ll. 13–14). While the lines assert the ascendancy of poetry over breed as a means to ensure the young man's immortality, one possible interpretation of the act of engrafting has the speaker promoting his addressee's survival by engrafting him to a wife.[33] This meaning is only revised towards the young man's imagined survival through writing by the opening lines of Sonnet 16: 'But wherefore do not you a mightier way / Make war upon this bloody tyrant, time' (ll. 1–2). What at first appears to be a rivalry between poetry and breed, then, looks on closer inspection like a merger of the two. Sonnet 16's apparent contrast of the poet's 'barren rhyme' (l. 4) with the 'maiden gardens yet unset' (l. 6) as an alternative means to ensure the young man's immortality goes on to juxtapose 'time's pencil' and the poet's 'pupil pen' (l. 10), and ends with an affirmation of the young man's reproductive powers, which are themselves figured as the product of the pen: 'And you must live drawn by your own sweet skill' (l. 14).[34] By the sonnet's close, procreation is conceived as the young man's self-authorship, a writing to counter and control time's pencil, while the poet's barrenness associates writing with the 'uneared womb', unblessed by the young man's prodigal self-love earlier in the sequence. This merger of procreation and writing continues when Sonnet 17 proposes a solution to the problem of the sonnet-as-tomb based upon the corroborating evidence provided by natural reproduction: 'But were some child of yours alive that time, / You should live twice: in it, and in my rhyme' (ll. 13–14). The lines imagine the poem and the heir as twins; both offspring enabled by the procreative powers of the young man, but delivered with the cooperation of different partners. When Sonnet 18 poses the question, 'Shall I compare thee to a Summers day' (l. 1), Shakespeare scripts the triumph of his 'pupil pen' (Sonnet 16, l. 10) and leaves behind the sterility of the procreation sonnets in the 'verbal progeny' of the sequence that follows.[35]

Rendering the womb an unproductive tomb, the procreation sonnets entertain a dream of autonomous self-creation and procreation like that envisioned in the myth of Prometheus in the 'Foure Epytaphes'. Thus Shakespeare promotes a parthenogenetic vision of the young man and the poet that would reproduce and immortalize them both without the participation of the womb. As the poems imagine childlessness as child-loss, as 'beauty's waste' (Sonnet 9, l. 11) that 'unbless[es] some mother' (Sonnet 3, l. 4) and causes the widowed world to 'wail' the young man's loss 'like a makeless wife' (Sonnet 9, l. 4), they explore alternative forms of child-birth enabled by their 'onlie begetter', at once the poet and his self-authoring subject. In doing so they blend natural and cultural categories and merge the subject and the text. It is no accident, then, that the young man is encouraged to reproduce himself as if he were a printed text, his offspring imagined as 'an endlessly reproducible commodity'.[36] Sonnet 11 argues, 'She [nature] carved thee for her seal, and meant therby, / Thou shouldst print more, not let that copy die' (ll. 13–14). Energizing this series of puns (on 'seal', 'die' and 'copy') that stress the procreative metaphors implicit in the language of early modern printing, Shakespeare 'delegitimizes' procreation by associating it with print, and blends notions of 'biological and aesthetic creation'.[37] He claims the right to immortalize the young man through poetry and urges the young man to exercise his procreative autonomy through the mechanical reproduction of the subject-text. The opening line of the sonnets, 'From fairest creatures we desire increase', suggests the mutual agency attending this merger of procreative and poetic powers in seeking to increase the young man himself, the sonnets that celebrate him, and the printed text that makes them both immortal.

Like the 'Foure Epytaphes', Shakespeare's sonnets stand in a troubled relationship to publication. The work came to press without the apparent involvement of its author and shares with the *Pandora* epitaphs a concern with rival claims for possession of its subject. These concerns lead in the 'Foure Epytaphes' to the creation of a feminine landscape in which the public and social forces which lay claim to the male child are challenged by maternal affect. The fragility of this landscape is apparent not only within the poems themselves, but also in the fragmented and unstable text which brings them to press. In the poems' narrative of textual provenance, as the maternal mourner surrenders her poems to publication, she also relinquishes her hold on her son's remains: he becomes the 'Lord Bulbecke' of Soowthern's title. Similar interests in the procreation sonnets lead Shakespeare to figure publication as at once establishing the poet as sole owner of the young man's literary remains (he lives only in Shakespeare's 'eternal lines,' Sonnet 18, l. 12), and as dispossessed of both his subject and the poems that create and contain him (since the written work, and thus its contents, can be considered Shakespeare's property only while it remains in manuscript).[38] Moreover, the poet's appropriation of the womb renders him, as the sequence proceeds, dependent upon his addressee. The poet becomes the vial to be filled by the young man's sexual and poetic potency and he struggles, unsuccessfully, to claim ownership of his subject until the sequence relinquishes him altogether in the fragmentary Sonnet 126. T. A. Birrell's characterization of quarto publications as 'self-destructing artefacts', owing to their material fragility, comments suggestively on the affinities between the poetic personae of the *Pandora* epitaphs and the procreation sonnets.[39] Alienated from an idea of feminine essence that constructs the speaker of the 'Foure Epytaphes', maternity's procreative power splits between the poet and his self-authoring subject, rendering them partners and rivals in the act of textual reproduction.

The ambiguities of authorship in these two texts – attendant upon attribution in the 'Foure Epytaphes' and deliberately crafted by Shakespeare's denaturalization of maternity in the sonnets – suggest means by which early modern texts, regardless of the gender of their authors, can both engage and illuminate constructions of masculinity and femininity pervasive in the culture. In Shakespeare's procreation sonnets the early modern project of establishing gender identity through parenthood – actual, failed or imagined – is examined, deconstructed and revised as the young man is cast at once as child, parent and partner in reproduction. While the 'Foure Epytaphes' portrays Anne de Vere among the ruins of domestic and religious orthodoxy, in the shadow of the broken household and in the threshold between life and death, Lord Burghley's monument to his daughter repairs these fractured foundations, much as the textual legacy of the sonnets repairs the work's fragmented speaker to construct the author 'Shakespeare'.[40] When the authors' personae, with their complex and shifting genders, are both crafted and undone within these texts, it is left to the reparative work of later readers to provide definition, shape and meaning to the lives of these wayward children within the canonical monuments erected upon their resilient, accommodating forms.

NOTES

I wish to thank the Melbern G. Glasscock Center for Humanities Research, Texas A&M University, for support while writing this chapter.

1 Hatfield MS 277.8; quoted in B. M. Ward, *The Seventeenth Earl of Oxford, 1550–1604 from Contemporary Documents* (London: John Murray, 1928), p. 288. Lansdowne MS 104, ff.195–214, also contains more than forty unpublished epitaphs for Anne de Vere.

2 On Oxford, see Ward, *Seventeenth Earl.*

3 Lansdowne MS 19.83, quoted in Ward, *Seventeenth Earl*, p. 122. See also Conyers Read, *Lord Burghley and Queen Elizabeth* (New York: Knopf, 1960), pp. 126–38, and Helen C. Payne, 'The Cecil Women at Court', in Pauline Croft, ed., *Patronage, Power and Culture: The Early Cecils*, Studies in British Art 8 (New Haven: Yale University Press, 2002), pp. 267–8.

4 Hatfield MS 9:1. See also Ward, *Seventeenth Earl*, p. 122, and Read, *Lord Burghley*, p. 135.

5 See Ward, *Seventeenth Earl*, pp. 232–3, and Thomas Birch, *Memoirs of the Reign of Queen Elizabeth*, 2 vols. (London: A. Millar, 1754), vol. 1, p. 31. This was the only son born to Anne and Oxford; his second wife, Elizabeth Trentham, gave birth to his heir in 1593.

6 Ward, *Seventeenth Earl*, p. 233.

7 John Soowthern, *Pandora, the musyque of the beautie, of his mistresse Diana* (London: John Charlewood for Thomas Hackett, 1584), C3v. The sonnets appear C3v–C4v. Subsequent citations are to this edition and appear in parentheses.

8 John Dart, *Westmonasterium: Or the History and Antiquities of the Abbey Church of St. Peter's Westminster*, 2 vols. (London: T. Bowles and J. Bowles, 1742), vol. 1, p. 137.

9 See Nicholas Abraham and Maria Torok, 'Introjection-Incorporation: Mourning *or* Melancholia', in Serge Lebovici and Daniel Widlocher, eds., *Psychoanalysis in France* (New York: International University Press, 1980), pp. 3–16.

10 Rosalind Smith, in her *Sonnets and the English Woman Writer, 1560–1621: The Politics of Absence* (New York: Palgrave, 2005), pp. 61–87, persuasively identifies Philippe Desportes's French poetry as the source for about one-third of the contents of the 'Foure Epytaphes', strongly supporting Soowthern's authorship. Feminist critics, following Ellen Moody, 'Six Elegiac Poems, Possibly by Anne Cecil de Vere, Countess of Oxford (with Texts)', *English Literary Renaissance* 19 (1989), 152–70, have accepted the poems as Anne's: see Louise Schleiner, *Tudor and Stuart Women Writers* (Bloomington: Indiana University Press, 1994), pp. 85–93; Marion Wynne-Davies, *Women Poets of the Renaissance* (London: J. M. Dent, 1998), pp. 343–54; and Patricia Phillippy, *Women, Death and Literature in Post-Reformation England* (Cambridge: Cambridge University Press, 2002), pp. 165–8. Smith follows Steven May, 'The Countess of Oxford's Sonnets: A Caveat', *ELN* 29 (1992), 9–20, in describing the poems as Soowthern's prosopopoeia, comprising original poetry interwoven with passages translated from Desportes. The innovation in *Pandora* is to place the elegies in the voice of the grieving mother: thus an emphasis on the lost infant as the mother's unique possession and the poems' appropriation of a discursive force understood as unique to the maternal mourner are original to the sequence. While this chapter thus reconsiders my earlier estimation of Anne's authorship in the light of Smith's evidence, I see the epitaphs as supporting, and exploiting, the commonplaces of maternal mourning and therefore as offering a performance of gender in relation to the absent child which is characteristic of the period.

11 Since he was buried on church grounds, the infant would probably have been baptized. See Will Coster, 'Tokens of Innocence: Infant Baptism and Burial in Early Modern England', in Bruce Gordon and Peter Marshall, eds., *The Place of the Dead: Death and Remembrance in Late Medieval and Early Modern Europe* (Cambridge: Cambridge University Press, 2000), pp. 266–87.

12 Ovid, *Metamorphoses*, trans. Frank Justus Miller, 2 vols. (Cambridge, MA: Loeb Classical Library, 1944), vol. 1, book 4, ll. 146–312.

13 Hatfield MS 8:24.

14 Ward, *Seventeenth Earl*, p. 285. Anne was carrying her daughter, Susan. Another daughter, Frances, died in September of that year, aged three.

15 See Smith, *Sonnets and the English Woman Writer*, pp. 79–87, on possible motives for Soowthern's publication.

16 Only two copies survive, one in the British Library (shelf mark C39.e35) and one in the Huntington Library (STC 22928). See Lansdowne MS 104, f.203, and see Smith, *Sonnets and the English Woman Writer*, pp. 64–5 and 72, for discussion

17 Thomas Wilson, *The Arte of Rhetorique* (London, 1553), 26v.

18 *Ibid.*, 28v.

19 *Ibid.*, 26.

20 See Naomi J. Miller, 'Playing "the Mother's Part": Shakespeare's Sonnets and Early Modern Codes of Maternity', in James Schiffer, ed., *Shakespeare's Sonnets: Critical Essays* (New York: Garland, 1999), pp. 347–67, on Shakespeare's engagement with early modern codes of maternity. See also Peter C. Herman, 'What's the Use: Or, The Problematic of Economy in Shakespeare's Procreation Sonnets', in Schiffer, ed., *Shakespeare's Sonnets*, p. 264, on 'Shakespeare's general interest in the deconstruction of cultural and generic forms'.

21 Margreta De Grazia, 'The Scandal of Shakespeare's Sonnets', in Schiffer, ed., *Shakespeare's Sonnets*, p. 105. For a similar view, see Valerie Traub, 'Sex Without Issue: Sodomy, Reproduction and Signification in Shakespeare's Sonnets', in Schiffer, ed., *Shakespeare's Sonnets*, pp. 431–54.

22 See also Sonnet 10, lines 8–9. De Grazia, in 'Scandal', pp. 102–3, argues that Shakespeare's original readers would have recognized his adoption of Erasmus's epistle 'as a blueprint for reproducing the fair values of the dominant class'.

23 Stephen Booth, ed., in his *Shakespeare's Sonnets* (New Haven: Yale University Press, 1977), pp. 152–3, suggests that 'here' in line 2 might also be read as 'heire': thus the young man is his own possession only as long as he continues to be his own heir.

24 See also Sonnet 2, l. 3.

25 See Herman, 'What's the Use', p. 275.

26 Traub, 'Sex without Issue', p. 436.

27 See De Grazia, 'Scandal', pp. 105–6, and Traub, 'Sex Without Issue', pp. 436–8.

28 See Herman, 'What's the Use', p. 268, on Shakespeare's reification of the womb.

29 Wilson, *Art of Rhetorique*, p. 31.

30 See also Booth's gloss, in *Shakespeare's Sonnets*, p. 138, of 'image' as: 1) memory, 2) mirror image, and 3) offspring.

31 See Miller, 'Playing "the Mother's Part"', pp. 357–8.

32 Traub, 'Sex without Issue', p. 440.

33 Booth, *Shakespeare's Sonnets*, p. 158.

34 For a similar discussion of the sonnet, see Miller, 'Playing "the Mother's Part"', p. 355.

35 *Ibid.*, p. 354

36 Herman, 'What's the Use', p. 268.

37 See Booth, *Shakespeare's Sonnets*, p. 151, for discussion of these puns, and see Wendy Wall, *The Imprint of Gender: Authorship and Publication in the English Renaissance* (Ithaca: Cornell University Press, 1993), for full discussion of the gendering of early modern print. See also Herman, 'What's the Use', especially pp. 269–78, for the former, and Traub, 'Sex without Issue', p. 441, for the latter argument.

38 See Margreta De Grazia, *Shakespeare Verbatim: The Reproduction of Authenticity and the 1790 Apparatus* (Oxford: Oxford University Press, 1991), p. 189, and Arthur F. Marotti, 'Shakespeare's Sonnets as Literary Property', in Elizabeth D. Harvey and Katharine Eisaman Maus, eds., *Soliciting Interpretation: Literary Theory and Seventeenth-Century English Poetry* (Chicago: University of Chicago Press, 1990), p. 143.

39 Quoted in Marotti, 'Shakespeare's Sonnets', p. 158.

40 See De Grazia, *Shakespeare Verbatim*, on the canonization of the sonnets.

PART 2

Children's Shakespeares

8

Introduction: reinventing Shakespearean childhoods

Susanne Greenhalgh

I

On three pages in a copy of the First Folio held by the Folger Shakespeare Library can be found several children's drawings. They appear as classic examples of juvenile artwork, depicting houses with smoking chimneys (one with a stick-figure in the doorway) and a room complete with table, chairs and pictures on the wall. Although the volume belonged to the same Warwickshire family for several centuries, we do not know whether there is any connection between these drawings and the inscription 'Elizabeth Okell her book 1729' which also appears in it, let alone the identity, age or gender of the child (or children) who once found amusement this way. Nor do we know whether the adult response to this youthful self-expression was one of anger or indulgence. We are left simply with the graphic evidence of a meeting point between Shakespeare and childhood, one in which Shakespeare was briefly appropriated and domesticated as part of a child's imaginative world, as a site of childish play.[1]

Here, dealing with an incident that probably took place at some point in the eighteenth century, it might seem that we are at last on familiar ground after the less travelled terrain of early modern childhood studies mapped by Kate Chedgzoy in the introduction to part 1. Shakespeare now exists as a magisterial and valued text, one becoming subject to the discoveries and refinements of scholarly editing, and developing into an increasingly significant force, first within British national culture and in due course internationally.[2] Historians also generally agree that this was the period in which 'a degree of sensitivity to childhood and to children' became apparent, at least in certain classes; one previously lacking in societies that had viewed childhood as primarily a time-limited passage either to adulthood or to heaven.[3] It is all too easy to imagine the unknown children doodling in the margins of Shakespeare's works as essentially like middle-class Western children of today. The very seductiveness of this image, however, underlines how concepts of childhood, as well as of Shakespeare, are intrinsically bound up with questions of ideology, especially with issues of class, and economic and cultural privilege. It is no accident that this piece of evidence originates in a home affluent enough to possess such a valuable collector's item; one where children had leisure for such play. The history of Shakespeare and childhood to some degree reveals the democratization of both these cultural formations over time.

This history is also one whose very terms require interrogation. Anna Davin has outlined the questions which must follow the fundamental one, 'What is a child?': 'In whose eyes? When? Where? What are the implications?'[4] These, too, are questions which must underlie any investigation of how Shakespeare has entered the lives of children during the past three centuries, and in the process been reinvented for them, within and through family life, performance, art, literature, education, mass media, and play. The essays in part 2 therefore place particular emphasis on the ideological purposes to which the shifting relationship between Shakespeare and childhood has been put, as the place of children in society – and the understanding of what childhood might be – have developed and changed.

The very concept of childhood is amorphous, just as the history of children is fragmented and often poorly documented.[5] As Chedgzoy pointed out in her introduction, the still-evolving multidisciplinary field of childhood studies has predominantly concerned itself with modern childhoods.[6] If the very existence of childhood remains cause for debate for scholars of medieval and Renaissance history, historians of the seventeenth century could find evidence in paintings and other representations of children (including the memoirs and diaries of parents and carers) that childhood was beginning to be viewed as a distinctive and valued phase of life, already open to the kind of adult nostalgia for its supposed innocent playfulness that Polixenes appears to express in *The Winter's Tale*:

We were, fair Queen,
Two lads that thought there was no more behind
But such a day tomorrow as today,
And to be boy eternal . . .
We were as twinned lambs that did frisk i'th'sun,
And bleat the one at th'other. What we changed
Was innocence for innocence. We knew not

The doctrine of ill-doing, nor dreamed
That any did (1.2.63–74)

Polixenes, however, goes on to invoke the doctrine of original sin which lay behind the conceptualization of the child as heir to an inherited 'disposition to evil', in need of vigilant discipline and moral guidance to prevent eventual perdition. Early modern concepts of childhood, whether humanist, Catholic or Protestant, focused on children's spiritual health, and the vulnerability and the value they represented was bound up with religious belief and symbolization, crucially influencing the representation of childhood to be found in Shakespeare's plays, as Catherine Belsey points out in chapter 3. The gradual secularization of Western cultures during the next three centuries, together with less rigid social stratification, improved economic conditions for some; and ethical shifts influencing theories of child-rearing and education, from John Locke to Jean-Jacques Rousseau, combined to make possible profound alterations in the meanings attached to childhood.

By the middle of the nineteenth century, the nexus of values and attitudes encapsulated in the term 'childhood' was a contested but powerfully influential force in Western societies; one that through the course of the twentieth century infiltrated other cultures as they became 'westernized' to varying degrees. Enlightenment esteem for scientifically observed nature had initiated the anthropological study of children, as a 'species' which preserved traces of the primordial past of the human race (a concept that influenced the Victorian association of fairies – or 'Old Ones' – with children; and which Robert Shaughnessy finds echoed in the ways in which *A Midsummer Night's Dream* has been linked with a sense of childhood as a foreign country).[7] The Romantic idealization of childhood, as not only a state of innocence but one of special insight into the workings of nature and the creative imagination, also began a slow process of popular 'sacralization' of the child. The 'discovery' of childhood, and the attendant abstraction and personification of the Child within the literary work of key figures such as William Blake, Samuel Taylor Coleridge, Johann Wolfgang von Goethe and William Wordsworth made possible conceptualizations of the child-figure as 'a central vehicle for expressing ideas about the self and its history'; above all the concept of an interior self, reconceived later in Freudian terms as 'the lost child within all of us'.[8]

Another key shift in thinking about childhood was to see it not as an unavoidable pit-stop on the race to maturity, best got over with as quickly as possible, but as a state imbued with the characteristics of progress, futurity and thus modernity itself.[9] All these developments were punctuated by intervals in which more religious or exploitative attitudes resurfaced – expressed to varying degrees in both sentimentality and harshness – and they never extended to all children. However, legislation and the introduction of universal education in most Western societies in the latter part of the nineteenth century brought about 'a profound transformation in [children's] economic and sentimental value – as they ceased to be wage-earners and became school-pupils'.[10] In principle at least, all children were now to be deemed 'priceless' social and emotional capital; worthy, too, of state investment – or at least potentially so.[11]

As childhood came to be perceived as a separate, highly significant, stage of life, it also increasingly became a site for debates about Shakespeare's place within this new world. Shakespearean works were also drawn upon for arguments and illustrations through which the experiences perceived as 'proper' to childhood could be defined, visualized and disseminated or censored. Previous scholarship has chiefly focused on the ways in which these concerns have been evident in the discourses and practices of education, and in literary – and later media – adaptation.[12] The still current formulation of Shakespeare as the 'best' that English culture has to offer, a heritage to which all children have a democratic 'right', has played an especially significant part in these processes, designed to produce a culturally informed future citizenry. However, much work remains to be done; for example, on the extent to which Shakespearean references and images found a place in the public rhetoric of social and political reform of the conditions of children's lives, which did so much to create the childhood that we recognize today.[13] Bound up as it was with the idea that the child was truly father to the man, the discourse of psychology has also frequently had recourse to the narratives and imagery of childhood provided by the Shakespearean text, not least in the work of Sigmund Freud himself. According to the controversial arguments of the 'psychogenic' school of historiography, a play such as *Hamlet* is a form of children's literature which reveals the hidden secrets of historical child abuse, part of a history of childhood to be regarded as 'a nightmare from which we are only just waking up'.[14]

The subjects and approaches explored in part 2 range selectively, yet widely, over a field which invites research and scholarship from the perspectives of many disciplines. Above all, these chapters do not merely seek to document the relationship *between* Shakespeare and childhood, but to acknowledge and explore the many ways in which Shakespeare has existed *within* changing cultures of childhood. In what follows, I point to a selection of materials and topics that will enable such documentation and exploration, and will repay future investigation.

II

Analysis of the visual arts has established itself both within childhood studies and Shakespeare studies but to date the two have rarely been brought together.[15] Whether or not modern childhood began in upper- and middle-class households of the mid-eighteenth century, this period saw the emergence of a significant aspect of Shakespearean iconography – the representation of Shakespeare himself as a child. Derived from classical sources that envisioned gods as growing gradually into their divine powers, the most influential expression of this trope was Thomas Gray's neoclassical framing of Shakespeare as a chief point of origin for the English poetic genius, in 'The Progress of Poesy: A Pindaric Ode' (1768).

> Far from the sun and summer-gale,
> In thy green lap was Nature's darling laid,
> What time, where lucid Avon strayed,
> To him the mighty Mother did unveil
> Her awful face: the dauntless child
> Stretched forth his little arms and smiled.
> 'This pencil take,' (she said) 'whose colours clear
> Richly paint the vernal year:
> Thine too these golden keys, immortal boy!
> This can unlock the gates of joy;
> Of horror that, and thrilling fears,
> Or ope the sacred source of sympathetic tears.[16]

The concept of Shakespeare as 'dauntless child' and 'immortal boy' was given further vividness and influence in the drawings, paintings and prints by George Romney that Gray's lines inspired. Modelled on classical and Renaissance artworks, Romney's allegorical images presented the infant Shakespeare as a child divinity, attended by personifications of Nature and the Passions or Tragedy and Comedy.[17] Theatre audiences in Dublin could also enjoy a drop scene of *Euterpe and Hercules conducting the infant Shakespeare to the Temple of Minerva*, by the Italian Gaetano Marinari.[18] Another theatrical example of the artistic conjunction of real child figures with the genius of Shakespeare is James Northcote's portrait of the child acting prodigy Master William Betty, portrayed as Hamlet ascending to an imaginary Shakespeare shrine (1804), now in the collection of the Royal

Shakespeare Company. The pose and setting are modelled on portrayals of David Garrick, so that Betty is subsumed into a series of subordinate relationships – with Shakespeare, the adult actor and the role itself – even as he is depicted mounting the steps of fame.[19]

Children are used traditionally, as images of transience, in Henry Wallis's *A Sculptor's Workshop, Stratford-upon-Avon, 1617* (1857), which depicts the carving of Shakespeare's memorial bust for the Stratford parish church. As Ben Jonson shows Shakespeare's death mask to the sculptor, three children play with wooden toy figures in a corner, their fleeting game of make-believe in poignant juxtaposition to the creative imagination being commemorated 'for all time'. In other nineteenth-century paintings, the 'immortal boy' appeared with a less mythic and more parochial aspect, often also maturing into an adolescent; now less a force of nature than a country lad wandering the woods of Warwickshire, and even poaching deer from them.[20]

Images of the child Shakespeare often illustrate, and sometimes inform, the biographical representation of Shakespeare, from the many nineteenth-century factual and fictional accounts to such recent scholarly undertakings as Stephen Greenblatt's *Will in the World: How Shakespeare Became Shakespeare* (2004) or media versions such as Michael Wood's *In Search of Shakespeare* (BBC 2003). In part a representation of the quest for Shakespearean origins, the Shakespeare-as-child figure is also, as Henry James recognized in his sceptical tale of bardolatry, 'The Birthplace', at the root of sentimental Shakespearean mythmaking. This story of an unsuccessful teacher's preferment to the post of custodian of the 'birthplace' of a world-famous writer, in return for nursing a child through a life-threatening illness, culminates in a parodic tour de force in which the guide 'brings to life' the writer's childhood for his tourist audience.

> It is in this old chimney corner . . . just there in the far angle, where His little stool was placed, and where, I dare say, if we could look close enough, we should find the hearthstone scraped with His little feet – that we see the inconceivable child gazing into the blaze of the old oaken logs and making out there pictures and stories, see Him conning, with curly bent head, His well-worn hornbook, or poring over some scrap of an ancient ballad, some page of some such rudely bound volume of chronicles as lay, we may be sure, in His father's window-seat.[21]

It is precisely because Shakespeare's childhood is 'inconceivable' that it continues to fascinate writers and artists, including those who write for children.[22]

The Romantic fusion of images of children as '*originary* models of ideal nature, unselfconscious and self-sufficient models of natural beauty, and irrepressible engines of vital power'[23] with constructions of Shakespeare as a unique embodiment of sublime Nature also informs representations of some of Shakespeare's child characters, as in Joshua Reynolds's portrait, *Puck* (1789), produced for the Boydell Gallery. This painting's disturbing vibrancy combines allegory of childhood as forceful nature with the social constraints of real children's lives. It was inspired by an earlier drawing of a child the artist had found sitting on his doorstep. It therefore has associations with the 'fancy' painting genre at which Reynolds excelled – depictions of poor or working children dressed (or undressed) in indeterminate settings and costuming suggestive of varying types of childhood innocence or poignancy and designed to evoke adult sensibilities.[24] The transformation of the child model into inhuman sprite lends him an eerie, changeling-like quality – one contemporary reviewer called it 'a portrait of a foetus'[25] – suggestive of the complex dynamics of adult appropriation and caring attention implicit in the genre.

Many other eighteenth- and nineteenth-century illustrations of the plays in editions and in prints intended for the home can be considered 'pictures of innocence', in which distinct conceptualizations of Shakespeare and childhood conjoin.[26] The victim children in *Richard III* and *King John* were especial favourites throughout the nineteenth century, a fashion paralleled and influenced by popular theatre productions by actor managers such as Garrick and Charles Kemble. Richard Northcote's *Murder of the Princes in the Tower* (1790) was one of the most popular of the Boydell prints, more for its poignancy than its historical insights. Painters such as John Millais and John Opie made these pathetic, often feminized, boys their subjects, and even Queen Victoria sketched Arthur after seeing Kate Terry (Ellen's sister) play the role at Windsor.[27] There are accounts, too, of children's own drawings of Shakespeare; for example, as a schoolboy at Charterhouse, William Makepeace Thackeray caricatured the Macbeths as a butcher and his wife.[28]

Shakespearean illustration also played its part in the idealization of girlhood that featured prominently in sections of Victorian society. In 1888 *The Graphic* weekly magazine capitalized on its reputation for publishing images of female beauty in the 'keepsake' tradition designed for private collection and display, by commissioning a selection of portrayals of Shakespeare's women. Available as expensive colour editions, they were also published in black-and-white versions, which could be coloured by children at home. In the latter part of the century, as both the school and home market for children's books grew, so, too, did the demand for illustrations; tailored, as children's films in the twentieth century would be, to a dual audience of adults and children. These ranged from the saccharine pictures of Shakespeare characters as toddlers that accompanied Edith Nesbit's retellings, to the visually striking and innovative images of Arthur Rackham and Edmund Dulac, designed as expensive gift items. Much work remains to be done to identify and study the range of artwork in which Shakespearean and childhood elements have been brought together, and how artistic conventions have interacted with the changing representations of gender, race and national identity offered to young people.[29]

III

Gary Taylor's assertion that Shakespeare was 'forcibly' transformed into a children's author in the nineteenth century constructs the works as both 'adult' in themselves and important sociocultural markers of maturity, and therefore intrinsically out of place in the world of childhood.[30] However, as Georgianna Ziegler has demonstrated, children were introduced to Shakespeare much earlier than the landmark year of 1807, which saw the publication of both the Lambs' *Tales from Shakespear* and Henrietta Bowdler's *Family Shakespeare*.[31] Rather than embark on a reprise of the story of these early, influential retellings and editions of Shakespeare for children, which are discussed in Naomi J. Miller's chapter and elsewhere, I want instead to highlight some aspects of the publications which helped to establish Shakespeare as 'a primary gentling and civilizing influence for children'.[32]

Whether edited, selected or adapted, most versions of Shakespeare for children involve abbreviation, and often annotation or commentary. The general critical assumption is that this entails dilution and distortion of the 'original', though neither in the theatre or the study was experience of 'whole Shakespeare' generally on offer before the nineteenth century. It is worth considering therefore what the effects of such repackaging might have been, beyond the imposition of adult interpretation on the reading experience of the child, or the offering of something that is 'not Shakespeare'. Although anthologies and collections of Shakespeare extracts have largely been dismissed as dutiful, coercive, or pointless cannibalizations of the Shakespeare corpus, they could also have a clear social role within the middle-class household or school. In many cases they had a strong performative dimension. As vehicles for the teaching and encouragement of good elocution, they not only provided exercises in confident and effective vocal delivery (an essential attribute for many professions, and regarded as desirable in wives and mothers), but also offered miniature scenarios in which model characters or situations might be absorbed through action and imitation. The opportunity to act out – or at least vocalize – Macbeth's dagger soliloquy or Mark Antony's masterclass in political manipulation must have been diverting as well as improving for the 'young ladies' of Mrs Bellamy's Boarding School in the early eighteenth century.[33]

In the United States the McGuffey Eclectic Readers (122 million copies of which were published between 1830 and 1920) consisted of extracts both from contemporary writers such as Harriet Beecher Stowe and Charles Dickens, and established literary classics by writers including Shakespeare and John Milton. First developed as a 'new form of pedagogy' by William Holmes McGuffey, a Presbyterian minister and Professor of Philosophy and Ancient Languages, they were published as a series between 1830 and 1857. They were consumer-tested on their intended audience, as McGuffey invited children to his home to gauge the suitability for specific ages and interests of his chosen extracts, intended to mirror and thus induce such virtues as independence, hard work, temperance and philanthropy. Such selections and anthologies either put diverse material side by side, or were available to be dipped into at will, rather than as a linear progression through an entire play. In this sense they could perhaps sometimes have operated in ways akin to those of the twentieth-century retellings of Shakespeare described by Miller, enabling forms of 'developmental autonomy, demonstrated in the capacity to act, and to learn through acting, in the dual senses of *taking action* and *dramatic performance*, both of which can occur through the medium of play'.[34]

The choice of particular extracts and plays also highlights the influence of constructions of national and gender identity. Where speeches from *Henry V* seem to have been favourites in England, the republican setting of *Julius Caesar* gave it special interest in the United States.[35] Jean-Baptiste Perrin's 1783 collection of *Contes Moraux*, compiled to aid language learning, and the selections made by the Lambs and the Bowdlers, all helped to initiate the creation of a 'children's canon' of plays, which has remained remarkably constant over the years. Those most retold and published appear to be, *Henry V*, *Julius Caesar*, *Macbeth*, *A Midsummer Night's Dream*, *Romeo and Juliet* and *The Tempest*, with *As You Like It*, *Hamlet*, *Henry IV*, Part 1, *Richard III* and *Twelfth Night* also appearing quite frequently.[36] As well as singling out plays with supernatural elements, the choice tends to fall on those that deal in some way with young people encountering the demands of adulthood, in the form of love and patriotic or family duty. A miniature canon of Shakespearean songs was also introduced by John Marshall's selection, published as the second part of *Mother Goose's Melody* (1797). Although this has been interpreted as an attempt to appeal to a more educated, elite market, the situating of Shakespeare alongside popular traditions of song opened up the possibility that his verse could be read – and perhaps even sung – with the emphasis on rhythm and rhyme, rather than meaning and morals. The role of Shakespeare-derived or Shakespeare-influenced music in the upbringing of Victorian children is another subject deserving of further investigation.

Accounts of children's first exposure to Shakespeare provide another productive field for research. In middle- and upper-class households, this often came about in the context of one-to-one or group readings within the family, usually with parents taking the lead. Mention of such activities is a convention of countless biographical and autobiographical accounts of writers, politicians, spiritual leaders and actors, but is also beginning to be identified and researched in otherwise unnoticed lives, especially those of working-class families.[37] Although often focused on how such experiences prefigure a glittering adult career, some anecdotes also reveal how domestic Shakespearean performances could be a form of emotional currency within the home, and remain a source of poignant memory in later life. Family readings were particularly important in households, often Methodist or Evangelical, whose religious beliefs precluded theatre-going. The actor Henry Irving grew up in such a family, as did Charles Dodgson (Lewis Carroll), who despite being intended for the Church, took full advantage of the opportunities for home-based *tableaux vivants* and puppet plays, some of them with Shakespearean themes.[38] Future acclaimed actors, from Charles Macready to Laurence Olivier, had their first heady taste of applause when they tried out their skills in scenes from the plays as schoolboy performers. Helena Faucit spent a childhood convalescence reading an acting edition of Shakespeare, and with her brothers staged a performance of scenes from *Cymbeline* for her governess's birthday.[39] She also, in a manner reminiscent of Anna Jameson's *Shakespeare's Heroines* (1832) and Mary Cowden Clarke's *The Girlhood of Shakespeare's Heroines* (1850) imagined herself into a daydreaming state of identification with Shakespeare's girls: 'I lived again and again through the whole childhood and lives of many of Shakespeare's heroines.'[40]

Private fantasies were not the only way children could make Shakespeare their own. Nathaniel Hawthorne, for instance, is depicted turning a dramatic highlight into a favourite game.

> When he could scarcely speak plain, it is recalled by members of the family that the little fellow would go about the house, repeating with vehement emphasis and gestures certain stagy lines from Shakespeare's *Richard III*, which he had overheard from older persons about him. One line, in particular, made a great impression upon him, and he would start up on the most unexpected occasions and fire off in his loudest tone, 'Stand back, my Lord, and let the coffin pass.'[41]

Not all children's imaginative encounters with Shakespeare were so enjoyable – both John Keats and John Ruskin recorded their youthful terror of *Macbeth*. More recently, Bob Smith has related how the reading of the opening line of *The Merchant of Venice*, 'In sooth I know not why I am so sad', at the age of eleven opened an imaginative escape route from the distress of living with a severely disabled sister and emotionally distant parents.[42]

In the case of a writer such as Dickens, for whom, as Valerie Gager has convincingly demonstrated, Shakespeare was a constant and deeply rooted influence, it has been suggested that early Shakespearean reading even helped to shape the direction of a successful career. In his story 'The Uncommercial Traveller', Dickens recounts a meeting in a coach with a 'very queer small boy' (probably a version of his younger self). The nine-year-old is portrayed as reading 'all sorts of books', evidently including *Henry IV*, since he knows of the connection of Falstaff with the house they are passing, called Gad's Hill, which will one day be the writer's famous home.[43] Occasionally, a child speaks to us directly at the time of first encounter. Emily Shore, the gifted daughter of a highly educated middle-class family, kept a diary until her death in 1839 at the age of nineteen. Along with her great passion for studying nature (and human nature) she records her developing response to Shakespeare. At thirteen her father's reading of *Julius Caesar* prompts a listing of her favourite characters, a judgement apparently based on their moral attributes: 'Brutus is my favourite . . . I am very fond of Portia also, but not Julius Caesar, nor Mark Antony.' As she gets older, *Hamlet* becomes her favourite play, and she proudly records her custom of spending twenty minutes reading Shakespeare before tea.[44] It is more than likely that these influences fed into the poems, plays and novels that she also wrote before she died. All these examples testify to the ways in which children have made Shakespeare a source for their own pleasure, inventiveness, and even self-preservation, even if first introduced to the works in the name of education or duty.

As Kathryn Prince demonstrates in chapter 10 in relation to Victorian periodicals and theatrical toys, during the course of the nineteenth century Shakespeare increasingly reached children in forms specifically designed for leisure and play. Those children whose families had the means began to be considered as potential consumers of a range of new products; paper dolls and scraps for decoupage, prints to decorate with tinsel, cigarette cards and postcards, boardgames and elaborate toy theatres. Often, these games and toys offered colourful versions of the kinds of nationalistic or melodramatic Shakespeares on offer in the contemporary theatre and press. Nineteenth-century mass media versions of Shakespeare, designed for a socially mixed and unequally literate audience, tended to draw on conventional discourses of patriotism, and fixed gender roles, thus contributing to the formation of 'a nascent sense of national identity among England's youth, embracing adventure, exploration, and conquest for boys, self-sacrificing daughterhood – and eventually motherhood – for girls'.[45] These tendencies continued in later magazine publications, such as the *Children's Newspaper* founded by Arthur Mee in 1919, and also featured in British postwar children's magazines and annuals, such as *The Young Elizabethan* and *Collins for Boys and Girls*. By the 1950s Shakespeare had been adapted into comicbook form in both the United States and Britain, and during the 1960s the *Children's Newspaper* and its successors – *Diana, Ranger* and *Look and Learn* – carried occasional 'picture-story' serials, comicstrip versions based on prose adaptations of the plays.[46]

But perhaps the most striking and influential way in which children might encounter Shakespeare was in the theatre. Nineteenth-century illustrations of theatre performances frequently show children in the audience of Shakespeare productions, especially the spectacular ones mounted by Charles Kean in the middle of the century. One of Queen Victoria's daughters was so struck by his version of *Richard II* that she spent weeks painting a picture of Bolingbroke's entry into London for her mother's birthday, even requesting a photograph of the scene in order to get the detail right.[47] Lewis Carroll frequently took his little middle-class girl friends to Shakespeare productions, as long as he was certain the play was suitable.[48] The theatre was also a place where children worked. Carroll much admired the childhood performances of Ellen Terry and her sister as Puck, Arthur and Fleance, and became an intimate of their family, as well as forming friendships with other child actors. In England the historical separation of the 'legitimate' theatres, able to stage play texts, and those licensed only for singing and dance, contributed to a form of class division in audience, actors and plays. Shakespeare was increasingly positioned in the 'higher' reaches of nineteenth century theatre, despite the long tradition of Shakespearean burlesques and the scheduling of performances of the (heavily cut) plays in double bills with pantomimes and other entertainments. Relatively few children were employed in the 'respectable' Shakespearean productions but, as with Terry, these roles often set them on the path to successful careers and enhanced social status. Many more children were featured as dancers and singers, in performances such as the pantomime version of *Henry VIII* which Carroll saw in 1856:

> [T]he dance in *Henry VIII* is acted in dumb show entirely by children. The prettiest thing I ever saw on the stage ... The little Queen Katherine was a merry little creature of about four years old, and pulled the ears of Anne Boleyn ... in anything but a malicious spirit ... Henry VIII became a tiny Harlequin, with Anne Boleyn as Columbine. The whole scene was a picture not to be forgotten.[49]

When legislation to control the hours and ages of children working in the theatre industry was debated by a parliamentary committee in 1889, the status quo was defended on the grounds that young children were required to portray the fairies in *A Midsummer Night's Dream* in a convincingly charming and diminutive manner. Carroll himself published an article on 'Stage Children' arguing for the propriety and usefulness of children working in the theatre, and its power to 'brighten' a child's mind.[50] The history of child performers of Shakespeare from the seventeenth century onwards still awaits intensive and systematic investigation.

There is no space here to do more than point to the extensive list of fictional 'reversions' of Shakespeare contained in the biographical appendix at the end of the book. The significance of Shakespeare as a source for new children's literature has so far been interrogated by scholars such as Megan Isaac, Naomi J. Miller and Pat Pinsent, and by Kate Chedgzoy in chapter 12.[51] The evidence is accumulating that Shakespeare-derived writing for children, whether in the form of rereadings of Shakespeare himself, of characters in the plays, or of the theatres in which the plays have been performed, need not be a vehicle for conservative ideologies of literary tradition and canonical authority, but can also form a vibrant space in which the complexities that children encounter in relation to gender, sexuality and social, family and racial roles, as well as first experiences of loss and love, can be entertainingly – and often powerfully – explored.

The consolidation of all these trends into consumerist niche markets, targeted at the 'media-rich' childhoods of the twentieth century, has produced a plethora of comics, films, animations and video games, in which Shakespeare is constantly remade, or simply meaninglessly cited in terms of contemporary youth mass culture.[52] Some media organizations, notably the BBC in the United Kingdom and PBS in the United States, retain a commitment to the literary and educational values of Shakespeare, producing inventive programmes for educational use, as well as those made to both entertain and teach younger age groups, such as *The Animated Shakespeare* (BBC 1992–4), several *Sesame Street* episodes, and the 'Dreaming Shakespeare' episode of the educational *Between the Lions* series (PBS 2000–). Despite such examples, Richard Burt argues in chapter 14 that the evidence of fragmented citation of Shakespeare in our contemporary mediatized culture shows how the very terms 'childhood' and 'adolescence' are degrading into the technologized indeterminacy of 'tween' culture, as are the distinctions between child and adult, and 'trash' and 'high culture' Shakespeare.[53]

The international rise of theatre companies or special events devoted entirely to performing versions of the plays for and with children may suggest a slightly different picture – one that Burt might label as hopeless nostalgia for the apparent authenticity and political effectiveness of 'liveness'. In such events Shakespeare is as likely to be 'by' kids as 'for' them, and often regarded as therapy rather than learning. Although many stage adaptations still aim at delivering a palatable and educationally useful version of Shakespeare's play, whether through abbreviation of the original or through prose retelling, others offer a wholesale restructuring, often from the perspective of minor characters – a kind of dramatic equivalent of 'history from below'. This appropriation of a historiographical enterprise which seeks to give a voice to those who have been ignored or silenced in history is an apt model for the kind of repositioning of Shakespeare within childhood culture that has taken place in recent years. *Fairy Monster Ghost* (2006), a trilogy of short plays for children by the Brighton-based performer-writer Tim Crouch, provides an especially vivid example. These three one-man shows – *I, Peaseblossom*, *I, Caliban* and *I, Banquo* – each offers young audiences a metatheatrical reflection of their own uncertainties, anxieties and resistance, in a world often controlled by others.[54]

Leah Marcus, in her study of childhood as a trope of cultural despair in the seventeenth century, suggests that the 'sudden appearance (or disappearance) of childhood as an important literary subject seems always to be a barometer for important cultural change'.[55] The frequent use of childhood motifs in late twentieth- and early twenty-first-century productions of Shakespeare for adults – in the form of fiction, films, artwork or performances – may represent a nostalgia-fuelled rejection of contemporary childhood experience, a fear of childhood's 'disappearance', or a blurring of any boundaries set between adulthood and childhood. Recently several filmmakers have made varied use of child figures, both as archetypal 'innocent victims' (Kenneth Branagh, *Henry V*, UK 1993; Richard Loncraine, *Richard III*, UK/USA 1995) and more complexly to explore childhood sexuality (Adrian Noble, *A Midsummer Night's Dream,* UK 1996) or childhood as both source of contemporary horrors and sole means of social redemption (Penny Woolcock, *Macbeth on the Estate*, BBC 1997; Julie Taymor, *Titus*, USA 1999).[56]

An equally ambiguous view of childhood experience, the responsibilities of the child as Shakespearean character, and the promise of futurity that childhood is currently meant to represent is offered in Matt Haig's novel *The Dead Fathers Club* (2006), a close retelling of *Hamlet*. Although written primarily for an adult audience, its first-person narration by an eleven-year-old boy aligns it with recent works which have also adopted a child's voice, and 'crossed-over' from child to adult readership, such as Mark Haddon's *The Curious Incident of the Dog in the Night-Time* (2004). It is quite likely that Haig's novel will be read by, and perhaps marketed to, adolescents who know the play's story. Like Hamlet, Philip Noble is haunted by his dead father, who claims that his brother, Alan, killed him to get possession of both his wife and the Castle and Falcon pub, and who is doomed to the 'Terrors' if he is not avenged. In place of princely 'melancholy', the novel gives us an ordinary child's mental breakdown – at each point it is open to us to read the ghost as Philip's own disturbed projection, which leads him to attempt to murder his uncle and finally to kill his girlfriend Leah's father accidentally in a garage fire. It is at this point, as children control the action, that the plot of the play seems open to rewriting. Philip confesses his crime to Leah's brother, Dane, but this Laertes pulls himself back from revenge killing. Although Leah throws herself into the river, and Philip nearly drowns trying to rescue her, both are saved by Alan. The novel ends indeterminately as Alan's life-support machine is tampered with – whether by Philip or the ghost remains unclear – and his life hangs in the balance. *The Dead*

Fathers Club presentation of the child as both victim and murderer encapsulates the contemporary ambivalence towards childhood, one that frequently colours the use of its motifs in relation to Shakespeare.

Concluding his survey of Shakespeare retellings for children, Stanley Wells declined to claim that such scholarship constituted a new field of Shakespeare studies.[57] The essays in part 2 of this book suggest that the 'rewriting' and 'reimagining' of Shakespeare for the young, together with the incorporation of children and child references into the textual, artistic and performance history of the plays, does indeed provide a promising seam for future critical investigation and research. Attention to this interplay of generational performances, perceptions and politics confirms that the reinvention of Shakespeare for children is a fascinating and significant aspect of Shakespeare studies, and one that has much to reveal about the hopes and anxieties that continue to circulate around childhood.

NOTES

1 *Mr. William Shakespeares comedies, histories, & tragedies: published according to the true originall copies*, printed by Isaac Jaggard and Edward Blount, 1623, A5r, A5r–i, A5r–ii (Folger copy 78). See www.folger.edu/imgdtl.cfm?imageid=1829&cid=1888 for an image of these drawings.

2 See Colin Franklin, *Shakespeare Domesticated: The Eighteenth-Century Editions* (Aldershot: Scolar Press, 1991).

3 Hugh Cunningham, *Children and Childhood in Western Society Since 1500*, 2nd edn (Harlow: Pearson Longman, 2005), p. 58. For the view that these transformations were led by the upper or middle classes, see Lawrence Stone, *The Family, Sex and Marriage in England, 1500–1800* (Harmondsworth: Penguin, 1977).

4 Anna Davin, 'What is a Child?', in Anthony Fletcher and Stephen Hussey, eds., *Childhood in Question: Children, Parents and the State* (Manchester: Manchester University Press, 1999), pp. 15–36 (p. 33).

5 Harry Hendrick, *Children, Childhood and English Society 1880–1990* (Cambridge: Cambridge University Press, 1997), pp. 1, 3.

6 For general histories of childhood, see James Walvin, *A Child's World: A Social History of Childhood, 1800–1914* (Harmondsworth: Penguin, 1982); C. John Sommerville, *The Rise and Fall of Childhood*, Sage Library of Social Research 140 (Beverley Hills: Sage Publications, 1982); Colin Heywood, *A History of Childhood: Children and Childhood in the West from Medieval to Modern Times* (London: Polity Press, 2001); and Hugh Cunningham, *The Invention of Childhood* (London: Ebury, 2006).

7 See Carole G. Silver, *Strange and Secret Peoples: Fairies and Victorian Consciousness* (Oxford: Oxford University Press, 1999), and Robert Shaughnessy, 'Dreams of England', in Sonia Massai, ed., *Worldwide Shakespeares: Local and Global Appropriations in Film and Performance* (London: Routledge, 2005), pp. 112–22, and 'Introduction', p. 2.

8 Carolyn Steedman, *Strange Dislocations: Childhood and the Idea of Human Interiority, 1780–1930* (Cambridge, MA.: Harvard University Press, 1998), pp. 5, 4. See also Judith Plotz, *Romanticism and the Vocation of Childhood* (Basingstoke: Palgrave, 2001), and George Dimock, 'Children's Studies and the Romantic Child', in Marilyn R. Brown, ed., *Picturing Children: Constructions of Childhood Between Rousseau and Freud* (Aldershot: Ashgate, 2002), pp. 189–98.

9 See Alan Prout, 'Children's Participation: Control and Self-Realisation in British Late Modernity', *Childhood and Society* 14:4 (2004), 304–15, and David Kennedy, *Changing Conceptions of the Child from the Renaissance to Post-Modernity: A Philosophy of Childhood* (Lewiston, NY: Edwin Mellen Press, 2006).

10 Harry Hendrick, 'Children and Childhood', *ReFresh: Recent Findings in Economic and Social History* 15 (1992), 1.

11 See Viviana A. Zelizer, *Pricing the Priceless Child: The Changing Social Value of Children* (Princeton: Princeton University Press, 1994).

12 See Naomi J. Miller, ed., *Reimagining Shakespeare for Children and Young Adults* (London: Routledge, 2003) for a collection of essays by teachers, authors and academics concerned mainly with modern adaptations. Janet Bottoms has written extensively on Shakespeare adaptations and education, including 'Representing Shakespeare: Critical Theory and Classroom Practice', *Cambridge Journal of Education* 25:3 (1995), 361–75; 'Of Tales and Tempests: The Problematic Nature of Prose Re-tellings of Shakespeare's Plays', *Children's Literature in Education* 27:2 (1996), 73–87; 'Familiar Shakespeare', in Erica Bearne and Victor Watson, eds., *Where Texts and Children Meet* (London: Routledge, 2000), pp. 11–25; and '"To Read Aright": Representations of Shakespeare for Children', *Children's Literature* 32:1 (2004), 1–14. On media versions, see Janet Bottoms, 'Speech, Image, Action: Animating Tales from Shakespeare', *Children's Literature in Education* 32:1 (2001), 3–15; and Laurie Osborne, 'Mixing Media and Animating Shakespeare Tales', in Richard Burt and Lynda E. Boose, eds., *Shakespeare the Movie II: Popularizing the Plays on Film, TV, Video, and DVD* (London: Routledge, 2003), pp. 140–53.

13 See Henry Cunningham, *The Children of the Poor: Representations of Childhood Since the Seventeenth Century* (Oxford: Blackwell, 1991).

14 See Lloyd de Mause, *The History of Childhood* (New York: The Psychohistory Press, 1974). For the 'psychogenic' reading of *Hamlet*, see Joseph L. Zornado, *Inventing the Child: Culture, Ideology and the Story of Childhood* (New York: Routledge, 2001).

15 See Catherine O'Brien, 'The Nature of Childhood Through History Revealed in Artworks?, *Childhood* 10:3 (2003), 362–78, for an overview and critique of the use of art history approaches in relation to childhood.
16 Thomas Gray, 'The Progress of Poesy: A Pindaric Ode' (1768), III.i. ll. 83–94.
17 Romney engraved the portraits in collaboration with Benjamin Smith as commissions for Boydell's ambitious publishing showcase, the Shakespeare Gallery (exhibitions 1789–1805; book versions 1792–1884). See Philip Edwards, 'The Image of Shakespeare in Romney's Time', *Transactions of the Romney Society* 1 (1996); Yvonne Romney Dixon, *Designs from Fancy: George Romney's Shakespearean Drawings* (Washington, DC: The Folger Shakespeare Library, 1998) and Stuart Sillars, *Painting Shakespeare: The Artist as Critic 1720–1820* (Cambridge: Cambridge University Press, 2006).
18 Jane Martineau, 'Bardolatry', in Martineau et al., eds., *Shakespeare in Art* (London and New York: Merrell, 2002), p. 203.
19 *Ibid.*, p. 203. On Betty, see Jim Davis, 'Freaks, Prodigies, and Marvellous Mimicry: Child Actors of Shakespeare on the Nineteenth-Century Stage', *Shakespeare* 2:2 (December 2006), pp. 179–93.
20 See, for instance, George Harvey's *Shakespeare Before Sir Thomas Lucy* (1836–7). The legend of Shakespeare's boyhood misdemeanour derived originally from Nicholas Rowe's *Some Account of the Life of Mr William Shakespeare* (1709).
21 Henry James, 'The Birthplace', in James, *The Better Sort* (London: Methuen, 1903), p. 216.
22 See, for example, Jan Mark, *Stratford Boys* (London: Hodder and Stoughton, 2003).
23 Plotz, *Romanticism and the Vocation of Childhood*, p. 6.
24 See Martineau et al., eds., *Shakespeare in Art*, pp. 104–5, for a reproduction and commentary. Also relevant is David Scott's *Puck Fleeing Before the Dawn* (1837), discussed by Martineau on pp. 226–7.
25 *Ibid.*, p. 104.
26 See Anne Higonnet, *Pictures of Innocence: The History and Crisis of Ideal Childhood* (London: Thames and Hudson, 1998).
27 Northcote's original is now destroyed. See the 'Shakespeare Illustrated' website, www.english.emory.edu/classes/Shakespeare_Illustrated/Northcote.Princes.html for a reproduction of another version, and Richard Schoch, *Queen Victoria and the Theatre of her Age* (Basingstoke: Palgrave, 2004), p. 54, for a reproduction of Queen Victoria's drawing.
28 Richard Foulkes, *Lewis Carroll and the Victorian Stage* (Aldershot: Ashgate, 2005), p. 29.
29 The children's writer and illustrator Marcia Williams has written an MA thesis, 'Messing with the Bard: Reimaging Shakespeare for Children', on the subject (University of Surrey Roehampton, 2002).
30 Gary Taylor, *Reinventing Shakespeare: A Cultural History from the Restoration to the Present* (New York and Oxford: Oxford University Press), 1989, p. 207.

31 See Georgianna Ziegler, 'Introducing Shakespeare: The Earliest Versions for Children', *Shakespeare* 2:2 (Winter 2006), 132–51. The first edition of *The Family Shakespeare*, published anonymously in 1807, was Henrietta Bowdler's work; subsequent modified versions included some input from her brother Thomas.

32 Charles H. Frey, 'A Short History of Shakespeare as Children's Literature', *New Review of Children's Literature and Librarianship* 7 (2001), 147–56. On the Lambs, see, for example, Stanley Wells, 'Tales from Shakespeare', *Proceedings of the British Academy* 73 (1987), 125–52, and Felicity James, '"Wild Tales" from Shakespeare: Readings of Charles and Mary Lamb', *Shakespeare* 2:2 (2006), 153–67. On the Bowdlers, see Michael Dobson, 'Bowdler and Britannia: Shakespeare and the National Libido', *Shakespeare Survey* 46 (1994), 137–44, and Stanley Wells, 'Making Shakespeare Decent', *Around the Globe* 15 (Autumn 2000), 32–3.

33 See Ziegler, 'Introducing Shakespeare'.

34 Naomi J. Miller, chapter 9, 'Play's the thing', p. 137.

35 See, for instance, Charlotte Yonge's depiction in *The Daisy Chain* (1856) of children choosing to read *Henry V* (cited in Ziegler, 'Introducing Shakespeare', 132). In his television drama series *The Lost Prince* (BBC 2002) about the British royal family at the end of the nineteenth century, Stephen Poliakoff depicted one of the children reciting Henry's Agincourt speech to his parents and assembled courtiers. See R. Raymond, *Shakespeare for the Young Folk* (New York: Fords, Hulbert and Howard, 1881) for discussion of the appeal of *Julius Caesar* for Americans.

36 In a 2002 Royal Society of Literature poll of the top ten 'classic' texts for children, the Poet Laureate, Andrew Motion, J. K. Rowling and Philip Pullman included a Shakespeare play. Motion and Rowling nominated *Hamlet*, Pullman *Romeo and Juliet*.

37 Andrew Murphy, 'Shakespeare Among the Workers', *Shakespeare Survey* 58 (2005), 107–17.

38 See Foulkes, *Lewis Carroll and the Victorian Stage*, pp. 8–26.

39 Theodore Martin, *A Life of Helena Faucit, Lady Martin* (London: William Blackwood and Sons, 1900), p. 4.

40 Helena Faucit, *Some of Shakespeare's Female Characters* (Edinburgh: W. Blackwood and Sons, 1885), p. 6. See Anna Jameson, *Shakespeare's Heroines: Characteristics of Women, Moral, Poetical, and Historical* (London: George Bell & Sons, 1832), and Mary Cowden Clarke, *The Girlhood of Shakespeare's Heroines* (London: W. H. Smith & Son, 1850).

41 James T. Fields, *Yesterdays with Authors* (Boston: J. R. Osgood and Company, 1872), p. 44.

42 Bob Smith, *Hamlet's Dresser: A Memoir* (New York: Scribner, 2003).

43 Valerie Gager, *Shakespeare and Dickens: The Dynamics of Influence* (Cambridge: Cambridge University Press, 1995), p. 25.

44 *The Journal of Emily Shore*, ed. Barbara T. Gates (Charlottesville, VA: University Press of Virginia, 1991), pp. 22, 223, 226.

45 Kathryn Prince, chapter 10, 'Shakespeare in the Victorian children's periodicals', p. 153.

46 Versions used included George Murray, *Let's Discover More Shakespeare* (London: Hamish Hamilton, 1960) and Ian Serraillier, *The Enchanted Island: Stories from Shakespeare* (Oxford: Oxford University Press, 1964).

47 Schoch, *Queen Victoria and the Theatre of her Age*, p. 188.

48 See Georgianna Ziegler, 'Alice Reads Shakespeare: Charles Dodgson and the Girl's Shakespeare Project', in Miller, *Reinventing Shakespeare for Children*, pp. 107–19, for an account of Carroll's plans for a Bowdlerized Shakespeare edition especially for girls.

49 Cited in Foulkes, *Lewis Carroll and the Victorian Stage*, p. 108.

50 *Ibid.*, pp. 109–11.

51 See Megan Lynn Isaac, *Heirs to Shakespeare: Reinventing the Bard in Young Adult Literature* (London: Heinemann, 2000); Pat Pinsent, '"Not for an Age but for all Time": The Depiction of Shakespeare in Selected Children's Fiction', *New Review of Children's Literature and Librarianship* 10:2 (2004), 115–26; and Kate Chedgzoy, chapter 12, 'Shakespeare in the company of boys', pp. 184–200.

52 See Richard Burt, *Unspeakable ShaXXXspeares: Queer Theory and American Kiddie Culture* (Basingstoke: Macmillan, 1998), and Jennifer Hulbert, Kevin J. Wetmore, Jr. and Robert L. York, eds., *Shakespeare and Youth Culture* (Basingstoke: Palgrave, 2006).

53 Richard Burt, chapter 14, 'Shakespeare (')tween media and markets in the 1990s and beyond ', pp. 218–32.

54 See the production website www.fairymonsterghost.co.uk/ for further information and scripts.

55 Leah Sinanoglou Marcus, *Childhood and Cultural Despair: A Theme and Variations in Seventeenth-Century Literature* (Pittsburgh, PA: University of Pittsburgh Press, 1978), p. 246.

56 See Carol Chillington Rutter, 'Looking Like a Child; or Titus: The Comedy', *Shakespeare Survey* 56 (2003), 1–26, 'Remind Me: How Many Children had Lady Macbeth?', *Shakespeare Survey* 57 (2004), 38–53, and *Shakespeare and Child's Play* (London: Routledge, 2007).

57 Wells, 'Tales from Shakespeare', p. 149.

9

Play's the thing: agency in children's Shakespeares

Naomi J. Miller

This chapter considers the creative and critical implications of changing constructions of the agency of the child as evidenced in written and illustrated adaptations of Shakespeare for children over the past two centuries in Britain and the United States. By 'agency of the child', I mean developmental autonomy, demonstrated in the capacity to act, and to learn through acting, in the dual senses of *taking action* and *dramatic performance*, both of which can occur through the medium of play. When associated with childhood – particularly of primary-school age – the term 'play' conveys a child's sense of pleasure and control over his or her actions at a level that can be guided without necessarily being overdetermined by adults. For this reason teachers and child psychologists have recognized 'play' as a crucial component in developmental learning.[1]

It is no coincidence, then, that dramatic 'plays', such as the works of Shakespeare, have been embraced by teachers and children's book authors in the twentieth and twenty-first centuries as providing an opportunity to engage children in learning through play. One term that can be applied to the effects of guided play that engages children with Shakespeare as agents of their own learning is *transformative initiation*, where the goal is not solely to connect children to Shakespeare, but to enable Shakespeare's plays to provide an environment where developmental 'sea changes' for individual 'actors' are possible. In Howard Marchitello's words, 'what becomes primary is the child's relation to Shakespeare and not Shakespeare as such: Shakespeare not as pedagogical object but rather as pedagogical site'.[2]

Of all new audiences for Shakespeare, children have been regarded as being at once the most enthusiastic and malleable and as potentially the most likely to be misdirected or even alienated by their initial encounters with the Bard. Adaptations of Shakespeare for children embody and respond to a variety of adult attitudes towards children and Shakespeare, whether informed by a disappointing first experience of Shakespeare that marked his plays as 'inaccessible' to the adult, or by an idealized conception of Shakespeare's works as 'high culture' which can be used to encourage the 'gifted child', or by a genuine yearning to connect children to the plays, emerging from the adult's own passion for Shakespeare. Marchitello points out that 'adapting Shakespeare for children is not only far more complex than is generally believed (by typical adult readers, at least), but is at the same time an intensive labor that hides its own traces'.[3] Here, I identify and explore some of the 'traces' of that labor, with the aim of considering changing constructions of childhood as well as of Shakespeare.

Children – or, more precisely, their parents, teachers and caregivers – presently represent an enormous potential market for Shakespearean material, through the school systems of Britain and the United States in particular. While there has been an enormous range of imaginative adaptations of Shakespeare for different audiences (including children) over the past century especially, from films and videos to boardgames and interactive websites, this chapter focuses on children's book adaptations in order to examine one particular thread of 'reimagining Shakespeare' over time. Adaptations currently in print range from illustrated reprints of such classic early versions as the famous *Tales from Shakespeare* written by Charles and Mary Lamb in the early nineteenth century, and Edith Nesbit's retellings in the early twentieth century, to late twentieth-century and early twenty-first-century adaptations by children's book authors as various as Lois Burdett, Bruce Coville and Marcia Williams.[4] Consequently, the present moment invites consideration of the evolution of 'children's Shakespeares' over the centuries. This chapter interrogates the creative and critical implications of that evolution as evidence of changing conceptions of the intellectual autonomy and agency of the child in the eyes of adult authors, illustrators, educators and parents.

For twenty-first-century children, opportunities abound to 'play with' Shakespeare. The pedagogical implications of such opportunities extend far beyond childhood alone into the production of a literate society. A first-year American college student attests to the immediacy of these implications in 2005 as follows:

> In third grade, as an eight-year-old, I once married the same boy, Robbie, twice in one day. My class, guided by our teacher, was putting on our own versions of Shakespeare's *A Midsummer Night's Dream, Julius Caesar*, and *Romeo and Juliet*. I was playing both Hermia and Juliet and Robbie was playing both Lysander and Romeo . . . For that semester, Shakespeare became my obsession: instead of bedtime stories, my father would quote lines from the plays, my dolls all took on

names of Shakespeare's characters, and I spent many hours contemplating his words and use of language . . . When I actually studied Shakespeare's *Romeo and Juliet* in my freshman year of high school, I felt as though I was returning not only to something which I knew well, but to *something with which I had played before, to something which was mine.*[5]

Having played with Shakespeare as a child, through performance as well as free play, this young woman could 'own' her knowledge of Shakespeare as an adult. This story suggests the importance not only of 'whose Shakespeare' we meet, but also of how our adult lives incorporate, from childhood, 'such stuff as dreams are made on' (*The Tempest*, 4.1.156–7).

STRATEGIES OF ADAPTATION

As critics such as Georgianna Ziegler have elucidated, early nineteenth- and twentieth-century adaptations commonly focused on bringing children to Shakespeare through frames of significance that reproduced adult concerns with the 'meanings' and 'messages' of the plays, reflecting the Lockean conception of children's minds as *tabula rasa*, or 'empty cabinets' to be filled.[6] Many late twentieth- and early twenty-first-century adaptations, on the other hand, endeavour to bring Shakespeare to children through 'play' and the concept of playing, involving a sea-change in notions of the agency of the literate child, where 'literacy' is associated not so much with literal 'knowledge' of quotable lines from 'high literature' as with comfort and active familiarity with the 'sounds and sweet airs' of the source (*The Tempest*, 3.2.131). Many contemporary adaptations offer children the opportunity to 'play with' Shakespeare, opening spaces for engagement through performance that can enable even the youngest audiences to choose their own entry-points into the plays, fostering versions of literacy that embrace playing as well as play-acting as an essential element of comprehension.[7] As Alison Lurie has observed, while 'run-of-the-mill children's literature tends to support the status quo', truly liberating literature for children is 'subversive' of 'the conventional adult world', possessing the ability to 'appeal to the imaginative, questioning, rebellious child within all of us, renew our instinctive energy, and act as a force for change'.[8] Shakespeare for children can be 'subversive' in precisely the sense in which 'child's play' itself can be 'subversive', allowing children to enter, temporarily, into an imaginative world marked by heroes and villains, conflict and misunderstanding, anxiety and hope, where outcomes are not always predictable but an ending is always attainable, and sometimes magic is present.

Moreover, a primary aim of such Shakespeare 'outreach' is to teach children not just the story, but also the 'sound' of Shakespeare, or the verbal texture of the plays. When one considers the necessary interdependence of the written and the spoken word in performing Shakespeare, it becomes evident that Shakespeare is already a player in educational initiatives and authorial outreach aimed at empowering children to become not just receptors but also agents of cultural literacy. Focusing on the primary school-age child, this chapter explores some of the ways in which William Shakespeare currently serves as a playing field for literacy and language arts, encompassing reading, speaking and listening, as well as for creativity and dramatic learning, in education both inside and outside the classroom.[9]

Importantly, when children are the intended audience, adaptations can reveal as much about the society's constructions of childhood as about notions of literary perfection or legitimacy. Consequently, a review of adaptations of Shakespeare for children over the past two centuries can contribute to our understanding of the evolution of conceptualized as well as experienced childhoods across time. As Susanne Greenhalgh notes in chapter 8, the place of children in society has changed and childhood has come to be perceived as a separate, highly significant and often idealized stage of life. If we consider not only the place of children in society, but also the interrelations of Shakespeare, pedagogy and play during the past two centuries, we can identify historical movement, if not precisely an evolution, between a desire for a formative model of education, and an interest in allowing children's autonomy to flourish.

Leah Marcus points out that in the sixteenth and seventeenth centuries, children were portrayed as miniature adults, and it was not until the eighteenth century that the first books for children's enjoyment were published.[10] Indeed, it was not until towards the end of the nineteenth century that primary school became compulsory and free, children were removed from full-time employment – with social consequences deeply inflected by class divisions – and 'juvenile' and 'adult' became distinguishable literary genres.[11] Sigal Benporath offers the cautionary observation that historically, Western society has embraced 'two flawed assumptions . . . first, that childhood is an impediment, a passing phase of impaired maturity, and second, that children benefit from the proliferation of rights assigned to them'.[12] Only when childhood is regarded neither as 'a stage nor an impediment', nor as 'a passage towards adulthood',[13] can we begin to explore the significance of differing historical attitudes to children's potential for agency and autonomy, including literacy.

NINETEENTH- TO TWENTIETH-CENTURY ADAPTATIONS

Both Edith Nesbit's adaptations (1900) and the slightly earlier *Phoebe's Shakespeare* (1894) by Adelaide Sim followed in the footsteps of Charles and Mary Lamb's influential *Tales from Shakespear* (first published 1807), as well as Thomas and Henrietta Bowdler's *The Family Shakespeare*, published in the same year, which exhibit a parallel confidence in the authors' adult wisdom as a superior vehicle for introducing Shakespeare to children's uninitiated minds.[14] A gendered concept of ownership emerges in the kindly but patronizing attitudes of the Lambs and the Bowdlers, introducing Shakespeare as if from an older brother to a younger sister, or from a gentleman to a lady, with tales in both cases written by a brother-sister pair. A less gendered and hierarchical but no less proprietary orientation can be identified in the 'gift' strategies of Nesbit and Sim, proffering their versions of Shakespeare to children in their own families, a rhetorical gesture indicative of the growing significance of the middle-class 'family', for whom adaptations of Shakespeare could offer a familial rather than solely individual experience.

Ziegler and Felicity James have pointed out that the Lambs' adaptations, while explicitly striving to highlight useful elements for moral instruction, also aspired to appeal to the imagination of the child.[15] Charles and Mary Lamb state clearly in their preface that they are endeavouring to make Shakespeare accessible to children in order to bring to '*young* readers' an appropriate level of instruction in values that they will later learn from Shakespeare as adults, such as 'courtesy, benignity, generosity, humanity'.[16] The narrative frame of the preface envisions a setting where an older brother reads aloud to a younger sister, 'carefully selecting what is proper for a young sister's ear' (p. viii) and thus maintaining an insistence on the essential innocence of children as distinct from adults, even while indicating an appreciation of what we might now term the child's 'agency', with one child reading to another. At the same time, the Lambs incorporate a commitment to maintaining, as much as possible, the 'native beauty' (p. vii) of Shakespeare's language, despite their transplantation of his poetic words into the less perfect soil of prose. Using a story format tailored to youthful rather than adult audiences, the Lambs rearrange some of the sequences of events in the plays so as to make the plays less confusing to children, and concern themselves with adjusting the plays so as not to be 'tedious to young ears', in order to give to children 'a few hints and little foretastes of the great pleasure which awaits them in their elder years' (p. ix). The Lambs' explicitly pedagogical approach becomes particularly evident in plays with a model young female character, such as Miranda in *The Tempest*, to such an extent that their story serves almost more as a vehicle featuring Miranda's youthful exemplary behaviour than as an exploration of Prospero's adult challenges and triumphs. James has made a compelling argument that the Lambs' *Tales* have 'a "divided energy", simultaneously radical and conservative, pushing against and maintaining boundaries' that reflects the Lambs' own efforts 'to achieve a careful and necessary balance between freedom and confinement, between childhood and adult responsibility' – and perhaps, I would add, between the agency of the child and the authority of the parent.[17]

Thomas and Henrietta Bowdler's adaptations, by contrast, tend to resist emerging social conceptions of childhood as distinct from adulthood, focusing less on children than on what can 'with Propriety be Read Aloud in a Family'.[18] Indeed, Thomas Bowdler's preface to the third edition asserts what he perceives to be his underappreciated aim of 'removing indecency from Shakespeare', allowing him to 'venture to assure the parents and guardians of youth, that they may read *The Family Shakespeare* aloud in the mixed society of young persons of both sexes, *sans peur and sans reproche*' (pp. vii–viii). Writing for the authoritarian family rather than the autonomous child, Bowdler tends to focus his adaptative emphasis on 'the erasure of the indecent passages', even in the 'most universally admired' of the plays, observing that 'there is not one that can be read aloud by a gentleman to a lady, without undergoing some correction' (p. ix). Moreover, it is Bowdler's sensibility that becomes the judge of what is or is not appropriate, so that even adult guardians of their children's sensibilities must accept the extended and fundamentally parental authority of Bowdler. His conception of Shakespeare seems less oriented to youthful sensibilities than desirous of avoiding any hint of sexual impropriety, for adults (particularly women) as much as for children. Thus Bowdler affirms that he is attempting 'to do for the library what the manager does for the stage' (p. ix), essentially echoing the omissions of contemporary performances, aimed at adults. By contrast with the Lambs, the Bowdlers' goals seem more explicitly moral than pedagogical, and in any case aim less to engage children with the worlds and words of the plays than to protect them from the consequences of being exposed too directly to such worlds.

Adelaide Sim, writing almost a century later, embraces the movement towards the fantastic in children's literature, with an investment in imagination and the fairytale realm that leads her to represent Shakespeare's evil characters as 'more comparable to trolls and giants in fairy tales than they are real representations of people'.[19] Not coincidentally, the publication of *Phoebe's Shakespeare* in 1894 places her project in direct historical proximity to the popularity of Andrew Lang's famous *Fairy Book* series (1889–1910), whose *Yellow Fairy Book* appeared in the same year as *Phoebe's Shakespeare*. Indeed, the emergence of fairy tales as part of the children's literature industry at the turn of the century signals an acceptance of the fantastical as appropriate for child readers, contextualizing such choices on Sim's part as the inclusion of *The Tempest* and *A Midsummer Night's Dream* as the first two plays in her collection of adaptations.

Although more akin to *Tales from Shakespeare* than *The Family Shakespeare*, because of its intent to introduce a younger generation to the plays, Sim's work offers a unique focus on one particular child rather than children in general. 'Aunt Addie' adapted the plays as a Christmas gift for her niece Phoebe, opening not with a formal preface that serves to introduce her purpose to adults, as in the examples of the Lambs or the Bowdlers, but with a letter to her niece that itself begins, in the best tradition of fairy tales, 'once upon a time'.[20] Sim states that she is interested less in imparting lessons than in telling 'beautiful stories – stories about Kings and Queens, and battles . . . about good, and noble, and brave, men and women, and wicked ones too' (p. iii). While Sim maintains the basic plots of the stories, she adds details and exaggerates settings in order to heighten the plays' fantastical elements. In *The Tempest*, which serves as the opening tale of her collection, Sim asserts that Prospero 'knew directly that he was in an enchanted country, and . . . understood all about fairies and their ways' (p. 3). And at the end of her retelling, Sim suggests that the island disappeared because 'the fairies gave it to the mermaids, who took it down to the bottom of the sea and used it for a palace' (p. 13). Personalizing Shakespeare by creating a role for him as the narrator of *A Midsummer Night's Dream* – explaining that 'a poet is a person who *can* see fairies' (p. 14) – Sim offers young readers the opportunity to form an imaginative relationship with the author, as character, that connects them to the plays, in a strategy that anticipates the personalized approaches of children's authors a century later. Juxtaposing enjoyment and education, Sim moves beyond purely pedagogical instruction or moral persuasion to engage children's imaginations.

Edith Nesbit similarly introduces Shakespeare's stories to her particular children by declaring that they are like 'fairy tale[s]', though she explains that 'the stories are the least part of Shakespeare'.[21] Akin to Sim in highlighting 'fairytale' aspects of the plays, Nesbit multiplies the presence of the fairies in *The Tempest,* for example, by recounting the tale of an enchanted island that 'for years had lain under the spell of an evil witch, Sycorax, who had imprisoned in the trunks of trees all the good spirits she found there'.[22] At the same time, she consistently grounds magical elements in relation to the real. In *The Tempest* she emphasizes that Prospero achieves his triumph not through magic but through forgiveness, giving him happiness on a human level more compelling than the magical power that he relinquishes. Iona Opie observes that Nesbit established 'what is generally agreed to be a new tone of voice for writing for children, one that was not condescending or preachy'.[23] Celebrating Nesbit's 'plain speaking' as 'the perfect antidote to the prevailing reverential attitude to Shakespeare's plays, which kills them dead', Opie affirms as an adult that Nesbit has given her 'a belated confidence and enhanced pleasure in probably the greatest playwright who ever lived'.[24] The staying power of the adaptations of the Lambs and Nesbit, still being reprinted in lavishly illustrated versions today, suggests that children's Shakespeares have the potential not simply to engage historically ephemeral audiences, but also to offer historically inflected experiences of transformative initiation to successive generations.

TWENTIETH- TO TWENTY-FIRST-CENTURY ADAPTATIONS

Just as the advent of the nineteenth century saw the emergence of adaptations by the Lambs and the Bowdlers, and the close of the nineteenth century brought the appearance of those by Nesbit and Sim, so the close of the twentieth century and the advent of the twenty-first has encompassed yet another resurgence of interest in children's Shakespeares, with the works of authors as varied as Leon Garfield, Bruce Coville, Bernard Miles, and Marcia Williams, as well as the spellbinding adaptations of Lois Burdett, who considers herself a teacher of children first and foremost. In the meantime, the evolution of children's literature as a field in its own right, as well as the increasing influence of secondary education and psychological research into the developmental stages of childhood, has produced a population of educators and parents, as well as authors, whose stated goal is to be attuned to the sensibilities of children as children, rather than regarding them primarily as 'nonadult' readers. Whether 'staging' the plays in the pages of a picture book or in the illustrated margins of the texts, the most successful recent adaptations of Shakespeare for children seek to engage young people with Shakespeare through adaptations of many of the dramatic portals offered so effectively by the plays.

Leon Garfield's *Shakespeare Stories* presents the plays in narrative form, in conjunction with watercolour illustrations by Michael Foreman that are dreamlike rather than realistic, and that serve to connect children more to moments of emotional intensity in the texts than to climactic details of the plot. In Garfield's text Prospero's all-seeing capabilities are connected to the 'mouse-eyed Ariel', so that Prospero, 'through the eyes of his servant, watched over all'.[25] In Foreman's illustration three pages later, the very hills appear like the head of a watchful giant, so that the foolish Stefano and Trinculo are pictured wandering into the all-seeing gaze of the magician.[26] Just as children might see monsters under the bed, they are brought into the Garfield/Foreman adaptation as into a world where nature itself is magical, possibly malevolent, and clearly enchanting. The briefly but intensely suggestive words of the author thus connect with the elusive and equally intense images of the illustrator to create an imaginative world where everything has 'suffer[ed] a sea-change / Into something rich and strange' (*The Tempest*, 1.2.404–5), and child readers or listeners, watching the pictures as the text is read aloud, can enter that world of their own volition.

While Bruce Coville's adaptations of different plays are accompanied by the images of different illustrators, to varying effect, his consistent authorial voice takes up the 'story' of the plays as 'the bait' for children.[27] Describing one of his most successful picture-book collaborations, with artist Ruth Sanderson on *The Tempest*, Coville acknowledges that 'just as a playwright must, at some point ... release the play to the director, eventually I have to release the text to the artist'.[28] This dialogic quality of voice and vision between author and illustrator in fact marks many successful picture-book versions of Shakespeare, indicating the extent to which, as suggested by Coville, a picture-book adaptation can function as a 'production' of the play. In the example of *The Tempest*, Coville chooses to tell (or 'produce') the story chronologically, rather than with the flashbacks employed by Shakespeare, so that the very first illustration, even before the opening page of text, portrays Prospero poring over his books as Duke of Milan, and the next illustration, following the text, shows the arrival of father and little daughter upon the island beach.[29]

Just as Sanderson's illustrations adopt a realistic versus fantastical style, in contrast with Foreman's illustrations of Garfield's text, so Coville's story at its climax makes visible not just Prospero's magical spells, but also his human emotions, with a light but highly effective narrative commentary that conveys, in brief, the heart of the story: 'For a long time [Prospero] was silent, for it was not easy to give up his anger.' Unlike Nesbit, who moves instructively and immediately to highlight the value of forgiveness, Coville first offers his young readers the chance to empathize with a magician, possibly recognizing moments when they, too, find it difficult to give up their anger. The final illustration, depicting Prospero high on a cliff, casting his staff down on the waters (and into the hands of Ariel), similarly provides an opportunity for children to experience imaginatively both power and its end, in a magical setting where the future holds boundless possibility rather than a single conclusion. In Coville's words, 'this book is not meant as a substitute for, but as an invitation to, the splendors that await in not only *The Tempest*, but all of Shakespeare's works'.[30] It is up to children to accept this invitation by entering the story as readers and viewers.

While Coville and Garfield remain as faithful as possible to the outline of Shakespeare's stories, Bernard Miles transforms the plot of a play such as *A Midsummer Night's Dream* in order to appeal to his young audience directly through play. Himself a Shakespeare character actor, and founder of the Mermaid Theatre in London, Miles is unusual in bringing a distinctly theatrical point of view to the project of adapting Shakespeare for children.[31] He opens his narrative with the workmen's play-within-a-play, making the story of the lovers secondary. Indeed, it has been aptly observed that Miles 'switches from having a play by workmen within a play about lovers to having a story about lovers within a story about workmen'.[32] Miles even introduces his story as a tale of friendship rather than love: 'Long, long ago, in a tiny village in the heart of Warwickshire, there lived two good friends, Peter Quince a carpenter, and Nicholas Bottom a weaver.'[33] Living in a setting closer to Shakespeare's England than the play's original setting of classical Greece, and inspired by a troupe of visiting actors, Quince and Bottom decide to stage their own play, based on Quince's retelling of their favourite story of Pyramus and Thisbe. The night before the opening performance, Bottom has a dream, which turns out to be a condensed version of Shakespeare's play about the lovers in the forest, including his own magical interlude with the fairy Titania. Waking up from the dream, he goes on to perform his part of Pyramus extraordinarily effectively, and it is only at the very end of the story that the narrator tells us:

> to this day no-one has ever discovered how Bottom came to wake up from his dream with a bunch of buttercups in his hand and his hair full of moss roses . . . And I don't suppose they ever will. But you and I know don't we? Nick

Bottom really had been on a trip to fairyland and he was lucky to get back so easily and lucky to find his own head on his shoulders again[34].

Ultimately, as in the fairytale-like adaptations of Nesbit and Sim, only the narrator and the child readers are in on the secret: that travel to fairyland is possible, and that dreams can be as real as waking life. In Miles's retelling of Shakespeare, all stories can be played with and each dreamer, whether adult author or child reader, can own his or her personal story.

Marcia Williams offers an entirely different approach to adapting Shakespeare for children from the authors surveyed above, not only because she is at once the author *and* the illustrator for all her adaptations, but also because her comic-strip format versions include both a running narrative summary of the story in consecutive panels, and multiple selections from the actual speeches in the plays, inserted as dialogue within the individual panels. Moreover, the borders of each page are framed by her drawings of imagined audience members at the Globe theatre, calling out commentary on the plays and judgements on the characters, as well as engaging in the business of theatre ('Ale for sale!').[35] Consequently, Williams's versions give her young readers a shared experience of viewing the plays alongside other audience members, encouraging their own right to involved commentary as much as Williams's audience members, whose remarks range from 'That duke is a softie. He must be in love' (p. 1) to 'I have no idea what's going on' and 'Disgusting! Kissing, yuk!' (p. 5). Her adaptations thus offer her young readers (or listeners, if her books are read aloud) a multivocal experience that leaves space for their agency and voices as individual audience members.

Williams herself observes of her childhood exposure to the Lambs' *Tales from Shakespeare*, that 'I had yawned and fidgeted through every page', and enquires, '[H]ow can you, particularly in this day and age, introduce children to plays without giving them a foretaste of the visual experience?'[36] At the same time, she acknowledges that the Lambs told the stories 'with loving care' and with a desire to share their passion, seeming 'innovative and lively' in comparison with the Bowdlers' approach (p. 31). Her point is that it is imperative to 'keep reimagining Shakespeare for a new audience' in order to 'speak directly to the modern child' (p. 31), so that just as children and childhood change and evolve, so must children's Shakespeares evolve alongside. Reflecting upon her own narrative and illustrative techniques, Williams explains that 'while the rest of the book may be considered my retelling of Shakespeare's conversation with his reader, the audiences' speech bubbles are my conversation with my reader, our personal interaction, gossip, backchat' (p. 34). Acknowledging that the Garfield/Foreman *Shakespeare Stories* can be termed the first classic retelling since the Lambs, she suggests that 'Garfield was a creative academic; I am a creative student. My place is still at the back of the class, doodling and wondering what is for supper. I need to write and illustrate for that student within me . . . and I hope that, if nothing else [my] pleasure will be shared with a few of my fellows at the back of the class' (pp. 33, 37). Williams's versions of Shakespeare's plays indeed respect children by offering a model of gleeful play at work. What better way to respect 'fellow' children than to play with them?

Finally, Lois Burdett's adaptations of Shakespeare provide truly inspired examples of what happens when children are respected for their own autonomy, as students, readers, actors, and persons in their own right.[37] As a primary-school teacher, Burdett integrated the study of Shakespeare into her grade two class of seven- and eight-year-olds at the Hamlet Public School in Stratford, Ontario, by writing and publishing a series of books entitled *Shakespeare Can Be Fun* (Firefly Books), which includes verse adaptations of Shakespeare plays along with illustrations and written responses by the children. Because the children's words and pictures are included, Burdett's students achieve the 'literacy standing' of published writers: agents of their own inventive adaptations. Speaking as an educator as well as an author, Burdett attests to the transformative power of bringing Shakespeare into the classroom with children:

> Shakespeare became not an end in itself but a means to an end, and the study went far beyond the plot line of a Shakespearean play. Shakespeare became a friend, not someone to be feared, and language took on a whole new dimension. Seven-year-old William wrote, 'The world would be less radiant without Shakespeare's plays, for he warms the world like a burning fire.' John, another grade two student, wrote, 'Shakespeare is like a never-ending song. His words are as powerful as a crocodile's jaws.' And Anika, age eight, shared her thoughts in her daily journal: 'Shakespeare is like a big piece of chocolate cake. Once you've started, you wish you could go on and on forever in a nonstopping dream.'[38]

Burdett involves her students from the start, as actors and audience members, authors and adaptors at once, by having them role-play and write letters to other students from the point of view of characters in each play. Observing their growth, Burdett comments, 'As they write diaries and letters pretending to be Shakespearean characters, the dramatic structure allows them to risk expressing their own emotions and thoughts. Their letters become rich in context and contain sensory details and deep insights' (p. 48). When Burdett took her students to the Ontario Shakespeare Festival to see a performance of *A Midsummer Night's Dream*, after they had written their own letters in Oberon's voice, the children heard the speech that they had put into their own words and 'gasped in unison and all turned to me with looks of sheer delight. They owned those words! It was one of those teaching moments that I will always treasure' (p. 50).

Just like the college student who was able to 'own' *Romeo and Juliet* in the third grade, Burdett's students know that Shakespeare belongs to them, even more viscerally and encompassingly than adults. In the voice of another of Burdett's students, 'William's incredible words are a velvet silk coat that wraps around his pure thoughts. His pen writes on like all the colours of the wind' (p. 54). No adult could say it better, and without meeting Shakespeare as a child, it is likely that no adult would.

PLAYING WITH SHAKESPEARE

To conclude with the words of Emily Schoch, the college student who met Shakespeare through play:

> While my third-grade class did not interact with the plays in the same ways that Burdett's class did, the effect was much the same. We understood the characters and the action, not by writing letters and drawing pictures reacting to them, but by creating our own versions of the plays, told through our own perspectives ... Then, when we encountered the 'real' Shakespeare later in our academic careers, far from being daunted, we felt as though we were dealing with something very familiar and comfortable.[39]

In the cases of Emily and many others, encountering Shakespeare as children in the twentieth and now twenty-first centuries through performance and their own creative interventions, plus the bold and imaginative adaptations of children's authors who respect the child as well as the playwright, agency and literacy go hand in hand with children's Shakespeares. Two centuries of reimagining Shakespeare for children attest to the evolution of pedagogical strategies and psychological theories focused on children's development. Even more significantly, however, reimagining Shakespeare for children across the centuries guarantees that new generations of children will grow to adulthood bringing with them a relationship to Shakespeare that depends, in Duke Theseus's words, upon 'a local habitation and a name' (*A Midsummer Night's Dream*, 5.1.16) that is grounded in their own childhood. May our children all be so lucky.

NOTES

1 See, for example, Michael Cole, foreword to Vivian Gussin Paley, *Mollie is Three: Growing Up in School* (Chicago: University of Chicago Press, 1986), pp. xi, xiv. Paley's work illuminatingly distinguishes between 'free play' and 'story-play', with the latter designating occasions when children are engaging with scripts, whether of their own or others' authorship, and consequently exploring developmentally advanced roles 'within the structure of the story'; see Paley, *Wally's Stories: Conversations in Kindergarten* (Cambridge, MA: Harvard University Press, 1981), p. 167.

2 Howard Marchitello, 'Descending Shakespeare: Toward a Theory of Adaptation for Children', in Naomi J. Miller, ed., *Reimagining Shakespeare for Children and Young Adults* (New York: Routledge, 2003), p. 186.

3 *Ibid.*, p. 181.

4 For a selection of essays covering an extensive range of adaptations for children, see Miller, ed., *Reimagining Shakespeare for Children and Young Adults.*

5 Emily Schoch, 'Playing with the Play: Transformative Adaptations for Children of Shakespeare's *A Midsummer Night's Dream* and *The Tempest*', manuscript essay (December 2005), p. 1 (italics mine).

6 See Georgianna Ziegler, 'Introducing Shakespeare: The Earliest Versions for Children', *Shakespeare* 2.2 (Winter 2006), 132–51.

7 Susanne Greenhalgh, 'The Eye of Childhood: Shakespeare, Performance, and the Child Subject', in Fiona Collins and Jeremy Ridgman, eds., *Turning the Page: Children's Literature in Performance and the Media* (Berne and Oxford: Peter Lang, 2006).

8 Alison Lurie, foreword to *Don't Tell the Grownups: The Subversive Power of Children's Literature* (Boston: Little Brown, 1990), p. xi.

9 For specific examples of adaptations for different ages of children, see the Bibliography in Miller, ed., *Reimagining Shakespeare for Children and Young Adults*, pp. 298–304.

10 Leah S. Marcus, *Childhood and Cultural Despair* (Pittsburgh: University of Pittsburgh Press, 1978), pp. 3, 25, 36–7.

11 Marilyn R. Brown, *Picturing Children: Constructions of Childhood between Rousseau and Freud* (Aldershot: Ashgate, 2002), p. xv; U. C. Knoepflmacher, *Ventures into Childland: Victorians, Fairy Tales, and Femininity* (Chicago: University of Chicago Press, 1998), p. xiii.

12 Sigal R. Benporath, 'Autonomy and Vulnerability: On Just Relations between Adults and Children', *Journal of the Philosophy of Education* 37:1 (2003), 127.

13 *Ibid.*, 131, 133.

14 I am indebted in many portions of the ensuing discussion to the work of my STRIDE research student at Smith College, Emily Schoch, in 'Seeing Children through Shakespeare: What the Nineteenth-Century Shakespeare Adaptations Say About Society's Constructions of Childhood', manuscript essay (Spring 2005).

15 Ziegler, 'Introducing Shakespeare', and Felicity James, '"Wild Tales": The Lambs, the Bad Baby, and the Child Reader', *Shakespeare* 2.2 (Winter 2006), 152–67.

16 Charles and Mary Lamb, preface to *Tales from Shakespeare*, illus. Arthur Rackham (New York: Crown, 1975), p. ix. Subsequent citations are to this edition and appear in parentheses.

17 James, '"Wild Tales"', p. 164.

18 Thomas and Henrietta Bowdler, *The Family Shakespeare* (London: Longman, 1823), title page. Subsequent citations are to this edition and appear in parentheses.

19 Schoch, 'Seeing Children through Shakespeare', p. 3.

20 Adelaide C. Gordon Sim, preface to *Phoebe's Shakespeare, Arranged for Children* (London: Bickers and Son, 1894), p. iii. Subsequent citations are to this edition and appear in parentheses.

21 Edith Nesbit, preface to *The Best of Shakespeare: Retellings of 10 Classic Plays* (Oxford: Oxford University Press, 1997), p. 9.

22 *Ibid.*, p. 49.

23 Iona Opie, 'Introduction' to Nesbit, *The Best of Shakespeare*, p. 6.

24 *Ibid.*, p. 7.

25 Leon Garfield, *Shakespeare Stories*, illus. Michael Foreman (London: Gollancz, 1974), p. 62.

26 Foreman illustration, *Shakespeare Stories*, p. 65.

27 Bruce Coville, 'Nutshells and Infinite Space', in Miller, ed., *Reimagining Shakespeare for Children and Young Adults*, p. 58.

28 *Ibid.*, p. 66.

29 Bruce Coville, *William Shakespeare's The Tempest* (New York: Doubleday, 1994), pp. 4, 7.

30 Coville, 'Author's Note', *Ibid.*, p. 40.

31 Bernard Miles, *Well-Loved Tales from Shakespeare*, illus. Victor G. Ambrus (Twickenham: Hamlyn Publishing, 1986).

32 Schoch, 'Playing with the Play', p. 11.

33 Miles, *Well-Loved Tales*, p. 36.

34 *Ibid.*, p. 59.

35 Marcia Williams, *A Midsummer Nights's Dream*, in *Mr William Shakespeare's Plays* (London: Walker Books, 1998), p. 1. Subsequent citations are to this edition and appear in parentheses.

36 Marcia Williams, 'Bravo, Mr. William Shakespeare!', in Miller, ed., *Reimagining Shakespeare for Children and Young Adults*, p. 29. Subsequent citations are to this edition and appear in parentheses.

37 See Lois Burdett, *A Midsummer Night's Dream for Kids* (Ontario: Firefly, 1997).

38 Lois Burdett, '"All the Colours of the Wind": Shakespeare and the Primary Student', in Miller, ed., *Reimagining Shakespeare for Children and Young Adults*, p. 45.

39 Schoch, 'Playing with the Play', p. 16.

10

Shakespeare in the Victorian children's periodicals

Kathryn Prince

Shakespeare's role in the formation of English national identity has already been well established by historians of Shakespeare reception, who have demonstrated that Shakespeare became recognized as England's 'national poet' in the eighteenth century, while under the Romantics this flourishing appreciation was magnified into that heightened reverence that George Bernard Shaw would later dub 'Bardolatry'. What has been generally overlooked, however, is the means by which this growing sense of Shakespeare's centrality and importance was transmitted in the nineteenth century beyond the purview of gentlemen, scholars and poets to members of society who might never choose to read poetry or literary criticism. As one component in a generalized popularization of Shakespeare during the Victorian era, the Victorian children's periodicals constitute a significant but unappreciated mechanism contributing to the rise of a popular Shakespeare. In return, Shakespeare as he was depicted in these periodicals helped to shape a nascent sense of national identity among England's youth, embracing adventure, exploration and conquest for boys, self-sacrificing daughterhood – and eventually motherhood – for girls.

The politicized nature of children's Shakespeare in the Victorian era is not solely a product of the periodicals, but because children's periodicals are largely a Victorian phenomenon, and especially because they reached a wider segment of Victorian society who would not have purchased the often lavishly illustrated, expensive books on the same subject, these periodicals merit investigation. At the same time, the periodical evidence needs to be situated within the context of Victorian children's appetite for Shakespeare more generally, both because this is unfamiliar territory for many Shakespeareans and because the whims of the Victorian marketplace are sometimes more evident in the books of the period, which are now more widely accessible. Thus, while the focus of this chapter is Victorian children's periodicals, its survey of several key periodicals also takes into account the interplay between periodicals and books to address both *how* Shakespeare was read by children in the Victorian era, and *why* adults published and purchased Shakespeare for children.

Any sense of how Victorian children experienced Shakespeare must take into account the legacy of Charles and Mary Lamb's *Tales from Shakespear* (1807), which continued to dominate the market in various guises throughout the period.[1] This is not to suggest, as most accounts of Shakespeare adaptations and interpretations for children have assumed, that the Lambs were either the first to adapt Shakespeare for children or an adequate synecdoche for the range of such adaptations before the twentieth century. The comparison of even a single one of the Lambs' *Tales* with any other prose adaptation reveals the nuances that make the Lambs far from representative. For instance, while the *King Lear* in *Tales from Shakespear* does not shrink from the death of Cordelia, the version of their immediate predecessor, from Jean-Baptiste Perrin's *Contes Moraux et Instructifs, à l'usage de la Jeunesse, tirés des Tragédies de Shakespeare* (*Moral and Instructive Tales for the Use of the Young, drawn from Shakespeare's Tragedies*, 1783), is more in keeping with the dominant nineteenth-century preference for Nahum Tate's 1681 Restoration adaptation. Like Tate and virtually all stage productions well into the Victorian period, Perrin allows Cordelia to survive and reign as queen to her husband Edgar's king. There is no way of knowing whether Perrin made this choice deliberately or because he was using one of the many acting editions that reproduced Tate's alterations unattributed, but the result is that in this instance the explicitly moral agenda in his *Contes Moraux* is less problematic than the troubled admission in the Lambs' version that virtue does not always prevail. The inadequacy of using the Lambs as a synecdoche for children's Shakespeares is all the more apparent when the canon is expanded to include the extensive variety of prose adaptations, criticism, biographies, short plays and parodies disseminated in the Victorian children's periodicals.

With that caveat in mind, it is nevertheless apparent that the Lambs were a significant factor in the rise of a thriving genre of Shakespeare reception for children. The sustained popularity of the Lambs' *Tales* undoubtedly contributed to periodical publishers' confidence that Shakespeare could appeal to children, and the publication of individual tales from the Lambs' book in chapbook format demonstrated that there was a market for this kind of material beyond the libraries of children whose parents could afford to purchase *Tales from Shakespear* at the rather high price of eight shillings when it was first published in 1807. The children's magazines of the Victorian period are deeply indebted to the chapbook form, and the chapbook publication of the Lambs' *Tales* is an example of the manner in which magazine publishers adopted successful approaches directly from the chapbook market. While several books published during these years emulated the Lambs' *Tales*, aimed at the same book-buying public that had bought the *Tales* in book form, the periodicals that published this kind of Shakespeare adaptation were pursuing a wider range of readers including those who had read the Lambs in the less expensive chapbook editions. Series of 'tales' from Shakespeare were published in children's periodicals because they had proven to be popular among a wide constituency of youthful readers and the adults who purchased reading material for them.[2]

Since the Lambs' *Tales* remained widely available to be purchased for Victorian children who did not already own a copy, periodicals were not particularly interested in replicating the Lambs' format and sought instead to produce equally successful variations on a theme. When *Little Folks* published a series of six 'stories' from Shakespeare over several issues in 1877, for example, the plays selected for inclusion were those featuring children as characters: 'Shakespeare's Little Folks'.[3] Rather than simply retelling Shakespeare's plays in an accessible style, as the Lambs had done, the *Little Folks* series went further in reshaping the plays to promote a sense of empathy among youthful readers. In Anna Buckland's hands Shakespeare's *Coriolanus*, *Cymbeline*, *King John*, *Richard III*, *The Tempest* and *The Winter's Tale* were reinvented as stories in which children became the chief protagonists in plots that promoted clearly articulated moral values in an entertaining format. Thus, for example, 'The Little Princes in the Tower' are models of bravery and virtue snuffed out by Richard III's villainy (July 1877, 78–81), and 'The Story of Miranda' (January 1877, 45–7) repeatedly focuses on Miranda's role as a dutiful daughter:

> If Miranda's love and smiles had comforted and saved her father when she was but a baby-child, we may be sure her sweetness and intelligence as she grew older – her tender concern for her father, and her sympathy and interest in all he taught her – must have been the very life of his life, and have kept him from hating all mankind on account of the way he had been treated by the world, or from sinking into wretchedness and despair. Perhaps it was seeing Miranda's unselfishness, and her pity and care for every living thing, that made Prospero feel that life is not meant to be spent only in pleasing ourselves, whether by giving up ourselves to study or to play. He may have perceived that Miranda's little, unselfish, loving services, had in them something nobler than some of his

intellectual pursuits, when these were sought only for the sake of the power they gave him, or for the indulgence of his own tastes. Prospero had now no State duties to take him from his studies, no fellow-creatures to disturb him; but he found that his life was not complete, for our lives never can be happy and true if we ever forget that others love us, and that they need our love.[4]

The other stories in the series adopt a similar approach, focusing on appropriately gender-specific virtues: duty to family, king and country in 'The Story of Polydore and Cadwal' and 'The Story of Young Marcius' (*Cymbeline* and *Coriolanus*), 'love to God, and love to every man' in 'The Story of Prince Arthur' (*King John*), and the feminine virtues of kindness and reserve which distinguish the noble Perdita from the rough shepherds and shepherdesses in 'The Story of Perdita' (*The Winter's Tale*).[5]

Like many other publishers of material for Victorian children, *Little Folks* recognized that Shakespeare was a valuable source of morality not only as an author but also as an exemplary Englishman. The Victorian fascination with Shakespeare's biography, well described by Gary Taylor in *Reinventing Shakespeare* (1989), serves a demonstrably ethical function in the children's periodicals.[6] While these periodicals exhibit something of the Victorians' need to see the trajectory of Shakespeare's career in terms of progression or evolution, in them the pinnacle of Shakespeare's success is reached not as an artist but as an Englishman. Indeed, Shakespeare's literary accomplishments, the cornerstone for his Victorian biographers, are often downplayed by children's biographers who seek to depict his accomplishments in familiar, and imitable, moral terms. For example, H. L. Hamilton's 'A Chat About Shakespeare' begins '"Our great Shakespeare!" That is what we love to call him. He is not only a great man and a great poet, but, say we – best crown of affection and pride – he is "ours".'[7] In this brief biography Hamilton stresses 'that it was not only as a poet that he was great, but that he must have been of a great noble heart, of a single mind, and of indomitable perseverance in and love for hard work; too great to think about himself at all'.[8] Shakespeare's status as a valuable possession – 'ours' – and his resemblance to a Victorian captain of industry in Hamilton's characterization supersede any interest Shakespeare might have had 'only as a poet'. H. P. Burke Downing takes a similar approach in one of the *Boy's Own Paper*'s very few articles featuring Shakespeare, an account of 'A Day in Shakespeare's Country' (10 June 1893, 584–6). Like Hamilton, Burke Downing emphasizes

Shakespeare's personal qualities, but here Hamilton's pride that he is 'ours' takes on a more precise meaning:

> the name of Shakespeare is as dear to the heart of true Anglo-Saxons as that of the protector saint on whose feast-day the great poet was born. To English boys, Shakespeare, it seems to me, is as much the great Englishman as the great poet, an embodiment of the national characteristics, and the feeling that they have for him forms part of their patriotism. He holds a place in their respect much more akin to that of a national hero than that of, as school boys might be inclined to express it, a mere poet, and disloyalty to the Queen would be as light an offense as disrespect for Shakespeare. Greater knowledge can only intensify such a feeling, so truly national is Shakespeare, so well does he agree with our English character.[9]

As this patriotic celebration suggests, in boys' magazines Shakespeare was depicted less often as a 'mere poet' than as an exemplar of English manliness. If those qualities that make Shakespeare 'an embodiment of the national characteristics' are never quite defined in Burke Downing's account, the general tenor of the *Boy's Own Paper* makes it clear that Shakespeare's three strengths mentioned in the *Little Folks* biography, that 'great noble heart', 'single mind' and 'indomitable perseverance', are no less crucial in the *Boy's Own Paper* for being implicit.

A final example of the purposes served by Shakespeare's biography, from *Boys of England*, is illustrative of the class interests that Shakespeare was made to serve. In contrast with the solidly middle-class values articulated in *Little Folks* and *Boy's Own Paper*, the short biography featured in *Boys of England* reinvents the Bard as a self-made man who rose from obscurity and the company of inappropriate youthful companions to employment in 'a very subordinate situation' in a play-house, where he 'worked his way up and eventually made a good fortune'.[10] For the imagined readers of *Boys of England*, 'returning from school, from the office, the work-room, or the shop, and taking up [their] weekly number of the 'Boys' to soothe and enliven [their] "care-tired thoughts"',[11] Shakespeare was depicted as a man whose struggles were much like their own and whose successes might also be theirs.

For boys toiling in these schools, offices, workrooms and shops, the publisher Edwin J. Brett offered an abundance of delight to leaven a modicum of instruction in a highly successful periodical that frequently verged on the luridness of the reviled 'penny dreadfuls' without ever quite tipping over into it.[12] Its treatment of *Othello*, published in instalments on the back page of five successive issues as one of the magazine's occasional 'sensation dramas', is an excellent example of the fine line that *Boys of*

England was always threatening to cross.[13] An account of the magazine's version of the play's final act gives a clear impression of the ways in which *Othello* was reshaped to appeal to boys. After Iago has shown Othello the handkerchief, here embellished with a message from Desdemona to Cassio written in invisible ink, Othello is determined to murder his wife. Desdemona goes to bed lamenting her husband's bad behaviour and vowing 'I'll never love another blackey', and Othello enters armed with a candle and a feather bed. After uttering a garbled version of the appropriate speech in Shakespeare's original, Othello smothers Desdemona with the feather bed, is stricken with remorse, and attempts to commit suicide with a dagger but fails because he has forgotten to unsheathe it. Then:

> the doors burst open, and all our characters rush on at once. Amid a chorus of anguish, they pulled her out, squashed so flat that it took the united exertions of everybody to bring her round again. At length, however, their restoratives were successful. Desdemona was herself again, but Othello, when he, too, was wakened up, thought she was somebody else, or her own ghost, for he was so confused he didn't know who was alive and who wasn't.[14]

The melodramatic nature of this *Othello* adaptation is more precisely understood when it is placed in its proper nineteenth-century context, not alongside the prose adaptations of the Lambs and their successors but rather among the hundreds of plays adapted for production in children's toy theatres earlier in the century.[15] Indeed, the history of the development of the juvenile drama is in some ways a microcosm of the trajectory by which Shakespeare was gradually adapted to the needs and interests of children. Illustrated sheets depicting London actors in costume were originally produced by enterprising publishers intending to furnish adult theatregoers with mementoes of performances they had seen. Eventually, perhaps when it became evident that the children of these theatregoers were making use of cast-off mementoes in an unexpected way, in effect as substitutes for the theatregoing experience rather than as souvenirs of one, publishers began to market their illustrations directly to children. As the juvenile drama became an established genre in the early decades of the nineteenth century, the illustrations moved away from carefully rendered portraits of actors because they no longer served to commemorate actual performances. Instead, accompanied by short dramatic versions of the plays intended for the use of juvenile puppeteers, the toy-theatre sheets became more cartoonlike renditions of characters and scenes from the plays, no longer specific to particular actors or productions. Just as Shakespeare for children eventually became its own branch of Shakespeare reception, with its own conventions far removed from the halls of learning or the theatres, so the juvenile drama took on a life of its own.

As his successful appropriation of the juvenile drama genre suggests, Edwin Brett had a keen eye for marketable material, so it is not surprising that his *Boys of England* furnishes an example of another characteristic type of Shakespeare adaptation in Vane St John's 'Wait Till I'm a Man', serialized in *Boys of England* (1867, nos. 43–58). 'Wait Till I'm a Man' is an unacknowledged adaptation of *Hamlet*, in which Reginald Fairleigh's father dies under mysterious circumstances while our young hero is away at school. Mr Fairleigh's steward inherits the dead man's estate, marries Reginald's mother, and is soon contriving to cheat Reginald out of the military career which the terms of his father's will had set out for him. In an ingenious solution to the perennial question 'Why does Hamlet delay?', St John suggests in his story that although something is very rotten in the estate of Fairleigh, Reginald will have to spend time away from home passing through the stages of a respectable boy's upbringing before he can take action against the usurping steward. It is only after a benefactor makes it possible for Reginald to attend the Sandhurst military academy and to obtain his first military position fighting in the Crimean War that Reginald is finally able to attain manhood and obtain his revenge.

'Wait Till I'm a Man' belongs among the coming-of-age stories which formed a significant proportion of the serial fiction appearing in the Victorian boys' magazines, characterized by the hero's education in what it means to be an Englishman and his triumph over the perils which threaten to prevent him from fulfilling his potential. Often, the threat depicted in these stories is related to class, as it is in this one when Reginald's parvenu stepfather attempts to prevent him from taking his gentlemanly place in the military. In merging contemporary concerns about masculinity with *Hamlet*, St John produced a Victorian adaptation very similar in technique to the treatment that Shakespeare's heroines were receiving in the girls' periodicals at that time, where they became the vehicles for less than subtle lessons about the feminine ideal.

Girls were by no means excluded from appreciating Shakespeare as a symbol of manliness and Englishness, not least because a contemporary survey demonstrated that, if most girls preferred reading *Girl's Own Paper*, *Boy's Own Paper* was their second choice, far ahead of the other magazines for girls.[16] In unisex publications for younger children such as *Little Folks*, too, girls absorbed the same kind of hagiography that encouraged their brothers to revere Shakespeare as a national icon.

However, while girls sometimes experienced Shakespeare as a historical figure embodying admirable characteristics, this was only one of a range of approaches to Shakespeare in the girls' periodicals. Where boys were generally encouraged to revere Shakespeare but not to read him, girls were exposed to a wide variety of Shakespeare's plays and poetry in the forms of quotation and criticism as well as biography. Girls and boys were expected to read Shakespeare in school, though, and after 1872 they were specifically required to be examined on his history plays if they continued their formal education long enough to reach Standard VI. However, since the legal age for leaving school was ten until 1893, when it was raised to eleven, many Victorian children would never be formally tested. Even for those who did achieve Standard VI, neither memorizing Shakespeare nor reading him aloud was quite akin to understanding him, and the connections between Shakespeare's plays and Victorian readers remained to be made by other, less formal engagements with his works.[17]

If Victorian girls were indeed reading Shakespeare more often than before, one significant reason is that Shakespeare had been reinvented as a moral writer. Whereas Shakespeare was held up to boys as an embodiment of English manliness, after the success of Anna Jameson's 1832 book *Characteristics of Women: Moral, Poetical and Historical* (later renamed *Shakespeare's Heroines*), girls were trained to view Shakespeare's heroines as exemplars for them to emulate. In order to discover the same moral usefulness that boys absorbed through reading about Shakespeare as a biographical figure, girls were required to read the plays themselves or character sketches derived from them. Mary Cowden Clarke articulates this approach to Shakespeare most clearly in her 1887 article for the *Girl's Own Paper*, 'Shakespeare as the Girl's Friend':

> To the young girl . . . Shakespeare's vital precepts and models render him essentially a helping friend. To her he comes instructively and aidingly; in his page she may find warning, guidance, kindliest monition, and wisest counsel. Through his feminine portraits she may see, as in a faithful glass, vivid pictures of what she has to evitate, or what she has to imitate, in order to become a worthy and admirable woman. Her sex is set before her, limned with utmost fidelity, painted in genuinest colours, for her to study and copy from or vary from, in accordance with what she feels and learns to be supremest harmonious effect in self-amelioration of character. She can take her own disposition in hand, as it were, and endeavour to mold and form it into the best perfection of which it is capable, by carefully observing the women drawn by Shakespeare . . . Happy she who at eight or nine years old has a copy of 'Lamb's Tales from Shakespeare' given to her, opening a vista of even then understandable interest and enjoyment! Happy she who at twelve or thirteen has Shakespeare's works themselves read to

her by her mother, with loving selection of fittest plays and passages! Happy they who in maturer years have the good taste and good sense to read aright the pages of Shakespeare, and gather thence wholesomest lessons and choicest delights![18]

As the author of that model of Victorian character criticism, *The Girlhood of Shakespeare's Heroines* (1850), Clarke had already established herself as an authority on the moral lessons to be learnt from Shakespeare's female characters. Her interest in the development of women's personalities through the exercise of external influences such as reading is everywhere apparent in the pages of her book; in her article the methodology she had used in her book to expand the characterization of Shakespeare's heroines is applied to real girls whose reading experiences will shape them in much the same way.

Like Clarke, the *Girl's Own Paper* took seriously the task of teaching girls how to 'read aright the pages of Shakespeare'. In 1888 it followed its publication of Clarke's essay with a competition on the theme 'My Favourite Heroine from Shakespeare'. In their overview of the entries received, the judges' fulsome praise for those which were clearly 'a labour of love' contrasts sharply with their dismay that:

A few of the girls wandered from the subject in a curious manner, and made their essays a vehicle for expressing their ideas on some social problem. The vexed question of 'women's rights' was answerable for four of these failures . . . How foolish girls are to become so exercised about one idea that they must fain 'drag it in', when it has nothing to do with the subject they are writing about. It is curious that both those who approve of and those who disbelieve in what are known as 'Women's Rights', should choose the same heroine, Portia, and draw from her character directly opposite conclusions.[19]

Girl's Own Paper readers, then, were encouraged to appreciate Shakespeare in what Isobel Armstrong, writing about women poets of this period, has dubbed the 'gush of the feminine', an ostensibly uncontrived outpouring of emotion.[20] Armstrong has demonstrated that this pose of an impulsive, uncontrolled outpouring of emotion was adopted by women writers to tailor their writing for a reading public which limited women's sphere of influence to the emotional realm and was unwilling to accept serious writing by women on any other terms. The emotional gush with which *Girl's Own Paper* readers are urged to respond to Shakespeare coincides with Armstrong's view of Victorian poetics, a view which she demonstrates with reference to contemporary reviews. I would argue, then, that in the *Girl's Own Paper* Shakespeare is packaged for Victorian girls much as Victorian poetesses were packaged for their readers.

As the most widely read girls' magazine, the *Girl's Own Paper* represents the dominant view of Shakespeare for girls, but not the only available one. In contrast with the emotional gush promoted in the *Girl's Own Paper*, *Atalanta* readers were invited to engage with Shakespeare on a more intellectual level. For example, when Shakespeare was the featured author in the '*Atalanta* Scholarship and Reading Union' for the October 1890–September 1891 year, the series of related articles included a general introduction by Lucy Toulmin-Smith (October 1890, 50–4) and eleven brief but critically astute analyses of Shakespeare's works divided along generic and chronological lines.[21] Each article concludes with a series of 'scholarship competition questions' designed to test readers' engagement with both the article and the plays it discusses.

The striking difference between the treatment accorded to Shakespeare in these two girls' magazines is most apparent when their essay competitions are juxtaposed. Unlike the emotional, appreciative, highly personal mode encouraged by the *Girl's Own Paper* judges, the prizewinning essay published in the March 1892 issue of *Atalanta* is a model of objective critical acuity. Susan H. Cunliffe's 'Is Shakespeare a Moralist?' situates the author in direct opposition to the approach advocated in the *Girl's Own Paper*. Although Cunliffe, too, eventually concludes that Shakespeare promotes morality in his plays, her essay relies on a careful analysis of the evidence rather than an emotional response. She considers several possible ways of answering the question, first dismissing the kind of decontextualized quotation evident in magazines like the *Girl's Own Paper* on the grounds that '[q]uotation is not a permissible method of confirming a statement when dealing with a dramatist, as there is no infallible test by which to decide positively when he speaks *in propria persona* and when in character'.[22] Moving from quotation to criticism, she argues that:

> though some German critics, indeed, would assert that each play is an ethical study, maintaining, for example, that *Cymbeline* is meant to illustrate fidelity, *The Merchant of Venice* man's duty with regard to wealth, and so on, such theories are as unsatisfactory in application as they appear farfetched. In no one case can the drift of the play be summed up in an aphorism which undeniably conveys the essence of the author's intention. It rather seems as if he made a point of abstaining from inculcating simple truths.[23]

Atalanta, then, offers an alternative to the more mainstream Shakespeare appreciation exemplified by the *Girl's Own Paper*, as well as an antidote to the morality-tale Shakespeare typified by *Little Folks*. *Atalanta*, however, cultivated a select readership of already literate girls, ones likely to embark on the ambitious series of readings recommended in the 1890–1 issues.

Yet if the *Girl's Own Paper* never attempted to scale the heights of Shakespeare criticism in quite the same way, it did succeed in introducing Shakespeare appreciation to a wider range of readers – for decidedly feminine ends. This ulterior motive is especially evident in an article on 'Our Shakespeare Society' (9 May 1885, 507–8) which describes how a *Girl's Own Paper* reader might form a mixed society for the purpose of reading Shakespeare aloud. The article narrates the experiences of 'Perdita', a young woman 'pretty, clever, and charming, the daughter of indulgent and sensible parents, with plenty of time at her command'.[24] Perdita's whim to form a Shakespeare reading group is eventually a success, despite the inconveniences arising from the fumblings of several unpractised readers as well as her lack of foresight in selecting the too-meditative *Richard II* for the group's inaugural reading. The real benefits of forming such a group are hinted at in the description of Perdita's increased esteem among the men of the circle, where she is now 'regarded with chivalrous allegiance by the gentlemen of the Society, who bow to her will as law'.[25] Or, as the magazine describes the merits of education more generally: 'Education increases your interest in everything . . . And it is *interest* in these things that is the never-failing charm in a companion. Who could bear to live life with a thoroughly uneducated woman?'[26]

The virtually incessant moralizing evident in much of the treatment Shakespeare was accorded by the Victorians is at least partially the result of the realities of the magazine publishing market. The bestselling Victorian children's periodicals, the *Boy's Own Paper* and *Girl's Own Paper*, had been founded by the Religious Tract Society in a thoroughly articulated plan to counteract the contaminating influence of popular, inexpensive reading material on the young. As part of its efforts to provide children with exciting yet wholesome alternatives to the penny dreadfuls and penny novelettes, Shakespeare was employed to promote ideals contrived to be at once appealing to children and acceptable to the society's members.[27] The success of the Sunday school movement earlier in the century had resulted in a tremendous surge in the number of literate children and a concomitant boom in the children's literature market. From its founding in 1799, the Religious Tract Society had recognized that the spread of literacy represented an opportunity as well as a challenge. An article in the *Evangelical Magazine* published that same year articulates the policy which would eventually help to shape the editorial policies of the *Boy's Own Paper* and *Girl's Own Paper*, that for 'thousands who would have remained grossly illiterate, having through the medium of Sunday schools been enabled to read, it is an object of growing importance widely to diffuse such publications as are calculated to make that ability an unquestionable privilege'.[28]

Victorian children were the beneficiaries of a publishing industry in which dozens of magazines competed for their weekly pennies. In the Victorian period, as never before, children from all classes had a range of reading choices available to them. With its two highly successful and enduring magazines, the Religious Tract Society captured the sustained interest of generations of children while continuing to promote the moral agenda which had prompted it to create these alternatives to the cheap but morally questionable periodicals with mass appeal. Although *Atalanta*'s approach is perhaps more appealing from a modern critical perspective, and *Boys of England*'s more multifaceted, the emphatically mainstream publications of the Religious Tract Society also taught children to care about Shakespeare, if only for less than literary reasons. While some of these children were no doubt satisfied with simply identifying Shakespeare as a national icon or a means of securing attention from the opposite sex, others, as the magazines' essay contests reveal, used this introduction as a springboard to more adult ways of understanding the man and his works.

Children's Shakespeare in this era, then, must be seen within the larger context of Victorian popular literature, disseminated chiefly in the periodicals, no less than in the context of the nineteenth-century theatre via the illustrations and playbooks published as children's toys or the 'family reading' of the middle and upper classes promoted in books such as *Tales from Shakespear*. From the popular periodicals and the toy theatre, children's publishers borrowed the sensationalism and sheer fun that gave Shakespeare an added appeal to young readers, while the 'family reading' Shakespeare of the Lambs contributed a moral focus. It is worth noting, by way of conclusion, that the impulse to extract a moral message from Shakespeare's plays was by no means the Lambs' invention, and is in fact evident in the earliest documents of Shakespeare reception history. When the Jacobean astrologer and physician Simon Forman recorded his impressions of *The Winter's Tale* produced at the Globe in 1611, he included a note to 'Beware of trusting feigned beggars and fawning fellows.'[29] Likewise, the title of the earliest known full-length book of Shakespeare for children, Perrin's *Contes Moraux*, indicates Perrin's explicitly moral, edificatory agenda. Tracing the trajectory of early contributions to the 'Shakespeare for children' genre from Perrin to Brett within the larger context of Shakespeare reception corrects the misperception that moral Shakespeare and children's Shakespeare are synonymous. It also renders more explicit the movement from the elite readership of Perrin's book, sold by subscription as a pedagogical aid for the governesses of wealthy children, to the increasingly demotic readerships of the Lambs' successive editions, the middle-class readers of early children's periodicals, and Brett's distinctly downmarket publications later in the century. When Perrin and the periodicals are included alongside the Lambs in a more complete history of the development of Shakespeare for children, the movement is clearly down the social scale, to include, by the middle of the nineteenth century, young readers from all social classes. By the end of the Victorian period, just as Shakespeare had been disseminated among a wide constituency of adult readers through periodicals for the working classes and women, so, too, in the children's periodicals, young readers were encouraged to find their own connections to Shakespeare.

NOTES

1 A letter in the 2 April 1898 issue of the *Girl's Own Paper* reminds us that the Lambs' *Tales* remained popular even at the end of the century: 'Will the Editor in Correspondence give a short account of Dante's "Divina Commedia"? Ordinary people never seem to know anything of Beatrice. Is there any book giving an easy interesting little tale from it in the way that Lamb's Tales do of Shakespeare's plays?' (431).

2 For example, Caroline Maxwell, *The Juvenile Edition of Shakespeare, Adapted to the Capacity of Youth* (London, 1828); Joseph Graves, *Dramatic Tales Founded on Shakespeare's Plays. To Which is Added, the Life of this Eminent Poet* (London, 1840); Mary Seymour, *Shakespeare's Stories Simply Told* (London, 1883); Charles Alias, *Scenes from Shakespeare for the Young* (London, 1885); Harrison Morris, *Tales from Shakespeare, Including Those by Charles and Mary Lamb, With a Continuation by Harrison S. Morris* (Philadelphia, 1893); Adelaride C. Gordon Sim, *Phoebe's Shakespeare, Arranged for Children* (London, 1894); Edith Nesbit, *The Children's Shakespeare* (London, 1895); Arthur Thomas Quiller-Couch, *Historical Tales from Shakespeare* (London, 1899); M. Surtees Townsend, *Stories from Shakespeare* (Warne, 1899).

3 The *Little Folks* series significantly predates Edith Nesbit's 1895 *The Children's Shakespeare*, a book often considered noteworthy because virtually all the characters are depicted as children in the illustrations.

4 Anna Buckland, 'The Story of Miranda', *Little Folks* (January 1877), 45–7 (46). Many of these periodicals are not readily available, even on microfilm or through interlibrary loan services, so I have been generous in my use of direct quotation where appropriate.

5 Anna Buckland, 'The Story of Polydore and Cadwal', *Little Folks* (*Cymbeline*; February 1877), 114–16; 'The Story of Young Marcius', *Little Folks* (*Coriolanus*; March 1877), 146–7; 'The Story of Prince Arthur', *Little Folks* (*King John*; April 1877), 225–8; 'The Story of Perdita', *Little Folks* (*The Winter's Tale*; May 1877), 269–71.

6 Gary Taylor, *Reinventing Shakespeare: A Cultural History from the Restoration to the Present* (London: The Hogarth Press, 1990).

7 H. L. Hamilton, 'A Chat About Shakespeare', *Little Folks* (July 1881), 104.

8 *Ibid.*

9 H. P. Burke Downing, 'A Day in Shakespeare's Country', *Boy's Own Paper* (10 June 1893), 584–6 (584).

10 *Boys of England* (21 September 1867), 277.

11 *Boys of England* (24 November 1866), 16.

12 Brett was a prolific publisher who recognized the profits to be made by marketing Shakespeare to boys in an easily digestible format. In 1881–2 he published the *Boys of England Stories of Shakespeare* series, a collection of twelve sixteen-page prose adaptations sold for a penny apiece: *Richard III* (1), *Hamlet* (2), *Macbeth* (3), *Henry IV* (4), *Romeo and Juliet* (5), *Othello* (6), *King John* (7), *King Lear* (8), *As You Like It* (9), *Henry V* (10), *Henry VI* (11), and *The Taming of the Shrew* (12). In contrast to the sensation dramas which appeared in the pages of *Boys of England,* these prose versions were serious and even sensitive adaptations rather than parodies.

13 November and December 1875, nos. 472–6.

14 *Othello, Boys of England Stories of Shakespeare* 6, p. 80.

15 As George Speaight explains in his history of the juvenile drama genre, between roughly 1810 and 1880 'some 324 plays were adapted for, and published as sheets of characters and scenery for, the Juvenile Drama. These sheets were sold originally for a penny plain or twopence coloured by hand, and their intended destiny was to be stuck on card and cut up, and for the characters to be moved across the boards of toy theatres' (*The Juvenile Theatre: A Union Catalogue* (London: The Society for Theatre Research, 1999), p. 2). Among the extant toy-theatre sheets housed in the collections canvassed in Speaight's catalogue are forty sets based on fourteen of Shakespeare's plays: *Antony and Cleopatra* (published by Jameson, no date); *Coriolanus* (West, 1824); *Hamlet* (Hodgson,1824; Jameson, 1818; Park, n.d.; West, 1819); *Henry IV* (W. Clarke, 1821; West, 1824); *Henry VIII* (Myers, n.d.); *Julius Caesar* (Hebberd, n.d.; Love, n.d.; West, n.d.); *King John* (Hodgson, n.d.); *Macbeth* (Hodgson, 1823; Smart, 1822; West, 1811); *The Merry Wives of Windsor* (Smart, 1822; West, 1815); *A Midsummer Night's Dream* (Jameson, 1813; West, 1817); *Othello* (Hodgson, 1823; M. & B. Skelt, n.d.); *Richard III* (Andrews, n.d.; Globe n.d.; Green, 1851; a second version by Green, n.d.; Hodgson, 1822; Jameson, 1815; Lloyd, 1830; Park, n.d.; Park and Golding, n.d.; Pollock, n.d.; G. Skelt, n.d.; M. & M. Skelt, n.d.; West, 1814); *Romeo and Juliet* (Hodgson, 1823; West, 1825); *The Tempest* (Hebberd, n.d.; Hodgson, 1823; Smart, 1822).

16 See Edward Salmon, *Juvenile Literature As It Is* (London, 1888).
17 Andrew Murphy, 'Shakespeare Among the Workers', *Shakespeare Survey* 58 (2005), 107–17.
18 Mary Cowden Clarke, 'Shakespeare as the Girl's Friend', *Girl's Own Paper* (4 June 1887), 562–4. I have taken my quotations directly from the periodical, but the article is reprinted in Ann Thompson and Sasha Roberts, eds., *Women Reading Shakespeare, 1660–1900: An Anthology of Criticism* (Manchester: Manchester University Press, 1997), pp. 101–3.
19 'My Favourite Heroine from Shakespeare', *Girl's Own Paper* (3 March 1888), 380–1.
20 Isobel Armstrong, 'The Gush of the Feminine: How Can We Read Women's Poetry of the Romantic Period?', in Paula R. Feldman and Theresa M. Kelley, eds., *Romantic Women Writers: Voices and Countervoices* (Hanover: University Press of New England, 1995), pp. 13–32.
21 Publication details and an inventory of plays covered in each article are: early comedy (George Saintsbury, 114–18: includes *The Comedy of Errors, Love's Labour's Lost, A Midsummer Night's Dream, Two Gentlemen of Verona*), early histories (George Saintsbury, 214–17: includes *Henry VI, Richard III*), early tragedy (R. K. Douglas, 273–7: treats *Romeo and Juliet* alone), middle history (Professor Church, 339–43: includes *King John* and *Richard II*), middle comedy (R. K. Douglas, 402–6: treats *The Merchant of Venice* alone), later history (Lucy Toulmin-Smith, 469–73: includes *Henry IV* (both parts) and *Henry V*), later comedy (Edward Garnett, 532–5: includes *As You Like It, Much Ado About Nothing, Twelfth Night*), middle tragedy (Professor Church, 597–601: includes *Hamlet, Julius Caesar*), later tragedy (George Saintsbury, 660–3: includes *Macbeth, King Lear*), historical classical tragedy (Edward Garnett, 726–9: includes *Antony and Cleopatra, Coriolanus*), romantic comedy (Edward Garnett, 786–90: includes *Cymbeline, The Tempest, The Winter's Tale*).
22 Susan H. Cunliffe, 'Is Shakespeare a Moralist?', *Atalanta* (March 1892), 347.
23 *Ibid.*, 348.
24 'Our Shakespeare Society', *Girl's Own Paper* (9 May 1885), 507–8 (507).
25 *Ibid.*, 508.
26 *Girl's Own Paper* (5 March 1892), 361.
27 See Patrick Dunae, 'The *Boy's Own Paper*: Origins and Editorial Policies', *The Private Library* 9 (1976), 123–58 for further details of the Religious Tract Society's struggles to balance its moral agenda with the demands of the Victorian children's periodical market. For contemporary views on the penny dreadfuls, see James Greenwood, 'The Penny Awfuls', *St Paul's Magazine* 12 (1873), 161–8; Alexander Strahan, 'Bad Literature for the Young', *Contemporary Review* 26 (1875), 981–91; Francis Hitchman, 'The Penny Press', *Macmillan's Magazine* 43 (1881), 385–98; Edward Salmon, 'What Boys Read', *Fortnightly Review* 39 (1886), 248–59; Bennett G. Johns, 'Literature of the Streets', *Edinburgh Review* 165 (1887), 40–65; Edward Lyttleton, 'Penny Fiction', *Quarterly Review* 171 (1890), 150–71. For the modern reader,

Kevin Carpenter, *Penny Dreadfuls and Comics: English Periodicals for Children from Victorian Times to the Present Day* (London: Victoria & Albert Museum, 1983) is an excellent overview of the penny dreadful's development.

28 *Evangelical Magazine* (1 July 1799), 2.

29 A transcript of Simon Forman's manuscript notes is printed in G. Blakemore Evans and J. J. M. Tobin, eds., *The Riverside Shakespeare* (Boston: Houghton Mifflin, 1974), pp. 1841–2. The quotation, in its original spelling, is at the end of the entry on p. 1842.

11

Growing up with Shakespeare: the Terry family memoirs

Pascale Aebischer

'REMEMBER ME': THE TERRY/CRAIG MEMOIRS

Ellen Terry was described in 1898 as 'the actress who in our time is most intimately associated with the impersonation of Shakespeare's Heroines'.[1] Her son Edward Gordon Craig is remembered for his avant-garde stage designs, his theory of the *Übermarionette* and his production of *Hamlet* for Stanislavsky at the Art Theatre in Moscow in 1912. Both are the authors of unusually vivid theatrical memoirs, which give us an insight into Shakespeare's role in shaping the narratives of the nineteenth-century childhood and adolescence of these theatre practitioners. Shakespeare, in these texts, is more than merely the creator of characters the playing of whom constitutes the pinnacle of an actor's career. His works can be seen to influence the way in which personal experience is conceptualized and the experience of growing up is understood.

Terry's 1908 *The Story of My Life*, written with the assistance of her daughter's partner Christopher St John (aka Christabel Marshall), has for many years been recognized as one of the few actors' memoirs to have genuine literary merit.[2] It forms the basis of and is reinterpreted by Gordon Craig in *Ellen Terry and Her Secret Self* (1931) and *Index to the Story of My Days* (1957).[3] While the first of Gordon Craig's books is ostensibly a biography of his mother which, with polemic heaviness, turns out to a large extent to focus on himself, the second is a quirky, highly selective autobiography which focuses to just as large an extent on his mother.[4] A further text considered here is the amplified and revised 1933 edition of Terry's autobiography published by Edith Craig and Christopher St John as *Ellen Terry's Memoirs*.[5]

In their idiosyncratic ways, the childhood and early adulthood sections of the Terry/Craig memoirs provide a uniquely complex intertextual case study of childhood involvement with and subsequent appropriation of Shakespeare by two giants of the late Victorian and early twentieth-century avant-garde theatre. While both Terry and Gordon Craig achieved their fame in adult life, their memoirs firmly ground their later successes and failures in their narratives of their childhood and early adulthood, turning these sections of their (auto)biographies into something of a foundation myth in which Shakespeare is deeply implicated. Terry's autobiography seems to have generated a family narrative that shaped the way her descendants recalled and understood their childhood. Shakespeare emerges from these texts as the only man Terry ever really loved and, as the creator of virtuous protagonists who could be used for the social vindication of the actors performing those roles, a relatively respectable means of earning a livelihood. Most importantly, Shakespeare is set up both as the contested property of Terry and, as Angela Carter was to do in her Terry-influenced *Wise Children* (1992), as the provider of plotlines according to which both the mother's and the son's self-perception and experience of growing up could be patterned or interpreted.[6] In a period in which Shakespeare was, as Kathryn Prince suggests in chapter 10, widely used in the formation of a national identity, the Terry/Craig memoirs demonstrate how he could be appropriated by theatre practitioners for the construction of a more personal, though no less public, identity.[7]

In *The Story of My Life*, Terry seems to identify phases of her girlhood with the Shakespearean child characters she played, leading to what appears to have been a lifelong fascination with Shakespeare's children. This is evident from the critical attention she lavished on Shakespeare's child characters in the lecture on 'The Children in Shakespeare's Plays' which she delivered on various tours between roughly 1911 and 1921.[8] The neglected subject of Shakespeare's children, Terry maintains, is appropriate for her as a novice lecturer precisely because she 'had begun life as an actress by impersonating one of the children in [Shakespeare's] plays' (*Four Lectures*, p. 25). However, far from basing her lecture on nothing but her girlhood performances of these parts, she brings to it a lifetime's experience of observing Shakespeare's children from both within and without. Recollecting her first theatrical engagement at the age of eight as Mamillius in Mr and Mrs Kean's production of *The Winter's Tale* at the Princess' theatre, she reveals that, during an offstage moment, she had 'made a slit in the canvas to watch Mrs. Kean as Hermione!' (*Story*, p. 8).[9] Similarly, in one of her last major appearances as a Shakespearean actress, she kept a sharp eye on Mamillius while playing Hermione. Her mature appreciation of the two roles, she implies, was thus formed through both a child's and an adult's perception. With hindsight, she muses in her lecture, 'When I spoke as a child and thought as a child I wonder whether I was able to reveal all I see now in this lovely child's part' (*Four Lectures*, pp. 26–7).

SHAKESPEARE AND THE CHILD ACTRESS

In Terry's *The Story of My Life*, the role of Shakespeare seems to be quite straightforward at first: his are the plays she first acted in and the ones to which she dedicated her life. The early part of her memoirs is filled with explicit references to Shakespeare's importance to her theatrical family and to her painstaking acquisition of her Shakespearean repertoire. Terry sees the fact that she was born in Coventry and thus in 'Shakespeare's own county' as 'a happy chance' (p. 3). Similarly promising, she feels, is the circumstance that Sarah Kemble married Mr Siddons in Coventry, thereby becoming the formidable Mrs Siddons who remained unrivalled in her interpretations of Shakespeare roles until Terry made those roles her own. Terry thus intimates an engagement with Shakespeare from the very moment of her Warwickshire birth. As a little girl, she was trained by her mother, who 'read Shakespeare beautifully', and her exacting father, who had played with Macready and 'would begin the day's "coaching" at breakfast' (pp. 8, 10). It is due to this early training, Terry surmises, that she obtained her first role as Mamillius with the Keans. She recalls that her 'heart swelled with pride when [she] was told what [she] had to do, when [she] realised that [she] had a real Shakespeare part – a possession that father had taught [her] to consider the pride of life!' (p. 8).

To judge from Terry's account of her early acting experience not only as Mamillius, but also later as Puck, Prince Arthur, Fleance and a number of walk-ons in *The Merchant of Venice, Richard II* and *Henry VIII*, performing Shakespeare's child roles was frequently the prerogative of girls, an appropriation of boys' parts which, in the eyes of Terry's son, was to become an obstacle to his own ambitions as a child actor.[10] Performing Shakespeare was hard and physically dangerous work for the child actress. When little Ellen failed to be properly terrified as Prince Arthur, Mrs Kean slapped her and was delighted with the resulting real distress. As Puck, Terry broke her toe when it was caught in the trap door but was (with the incentive of a doubled salary) made to finish the performance, and as the 'top angel' in a vision in *Henry VIII*, being rigged up near the gaslights made her sick at the dress rehearsal. In spite of these moments of physical distress, Terry says she 'was a very strong, happy, and healthy child', who, though she had experience in acting in contemporary drama, farce, and burlesque, felt 'more at home in Shakespeare than anything else' (pp. 10, 29). In her early teens, while she was '"in standing water", as Malvolio says of Viola when she is dressed as a boy' and 'neither child nor woman' (p. 22), Terry started to add to her repertoire of boys' roles the parts of Shakespeare's women. She learnt the words 'of every female part in every play in which [she] had appeared at the Princess'(p. 21), so that by the age of eighteen she 'knew the words and had *studied* the words – a very different thing – of every woman's part in Shakespeare' (p. 41). She scared herself when studying the role of Juliet in the 'Stalactite Caverns' of the Colosseum in London, performed the part of Titania at the Theatre Royal in Bath in 1862 and played Hero in *Much Ado About Nothing* at the Haymarket theatre in London the following year.

In view of Terry's early enthusiasm for her profession and her widely acknowledged success in it, it is strange that, before the age of twenty, she should have left the stage twice. She first left it to be married, at 'not quite sixteen years old' (*Story*, p. 33), to George Frederic Watts, the Pre-Raphaelite painter thirty years her senior. After less than a year, Watts sent his child-bride back to her parents.[11] She half-heartedly resumed her stage career for a while before abandoning it a second time to start a new life in the country with the aesthete and architect Edward William Godwin, with whom she had two illegitimate children: Edy (Edith Craig) and Teddy (Gordon Craig). Six years later, she returned to the stage in order to ward off the bailiff, and she and Godwin separated the next year.[12]

It is at the point when Terry begins to write about her life with Watts and Godwin that Shakespeare almost entirely vanishes from the overt narrative of her memoir and starts appearing as a strange *déjà-vu* effect instead. This relegation of Shakespeare to the subtext in the sections of *The Story of My Life* dealing with Terry's teens is surprising since, elsewhere, she identifies precisely this period in her life with the beginning of her exclusive love of Shakespeare. She is reported to have told Henry Irving, 'When I was about sixteen or seventeen and very unhappy, I forswore the society of men . . . Yet I was lonely all the same. I wanted a sweetheart. Well, Shakespeare became my sweetheart! I read everything I could get hold of about my beloved one. I lived with him in his plays.'[13] In the context of her account of that same period in *The Story of My Life*, however, and in spite of her earlier assertion that '[t]he parts we play influence our characters to some extent' (p. 12), Terry remains oddly silent about an obvious link between her marriage to Watts and her last role in a Shakespeare play before her marriage, that of Hero in *Much Ado About Nothing*. The shock Terry registers in her memoir at her rejection by her husband, saying that she was 'thunderstruck', 'miserable, indignant, unable to understand that there could be any justice in what had happened' is a replay of the role of the repudiated bride she admits she had played 'beautifully!' at the Haymarket theatre (pp. 37, 38, 32). Hero is also one of the very first roles (and the first Shakespearean part) she played again upon her return to the stage, so that her real-life repudiation is disconcertingly bracketed by her public enactment of it through the medium of Shakespeare's wronged adolescent heroine.

More striking yet than this echo of *Much Ado About Nothing* is the intrusion of another Shakespearean plot and adolescent heroine that Terry almost pointedly fails to highlight. Whereas her account of her marriage to Watts is as open as her delicacy and enduring respect for him allow, her handling of the years she spent with Godwin is much more oblique and allusive, giving some of her chosen reminiscences symbolic power. As Nina Auerbach notes, in *The Story of My Life*, '[o]nce [Terry] falls in love, her narrative method changes: she moves from bold and powerful vignettes to suggestion and indirection'.[14] In the brief chapter entitled 'A Six-Year Vacation: 1868–1874', Godwin remains unnamed and Shakespeare is evoked only negatively in her assertion that she 'studied cookery-books instead of parts – Mrs. Beeton instead of Shakespeare!' (p. 50). For the expected narrative of her life with Godwin and a straightforward acknowledgement of her continuing engagement with Shakespeare through her work with Godwin, Terry substitutes the following:

> a dreadful thing happened. A body was found in the river – the dead body of a young woman, very fair and slight and tall. Every one thought it was my body.
>
> I had gone away without a word. No one knew where I was. My own father identified the corpse ... the news came to me in my country retreat that I had been found dead, and I flew up to London to give ocular proof to my poor distracted parents that I was alive ... You see, they knew I had not been very happy since my return to the stage, and when I went away without a word, they were terribly anxious, and prepared to believe the first bad tidings that came to hand. It came in the shape of that most extraordinary likeness between me and that poor soul who threw herself into the river. (p. 48)

While the 'ocular proof', borrowed as it is from *Othello*, betrays the latent presence of Shakespeare in this passage, the Shakespearean plot behind the episode appears to be the suicide of Ophelia – another girl whose transition to adulthood and marriage is hampered by the imputation of unchastity – following her rejection by Hamlet. The role of Hamlet seems to be taken on by Watts, the man for whose paintings, just before her repudiation, she had posed as Ophelia, and whose desire to shut her into a nunnery (he paid her the allowance agreed in the terms of their separation only as long as she remained chaste) she had frustrated by choosing to live with Godwin. Tainted with sexual experience and rejected by her husband, the plot Terry was clearly expected to enact was that of the stereotypical Victorian 'fallen woman' who, inspired by Ophelia's exemplary fate, seeks her watery death in the Thames.

What makes the whole episode stranger still is that her parents' mistake partly originated from the fact that it is Terry who first seems to have thought of herself as a drowned fallen woman. It is she who, when she left home to live with Godwin, had apparently stuck a note reading 'Found Drowned' on a portrait of Watts, leading her parents to believe that she had sought to commit suicide. Watts, in turn, had almost prophetically immortalized the supposed fate of his wife in paint in the 1850s in a work entitled *Found Drowned* which depicts the corpse of a girl who has been pulled from the river and which must have provided the inspiration for Terry's farewell note. Neither of these facts, nor the circumstance that Terry heard of her 'death' when a detective hired by her brother-in-law tracked her down in the country, is mentioned in Terry's version of the events.[15] As presented in the memoirs, the episode of the drowned woman is mysterious enough to warrant a reading that goes beyond the factual to the symbolic. Terry's rendering of the story makes most sense when read as a melodramatic displacement of the stereotypical fate of the fallen woman from Terry on to a surrogate body. This enables Terry to emerge from the episode, if not cleansed of sexual wrongdoing, then at least alive enough to make her parents acknowledge her existence in spite of their estrangement from her.

In real life Terry resisted the roles of Shakespeare's maligned adolescent heroines to the point that in her memoirs she never openly acknowledges the Shakespearean plotlines of swooning Hero and suicidal Ophelia that pervade her early life. In her lecture on Shakespeare's 'Pathetic Woman', Terry even ended up taking an openly critical stance towards Ophelia, stating that '[t]he whole tragedy of *her* life is that she is afraid . . . She is scared of life itself when things go wrong. Her brain, her soul and her body are all pathetically weak' (*Four Lectures*, p. 165). It would seem that Terry herself was neither afraid nor weak when she was sent home by Watts and then separated from Godwin. Instead, she found consolation in her work as epitomized by Shakespeare's plays. Artistically, she says, her 'fires were only just beginning to burn' (*Story*, p. 66) at the time of her rift with Godwin. She worked with the Bancrofts, the influential actors and theatre managers, for a year before her big breakthrough came in 1878 in the shape of an offer, from Irving, to join his company, become his leading lady and play . . . Ophelia.

It is as Ophelia, the pathetically weak, scared girl she despised, that she achieved her greatest popularity, leading a contemporary to eulogize:

> Ophelia, then, is an image or personification of innocent, delicious, feminine youth and beauty, and she passes before us in the two phases of sanity and delirium. Ellen Terry presented her in this way. The embodiment is fully within her reach, and it is one of the few unmistakably perfect creations with which dramatic art has illumined literature and adorned the stage. Ellen Terry was born to play such a part, and she is perfect in it.[16]

The bulk of Terry's theatrical career and her increasing social respectability were thus founded on the public perception of her 'perfect' impersonation of the 'feminine youth and beauty' of Ophelia, which could be achieved only by one 'born to play such a part' and therefore, by implication, as wrongly accused of sexual misdemeanour as Shakespeare's 'innocent, delicious' young heroine. It is symptomatic of the redemptive symbolism of Terry's impersonation of Ophelia that Watts seems to have almost obsessively seized on his fallen wife's performances in the 1870s and 1880s to return to a sketch of Terry as Ophelia that he had drawn during their year together. As if to make Terry drown in art if she would not drown in life, he now elaborated the drawing into a cycle of paintings of 'the water-haunted Ophelia who was so indelible a part of Watts's imagination of Ellen Terry'.[17] On his part, Gordon Craig's fantasy of a fusion between his mother and Ophelia, which started as a child when he addressed Terry in a letter as 'Sweetest – beautifulest & Kindest & Bestest = Ophelia',[18] appears to have been realized only very briefly in or around 1906. At that time he saw the 58-year-old Terry perform Ophelia one last time and, he says, 'she was the thing itself. All was faultless – and all I could do was to look and listen and look again, and murmur in between times a prayer for forgiveness' (*Secret Self*, p. 172). What he needs to be forgiven for, he does not say.

'ALWAYS I HAVE BEEN HAMLET': GORDON CRAIG'S WAR OF THE MEMOIRS

Terry's appetite for life and her ability to disentangle herself from the Shakespearean plots that would prescribe either permanent retirement or suicide are at the heart of her son's resentment of her. Together, Gordon Craig's two memoirs constitute a wholesale rewriting of his mother's *The Story of My Life*, covering almost precisely the same time span from Terry's youth to her jubilee performance in 1906. In the *Index to the Story of My*

Days that he wrote in his eighties, Gordon Craig revisits the scene of the suicide of Terry's alter ego when he states that it is '[s]trange to realize . . . that she did not kill herself' rather than 'work on'. 'Is it that she was made of more clay than spirit?' he asks (*Index*, p. 21). At the end of his life, Gordon Craig clearly still finds it hard to forgive his mother for refusing to become a latter-day Ophelia and opting to *play* Ophelia instead.

In the *Hamlet*-inspired psychodrama that unfolds in Gordon Craig's *Index to the Story of My Days* even more than in his earlier biography *Ellen Terry and Her Secret Self*, he portrays himself as 'the young Lord Hamlet', as he was called by Irving.[19] This identification is partly based on his sense that he, in his idleness and lack of direction, belongs to the group of 'English Impossibles' of the turn of the century who, like Hamlet, '[lack] *technique* and advancement – a sense of business' (*Index*, pp. 247–8). Even more than Gordon Craig's 'antiestablishment' attitude and idleness, what allows him to identify thoroughly with Hamlet is that he sees himself as the only true upholder of his father's memory, the brilliant, lonely youth who is kept in a state of inability to act because of his father's obliteration. Terry, in this scenario, relinquishes her devoutly to be wished-for identity as innocent girlish Ophelia to become the sexually mature, immoral and vaguely threatening Gertrude whose sins are blamed for her son's failure to become a responsible, purposeful adult. The memoirs are full of complaints about being surrounded by 'so many dear women . . . [who] all avoided speaking tenderly or wisely about the poor man no longer there. He was alive – I suppose that in itself was, in their minds, "dreadful"' (*Index*, p. 48). In what W. D. King has aptly dubbed Gordon Craig's 'Oedipal melodrama',[20] Terry is thus portrayed as the fickle woman who, Gordon Craig seems to think, wished his father dead and who later perpetrated a similar betrayal of the father-figure that Irving had become in the meantime.[21] As Gordon Craig 'rambled' (his own word) in an *Index* entry supposedly concerned with finding lodgings while touring in 1894:

> Yes, this dear strange, so easily understood, nature – this Hamlet – and his mother – when as a young man I acted him I remember how much I loved my mother – I mean Queen Gertrude – I loved to be with her on the stage – but why was she so cross? The scenes where we were together, more especially in that lovely scene when there came to us into the room my father – his so pale and glaring eyes fixed upon us both. Poor dear – she, my mother I mean – she could not see him – she saw the chairs and the table – the bed – but not him – Heard nothing, heard only my words not his . . .
>
> . . . *Hamlet* was not only a play to me nor he a rôle to be played – I somehow or other lived Hamlet day by day. Since I was so much like Hamlet myself I *had*

to – not only were my weaknesses his, but his situation was almost mine.

I too had lost a father – I too saw my mother married to another [the actor Charles Wardell] …

Always I have been Hamlet, and now, as Hamlet aged, 'reporting myself to the unsatisfied', telling something of my own story and reporting my cause too, as in the play I asked Horatio to do. (*Index*, pp. 162–5)

Evidently, though Terry's use of *Hamlet* to convey the more painful experiences of her girlhood can be seen to have generated Gordon Craig's *Hamlet*-inflected interpretation of his adolescence, the delicate allusiveness of Terry's evocation of Ophelia in *The Story of My Life* is not to her son's taste.

Particularly intriguing is the way Gordon Craig's relationship with both his parents is negotiated through the figure of Shakespeare, whose ownership Gordon Craig seeks to establish. Sometimes Shakespeare is attributed to his father, the author of a series of thirty articles on 'The Architecture and Costume of Shakespeare's Plays' in *The Architect* (1874–5). Sometimes he is identified with 'Nelly', 'a very small person, not a famous person – the little mother' on whose 'sensitive nature … the big and vibrating lines of Shakespeare played' (*Secret Self*, pp. vii, 23). Most frequently, however, Shakespeare is associated with his 'mother-in-art' 'ET', the 'great and famous actress – the important figure' for whom 'Shakespeare was the wood, the earth, the air', who was 'possessed … of a unique and driving genius for acting Shakespeare' and who 'loved [Shakespeare] possibly most of all [men]' (*Secret Self*, pp. 67, 11, 15, 29, 48). Gordon Craig even pens a fanciful dialogue between the loving mother Nelly and the ambitious actress ET in which Shakespeare tellingly intrudes into their quarrel over the two children:

Nelly Terry.	What on earth do you think you are doing?
Ellen Terry.	Mind your own business – I have made up my mind.
Nelly Terry.	I don't think you've got a mind worth making up.
Ellen Terry.	The playing of Shakespeare improves a woman's mind far more than washing a couple of brats.
Nelly Terry.	Yes – if you look on them as brats. I have two children –
Ellen Terry.	They aren't yours – they're mine.
Nelly Terry.	You take one, I'll keep the other.
Ellen Terry.	Yes, we will toss up!
Nelly Terry.	No, we won't. You've got such grand ideas of what women should be. Suppose you experiment on the girl.

(*Secret Self*, pp. 63–4)

The gift of Edith Craig by Nelly to the Shakespearean sophisticate ET to be experimented on is unexpected in itself. It is yet more unsettling if seen in the context of the fact that when Godwin had tried to abduct Edith after his separation from Terry, Terry had by her own admission '*offered* to let him have the boy'.[22] Although Gordon Craig was never told of this episode of maternal rejection, an uncanny inverted trace of it lingers in this dialogue, mixed in with his mother's absorption in Shakespeare, to suggest his deep-seated unease about the firmness of her affection for him and his suspicion of Shakespeare's role in her life as a rival for his affection and the obstacle to maternal love. Where for Terry, Shakespeare was the benign author of a respectable repertoire, the creator of a number of male and female characters with whom she could identify for the duration of a production, and the friend she turns to in times of emotional need, for Craig-as-Hamlet he is the threatening stranger who breaks up the nuclear family by appealing to Terry's mind and claiming her for himself.

It is ET's preference for Shakespeare and the theatre over Gordon Craig and his father that leads to his strongly ambivalent stance towards the figure of Shakespeare and the acting profession as jointly and seemingly inseparably embodied by his mother. He quotes from his mother's memoir and her account of how the threat of the bailiffs forced her back to the stage in order to deny the veracity of her version of events:

> What I think is something not exactly like the truth and nothing but the truth, is that she 'remembered the bailiff in the house'. I think the truth is that she remembered the stage, and had all at once felt the full force of the pull of that damnable magnet, the theatre, which had been attracting her from a great distance for the last two years (p. 36).

In Gordon Craig's emended version of Terry's account, his glorified father is guilt-free and the theatre (and, by implication, Shakespeare) alone is responsible for Terry's return to the stage. In fact, in Gordon Craig's rendering of the events in *Ellen Terry and Her Secret Self*, the break-up of his parents' relationship is elided and replaced by Terry's resumption of her career and her concomitant abandonment of her children to a minder, shifting the blame for his loss of a father entirely on to his mother and the 'damnable magnet' of the theatre.

Not surprisingly, in view of Gordon Craig's bitter chronicle of his childhood and his mean-spirited attacks on his sister (let alone his not too subtly implied indictment of his late mother for 'murdering' his fathers Godwin, Kelly/Wardell and Irving), Edith Craig and Christopher St John jointly attempted to defend Terry's cause by letting her, once more, tell her story.[23] The result is the voluminous *Ellen Terry's Memoirs: With Preface, Notes and Additional Chapters by Edith Craig and Christopher St John*, a reframing of *The Story of My Life* which leaves Terry's words largely unaltered while providing a critical framework that, for the most part, supports Terry's own rendering of her life.[24] In the margins of Terry's text, the women's notes mushroom into a rich addition to Terry's self-portrait. In their preface Craig and St John make it obvious that the *Memoirs* constitute a defensive strike in the children's undignified battle over their mother's corpus.

By contrast, Gordon Craig's last tribute to his mother in *Index to the Story of My Days* must be read as his final, bitter attempt to reclaim control over his mother's life and counter Edith and St John's affirmation of Terry's independence. Hence the ranting tone of this memoir, hence also the Hamletian diatribes that invade the later index entries to deny his sister any importance in his formative years. In *Index* Gordon Craig turns his entire life-writing into the intimate, archetypal, Shakespearean struggle between mother, son and discarded father.

It is the *Hamlet*-inflected nature of the later parts of this memoir, however, which, at a second reading, makes one feature of Gordon Craig's narrative of his boyhood stand out more than it otherwise would have done. That his youth was deeply marked by Shakespeare cannot be in doubt. Both Terry and Gordon Craig's son Edward (aka Edward Carrick) write in their memoirs of Gordon Craig's early love of Shakespeare, and Gordon Craig himself, in his biography of Irving, vividly describes several productions that he saw as a child.[25] It is therefore all the more remarkable that his *Index to the Story of My Days* opens almost directly with a defiant assertion that he has '*not* read all the plays of w.s. . . . Here's a confession for you, if you like. That one could have read the *Daily Mail* for twenty minutes each day for eight or ten years and not read the *C. of E.* by w.s.!' (*Index*, p. 4). In a book which is full of initials – his own, his mother's, Irving's, Godwin's – Shakespeare's are the only ones that Craig repeatedly prints in lowercase, as if to signal a contemptuous refusal to grant him proper status. Indeed, in contrast with Terry's constant, unselfconscious and admiring references to Shakespeare throughout the childhood section of her autobiography, in the corresponding section of the *Index* Shakespeare appears only in passing. He surfaces in occasional very brief references to parts that Terry played, but more often than not the references are undercut by a refusal to discuss the plays mentioned. Thus for 27 February 1880 the *Index* entry reads:

I went with E.T. to see 'As You Like It' at the Aquarium Theatre, Westminster ... It was a matinée, and the old custom of cake and tea in the Green Room was revived ... I remembered and still recall the teacake – it was warm cake – and much of the afternoon show I can recall. Cake makes such a difference at eight years old. (p. 47)

Lured into thinking that we will be told about this memorable performance of *As You Like It*, what we are offered instead is the story of a cake. Shakespeare, then, while essential for Gordon Craig's indulgence in his 'Hamlet-complex', is present in his account of his youth in the *Index* only by his conspicuous absence and Gordon Craig's denial of his importance. In Gordon Craig's view of his childhood, Shakespeare is pointedly refused the formative status he had held in Terry's memoir.

The absence of Shakespeare is, in the early parts of the *Index*, coupled with the absence of Gordon Craig's involvement in the theatre. Both of Gordon Craig's memoirs are full of resentment at the way he feels his mother deprived him of proper training by sending him to school rather than letting him go on the stage from an early age. It is as though the monstrous ET had not only deprived Gordon Craig of his father, but had also appropriated Shakespeare to such an extent that acting became impossible for him. It must be remembered here that during *her* formative years, Terry had made Shakespeare's boy roles her own and thus 'usurped' the parts her young son would have liked to play on a London stage. Significantly, when Terry did allow her son to appear alongside her in a boy role, the location was the United States and the role was not Shakespearean. Gordon Craig sums up his predicament as follows: 'Born of the flesh and blood of a woman of the stage, my vocation, calling, job would seem to be hers – the stage. But whereas she was an actress, my father was an architect. My vocation, calling, job could therefore easily seem to be his – architecture' (p. 101).[26] With Shakespeare and the acting profession identified with his mother, Gordon Craig presents it as almost a logical conclusion that he should have given up the stage only a few years after first treading the boards, and that he should have left it to follow in his father's footsteps. In W. D. King's words, Gordon Craig 'took up the legacy of his father, a tradition of running away, of being remembered for his absence'.[27] As if deliberately to upset the mother who had told him that 'anything [is] better than theorize – Talk & not do = It's bad in a woman, but terrible in a man',[28] Gordon Craig spent the rest of his life devising a theory of the theatre which has been described as 'so radical that it seemed to have no place for the actor at all'.[29] While Shakespeare did have a place in Gordon Craig's life away from his mother, culminating in his influential avant-garde *Hamlet* for Stanislavsky, his was not Terry's embodied Shakespeare but rather his father's theoretical, conceptualized, designed Shakespeare. Gordon Craig's is a Shakespeare that could properly be his only when his works had been freed from their perceived imprisonment in the bodies of actors, the body of Terry.

As a child, Terry had embodied Shakespeare's characters to the extent of breaking her bones for the sake of a role. But away from the stage, she held back from total identification with her roles, even when she used them, as she did Ophelia, to structure her experience and say the unspeakable: that she refused the role of the stereotypical 'fallen woman' and would seek professional success instead, putting the need to provide for her children above conventional conceptions of feminine duty and honour. When her son uses Hamlet/*Hamlet* to structure his experience and narrative, his almost obsessive psychological rather than physical identification with the role, by contrast, becomes his preferred way of articulating his feelings of resentment towards his mother and towards Shakespeare as the rival who deprived him and his father of Terry's love. While Gordon Craig's identification with Hamlet is much more overt than Terry's allusion to and rejection of Ophelia, it is also a strikingly intellectual, rather than physical, identification. Even Terry's Ophelia-like double, while a narrative strategy, is also a tangible corpse. Gordon Craig's Hamlet, by contrast, is a child of the mind, a disembodied idea of how a brilliant son could be stifled in his creativity by his mother and her beloved Shakespeare. In Terry's and Gordon Craig's respective memoirs, we can thus trace an evolution from the businesslike attitude towards Shakespeare of the mid-Victorian girl actress, who saw him as the provider of a variety of roles and role models that could be adopted and/or rejected to suit her own needs, towards an internalized Shakespeare whose conflicted relationship with the young Gordon Craig led to a conceptualization of *Hamlet* and Shakespearean staging that ushered in what Robert Smallwood has called 'director's Shakespeare',[30] the intellectualized, problematic Shakespeare of directors and designers (rather than that of actors and actor-managers) that has predominated in the twentieth century.

NOTES

1 Charles Hiatt, *Ellen Terry and Her Impersonations: An Appreciation* (London: George Bell and Sons, 1898), p. 3.

2 Ellen Terry, *The Story of My Life* (Woodbridge: Boydell and Brewer, 1982). Subsequent citations are to this edition and appear in parentheses. On Terry,

see also Virginia Woolf, 'Ellen Terry', in *Collected Essays*, 4 vols. (London: Hogarth Press, 1967), vol. 4, pp. 67–72; Nina Auerbach, *Ellen Terry, Player in Her Time* (New York: W. W. Norton & Co., 1987), p. 36, and Sandra Richards, *The Rise of the English Actress* (Houndmills: Macmillan, 1993), p. 134.

3 Edward Gordon Craig, *Ellen Terry and Her Secret Self* (London: Sampson Low, Marston & Co. Ltd, 1931) and *Index to the Story of My Days: Some Memoirs of Edward Gordon Craig: 1872–1907* (London: Hulton Press, 1957). Subsequent citations are to these editions and appear in parentheses.

4 Auerbach, *Player in Her Time*, p. 269.

5 Ellen Terry, *Ellen Terry's Memoirs: With Preface, Notes and Additional Biographical Chapters by Edith Craig and Christopher St. John* (London: Victor Gollancz, 1933).

6 Carter's debt to Terry is evident in one of her three epigraphs to the novel, which quotes Terry's observation 'How many times Shakespeare draws fathers and daughters, never mothers and daughters'. Angela Carter, *Wise Children* (London: Vintage, 1992).

7 Kathryn Prince, chapter 10, 'Shakespeare in the Victorian children's periodicals', pp. 153–68.

8 Christopher St John in Ellen Terry, *Four Lectures on Shakespeare*, ed. and intr. St John (London: Martin Hopkinson Ltd., 1932), p. 7. Subsequent citations are to this edition and appear in parentheses.

9 Throughout this chapter, I shall adopt Terry's own conception of her birthday as being 27 February 1848. In fact, it seems that she was born on 27 February 1847. See Roger Manvell, *Ellen Terry* (London: Heinemann, 1968), p.vi.

10 For an account of the rise of the cross-dressed girl on the Victorian stage, see Lesley Ferris, 'The Golden Girl', in Viv Gardner and Susan Rutherford, eds., *The New Woman and Her Sisters: Feminism and Theatre 1850–1914* (London: Harvester Wheatsheaf, 1992).

11 The fullest accounts of Terry's poorly documented marriage to Watts can be found in Edward Craig, *Gordon Craig: The Story of His Life* (London: Victor Gollancz, 1968), pp. 35–7, Manvell, *Ellen Terry*, pp. 47–53 and Auerbach, *Player*, pp. 90–113 *passim*.

12 See, especially, Craig, *Gordon Craig*, pp. 38–48.

13 Terry, quoted by Christopher St John in the 'Introduction' to Terry, *Four Lectures*, p. 16.

14 Auerbach, *Player in Her Time*, p. 148.

15 Tom Prideaux, *Love or Nothing: The Life and Times of Ellen Terry* (London: Millington, 1975), p. 73.

16 Quoted (anonymously) in Edgar T. Pemberton's authorized biography *Ellen Terry and Her Sisters* (London: C. Arthur Pearson, Ltd., 1902), p. 301.

17 Auerbach, *Player in Her Time*, p. 105.

18 *Ibid.*, p. 237.

19 This is how Henry Irving addressed Craig in his inscription in the second volume of the *Irving Shakespeare* (Gordon Craig, *Index*), p. 85.

20 W. D. King, *Henry Irving's Waterloo: Theatrical Engagements with Arthur Conan Doyle, George Bernard Shaw, Ellen Terry, Edward Gordon Craig: Late-Victorian Culture, Assorted Ghosts, Old Men, War and History* (Berkeley: University of California Press, 1993), p. 216.

21 See, for example, Gordon Craig, *Index*, p. 47.

22 From a letter by Ellen Terry quoted by Edward Craig in *Gordon Craig*, p. 46.

23 On this mild retaliatory act, see Katharine Cockin, *Edith Craig (1869–1947): Dramatic Lives* (London and Washington: Cassell, 1998), pp. 7–8.

24 Gail Marshall argues that 'small though the alterations made to the 1908 text may seem individually, the number of them is so great that their cumulative effect, along with the editors' adherence to a more strictly chronological narrative, represents a substantial re-writing of Terry's story'. Nevertheless, Edith Craig and Christopher St John's treatment of Terry's text is, on the whole, more discreet and respectful than Edward Gordon Craig's aggressive remodelling of Terry's life. See Gail Marshall, *Actresses on the Victorian Stage: Feminine Performance and the Galatea Myth* (Cambridge: Cambridge University Press, 1998), p. 184.

25 See, for example, Edward Gordon Craig, *Henry Irving* (London: J. M. Dent and Sons, Ltd., 1930), p. 10.

26 On Gordon Craig's intellectual relationship with his father's work, see Christopher Innes, *Edward Gordon Craig* (Cambridge: Cambridge University Press, 1983), pp. 27–8.

27 King, *Henry Irving's Waterloo*, p. 213.

28 Quoted in Cockin, *Edith Craig*, p. 36.

29 Innes, *Edward Gordon Craig*, p. 1.

30 Robert Smallwood, 'Director's Shakespeare', in Jonathan Bate and Russell Jackson, eds., *Shakespeare: An Illustrated Stage History* (Oxford: Oxford University Press, 1996), pp. 176–96.

12

Shakespeare in the company of boys

Kate Chedgzoy

In palaces and on battlefields, in woods, on remote hillsides and in the streets of London, boys swarm through Shakespeare's plays just as they thronged the public and private spaces of early modern England. From the blushing page who accompanies Bardolph (*2 Henry IV* 2.2) to the 'youthful parcel / Of noble bachelors' arrayed for Helena to choose from, dismissed as beardless boys by Lafeu (*All's Well That Ends Well* 2.3.49–50); from Constance's lament for her 'absent child' (*King John* 3.4.93) to the 'very pretty boy' admired for tearing a butterfly apart with his teeth (*Coriolanus* 1.3.54–5), boys in Shakespeare's plays inhabit a wide range of social and dramatic roles. Revealing that masculinity and youth could intersect in diverse ways in early modern culture, Shakespeare's boys are variously associated with incipient sexuality, play, work, schooling and violence. They are contested objects of desire, devoted servants, singers and messengers.

The history of childhood has often been seen as close kin to the history of the family. But Shakespearean boys, present in families and workplaces, in domestic locations and in the public realm, show that the geographies of childhood and youth extended beyond the home. In particular, the theatre, as a public site where boys played an active and distinctive role, was a cultural space that enabled fantasies and anxieties about boys and their places in the family and in the wider world to be played out. Examining a corpus of modern novels for young readers which take the Shakespearean theatre as the scene for boys' journeys towards adulthood, this chapter traces some of the legacies of those sites of fantasy and considers their implications for the continuing cultural work of reimagining boyhood.

I

The early modern boy is an analytically significant figure for any study of childhood in history, for he offers the chance to explore and test the often labile boundaries between childhood and the following life-stage.

The term 'boy' in Shakespeare's England was almost always used to describe a male youth aged between ten and eighteen, and with a few possibly younger exceptions (most strikingly Mamillius), most of the boys who appear in Shakespeare's plays fall into this age band.[1] Yet as the Shakespearean examples with which I began make plain, this span of years did not constitute a single, coherent age group for early modern society. Rather, it embraces the blurred overlapping of the latter years of childhood with the first phase of youth, understood as a transitional time of apprenticeship to adulthood. Because of this liminal nature, older boyhood and youth were, as Lucy Munro demonstrated in chapter 6, seen as potentially dangerously unstable, prone to 'getting wenches with child, wronging the ancientry, stealing, fighting' (*The Winter's Tale* 3.3.60–1). But this phase could also be perceived as a time of burgeoning potential and hope for the young man's future.

This time of as yet unachieved manhood was also associated with gender liminality. As boys made their journey away from the female-dominated realm of early childhood to adult masculinity, they could be seen as still partaking of femininity, as Rosalind/Ganymede's derisive remark that 'boys and women for the most part are cattle of this colour' (*As You Like It* 3.2.571) highlights. Indeed, in the Shakespearean context the term 'boy' frequently brings together age and gender, when it is used to denote the young male actors who performed female roles.[2] Women and children (of either gender) occupied a space of relative disempowerment compared with adult men in early modern society, and the category 'boy' is also one that signals status, denoting subordination to adult male authority and a lack of autonomy. Unlike women and girls, however, boys could at least hope that their progress through the masculine life cycle would enable them in time to accede to a position of masculine independence and authority. The prospect of change over time in an individual life – of growth to manhood – is thus of formative significance in shaping the meanings and experience of boyhood.

Gender and life-stage remain intricately intertwined in the production of the meanings of boyhood. The influential masculinity theorist Bob Connell places the contemporary upsurge of 'concern with questions about boys' in the context of the critical reevaluation of masculinity prompted by feminism.[3] In the light of changing perceptions of masculinity, the centuries-old association of adolescent boys with relatively ungoverned behaviour has been newly problematized. Although some of the attributes associated with boyhood in the early modern period are still in play, a crucial difference is that contemporary parents, educators and commentators lack the Renaissance's confidence – illustrated, in this volume, in A. J. Piesse's investigation of early modern pedagogies – that it knew how these boys should be formed and disciplined in order to turn them into acceptable adult men.[4]

This chapter examines a group of novels for young readers which employ an early modern setting to test and model a range of ways in which late modern boys can become men, in a context in which the relations between boys, literacy and their social behaviour in the transition from childhood to adulthood have become matters of considerable concern. In this they are typical of much modern children's literature, which is often didactic not in the traditional sense of seeking to impart particular doctrines or values, but in terms of taking upon itself the responsibility of fostering the development of emotional literacy and social competence on the part of its readers. Many of them show signs of the tendency noted by the children's literature critic John Stephens in recent fiction for pre-adult readers to engage with anxieties about boyhood, and with uncertainties about how boys should be treated, educated and represented, by diversifying the kinds of youthful masculinity depicted.[5] Combining an exotic setting, a suspenseful narrative and pleasurable identification with a complex but adventurous male protagonist (who is often also the first-person narrator), and asking narrator and reader to discriminate between both positive and negative adult male role models, these texts are faithful to the tradition of children's Shakespeares outlined by Naomi J. Miller in this volume in providing a blend of entertainment and instruction.

It is frequently noted that from the Lambs' *Tales from Shakespeare* (1807) onwards, adaptations of Shakespeare for children have addressed themselves in particular to girls.[6] But these recent fictive appropriations are overtly concerned with boyhood, and their settings, themes, characterization and marketing all appear to indicate that the implied reader is a boy. Girls may certainly read and enjoy the novels, but they will be reading against the grain, for as Erica Hateley argues, these fictions are thematically and structurally predicated on the depiction of Shakespeare as an idealized father figure for sons, a 'symbolic parent-instructor for the *masculine* reader'.[7]

II

Since the mid-twentieth century, enough novels have taken the Shakespearean theatre as their setting and a boy actor as their protagonist to constitute a subgenre of historical fiction. These range from Geoffrey

Trease's *Cue for Treason* (1940), via Marchette Chute's *The Wonderful Winter* (1954), and Antonia Forest's paired novels *The Player's Boy* (1970) and *The Players and the Rebels* (1971), to a recent flurry of works including Pamela Melnikoff's *Plots and Players* (1988), *On a Scaffold High* (1993) by Gweneth Lilly, Susan Cooper's *King of Shadows* (1999), Lynn Kositsky's *A Question of Will* (2000), in which a time-travelling girl is mistaken for a boy actor, and Rosemary Linnell's *Robin Babb, Actor's Apprentice* (2003). The subgenre is evidently considered sufficiently appealing to young readers for two series to be under way in the expanding children's books market at the turn of the century: Gary Blackwood's novels about Widge, *The Shakespeare Stealer* (1998), *Shakespeare's Scribe* (2000), and *Shakespeare's Spy* (2003), and J. B. Cheaney's Richard Malory books, *The Playmaker* (2000), and *The True Prince* (2002).[8]

Typically in these fictions an isolated and deracinated, often orphaned, boy in his early teens makes his way to London from the countryside (a plausible enough journey, given the huge scale of rural migration into London in the early modern period), and finds a home and job with Shakespeare's theatre company. This environment offers him emotional and material sustenance, as well as the opportunity to discover a talent for acting – which in turn provides a site for testing and discovering the emergent adolescent male self. Frequently, the young actor also has to use his newly acquired theatrical skills to accomplish a mission of some personal and political danger, entailing secrecy, performance and disguise: the Elizabethan England in which all these novels are set is a world of plots, mistaken identity, religious persecution and treason, in which the theatre is implicated as a thoroughly political phenomenon. Yet it is also a world worth fighting for: the plots and treachery must be opposed to safeguard the golden worlds of masculine comradeship and heroic achievement represented both by the Shakespearean theatre and by Elizabeth's reign as a unique moment in time.[9] The quests for information and tests of loyalty, courage and integrity with which the protagonists are frequently charged endow the novels with a strong element of the historical adventure story, so that although the world of the theatre appears initially as a haven, it is also a place of risk. Similarly, Elizabethan London is ambivalently presented, both as a locus of creative energy and openness to strangers, and as a dirty, dangerous place – plague, stinking streets and the display of decapitated heads on London Bridge are invariably mentioned. Provincial tours feature in several of the novels, varying the settings within the series fictions but also ensuring that

England as a nation is brought under the sign of the cultural and political power iconically represented by the Elizabethan Shakespeare.

The world of these fictions is poised between a nostalgic evocation of a past golden age, and an implicit sense of the deficiencies of the past in comparison with the reader's present. This ambivalence is voiced most powerfully in Cooper's *King of Shadows*, discussed in detail below, which as a time-travel novel engages directly with the tensions between past and present. Cooper's novel is also unusual with regard to the nature of the journey undertaken by its protagonist, who traverses the Atlantic and crosses four centuries, but once arrived in Shakespeare's London remains staunchly in Southwark.[10] The historical setting of the novels thus combines an instructive celebration of the English past with the theatre's distinctive capacity to sustain narratives of the development of self through language, performance and social interaction.

Neither adaptations nor appropriations of individual Shakespearean dramas, nevertheless in their themes and verbal textures these fictions play with dramatic situations, characters and language to weave intertextual relationships with multiple Shakespearean pre-texts. In each novel the performance of one or more Shakespeare plays, in which the protagonist plays a significant role, is important both in the unfolding of the plot and in facilitating the protagonist's emotional, social and personal learning and development, as boy and as actor. In *The Playmaker*, for instance, the narrator Richard Malory's performance as Constance in *King John* enables him to make a breakthrough in his hitherto stuttering development as an actor. More important, it prompts a powerful emotional coming to terms with the death of his mother and his abandonment of his sister Susanna when he ran off to London to seek both his fortune and his long-lost father. Identifying with the grieving mother Constance across differences of age, gender and familial status, Richard learns something about himself, his craft and his female relatives by performing an emotion that dissolves the gap between theatre and life, in the context of the novel's thoroughly modern conceptualization of acting.

The crucial roles performed by the protagonists of these novels are, as in this example, inevitably female ones, and these texts have a complex relationship with the possibilities for playing with gender thus opened up. *Cue for Treason* and *The Shakespeare Stealer* meditate on the relations between the gender of the actor and of the role by featuring an exceptionally talented performer of female roles, who is eventually unmasked as a girl. They combine an implication that the correspondence of gender with role facilitates the accuracy of the performance with an endorsement of the young actress's exceptional theatrical skill. Elsewhere, the boy actor can identify with his role because of commonalities of experience that transcend the difference of gender – having worked with Shakespeare on the script of *All's Well That Ends Well*, Widge comes to feel 'a kind of kinship' with Helena, a role he desperately wants to play, because of similarities in their personal histories.[11] Or, like Richard Malory as Constance, he finds that the experience of playing a female role extends and enriches his sense of what is possible for him as a young man.

Characteristically, then, these novels use the convention of cross-gendered performance on the Renaissance stage to contribute to the production of an enhanced version of postfeminist heterosexual masculinity. They deemphasize the boy actor's potential to explore the instabilities of gender in formation by insisting on the purely conventional nature of boys' performances of female parts. The association of boy actors with gender instability has generated much recent academic discussion of the erotic dynamics of their cross-gender, cross-age performances. Such playful, knowing eroticism as scholars have attributed to many of the roles and scripts associated with boy actors would sit uneasily in novels aimed mainly at preteen readers; nor are romance and sexuality particularly frequent themes in novels aimed at boys of this age group, whatever their setting. Moreover, as Douglas Lanier points out, even in adult fictions where Shakespeare appears as a character, he almost invariably 'is identified with and functions as a mainstream icon for heteronormative sexuality'.[12] With a few exceptions – notably Trease's *Cue for Treason* (where a wholesomely Shakespearean romance is allowed to blossom between the hero, Peter, and his acting rival Kit, eventually revealed as a young woman disguised as a boy player to escape a coerced marriage), and Cooper's *King of Shadows* (of which more below) – these novels pass in silence over the question of the eroticization of the boy player, whether as subject or object of desire.

Yet if direct treatment of potentially troubling aspects of the formation of adolescent masculinity is eschewed, it is nonetheless clear that the world of the boy actor does not merely provide an appealing setting for an adventure novel that facilitates the young heroes' free movement through diverse social spaces in London. The boy actor's commitment to performance and self-transformation holds deeper significance in these novels. Fictions of the Shakespearean boy actor's life both expose the extent to which masculinity and femininity alike may be understood as social performances subject to constant reenactment, rehearsal and development and reveal the unique value – developmental and emotional, but also in terms of the pure intrinsic pleasure of play – of performance as that which does not merely reiterate a particular social self, but offers the temporary provisional opportunity to inhabit another self in the act of pretending to be someone else, acting a theatrical role, and thus expands the performer's sense of the possibilities of selfhood.

It is as a facilitator of the social and theatrical performance of selfhood that Shakespeare figures most powerfully in these novels, playing an invariably benign and enabling role in relation to the young hero's journey towards the acceptable form of adult masculinity modelled by the playwright, which forms the central dynamic of the plot. Where the real fathers of the boy protagonists are absent, dead, unknown or untrustworthy, Shakespeare stands in the place of an ideally nurturing father figure, or perhaps a good uncle,[13] giving the novels a strong flavour of the family romance.[14] Yet in these fictions where boys interact with adult men in a homosocial environment detached from the family, such kinship terms are only obliquely and problematically appropriate. Boys in these works are liminal figures, dislocated from the conventional family and forced to negotiate the passage from childhood to adulthood in isolated and traumatic circumstances. These novels thus play variations on the themes of lost children and fractured families that recur in Shakespeare's late romances. But whereas the lost daughters of *Pericles* and *The Winter's Tale* and the lost sons of *Cymbeline* and *The Tempest* are safely restored to their families of origin, in these postmodern fictions of Shakespearean surrogate sonhood, the importance of the heterosexual family as a site where boyhood and the transition from childhood to adult status are experienced and negotiated is reconfigured. With the exception of Cheaney's novels, where the warmly affectionate and quasi-maternal atmosphere of Richard Malory's lodgings with the Condell family is evoked, these lost boys are offered respite and succour by the predominantly homosocial environment of the theatre, which in providing them with quasi-paternal love and care replaces the family. In some ways, then, these fictions of lost and lonely boys are symptomatic of a larger trend in children's literature diagnosed by James Holt McGavran, namely the articulation of a homophobic, patriarchal affection for 'texts like *Peter Pan* and *Huckleberry Finn* that give simultaneous narrative space . . . to the conflicting demands of homeless boyhood, with its autoerotic and homoerotic tendences, and of . . . domesticity'.[15] The idealized all-male community of the Shakespearean theatre offers a provisional, precarious way of reconciling these conflicting demands for the lonely boys who take refuge in it.

The texts I discuss here show that the achievement and maintenance of alternative kinds of masculinity can be an uneven, contested, painful process. Shakespeare is invoked as an idealized guide and companion on the boy's 'journey from adolescent to adult',[16] but the complexities and ambivalences of his own position – a man whose family have been abandoned in the provinces while he pursues his uncertain ambitions in London – mean that this journey is not presented as unproblematic. Preoccupied with the fashioning of the young male protagonists' subjectivities (and, through comparison and contrast, those of the other young men around them, who tend to model a range of ways of being male and youthful), these novels seek to construct versions of young male selves acceptable to boys, parents and educators in a broadly postfeminist context, while diminishing the appeal of nonfeminist versions of hegemonic masculinity by marginalizing them or endowing them with negative connotations. In Blackwood's novels, for example, machismo is most closely associated with the violent and unreliable figure of Jamie Redshaw, who claims to be the long-lost father of the apparently orphaned protagonist Widge. This strategy enables Blackwood to acknowledge the appeal of a macho identity, while distancing and critiquing it: Redshaw's lack of integrity and glamorization of brawling and drunkenness are harshly judged by the adult actors Widge admires so much, and whom he aspires to resemble. And among these actors the figure of Shakespeare above all serves to embody a very different, more positive model of adult masculinity. The emotional complexities attendant on the relationships between Shakespeare and the boy actors inspired by him are most richly explored in Cooper's *King of Shadows*, the subject of the next section.

III

Nat Field, the protagonist of *King of Shadows*, temporarily inhabits a world of boys as a member for one summer of an all-male theatre company visiting London in 1999 to perform in the newly rebuilt Globe theatre. A single-sex institution with elaborate rules, divorced from families and the wider social world, the Company of Boys is reminiscent of the enclosed environments of the traditional school story.[17] Yet it is also, according to 'bossman' Arby, 'a family, a big family' – a substitute for the traditional family as well as an alternative to it.[18] As Julie Sanders points out, this theatrical family has a compensatory quality for the novel's adolescent protagonist, whose family has been destroyed by his mother's death from cancer and his father's subsequent grief-stricken suicide.[19]

The ideally nurturing and protecting quality of the Company of Boys is foregrounded in the novel's opening pages, in the playing of a trust game which acts out Nat's personal history. Playing the game 'flick[s Nat] back to being a very little boy', reminding him of the shadowy, long-lost figure of his mother, and of 'how safe she made [him] feel' (p. 3). When another player allows him to drop to the floor – 'not saved, but still falling' – the traumatic betrayal of Nat's trust in his father by the latter's suicide is replayed. But this boy is promptly expelled from the group, reaffirming the Company of Boys as a surrogate family that will prove safer and more reliable for Nat than his birth family.

Yet Nat's meditation on the theatre as a refuge for a damaged boy is immediately countered by the invocation, in a conversation between several of the young actors, of the common cultural fantasy of theatre as a dangerous place, where boys in particular are at risk of specifically sexual kinds of damage. Gil Warmun counters Eric's mother's belief that 'theatre's *dangerous*' with the dubious reassurance that Eric's red hair saves him from being a 'beautiful little boy' vulnerable to 'nasty molesters' (p. 11). In view of Gil's parodic echoing of Arby's assertion that 'This company is a family! ... Families only have one set of parents!' (p. 11), the fact that it is a mother who expresses this anxiety about the dangers of the homosocial world of the theatre is salient. For women are marginalized in this novel populated by motherless boys being raised by surrogate fathers and gangs of substitute brothers. The Company of Boys, in practice, does not have only 'one set of parents', but one parent, and that one a father, Arby. His partner Julia never speaks, is only mentioned a couple of times, and indeed seems to be in the novel solely for the purpose of protecting Arby from the taint of homosexuality. To this extent, *King of Shadows* differs from most of the other novels of boy actors, in which women appear in a number of emotionally, thematically and narratively significant roles: as mothers and sisters of company members, as important friends and co-conspirators for the protagonist, and as hopeful young actors, disguised as boys in the pursuit of a theatrical ambition they share with the protagonist.

In its focus on homosocial relationships among men and boys, its near-excision of women, and its anxiety about the homoerotic, *King of Shadows* exemplifies McGavran's diagnosis of a particular kind of female-authored novel about boys as 'strangely sexless yet strenuously gendered texts'.[20] In its desexualization of theatre – which contrasts strikingly, in the

Renaissance aspect of the fiction, with the early modern antitheatrical discourse of the theatre as a lubricious and frequently sodomitical site[21] – the novel seeks to keep the concerns expressed by Eric's mother at bay. The marginalization of female figures supports this, by normalizing the predominant homosocial interactions between boys and men. Cooper thus invokes modern anxieties about the theatre as a transgressively sexualized location in order to dispel them. Yet the relationship between Shakespeare and Nat which unfolds later in the novel will prove to be precariously evocative of early modern versions of the homoerotic anxieties that Cooper is at pains to disavow in the contemporary passages of the novel.

The crucial link between the 1999 teenager Nat Field and William Shakespeare in 1599 is provided by twin productions of *A Midsummer Night's Dream*, in both of which Nat plays Puck. As the Company of Boys begins rehearsing its modern production in the Globe, a playful father-son dynamic starts to emerge between Nat and the older boy, Gil, who plays Oberon. When Gil, in role as Oberon, teases Nat about uttering Shakespeare's lines in his North Carolina accent, Nat camply returns the joke by calling Gil '"Poppa!" . . . in a high falsetto' and flinging his arms round Gil's waist (p. 17). Later, Gil cups Nat's head with his hand, summoning up the ghostly body-memory of Nat's dead father, who used the same affectionate gesture: 'I got goosebumps from the feel of it' (p. 24). Aware of the connections and disjunctions between the performance and his own life, Nat slips in and out of role, sometimes speaking as Puck of 'my master Oberon' (p. 24) and sometimes in his own persona. Saying Puck's line 'Naught shall go ill' brings Nat to a traumatic realization of the faultlines between Shakespearean art and late twentieth-century reality: '*All shall be well.* I knew as I said it that it was a lie, Shakespeare's lie, because I knew from my own life that all does not go well, but that terrible things happen to people and cannot be put right, by magic flower-juice or by anything else in this world' (p. 27). This moment of traumatic recognition widens the faultlines between past and present a little, preparing the way for Nat to slip through a crack in time and back to the sixteenth century. There he will find that sometimes terrible things can be, if not actually put right, at least averted; and that healing and recovery from those terrible things that could not be prevented is also possible. As Richard Burt notes in chapter 14 of this volume, time-travel narratives 'link Shakespeare's transmission through various past and present media to the transition from child to adulthood':[22] in *King of Shadows* Nat's time-travelling encounter with

Shakespeare is precisely what will enable him to continue to grow towards adulthood.

Shakespeare echoes the novel's opening insistence on the theatre as surrogate family when he kindly tells Nat, who is being bullied by another boy actor, 'This company is a family, close and closeted' (p. 69). The remark is clearly intended to console Nat with the knowledge that his misery is known and observed, but also carries the implication that families are less than ideal places, in which power inequalities and cruelties may lurk. The use of the term 'closeted' here, which in Shakespeare's time evoked a kind of privacy unobtainable in the theatre, and in ours implies repressive secrecy about sexuality, disconcertingly highlights the proximity of dynamics and spaces which the novel is generally at pains to keep apart. The phrase may also, for expert readers of the novel, summon up the 'closet' scene in *Hamlet*, a scene preoccupied with family secrets, confrontations and death in a play that haunts Cooper's novel without ever taking centre stage as one of its Shakespearean intertexts. Shakespeare's kindness releases Nat's 'terrible buried sorrow' (p. 70) in unstoppable tears, and the boy ends up confessing the source of his grief: his father's choice to follow his mother into death, rather than to stay alive and love his son. By way of reciprocation and consolation, Shakespeare tells Nat about the death of his son Hamnet, offering the fatalistic analysis that 'Some things are beyond our command . . . Men will destroy much for love, even the lives of their children, even their own lives' (p. 72).

The exchange concludes with Shakespeare offering to copy out a poem for Nat which, it is implied, will help him to come to an accommodation with his losses, and which he is to 'read and remember. *Remember*' (p. 72). Echoing Hamlet's self-exhortation to remember and memorialize his own dead father, this emphasis on remembering counteracts Nat's desire to forget. Theatre, for Nat, is above all a way to escape through fantasy and play the painful realities of his life; it is a means to forgetting. Evading his fellow actors' concerned questions about his parents, he wonders, 'If you have to answer questions every time, how are you ever going to learn to forget?' (p. 12). He wants quite literally to lose himself in his role – he looks forward to belonging to the Company of Boys and performing in London because 'I wouldn't be Nat there, I would be Puck' (p. 12). The annihilation of Nat in his identification with Puck is powerfully seductive because of what Nat perceives as the character's invulnerability, for as Shakespeare himself points out to Nat, Puck 'has no heart' and no ability to '*feel*, like you or me' (p. 123). But by playing Oberon to Nat's Puck,

Shakespeare will teach him not to forget, but to remember. Shakespeare, bereaved of a son, acts as a temporary substitute father figure for Nat, and in doing so gives back to Nat the memory of his real-life poet father who lives on through the poems that Nat will now read for the first time (p. 175), inspired to do so by Shakespeare's gift to him of the capacity to understand the sonnets as documents of love, loss and endurance that can help him make sense of his own life: '*So long as men can breathe or eyes can see, / So long lives this, and this gives life to thee*' (p. 174).

Nat's recovery of a memory of his father that is not traumatically associated with his suicide is facilitated by a tiny, private performance, when Shakespeare comes to him one night, kneels at his bedside, and reads aloud Sonnet 116 ('Let me not to the marriage of true minds / Admit impediments'). In this scene Cooper appears to evoke the homoerotic potential of the relationship between Nat and Shakespeare, only in order to repudiate it. As I argued in *Shakespeare's Queer Children* (1996), this poem is central to the queer vision of Shakespeare that Oscar Wilde articulated in his novella *The Portrait of Mr W. H.* (1889), which imagines a homoerotic 'marriage of true minds' binding the playwright to boy actor Willie Hughes, a union of which such great female Shakespearean roles as Beatrice, Juliet, Ophelia and Rosalind are the offspring.[23] In gay genre fiction this candlelit poetic encounter in the boy's bedroom would undoubtedly have an erotic conclusion, but in this young adult novel Shakespeare merely hands Nat the poem, kisses him on the forehead, and goes: 'The shadows flickered away with him, and left the room dark' (p. 102).

Cooper's use of Sonnet 116 focuses not on the marriage metaphor central to Wilde's deployment of the poem in *The Portrait of Mr W. H.*, but on the poem's evocation of the endurance of love over time, beyond death. Shakespeare interprets it to Nat, saying, 'I do know thy father's love for thee did not die with him, nor thine for him . . . Love is love. An ever-fixed mark. Remember that, and try to be comforted' (p. 102). The poem itself becomes a site of memory, reminding Nat after he returns to his life in 1999 of his encounter with Shakespeare, and what he has learnt from it. Nat loses the 'stiff, curling paper' (p. 102) on which Shakespeare copied out the poem for him, just as he loses Shakespeare himself, in what at first threatens to be an agonizing recapitulation of the loss of his father. However, in losing the paper but finding the words of the poem in a modern edition of Shakespeare, he comes to realize, in a scenario that offers a concrete metaphor for the larger lesson he learns from his experiences in 1599, that the loss of a beloved object can be endured, and the memory of it can in turn offer enduring consolation.[24]

Nat, player of Puck and 'aerial sprite', has carefully made clear that he 'never fancied the lovey-dovey parts' (p. 82). So the role that will be the child of his brief theatrical union with Shakespeare will be androgynous Ariel, who shares with Puck not only his uncanniness – the term 'sprite' is insistently used to connect Ariel, Puck and Nat – but also his involvement in a master-servant relationship with his beloved creator. As a performer in *A Midsummer Night's Dream*, Nat is brought into close theatrical proximity with another orphaned boy transported to Shakespearean England from a distant colonial location, the Indian child whom he, intriguingly, identifies as a servant. Nat's characterization of the boy as a servant highlights both the fact that the dividing lines between children and servants as status groups were far from clear or stable in early modern England, and the disconcerting presence of an erotics of domination behind Puck/Nat's eager embrace of Oberon/Shakespeare as his master. Mario DiGangi has richly explored 'the homoerotic potentiality within the master-servant power structure',[25] but his focus on the homoeroticism of master-servant relations within the context of satirical comedy did not address age differences as a factor in this power structure. Yet age difference has of course been key to the history of male homosexuality in the West for many centuries; and its increasingly controversial significance in our own time is what makes Cooper's handling of the master-servant theme within the strenuously desexualized relationship between Nat and Shakespeare so remarkable. Likewise, Cooper's repeated evocation and disavowal of the homoerotic associations of theatre form an intriguing and unsettling frame for her handling of the love between Nat and Shakespeare.

These charged textual moments must, I think, be read as symptoms of a larger cultural discomfort with the idea of a loving relationship between man and boy which is not straightforwardly reducible to that between father and son. Simultaneously complicating the gender politics of this union between playwright and boy actor and disembodying it, the substitution of Ariel for Juliet, Rosalind et al. offers an ostensibly desexualized, but in effect complexly homoerotic recasting of Wilde's appropriation of Shakespeare's sonnets.

'The shadows flickered away with him, and left the room dark' (p. 102). The king of shadows of the novel's title is both Shakespeare, as this moment makes plain, and Oberon, designated thus by his Puck (3.2.348). The shadows themselves are simultaneously the fairy subjects of Oberon's kingdom and the actors apologetically foregrounded by Puck's Epilogue: 'If we shadows have offended / Think but this, and all is mended'. Shadows, of course, are evocative, in Shakespeare's plays as in English literary culture more generally, of mortality, as Macbeth's metaphor of the actor as shadow reminds us: 'Life's but a walking shadow, a poor player / That struts and frets his hour upon the stage / And then is heard no more' (5.5.23–5). Although Puck's assurance that 'Naught shall go ill ... all shall be well' (3.3.46–7) was a source of distress to Nat early in the novel, marked as he was by the shadows of mortality cast by his parents' deaths, by its end he finds that something has indeed been mended by his encounter with the king of shadows.

The emotional and dramatic climax of the plot comes with the production of *A Midsummer Night's Dream* in which Nat plays Puck, proud servant to his master Shakespeare's Oberon. For Nat, Shakespeare as Oberon is 'King of Fairyland and of the whole world, as far as I was concerned ... he had an eerie authority that made me, as Puck, totally his devoted servant' – while as Nat, the delight of service to such a charismatic master 'put spring into my cartwheeling exit' (p. 120). The homoerotic potential of this theatrical master-servant relationship is thus aligned with the uncanniness of fairyland, distancing it safely from Nat's pleasure in his filial intimacy with Shakespeare. Voicing Puck's Epilogue at the end of this magical production, Nat comes to the realization that in the theatre he need not seek solace only in the form of self-cancellation, but that by playing others he, like Robin Goodfellow, can 'restore amends' and achieve the recuperation of love and loss. Nat ends the novel mourning the loss of Shakespeare, that painful reiteration of the first loss of his father, but he also learns that by playing Ariel, the role Shakespeare wrote as a memorial to his 'aerial sprite' (p. 180), he can, for a while at least, restore lost fathers and lonely boys to each other, and thereby free both himself and Shakespeare from grief. *King of Shadows* uses a love story to redeem loss, a narrative strategy often employed in children's fiction.[26] But that redemption remains haunted by the shadowy ambiguities attendant on the nature of the love between the man and the boy at the heart of the story. In *King of Shadows* the fiction of the Shakespearean theatre company as surrogate family combines with the emotional investment of Western culture in the fantasy of Shakespeare himself as idealized father figure to produce an uneasy meditation on the repressions and exclusions of gender and sexuality that have to be performed in order to sustain those fantasies.

IV

Of all the novels considered here, *King of Shadows* is the most complex, ambitious and open in its use of Shakespeare's iconic image and works to explore the performance of boyhood, and the relationships between boys and the men who are both responsible for such love, care and education as they receive, and provide the models of the adult masculinity that lies ahead of them. Although none of the other books I have considered is as bold or imaginative in its reimagining of Shakespearean boyhood, each of them does recognize the variety and complexity of the social and cultural demands placed on boys faced with the task of making sense of their changing masculinity as they move through the space between childhood and adulthood. And each employs the Shakespearean theatre as a site that can do justice to that complexity, acknowledging that there may be as many different ways of performing masculinity as there are actors – boys and men – taking up their places on that stage. At the end of *Shakespeare's Scribe*, it is through acting the role of Helena in *All's Well That Ends Well* that Widge is able to arrive at an accommodation with his precarious sense of self, and his place in the theatre company. Mr Armin congratulates him, remarking, '[W]hen an actor truly shines in a role for the first time, we say that he's found himself. Well, it seems to me that you've found yourself.'[27] The player's self that Widge has found exists in the movement between boy actor and role; in the processes of identification and differentiation that enable Widge to recognize the ways in which he is and is not Helena. It is perhaps in this comprehension of the mobility and multifacetedness of masculinity and selfhood that these readable, enjoyable books for boys are most productively Shakespearean.

NOTES

1 Paul Griffiths, *Youth and Authority: Formative Experiences in England 1560–1640* (Oxford: Clarendon Press, 1996), p. 24.

2 Edel Lamb, *The Early Modern Children's Playing Companies: Childhood, Theatre and Identity, 1599–1613* (PhD thesis, Queen's University Belfast, 2005), pp. 37–8.

3 R. W. Connell, *The Men and the Boys* (Berkeley: University of California Press, 2001), p. 3.

4 Chris Haywood and Mairtin Mac an Ghaill, 'Schooling Masculinities', in Mac an Ghaill, ed., *Understanding Masculinities* (Buckingham: Open University Press, 1996).

5 John Stephens, ed., *Ways of Being Male: Representing Masculinities in Children's Literature and Film* (New York: Routledge, 2002), preface, pp. ix–xiv (p. ix).

6 Jean I. Marsden, 'Shakespeare for Girls: Mary Lamb and *Tales from Shakespeare*', *Children's Literature* 17 (1989), 47–63.

7 Erica Hateley, 'Gary Blackwood's *Shakespeare* Trilogy: Cultural Literacy and Gendered Adolescent Subjectivity', unpublished paper, p. 2. I am grateful to Dr Hateley for sharing her work in progress with me.

8 For reflections on the writing of these recent fictions, see the chapters by Gary Blackwood and J. B. Cheaney in Naomi J. Miller, ed., *Reimagining Shakespeare for Children and Young Adults* (New York: Routledge, 2003).

9 Compare the fictions, mainly aimed at adult readers, in which Shakespeare appears as a character discussed in Michael Dobson and Nicola Watson, *England's Elizabeth: An Afterlife in Fame and Fantasy* (Oxford: Oxford University Press, 2002), pp. 121–38.

10 Emphasizing American Nat's crosscultural journeying, Erica Hateley sees the novel as enacting a 'postcolonial annexing of Shakespeare' in her 'Shakespeare as National Discourse in Contemporary Children's Literature', *Papers: Explorations into Children's Literature* 13:1 (2003), 11–24 (22).

11 Gary Blackwood, *Shakespeare's Scribe* (New York: Dutton's Children's Books, 2000), p. 255.

12 Douglas Lanier, 'Shakespeare™: Myth and Biography', in Robert Shaughnessy, ed., *The Cambridge Companion to Shakespeare and Popular Culture* (Cambridge: Cambridge University Press, 2007).

13 Pat Pinsent, '"Not for an Age, but for All Time": The Depiction of Shakespeare in a Selection of Children's Fiction', *New Review of Children's Literature and Librarianship* 10:2 (2004), 115–26 (115).

14 Freud's term for the widespread childhood fantasy in which the child replaces unsatisfactory parentage with an idealized version. For a discussion of its Shakespearean resonances, see my *Shakespeare's Queer Children: Sexual Politics and Contemporary Culture* (Manchester: Manchester University Press, 1996).

15 James Holt McGavran, 'Wordsworth, Lost Boys, and Romantic Hom(e) ophobia', in McGavran, ed., *Literature and the Child: Romantic Continuations, Postmodern Contestations* (Iowa City: University of Iowa Press, 1999), pp. 130–1.

16 Hateley, 'Blackwood's *Shakespeare* Trilogy', p. 11.

17 See, for example, Jeffery Richards, *Happiest Days: The Public Schools in English Fiction* (Manchester: Manchester University Press, 1988).

18 Susan Cooper, *King of Shadows* (London: Puffin Books, 2000), pp. 1–2. Subsequent citations are to this edition and appear in parentheses.

19 Julie Sanders, *Novel Shakespeares: Twentieth-Century Women Novelists and Appropriation* (Manchester: Manchester University Press, 2001), p. 93.

20 James Holt McGavran, 'Wordsworth', p. 137.

21 Lamb, *Early Modern Children's Playing Companies*, pp. 90–4.

22 Richard Burt, Chapter 14, 'Shakespeare (')tween media and markets in the 1990s and beyond', pp. 218–32.
23 Chedgzoy, *Shakespeare's Queer Children*, pp. 160–1.
24 My thinking about this issue is indebted to Peter Sacks, *The English Elegy: Studies in the Genre from Spenser to Yeats* (Baltimore: Johns Hopkins University Press, 1985).
25 Mario DiGangi, *The Homoerotics of Early Modern Drama* (Cambridge: Cambridge University Press, 1997), pp. 64–99.
26 Michael Rustin and Margaret Rustin, *Narratives of Love and Loss: Studies in Modern Children's Fiction*, 2nd edn (London: Karnac Books, 2001).
27 Blackwood, *Shakespeare's Scribe*, p. 265.

13

Dream children: staging and screening childhood in A Midsummer Night's Dream

Susanne Greenhalgh

What does it mean for a child to act or for an audience to watch that performance? Many attempts to answer these questions have focused on the child performers of the early modern stage, the 'play-boys' of the adult companies, with all their enticing ambiguities of sexuality and gender, or the highly schooled performers of the children's companies, with their repertoire dominated by comedy and satire. Discussion of the boy players in the adult companies has tended to alternate between their possible impact on the nature of the female roles written for them, and attention to their erotic effect when playing those roles. However, as Lucy Munro argues in chapter 6, juvenile acting out of masculine political authority by the children's companies could take on a subversive force precisely by means of the distance between the young actors' physicality and cultural status and the dramatic roles they played. If the Shakespearean roles created for boys to play only rarely made use of such sharp, satirical disjunctions between the age of the actor and the nature of the part, the child characters and their performers are more than incidental insertions into the narrative, or sentimentalized supernumeraries to the main action. The Shakespearean child has often been viewed as archetypal 'innocent victim', on the assumption that the meanings of childhood are themselves stable, and thus available as a mode of unproblematic symbolization.[1] However, as Carolyn Steedman points out, by the nineteenth century children on stage also embodied the question of how childhood itself was to be seen, 'literally and figuratively'.[2] It is this chapter's contention that attending to child actors of Shakespeare, as well as to their roles, reveals how the shifting constructions of childhood current in different eras have been refracted, and perhaps reformulated, through Shakespearean performance.

Such an approach considers not only the meanings that children have embodied for adult audiences, but how far children have power over their own performances. Some critics have argued that children are intrinsically anomalous and even resistant elements within the illusion-making processes of theatre. With the children's companies primarily in mind, Bert O. States draws on phenomenology to argue that there is a basic mismatch between the child and acting: 'There are permanent quotation marks around the concept of children as "actors", and their performances provocatively "flaunt" their insincerity.' At the same time, child actors are 'naturally' seductive, carrying to perfection 'the titillating potential of a medium that by its very nature inoculates the audience against belief'.[3] Paradoxically, child performance becomes both the quintessence of artificiality and manipulation, and a fulfilment of adult desire to surrender to the pleasures of dramatic illusion.

This is evident in Alan Read's description of a child's first entry into performance as an interplay of seductive and wistful gazes.

> A child of 4 years . . . walks from somewhere off to somewhere on and accustoms herself to being watched. This acclimatization has already begun between the off and the on and first manifests itself in her eyes. They are averted from the habitual assimilations of childhood that links foreground and distance, a visual dexterity that can give the youthful that magical air of insouciance just beyond and out of reach of the adult in a zone of myriad pleasures and fears.[4]

For Read, as for States, the performing child is an icon of adult desire. Although her active gaze back at the audience is acknowledged, 'acclimatization' to performance is understood as an imposition of surveillance (and increasingly self-surveillance) on to the magically insouciant 'visual dexterity' of childhood, a process enacted through the operations of Read's own nostalgic gaze. The complex dynamic by which the performing child is simultaneously gazing subject and object of the gaze is well captured in Pascale Aebischer's account in chapter 11 of the eight-year-old Ellen Terry. While acting Mamillius, she made a peephole in the backcloth in order to watch the actress playing her mother, but when performing the role of Hermione as an adult she herself kept a 'sharp eye' on the child actor – just as Mrs Kean had overseen her. Terry was also urged to create convincing pathos as Arthur in *King John* by recalling her own tears of distress after a hard slap. Such anecdotes insist on the uneasy tension between the performing child's active gaze, desire to learn and potential autonomy, and the constant adult surveillance she attracts – whether by audience or fellow actors. The child's corporeality – its 'childness' – at one and the same time threatens to subvert or destroy dramatic illusion, and tempts adults to shape satisfying representation through that body, by imposing real physical or emotional experience, even to the verge of actual child abuse.

Film adds another layer to these concerns about illusion, desire and the extent to which child performance satisfies or frustrates adult expectation. Children's theatrical performance, in whatever period, is commonly regarded as requiring maturity, discipline and practice, and thus a degree of art if not actual professionalism: child stage actors are often older than they try to appear.[5] From its earliest days, by contrast, film takes and editing made it possible for even infants to take significant roles on screen, their moments of poignant emotion in front of the camera often actually generated by some entirely different scenario, 'real-life' situation, or even the use of twins.[6] This concealment of the illusion-making process significantly complicates the dialectic of 'artful'/'artless' that is often – more or less unconsciously – regarded as the repertoire of the child performer.

Theorizations of the child figure on film echo those of theatre and the visual arts. The child is depicted as 'innocent, as silent, as a site of memory, or as an anterior to rational thought', and childhood as a 'transcendent period of human life', outside society and even history. Ultimately, the child's role in film is to carry the 'burden of signification' for the adult spectator; to act, in Thomas Jousse's phrase, as 'a sheer capability of gazing'.[7] Such arguments are thus not really about children in film at all but rather about how adults project themselves on to and into the position of the child.

As Barbara Hodgdon has argued, however, the 'Shakespearean body on screen' is a form of 'distilled portraiture' that is also a 'socio-aesthetic-historical entity'.[8] When the 'Shakespearean body' screened or staged is that of a child, not only does it raise the questions concerning dramatic illusion already discussed, it inevitably becomes implicated in the complex and evolving discourses of childhood. The idea that natural-appearing performances by children can arise from artifice makes problematic the notion of 'natural' childhood innocence, which, as cultural historians have shown, began to become dominant in Europe from the seventeenth century onwards, and culminated in the still powerful visual icon that Anne Higonnet calls the Romantic Child. Characterized either by costuming in a nostalgic evocation of some form of historical dress, or by association with nature, including animals, the Romantic Child is above all conceived of as innocently nonsexual, though implicitly vulnerable to violation.[9] This concept is also intrinsically theatrical: the social or emotional realities of individual children's lives are disguised, dressed up or altered by the *mise en scènes* in which an idealized childhood is staged.

A Midsummer Night's Dream provides a particularly appropriate text through which to pursue questions of child performance, infused as it is with the imagery of both theatre and childhood. As Samuel Crowl summarizes, the *Dream*

> isn't just child-friendly – it is child-inspired. The text abounds in references to children: winged Cupid painted blind; schoolgirls; waggish boys; and the little changeling boy. Love, imagination, and the creative spirit are all linked with that prelapsarian state we associate with childhood. Dreams are the adult's pipeline back to innocence and delight.[10]

The play's performance history can be charted through the fluctuations in the casting of the roles of Puck and the other fairies, as adults or children, as well as male or female. Since the nineteenth century, the changeling boy, only referred to in the play, has often appeared on stage as a centrally emblematic character, signifying the ways in which different productions have understood childhood and even becoming a play's protagonist in *The Indian Boy* by Rona Munro (RSC 2006).[11] Writers such as Thomas Hood and Charles Lamb stressed the link between the creativity of early childhood, the Romantic concept of imagination, and the 'fairy kingdom' of Shakespeare's *Dream*.[12] In turn, the play, as both literature and theatre, also helped to inspire a nineteenth-century genre of fairy paintings, which presented 'images not only of lost or enchanted childhood, but also of hidden sexuality and retreat into secret, even taboo, sexual worlds and activities of "little people", both fairies and the young'.[13] Despite these darker attributes, the play has also been regarded as especially suited to a child audience, whether in performance or print. From the Lambs' adaptation on, it has often been used as a child's first introduction to Shakespeare. By the beginning of the twentieth century, as Gary Jay Williams concludes from his study of its stage history, its performance, 'whether in an outdoor summer theatre or as a Christmas fairy fantasy', had become a common part of upper-and middle-class childhood experience of Shakespeare.[14]

The effects of that experience are evident not only in the continuing frequency of illustrations and adaptations, but also in *A Midsummer Night's Dream*'s appearances within new texts for both child and adult audiences. The children in Rudyard Kipling's *Puck of Pook's Hill* (1906) summon up the original of Shakespeare's character by acting out parts of the play on Midsummer's Eve, a story originating in Kipling's own family theatricals. In Noel Streatfeild's *Ballet Shoes* (1936), performing as fairies in an avant-garde production in the West End proves a crucial turning point in the fortunes of the story's heroines. As Kate Chedgzoy explores in chapter 12, the play not only provides the title for Susan Cooper's *King of Shadows* (1999) but her young hero's performance in the role of Puck is at the heart of the emotional journey which structures the novel. Other examples of the play's enduring currency in crossover or adult-targeted work include Benjamin Britten's operatic version scored for numerous boys' voices (1960), Neil Gaiman's graphic novel *Dream Country* in *The Sandman* series (1991), and the film comedy *Get Over It* (USA 2001) in which teen romances develop while preparing a performance.

Given this theatrical and cultural afterlife, it is no surprise that several film versions of Shakespeare's play have also chosen to emphasize childhood elements, through casting, or the addition of child figures, or even by giving the whole film over to the young.[15] The two by Max Reinhardt and Walter Dieterle (USA 1935) and Christine Edzard (UK 2001) make a particularly useful comparison of how the performance of childhood has been constructed in different periods and cultures. While both illustrate Higonnet's thesis that the Romantic discourse of childhood innocence always invokes a dark side of violence and eroticism, there are crucial differences in their treatment of this theme. The 1935 film, though aimed at a family audience and subject to censorship, remains bound by the traditional concepts of child gaze and performance already outlined. The key figures of Puck and the Indian Boy present two aspects of performance, the 'professional' and the 'natural', and two aspects of the gaze; one marked out as precociously voyeuristic and associated with adult sexuality, the other that of a tearful love object. In Edzard's *The Children's Midsummer Night's Dream*, a film made for and to a degree by children, on the other hand, the children's performances are portrayed as free of adult control; they are also implicitly envisaged as therapy for damaged childhoods. Although the children start the film in the role of audience, they gradually take over the performance, a rebellion signalled, significantly, by Hermia's line 'I would my father looked but with my eyes' (1.1.56). Where the Reinhardt-Dieterle film privileges the male child's gaze and finally subsumes it into that of masculine adulthood, Edzard creates a female resistant gaze which comes to stand for the autonomy of child actors of both sexes, replacing adults' gratification with the ideal of 'true delight' embodied in 'unharden'd youth' at play through performance (3.2.455).

LOVE'S SIGHT: A MIDSUMMER NIGHT'S DREAM (1935)

Reinhardt's vision of the play, as a spectacular fantasy in which dozens of dancing, half-naked children were a key element of both choreography and interpretation, was developed from the early 1900s in at least thirteen stage versions until the director was driven into exile after the Nazis took power in Germany.[16] In 1934, after a festival production at the Hollywood Bowl, the Warner Brothers studio, noted for its exploitation of the newly developed technologies of sound in musicals and animations, commissioned a film version designed both to improve its standing in the 'quality' stakes and to appeal to American middle-class family audiences. The project may also have formed part of a more or less conscious policy, at a time when the Hays censorship code was being introduced, to distance the studio from its gangster films, then attracting condemnation, especially as viewing for the young. Some of the film's marketing was aimed specifically at children, for instance through a poster of Mickey Rooney as Puck, which in turn was used on the cover of a children's book version of the film.[17] Reinhardt's basic concept – infused with Grimm-like ideas about childhood and fairy tale, and influenced by Arthur Rackham's illustrations – remained intact. But constructions of childhood residually derived from literary sources were now juxtaposed with those emergent within the new medium of sound film, especially the developing codes of animation, in a context of cultural unease about American youth growing up 'too fast' in an increasingly violent society.

Rooney's performance, at the age of what most writers put at thirteen but which was probably closer to fifteen, is at the centre of these concerns.[18] As one of his biographers commented, 'Mickey didn't actually have much childhood.'[19] By 1935 Rooney was well established as a performer, having begun his career in vaudeville as a toddler, and was currently best known for his roles as 'tough' kid brother to gangsters. He was also one of the most experienced members of the cast, having played Puck to good reviews in the Hollywood Bowl production. The epitome of the Professional Child Actor, he could also be characterized as what James R. Kincaid terms a 'bad child' and John Collick and Higonnet a 'knowing child'.[20] But his urchinlike persona is layered with other constructions of childhood, notably that of the 'magic child'. Rooney's physical energy on screen becomes in a sense an embodiment of the new potential of animation to which much of the film's cinematography pays homage. The frightening Grimms' fairy tale aspects present in Reinhardt's previous productions are intensified through echoes of 'the destruction, fragmentation and extreme distortion of form that occur in early animated films', which Collick argues are similar to the displacement processes identified in Freudian dreamwork, creating a world of 'vicious and nightmarish childhood' of which movement is a key signifier.[21]

Yet much of Rooney's dynamism, in the last part of the film at least, is cinematic illusion. Having disregarded the usual contractual obligations to avoid dangerous activities while shooting, his real-life 'bad boy' behaviour resulted in him breaking his leg in a tobogganing accident, so that he had to be moved on a platform, his plaster cast tucked out of sight or disguised by greenery.[22] It is no accident that his characterization is linked with nature and animals, as well as movement. In effect, he is a feral version of the Romantic Child, whose bare torso and strange animal cries deliberately invoke the neo-Romantic figure of Tarzan, already an iconic child of nature in popular culture.[23] Kenneth Kidd argues that the '[f]eral child narrative guarantees the legibility of childhood itself, implying deviance from a normative path of human development'.[24] Cinematic trickery and the allusions to animation manipulate Rooney's Puck into appearing to generate and command narrative energies, while simultaneously disguising and containing the disruptive evidence of deviance. The mixed, and potentially disturbing, constructions of childhood at play in Rooney's performance thus throw into sharp relief what appears at first sight to be the more 'normative' portrayal of the changeling boy.

Portrayed as a chubby American preschooler dressed up as a tiny Indian rajah, the latter is a deracinated and vulnerable victim, driven with alternately playful and spiteful insistence through the forest into the arms of a maternally envisioned Titania. Although she puts the little boy to sleep in her bed, her enchantment with Bottom causes her to abandon him in tears, allowing Victor Jory's scary Oberon to snatch him away in triumph. In the child's next appearance, the garland of flowers with which the fairy queen crowned him has been exchanged for a headdress that echoes the phallic horns of Oberon and his dark, quasi-fascistic henchmen. This juxtaposition of stereotypically childish face and sexually symbolic costume creates a disturbing effect that mirrors the ambiguities surrounding the casting of the changeling boy. It has been suggested that the uncredited child was in fact female, but more credence is given to the idea that the role was performed by the young Kenneth Anger, who would go on to become an influential avant-garde director of films combining gay and occultist themes with innovative cinematography.

Anger (the name is assumed) is quoted as recalling his *A Midsummer Night's Dream* experience as a 'rite of passage', in which 'scampering in spangles and plumes through Reinhardt's enchanted wood remains the shining moment of my childhood'.[25]

This account constructs childhood in nostalgically Romantic terms but also implies that the film experience was a liminal one, in which the child actor undertook some kind of transformative journey. It also suggests a separation between the performer and the film role, which, as already noted, in fact required displays of distress as well as delight. It is impossible to know whether the tears shed in the character of the changeling boy resulted from his own powers of imagination or artifice, or from directorial manipulation. It is certainly tempting to interpret Anger's first film, made at the age of 17, in which he himself played a dreamer plunging into a male world of violence and eroticism, as an acknowledgement of darker elements within the earlier 'dream' experience. Anger also used Puck as his company's logo and included frames of Rooney's performance in his best-known film, *Scorpio Rising* (USA 1964). If Anger's claim that he acted in *A Midsummer Night's Dream* is more than personal myth-making, both his own supposedly 'shining' childhood experience and Rooney's contrasting performance evidently left their mark on the adult cinematic gaze he went on to develop.

Anthony R. Guneratne has suggested that the theatre production's sexual allusions were censored for the screen version.[26] It is significant, however, that the film's action was originally intended to be framed entirely by child figures.[27] The first sequence would have featured Cupid firing his arrow at the 'little western flower', while the film would have ended, in a final flourish of animation's powers, with Puck miniaturized into a tiny figure on the doorknob of the lovers' nuptial chamber, locking himself and the audience out of its sexual intimacies. The final cut seemingly rejects this technical and narrative reassertion of filmic 'innocence'. Puck's parting bow straight to camera not only emphasizes him as performer, but also reconfirms him as a precocious voyeur, whose gaze, as Laurie Osborne has argued, has previously been assimilated through editing and camera point of view with the sinister, controlling vision of Oberon.[28] Having dogged the lovers' steps through the forest, revelling in his power over them, Puck ends the film by plunging them into darkness, scaring them to their beds, *opening* the door and provocatively enticing the audience's imagined gaze to intrude with him on a scene of adult sex. In the violence-haunted world from which the film's fantasy emerges, the possibility of an innocent child (or cinematic) gaze, independent of adult looking, is evoked only to be denied. Together, in fancy dress and 'natural' undress, vulnerable and vicious, amateur and professional, the two child actors represent the dual faces of the Romantic vision of childhood, of nurture and nature, the Edenic and the primordial. However, as 'distilled portraits' captured on film, they also hint disturbingly at the ambivalent – and sometimes abusive – attitudes that shadowed childhood and child performance in 1930s Hollywood.

INTO THE WARDROBE: THE CHILDREN'S MIDSUMMER NIGHT'S DREAM (2001)

Edzard, as was Reinhardt, is a director-designer, one never comfortably assimilated into the British film industry despite the success of her Oscar-nominated film of Charles Dickens's *Little Dorrit* (UK 1987). With the exception of *As You Like It* (UK 1991), performed in modern dress in the dockside surroundings of Southwark and Rotherhithe where her studio is based, her films have almost entirely centred on child-related subjects. These include script and designs for a ballet version of the *Tales of Beatrix Potter*, stories by Hans Christian Andersen, a children's opera *Amahl and the Night Visitors* (1996), and a nonballet 3-D version of *The Nutcracker* (1997) for IMAX, set in contemporary London. Her version of *A Midsummer Night's Dream* was developed between 1998 and 2000, in collaboration with the local education authority in south London. Eventually, the project involved more than 350 children from seven primary schools, comprising a wide range of cultures and ethnicities. The resulting film is almost entirely set in a miniature auditorium, a composite studio reconstruction of seventeenth-century indoor playhouse and aristocratic marionette theatre, and presents a largely uncut version of the play. Its three-part action begins with the modern schoolchildren restively watching a sonorous puppet performance of the first act, until the girl who will play Hermia takes over her character's lines. Gradually, all the children are absorbed into the world of the play as the theatre is transformed into a kind of secret garden, where, in Elizabethan dress, they gravely act out the middle part of the play, resuming their identity as contemporary audience for the performance of *Pyramus and Thisbe*. Here, although puppets again represent the lovers, the boy mechanicals retain their roles and costumes, as do the fairies in the film's closing moments.

As Douglas Lanier has pointed out, the film's structure thus presents a nested sequence of different spatial and temporal locations.[29] The action moves from the present-day collective 'school outing' scenes, to private moments in children's bedrooms or the local park. Stop-animation and jump-shot techniques signal entry into the fantasy world of the play, and the return to the present in which a rearranged theatre allows for a more participatory and pleasurable performance of the play within the play. In effect, the film borrows the same narrative structure of 'time-slip' children's literature employed in *King of Shadows*; a genre in which, as Julie Sanders has argued, the 'presentness' and immediacy of theatre can provide 'the most amazing time travel of all'.[30] Previous readings of the film have discussed its use of child actors in terms of what they may symbolize, especially as embodiments of nostalgia for a 'popular' communitarian Shakespearean theatre of the past.[31] More relevant to Edzard's film, in my view, is Tess Cosslett's analysis of the time-slip narrative as one that 'critiques empty reconstructions of the past; and because of the way it constructs childhood . . . evades the dangers of nostalgia'.[32]

If Reinhardt-Dieterle's Hollywood version of Germanic fantasy created a neo-Romantic vision of childhood, Edzard's interrogates as well as employs such visual representations. Her beautifully designed clothes, derived from engravings, pictures and masque costumes, turn her child performers into 'distilled portraits' in a literal sense. Lanier argues that the film's representation of Shakespearean theatricality can be linked to a nostalgic referencing of 'Victorian fairy lore . . . and such books as E. Nesbit's illustrated *Children's Shakespeare* (1900)',[33] while Crowl detects the influence of John Singer Sargent's Victorian painting of children with lanterns, *Carnation, Lily, Lily, Rose* (1886).[34] However, the primary source for Edzard's concept was early modern portrait miniatures, in which she found 'a very particular mixture of stiffness, clumsiness even, and ferocious, unforgiving realism'.[35] By thus situating her reading of the core of the play in a period immediately prior to the historical moment when, according to many historians, children were first recognized as separate entities from adults, Edzard places her child actors on an equal footing with the adult world.[36] Although the accustomed prelapsarian rhetoric of childhood is still present in Edzard's account of her young cast as 'personalities . . . as yet untampered with', possessing 'an awkwardness and passion like no adult actor ever could have . . . new, raw, fresh – and innocent', her insistence on children's own participatory performance crucially modifies the codes of Romantic childhood.[37] They become more than portrait miniatures, mere 'pictures of innocence', or actors there to 'accustom themselves to being watched', but are present, and presented, as auditors and spectators, and as such are invested with representational power.

Although the children's costumes remain a form of fancy dress, their style is far removed from that of the regimented muslin-clad child troupes of the Victorian theatre or Reinhardt's film. Stella Bruzzi has examined the relation between costume and gender ideologies in period-based films, drawing a key distinction between screen costumes that demand to be looked *at*, and those to be looked *through*, to the eroticized bodies beneath. Edzard's costuming is deliberately nonerotic, even curiously androgynous, despite the clear gender codings carried by its reconstruction of early modern adult dress (and fancy dress). These are not gauzy costumes to be looked through, to the potentially sexualized bodies beneath, but are rather emblematic of 'iconic historical possibilities, a collective ... cultural and political history' carrying information about 'country, class and period'.[38]

Here the context of the film's reception is important. Much journalistic writing on the film delineated the children's backgrounds as marked by family breakdown and violence, as well as cultural difference. There were frequent references to the recent killing of a Nigerian boy, Damilola Taylor, possibly by other children on the North Peckham estate from which some of the actors came,[39] while Edzard herself refers to an incident of child-on-child rape at one of the schools involved. These media accounts treated the children not as ideal Romantic children, but as already damaged beyond repair, often with an underlying viewpoint that bringing film 'magic' into their lives would only leave them more bereft when the 'dream' was over. Edzard's view was quite the opposite. 'Between their block of flats, school and TV, they have become cut off from reality', she said, implying that her project had opened a doorway, not to artifice but to an authenticity otherwise missing from their lives.[40]

Her film deliberately takes these 'ordinary' children from multicultural schools in a deprived part of London on a journey into another reality. Their different school uniforms, regarded within the ideology of British state education as tools of equality to erase distinctions of class, income or sexual maturity, also encode the distinct religious, geographical and cultural affiliations of the present, and thus tacitly acknowledge that difference may sometimes become a pretext for violence. The Elizabethan costumes worn for much of the film set such concerns aside. Instead, they replace contemporary social markers with distinctions between the scrupulously researched clothes of the lovers and mechanicals (reminiscent of the 'authentic' dress worn at educational period reenactments in stately homes and at other heritage sites) and the more fantastical, masquelike style of the fairies. Thus the 'greenwood' costume worn by

Puck (Leane Lyson) evokes both the flute-playing Dickon who is the presiding spirit of nature in Frances Hodgson Burnett's *The Secret Garden* (1911) and the hugely popular Edwardian children's print *The Piper of Dreams* by Estella Canziani (1915). That of Oberon, played by an Afro-Caribbean child, may recall the 'orientalist' changeling boy in the 1935 film, but its associations are not confined to that text's racial discourse. At the end of her survey of time-slip writing for children, Cosslett questions the lack of examples in which immigrant child protagonists explore the 'heritage' of their new surroundings.[41] The film's utopian, time-shifting blend of history and fantasy, theatre, literature and cinema, does not deny differences of race, gender and cultural history, but leaves them thematically unmarked. The empathetic experience the film provided by the wearing of such costumes and the playing of such roles becomes in effect an exercise in 'living history', allowing both native and immigrant children 'to play games with the past and to pretend that [they were] at home in it, ignoring the limitations of time and space'.[42]

Equally significant is the way in which allusions to sexuality are kept within bounds, and, in contrast to the 1935 film, do not reemerge in the visual text. As Mark Thornton Burnett points out, the casting of year seven children as the lovers evokes the theme of a rite of passage between childhood and adolescence. However, the reallocation of some of their lines to the younger fairy chorus acknowledges that there are 'realms of experience still to be encountered . . . areas of discovery and autonomy that culture and time have not yet made permissible'.[43] When the child lovers first wake and discuss the visions they have seen, they are back in uniform. They are soon replaced on stage by the puppet versions and return to being part of the contemporary child audience that watches their still-costumed fellow performers present *Pyramus and Thisbe*, as theatre in the round. Unlike Rooney's Puck, these child performers are separated from the final act's atmosphere of sexual expectancy. The film ends with children still acting for children, in a theatre that retains its fairy magic, in which, as Stephen Orgel argues about Elizabethan theatre, costume has been the chief means of transformation – however temporary – of social, as well as gendered, identities.[44]

The use of an unabbreviated version of the play distances it from conventional editions for the child audience, whether the Lamb retellings and their progeny discussed by Naomi J. Miller in chapter 9, or such contemporary versions as the *Animated Shakespeare*. Even the lack of animation and movement in the performance, disliked by many critics, can be read as Edzard's deliberate avoidance of elements now associated with 'kiddie culture' mediatizations. The film insists on the 'serious work' undertaken by the featured actors, as well as implicitly by the hundreds of other children involved in workshops and classroom activities. This concept of child culture is the opposite of the 'childish, regressive, immature and infantile' modes, based on rejection of 'mastery' and 'knowledge', that Richard Burt associates with the 'diminishing expectations' of the 1990s, and finds reflected in popular television's representations of Shakespearean performance in schools.[45]

Another key ingredient in Edzard's representation of an autonomous childhood is the replacement of adults by puppets, who consequently have only the illusion of a gaze. Edzard's film insists on children's own seeing throughout the film, not just when watching the performances that begin and end it. In this sense it is a 'children's film' as defined by Ian Wojcik-Andrews in his book on the genre, offering a 'dual vision' addressed jointly to child and adult audiences. Such films characteristically contain such elements as journeys; presence of an alternative world; a setting in and around small and or enclosed spaces; the child's body itself as the source and scene of exploration; discovery and transformation; and, finally an intrinsic metafilmicity which lays bare its conditions of artifice and plays with the conventions of cinema, often through introduction of the theatrical.[46] Edzard's *A Midsummer Night's Dream* features virtually all these elements. Wojcik-Andrews also finds similarities between women's film and children's cinema, in particular a degree of antirealism; a focus on female, rather than male, bonding; and the absence of a controlling male gaze.[47] These categories, too, are more or less applicable to Edzard's film, which, for instance, highlights Hermia's and Helena's roles by showing them in their bedrooms before the transition to the woods. Perhaps the overt hostility with which many (mainly male) reviewers greeted the film was prompted partly by a recognition that their gaze is not essential to the film's meaning.

Such a child-centred approach to performance is still rare in Shakespearean films or theatre productions that highlight the presence or associations of childhood. More frequently, children are subsumed into the play's overall symbolic structure, and it is their visual impact rather than their speech or action that is made significant. Kincaid has characterized contemporary childhood itself as 'a self-contained leisure-time industry', in which child-watching, whether in the form of amateur or professional 'shows', has become a favourite form of adult entertainment.[48] Child actors of Shakespeare are thus doubly performers; both of the roles they play, and by virtue of simply being children. In this sense it might seem that they are always dream children, seen 'with parted eye, / When everything seems double' (4.1.188–9).

Children are much more than this, of course, and always have been, whether in Shakespeare's day, the 1930s, or the beginning of the twenty-first century. By putting the Reinhardt-Dieterle and Edzard films of the same child-infused Shakespearean text side by side, the differences within and between historical childhoods can come into sharper focus. It is one thing to identify the multiplicity of discourses – social, aesthetic, cultural, literary – out of which both *Dreams* construct their distilled portraits of childhood. It is less easy to uncover the traces of the child performers, amateur or professional, who flicker so enticingly across stage or screen. Nonetheless, recovery of the hidden histories of how Shakespearean performance of childhood was enacted by real children, and how this in turn both reveals and reforms dominant understandings of childhood at a given historical moment, is a challenging but necessary task, if criticism is to do more than reproduce the very operations of child-gazing it seeks to observe.

NOTES

1 R.S. White, *Innocent Victims: Poetic Injustice in Shakespearean Tragedy* (London, Athlone Press, 1986). See also Ann Blake, 'Shakespeare's Roles for Children: A Stage History', *Theatre Notebook* 48 (1994), 122–37.

2 Carolyn Steedman, *Strange Dislocations: Childhood and the Idea of Human Interiority 1780–1930* (Boston, MA: Harvard University Press, 1998), p. 141.

3 Bert O. States, *Great Reckonings in Little Rooms: On the Phenomenology of Theatre* (Berkeley: University of California Press, 1985), pp. 31–2.

4 Alan Read, 'Acknowledging the Imperative of Performance in the Infancy of Theatre', *Performance Research* 5 (Summer 2000), 61.

5 See Catherine Belsey, 'Shakespeare's Little Boys: Theatrical Apprenticeship and the Construction of Childhood', in Bryan Reynolds and William N. West, eds., *Rematerializing Shakespeare: Authority and Representation on the Early Modern English Stage* (London: Palgrave, 2005), pp. 53–72, and chapter 3, 'Little princes: Shakespeare's royal children', pp. 43–5.

6 Children occasionally appear in silent films such as the Vitagraph *Julius Caesar* (USA 1908), and *A Midsummer Night's Dream* (USA 1909) and *A Winter's Tale* (USA 1910).

7 Joe Kelleher, 'Face to Face with Terror: Childhood in Film', in Karín Lesnik-Oberstein, ed., *Children in Culture: Approaches to Childhood* (Basingstoke: Macmillan, 1999), pp. 29–55.

8 Barbara Hodgdon, 'Spectacular Bodies: Acting+Cinema+Shakespeare', in Diana E. Henderson, ed., *A Concise Companion to Shakespeare on Screen* (Oxford: Blackwell, 2006), pp. 96–111 (97–8).

9 Anne Higonnet, *Pictures of Innocence: The History and Crisis of Ideal Childhood* (London: Thames and Hudson, 1998).

10 Samuel Crowl, *Shakespeare at the Cineplex: The Kenneth Branagh Era* (Athens, OH: Ohio University Press, 2003), p. 168.

11 Miranda Johnson-Haddad uses the term 'shadow children' for these extratextual insertions. See her 'Childhood Dreams and Nightmares: Children in Productions of *A Midsummer Night's Dream*', in Paul Nelsen and June Schlueter, eds., *Acts of Criticism: Performance Matters in Shakespeare and his Contemporaries: Essays in Honor of James V. Lusardi* (Cranbury, NJ: Associated University Presses, 2006) pp. 232–44.

12 Darlene Ciraulo, 'Fairy Magic and the Female Imagination: Mary Lamb's *A Midsummer Night's Dream*', *Philological Quarterly* 78:4 (Fall 1999), 439–53.

13 Susan P. Casteras, 'Winged Fantasies: Constructions of Childhood, Innocence, Adolescence, and Sexuality in Victorian Fairy Painting', in Marilyn R. Brown, ed., *Picturing Children: Constructions of Childhood Between Rousseau and Freud* (Aldershot: Ashgate, 2002), pp. 126–42 (p. 127).

14 Gary Jay Williams, *Our Moonlit Revels: A Midsummer Night's Dream in the Theatre* (Iowa City: University of Iowa Press, 1992), p. 139.

15 Other *Dream* films with numbers of fairy children, often deliberately invoking visual references to the Victorian genre of fairytale paintings, include those of Peter Hall (UK 1968) and Elijah Moshinsky (BBC 1981). See my essay 'The Eye of Childhood: Shakespeare, Performance and the Child Subject', in Fiona Collins and Jeremy Ridgman, eds., *Turning the Page: Children's Literature in Performance and the Media* (Berne: Peter Lang, 2006), pp. 269–86, for discussion of Adrian Noble's film version (UK 1996), which employs a child's dream as narrative frame.

16 Williams detects a 'darker' note creeping in during the 1930s as the Jewish Reinhardt began to experience the impact of Hitler's rise to power in Germany.

17 See Michael P. Jensen, 'Fragments of a Dream: Photos of Three Scenes Missing from the Reinhardt-Dieterle *Dream*', *Shakespeare Bulletin* 18 (Fall 2000), 37–9 for a reproduction.

18 Judith Buchanan suggests influence from a 1913 Italian film, which also featured a boy Puck. See Buchanan, *Shakespeare on Film* (Harlow: Pearson Education Ltd., 2005), p. 129.

19 Norman J. Zierold, *The Child Stars* (London: Macdonald, 1965), p. 228.

20 James R. Kincaid, *Child-Loving: The Erotic Child and Victorian Culture* (New York: Routledge, 1992), pp. 93–5, and John Collick, *Shakespeare, Cinema and Society* (Manchester: Manchester University Press, 1989), p. 81.

21 Collick, *Shakespeare, Cinema and Society*, p. 86.

22 Robert F. Willson, Jr., 'Break a Leg: Mickey Rooney's Lame Puck', *Shakespeare Bulletin* 10 (Fall 1997), 41. Buchanan states that the accident happened on set (*Shakespeare on Film*, p. 148, fn.9).

23 See Jerry Griswold, *Audacious Kids: Coming of Age in America's Classic Children's Books* (New York: Oxford University Press, 1992).
24 Kenneth Kidd, 'Men Who Run with Wolves and the Women Who Love Them: Child Study and Compulsory Heterosexuality in Feral Child Films', *The Lion and the Unicorn* 20:1 (1996), 90–112 (93).
25 Cited from a National Film Theatre programme, in Robert A. Haller, 'Kenneth Anger' (*Filmmakers Filming*, New York: Walker Art Centre, 1980), rpt. www.geocities.com/Hollywood/Lot/1162/HCAngerBio_html.html.
26 Anthony R. Guneratne, '"Thou Dost Usurp Authority": Beerbohm Tree, Reinhardt, Olivier, Welles, and the Politics of Adapting Shakespeare', in Henderson, ed., *A Concise Companion to Shakespeare on Screen*, pp. 31–53 (p. 44).
27 See Russell Jackson, 'A Shooting Script for the Reinhardt-Dieterle *Dream*: The War with the Amazons, Bottom's Wife, and Other "Missing" Scenes', *Shakespeare Bulletin* 16 (Fall 1998), 39–41.
28 Laurie E. Osborne, 'Constructing Female Desire and the Female Gaze in the *Dreams* of Reinhardt, Hall and Papp', *Shakespeare on Film Newsletter* (December 1995), 5.
29 Douglas Lanier, 'Nostalgia and Theatricality: The Fate of the Shakespearean Stage in the *Midsummer Night's Dreams* of Hoffman, Noble and Edzard', in Richard Burt and Lynda E. Boose, eds., *Shakespeare the Movie II: Popularizing the Plays on Film, TV, Video, and DVD* (London: Routledge, 2003), pp. 154–72 (p. 161).
30 Julie Sanders, *Novel Shakespeares: Twentieth-Century Women Novelists and Appropriation* (Manchester: Manchester University Press, 2001), p. 96.
31 See Lanier, 'Nostalgia and Theatricality'; Crowl, *Shakespeare at the Cineplex*; and Mark Thornton Burnett, '"Fancy's Images": Reinventing Shakespeare in Christine Edzard's *The Children's Midsummer Night's Dream*', *Literature/Film Quarterly* 30:3 (2002), 166–70.
32 Tess Cosslett, '"History from Below": Time-Slip Narratives and National Identity', *The Lion and the Unicorn* 26 (2002), 243–53 (244).
33 Lanier, 'Nostalgia and Theatricality', p. 162
34 Crowl, *Shakespeare at the Cineplex*, p. 167.
35 Christine Edzard, *The Children's Midsummer Night's Dream: Director's Notes on the Film* (London: Sands Films, 2001), n.p.
36 See Belsey, 'Little princes', pp. 33–4.
37 Edzard, *Director's Notes*, n.p.
38 Stella Bruzzi, *Undressing Cinema: Clothing and Identity in the Movies* (London: Routledge, 1997), p. 36
39 The murdered boy was caught on CCTV cameras playing outside Peckham Library shortly before his death, and this footage rapidly became iconic of the contrast between childhood innocence and 'evil' in media coverage.
40 Edzard, *Director's Notes*, n.p.
41 Cosslett, '"History from Below"', 221.

42 Raphael Samuel, *Theatres of Memory*, 2 vols. (London, Verso, 1988), vol. 1, p. 196. Cited in Cosslett, '"History from Below"', 247.
43 Burnett, '"Fancy's Images"', 169.
44 Stephen Orgel, *Impersonations: The Performance of Gender in Shakespeare's England* (Cambridge: Cambridge University Press, 1996), pp. 100–5.
45 Richard Burt, *Unspeakable ShaXXXspeares: Queer Theory, and American Kiddie Culture* (Basingstoke: Macmillan, 1998), p. 9. See also his chapter in this volume, pp. 225–9.
46 Ian Wojcik-Andrews, *Children's Films: History, Ideology, Pedagogy, Theory* (New York: Garland, 2000), pp. 9–11.
47 *Ibid.*, pp. 149–50.
48 Kincaid, *Child-Loving*, pp. 363–4.

14

Shakespeare (')tween media and markets in the 1990s and beyond

Richard Burt

The Shakespeare industry[1] has recently achieved striking market penetration in the United States, the United Kingdom and elsewhere into 'niche markets'[2] of earliest childhood, including, to name just a selection, videos such as *Baby Shakespeare*, which has a recitation of Oberon's 'I know a bank where the wild thyme blows'; Fox Network and Disney animated cartoons and television situation comedies that cite or thematize Shakespeare; Shakespeare episodes of Public Broadcasting Service (PBS) puppet shows such as *Between the Lions* and animated cartoons such as *Seven Little Monsters*; 'family' films such as *Dazzle* (dir. David Lister, USA 1999), about a widower who meets a fairy and a teacher; and made-for-television film retellings of fairy tales starring adults such as *Jim Henson's Jack and the Beanstock: The Real Story* (dir. Brian Henson, USA 2001), with a mention of *Romeo and Juliet* and a shot of an old edition of Shakespeare's collected works in the giant's library; activity products such as pop-up books on Shakespeare's life; a Treasure Chest 'book' called *Shakespeare* complete with printing set and model Globe theatre; scattered references throughout Lemony Snicket's ten-volume *A Series of Unfortunate Events*; a Shakespeare action figure with detachable quill and book; plush Shakespeare beanie dolls; and even Mickey and Minnie Mouse and Barbie and Ken dolls dressed as Romeo and Juliet.[3]

At the same time that children's Shakespeare has unquestionably become part of the Shakespeare industry, the political right in the United States has mobilized a public relations campaign around a civic Shakespeare centred on the education not of college students (the terrain of the 1980s culture wars) but of elementary and middle-school children. Appearing on talk shows and sponsoring school programmes and television documentaries, First Lady Laura Bush, conservative Professor Abigail Thernstrom, and Dan Goia, chair of the NEA (National Endowment of the Arts) and sponsor of 'Shakespeare in American Communities', have all targeted school children as juvenile custodians of the right's preservation of the Western canon.[4] One could easily imagine a Marxist-inflected cultural studies account of these developments in marketing and public relations that would regard them as yet another version of the Shakespeare myth, the Shakespeare trade, and capitalist-driven cultural hierarchies, the aim of the account being to harness a progressive Shakespeare for children.[5] However, such an account of a political contest over 'Shakespeare' would fail to consider the dispersion of 'Shakespeares' into a series of fragments, remains and residues, usually positioned within a framing symbolic narrative that does not entirely arrest Shakespeare's slide into a cultural imaginary of psychotic citation.[6]

In this chapter I want to examine Shakespeare's citation and circulation in a number of child-related 1990s and millennial films and television shows from a perspective derived from deconstruction and media theory. I regard Shakespeare and childhood as always already technologized, part of discourse and media networks to which Sigmund Freud and Jacques Lacan drew analogies with the psyche.[7] Rather than assume that Shakespeare's corporatization is smoothly accomplished via capitalism, I want to take Shakespeare's incorporation in media as a problem of metabolization, assessing what gets lost or derailed and what won't go down into the symbolic.[8] My aim is not to do a political reading of television tween Shakespeares so much as to suggest what gets repressed in the name of political readings, or readings of Shakespeare that call themselves political.

The title of my chapter both marks Shakespeare's position between ('tween) media markets and also describes a new space that Shakespeare inhabits between childhood and adolescence, namely the tween (no apostrophe), a space that marks the fluidity of both terms that flank it. If the marketing of a civic 'Shakespeare' has made his works and iconic status increasingly more fragmented and less meaningful, on the one hand, yet more global and ever present, on the other, it may reasonably be said that the niche market of the tween, made up of eight- and twelve-year-olds ('tween' as in 'between childhood and adolescence'), has increasingly destabilized and even collapsed the distinction between child and adult. What emerges in the tween market is less the disappearance of childhood than the disappearance of adulthood: the tripartite distinction between child, teenager and adult is displaced by a new tripartite distinction between child, tween and teenager. Shakespeare's economic and cultural capital, or lack thereof, is all the more firmly established by youth culture as its evaluative terms have migrated downwards into (')tween and child culture.

Shakespeare's mediatization has meant that questions of aesthetic and educational value have been largely displaced and subordinated by a question of coolness and uncoolness, terms that traverse political divides. As Alan Liu writes, 'Cool is the techno-informatic vanishing point of contemporary aesthetics, psychology, morality, politics, spirituality, and everything. No more beauty, sublimity, tragedy, grace, or evil; only cool or not cool.'[9] The writer of the *Between the Lions* 'Dreaming Shakespeare' episode confirms Liu's point when describing the impact of the show in an interview: 'We really do think we've made Shakespeare accessible to kids. I think they'll know who Shakespeare is by the end of the show.'[10] Liu adds that 'research has shown that older children think the show is cool; it held their attention better than *Pokemon*.'[11] Yet if Shakespeare can be plugged into a mediatized children's (cultural) literacy network designed to further the interests of capital and the right because he can be made cool even to toddlers, Shakespeare's subjection to the laws of cool destabilizes not only his value but the project of cultural literacy (either for the right or the left) as well. The very capaciousness of cool blurs distinctions between trash and culture (literary classics, art, performance, and so on) and between losers and winners as success is defined not by academic or literary success but by the (anti-)star who wins/cashes in by (apparently) losing.

A fuller understanding of the complexity of Shakespeare (')tween media and markets demands that we adopt a transmedia approach towards Shakespeare's relation to literature and visual and electronic media, and to the dissemination of literary culture via other media such as film and television. As literature and literary culture are transposed, constructed, and framed in other rival media, and as classics are adapted in animated television shows, comics and biopics about writers, the lines between literature, comics, animation, film and so on are redrawn as much as they are blurred.[12] What Fredric Jameson says of film's 'rivalry' with other media may be generalized to include the way all media frame competing media: 'whenever other media appear in film, their deeper function is to set off and demonstrate the latter's ontological primacy.'[13] When Shakespeare enters 'children's' media, the rivalry between media tends to take a heightened narrative form.

Television, the medium on which I focus primarily in this chapter, occupies an interestingly transitional site within remediatizing networks. In many television programmes we may see an investment in various cultural hierarchies, hence the frequency with which Shakespeare, as icon of high culture, is cited and referenced. Yet in the case of (')tween

Shakespeares (and the point arguably holds for television Shakespeare generally), there is a corresponding disinvestment in these same cultural hierarchies. The citation tends towards the psychotic in being of little value even as it is revalued as cool (the toggle switch for 'whatever'). The parody is too obvious for adults and perhaps not receivable for kids. The television transmediatization of Shakespeare involves the loss of Shakespeare as he moves from one medium to another: the loser, as child or adult doing Shakespeare, allegorizes a failed crossover, something more like a crossing of wires, a flipped-off switch that interrupts a performance before it is finished. It doesn't matter how much of Shakespeare's language is used, that Shakespeare has been reduced to the most familiar quotations. Poised between precious sentimentality (the children are our future) and total abjection ('Is our children learning?', as President George W. Bush once ungrammatically asked), television (')tween Shakespeare may rightly be considered the loser of the losers, reducing live theatre to the children's amateur Shakespeare production of interest only to the parents in the audience. Any political reading of (')tween Shakespeare needs to take into account these losses in Shakespeare's transmission, the way his reception involves an implosion into insignificance.

To be sure, the distinction between childhood and adulthood is never secure, particularly when viewed from a transmedia perspective attuned psychoanalytically to static, loss and resistances in reception as well as transmission. Childhood, like the unconscious, is timeless. In an episode of the television sitcom *Cosby* entitled 'Will Power', for example, Bill Cosby dreams that he encounters Shakespeare, whose writings he has not learnt to appreciate, and meets his grade-school teacher while riding a child's tricycle as he gets yet more instruction on Shakespeare's value. Yet Shakespeare can still satirically serve 'antifamily' values, as in the school-play version of *Macbeth* put on by Wednesday and Pugsley Addams in the film *The Addams Family* (dir. Barry Sonnenfeld, USA 1991). The Shakespeare skit is clearly contrasted for maximum comic effect with the 'Getting to Know You' number (performed by all the other school-children) that precedes it, and the contrast is heightened by reaction shots from the audience members, many of whom, covered in fake blood, look horrified, and the other Addams family members, who give their children a standing ovation.

In more recent television shows, however, distinctions between Shakespeare as a token of high culture or as an agent of subversive parody have largely ceased to operate, and are hardly intelligible in terms of a narrative of sacralization and desacralization of the sort that Lawrence

Levine adopts in *Highbrow/Lowbrow: The Emergence of Cultural Hierarchy in America* (1988).[14] In the episode of *The Simpsons* entitled 'Tales from the Public Domain' and involving *Hamlet*, for example, Shakespeare and classic literature (collapsed with historical biopics as well) are devalued.[15] The episode begins as Homer Simpson, a loser and rather neglectful father, gets an overdue notice from the library for a book of 'classics' that he checked out just before his son, Bart, was born; gathering dust ever since, it is found by his daughter Lisa. *Hamlet* is retold with Bart and Homer playing Hamlet and Old Hamlet, while Lisa and her mother Marge play Ophelia and Gertrude. The retelling of *Hamlet* is quite funny, but it lacks any meaningful parodic force, owing in part, no doubt, to the lack of Oedipal parallels, in the absence of murderous and incestuous desires, between the Simpson family and Hamlet's. The classics are recycled here not because they constitute symbolic capital or signify class status but because, more cynically, they are a cheap source of adaptable materials since they are not protected by copyright but instead are part of the public domain. Yet the public domain is not simply opposed to the commercial, since public tales can be reterritorialized and privatized by a commercial television network show. *Hamlet* implicitly becomes a metaphor for Shakespeare's continual reanimation in post-Oedipal networks, but now with Shakespeare regarded as being both trash and profitable.

We can begin to grasp more concretely some of the implications of the way television (')tween Shakespeares break down the opposition between Shakespeare as token of high culture and target of parody into paradoxically profitable trash by examining four examples of (')tween Shakespeare media networks, the first example dealing with Shakespeare's commercialization in relation to time travel, the others with child stars and talent-show losers. A number of time-travel narratives in various mass media involve Shakespeare, taking the reader or viewer back to Shakespeare's future not so much to restore the past as to link Shakespeare's transmission through various past and present media to the transition from child to adulthood. Consider an episode of the animated cartoon *The Time Squad*, entitled 'Child's Play' and targeted at tweens. In this series the three members of the squad – a muscular, dumb cop named Buck Tuddrussel; a moralistic robot named Larry; and a bright, informed eight-year-old orphan boy, Otto Osworth – go back in time to 'enforce the past to protect the future'. In the 'Child's Play' episode, the squad meet Shakespeare at the Globe theatre where he is doing plays for children which apparently bore them and frustrate him by imposing artificial constraints on his creativity.

Shakespeare's authority as an author is clearly upheld in the episode. Before the squad go back in time to Shakespeare's London, Otto says, 'We're going to meet one of the greatest writers of all time.' Literary value and commercial value immediately collide as mass-market success clashes with canonical greatness. Before Otto can identify the world's greatest writer as William Shakespeare, Buck asks if they will meet Danielle Steele and Larry follows with Jackie Collins. When the squad characters use their machine to return to Elizabethan London, however, the historical past is made openly anachronistic in order to comment on the present. The episode satirically uses Shakespeare to point out problems with producing art or literature in the present commercial age (much like *Shakespeare in Love* (dir. John Madden, UK/USA 1998)). When the squad first find Shakespeare, he is watching an actor perform the role of Richard III for an audience of children, and after 'a horse, a horse, my kingdom for a horse', a bunny hops out and the two characters embrace. Shakespeare complains to the manager, Lance 9 Trillion, ''Tis awful. It's drek. It stinketh', and pleads 'What of art, that fickle muse that doth illuminate and nourish the soul?' But Lance responds, 'Two words, Bill: "youth market". Bunnies sell. It's where the green's at, booby.' ('Green' is American slang for 'money'.) Initially, it seems as if the show's satire is directed at the limits of crass commercialism as defined by action figures. Buck can only say over and over again his tagline: 'It's go time' and his philistine sensibility is indicated by his preference for the new play *Timeth Squad* over *Hamlet.*

The squad is as much a problem in the episode as a solution, however, in helping to make sure that Shakespeare writes Shakespeare. While Lance represents crass commercialism and Shakespeare high-minded art, a fresh threat to art arises in the form of market censorship. Both Shakespeare and Lance see a new opportunity in using the squad as actors for a new play that Shakespeare calls *Timeth Squad.* Larry is happy with the commercial prospects: 'Caw-ching! Caw-ching! I smell green ... The cop [Buck] appeals to adults 19–35. Boys 3–11 will go for the robot. And for girls 6–9 we got an attractive lead.' And Shakespeare is similarly enthusiastic: 'Thine story hath everything. With *Timeth Squad* I have finally created a masterpiece.'

Yet this initial reconciliation of art and commerce is thwarted by anticommercial forces in the name of children's values. Larry's interventions in Shakespeare's rehearsals and his script editing are satirized. When Shakespeare starts rehearsing *Timeth Squad*, Larry tells Shakespeare what he can't do because his audience are children: 'No pie throwing, no water in the face, no baseball bat.' Larry tears out page after page of

Shakespeare's *Timeth Squad* book as Shakespeare barely contains his anger. Larry and Lance then join forces as Lance uses Larry 'to make sure we are being sensitive, head off lawsuits'. Larry quickly becomes the star. 'You move these toys [robot dolls],' Lance tells him, and 'you've done your job.' Market censorship leads to a breakdown as Shakespeare, now a loser, walks off in disgust.

The episode ends saving both art and commerce by appealing to Shakespeare's universality. Otto tells Shakespeare, 'You were meant to write something else: Plays with tragedy, betrayal, love, war, plays about the human condition.' Acknowledging the pressure of markets, Shakespeare asks with some trepidation, 'But what of selling plush toys?' Otto responds reassuringly, 'Trust me, you write what you're supposed to and you're going to be just fine.' As we cut back to the Globe theatre, we see that Shakespeare has succeeded in producing Shakespeare. *Hamlet* is being performed before a larger audience composed of adults and children. Larry objects even to Shakespeare's 'original' version: 'Ahckkkk!!! A skull?!! The children will have nightmares!' Yet Otto overrides and effectively censors Larry, the market censor: 'Calm down, Larry. This is not a kid's play. It's called *Hamlet* and it's for all generations, all ages.' Art and commerce appear to be compatible. Lance adds, 'I just hope these Hamlet plush toys sell', as he pulls the doll's string and it says, 'To be, or not to be.'

The episode's final and tentative reconciliation of art and commerce both dissolves distinctions between adults and children and redraws them. On the one hand, Shakespeare moves beyond 'kid's' plays (and the niche divisions of marketing and ratings systems of market censorship) as the Globe is transformed from a children's theatre into a theatre for all ages. On the other hand, the child character, Otto, is the character who legitimates Shakespeare's universalization even as the episode discloses that Shakespeare has lost out to commercialization. The boy is the only one of the three who knows anything about Shakespeare (or history).

Yet Shakespeare's universalization collapses his plays into the kinds of lowbrow, trashy, 'childish' entertainment that the episode satirizes as a timeline becomes a tagline. Larry rolls his eyes when Buck practises his catchphrase 'It's go time' over and over again, a line that ends this episode as Buck says repeatedly 'It's goeth time.'[16] *Richard III* and *Hamlet* are similarly reduced, however, to taglines ('A horse, a horse' and 'To be, or not to be: that is the question'). Although one would not expect much in the way of Shakespeare citations from a cartoon show aimed at tweens, the episode's claim for Shakespeare's restoration and maturation into a universal theatre or removal from the scene of authorship need not self-deconstruct. In earlier versions of the Shakespeare time-travel story – such as the 1949 *Superman* comic entitled 'Shakespeare's Ghost Writer' and a '*Mr. Peabody and the Wayback Machine*' segment of a *Rocky and Bullwinkle Show* episode entitled 'William Shakespeare' – an adult either writes for Shakespeare his plays as we now have them or shows that someone else from early modern England did.[17] Superman manages to write *Macbeth* for Shakespeare, himself at a loss for a new plot, since Superman has 'seen and read every play [Shakespeare has] written many times!' Similarly, the *Rocky and Bullwinkle* episode addresses the Shakespeare authorship controversy and exposes Shakespeare as a fraud. Sir Francis Bacon arrives at the Globe theatre in drag and smashes a pot on Shakespeare's head in revenge for stealing Francis Bacon's play, *Romeo and Zelda*. And in the epilogue Mr Peabody, the 'adult' and very witty god, reveals to his young student, Sherman, that Shakespeare was not '*the* bard of Avon' but 'barred in Avon'. Even as it approaches a zero point of reception, a tween episode like *Time Squad* may allegorize something significant about Shakespeare's loss, a loss that accompanied even earlier transmissions for children.

I want to turn now to my other three examples of media network reconfigurations of Shakespeare in terms of childhood, those focusing on child stars and variety-show losers.[18] These 1990s and millennial tween television Shakespeare episodes bring together child film stars, professionals with agents; talent shows, with telephone votes for their winners and losers, who may become famous by losing; and school theatre productions (by definition, amateur productions). A brief genealogy of child stars and talent shows may be of some help. Broadly speaking, child stars and Shakespeare could at an earlier historical moment be seamlessly integrated into Shakespeare film adaptations. When Mickey Rooney played Puck in Max Reinhardt and Walter Dieterle's *A Midsummer Night's Dream* (USA 1935), he was just one Hollywood star among others. Conversely, the child star and Shakespeare could be easily disintegrated, as in Kenneth Anger's use of a clip of Rooney as Puck before cutting to Hitler and Nazi soldiers in his avant-garde film *Scorpio Rising* (USA 1964).[19]

Similarly, the talent show has a long history in American culture from Major Bowes's *The Original Amateur Hour* and Arthur Godfrey's *Talent Scouts* radio shows (1930s and 1940s) to television programmes including Ted Mack's *Amateur Hour* (1960s), Chuck Barris's *The Gong Show* (1970s), Ed McMahon's *Star Search* (1980s) and the more recent *American Idol* and *Are You Hot?* Shakespeare shows up in an animated cartoon entitled 'Hamateur Night' (dir. Tex Avery, USA 1939) that parodies American talent shows. All of the talent and all of the audience are animals. The actor doing Hamlet's 'To be, or not to be' soliloquy only manages to get out 'To be, or not to be' before being pelted with something rotten, and after he finishes the first line he is dropped through a trapdoor. The *Romeo and Juliet* balcony scene that follows has no lines from the play at all. In this cartoon neither 'authentic' Shakespeare nor modernized, translated Shakespeare wins. Both are trashed.

The television school play genre fuses facets of these shows in making the central character a loser figure (untrained and unprofessional) who may achieve fame through Shakespeare. In three Disney Channel television shows involving school productions, Shakespeare appears in transmediated forms and is neither trashed nor entirely upheld as a traditional value. *The Famous Jett Jackson* episode entitled 'A Tragedy in Two Parts' uses Shakespeare's *Julius Caesar* to put in play two opposed ideas of acting, one for television and the other for live theatre, which compete in value. Jett Jackson is an African-American middle-school pupil who stars in an action television series called *Silverstone*. When his friends comment that a white student named Rudy who loves Shakespeare and wants to act in the school production of *Julius Caesar* can do 'real acting', as in Shakespeare, Jett is provoked and decides to audition himself. Mr Dupree (Robert Bockstael), the high-school teacher and director, is overjoyed when Jett appears for the auditions and casts him immediately, even though Jett's line readings are atrocious, in contrast with the 'good' line readings of the white student. Static in the form of racism (black boys sure can't do Shakespeare) is generated in a television show that is avowedly antiracist as the episode reveals Jett's inability to cross over from television (where he is a star) to live theatre (where he is a loser), as well as the fundamental incompatibility of television and live theatre.

The values of television threaten to overwhelm live acting in several respects. Jett is distracted from his television role by the time he spends learning his lines in *Julius Caesar*. When Dupree asks the show's director, a woman, if she would be willing to shut down production of the show until after the play, she refuses, saying that her sixty-person crew and commercial investors are more important than a school play. Jett's television stardom also threatens to overshadow the play. Dupree casts Jett largely because he will draw an audience and help to promote Dupree's ambitions to work in television, and the play is advertised as 'Jett Jackson's *Julius Caesar*' in large letters on top and 'by William Shakespeare' in small letters on the bottom. Similarly, Jett's family and a friend help to publicize the production with T-shirts and caps with Jett's name prominently on them. Shakespeare is positioned as white and traditional (the production is done in period dress), and television as black and commercial. Yet Shakespeare's value can be reasserted only through a radical truncation and misreading of *Julius Caesar* as an endorsement of Caesar's willingness to sacrifice himself for his country and through the use of special effects borrowed from television. In the end, realizing that he cannot act Shakespeare well, Jett 'sacrifices' himself for the good of the performance. A white friend in charge of special effects on the television show use spurts of fake blood to make it appear that Jett has had a serious accident minutes before the performance of *Julius Caesar* is set to begin.

We then see Caesar (played by Rudy) assassinated in the production, which ends with his death. The audience applaud enthusiastically. Although the episode seems to place a white Shakespeare and live theatre above a black action series and television acting, it also has mixed feelings about both. The episode is clearly indifferent to a distinction between authentic Shakespeare and modern Shakespeare, with a schlocky reading of Julius Caesar as a heroic leader being represented as the original.

A similar framing of Shakespeare by rival media and (')tween pop stardom shapes 'Romeo Must Wed', an episode of the animated cartoon series *The Proud Family*. The episode derives from the action film *Romeo Must Die* (dir. Andrzej Bartkowiak, USA 2002), a very loose, modernized spin-off of *Romeo and Juliet* that marries hip-hop (through the now deceased African-American dancer and singer Aaliyah) with the Hong Kong kung fu action film (through film star Jet Li). Whereas virtually no mention is made of *Romeo and Juliet* in *Romeo Must Die*, the play is very much the focus of 'Romeo Must Wed'. Penny Proud, the daughter and central character of the middle-class African-American Proud family, and Kwok, a Chinese immigrant boy from Hong Kong whose parents want to arrange his marriage, begin rehearsing their respective roles as Romeo and Juliet for the school play and quickly fall in love. During the balcony scene of the live performance of the play, Penny and Kwok break out of character. Penny then jumps down into Kwok's arms and the two exit while the teacher/director and both sets of parents gasp in disbelief. The play is largely performed with period dress and staging, and accurate quotations from the play are clearly differentiated from the interpolated lines.

When the performance begins again after a commercial break, Penny is performing Juliet's lines in the final tomb scene after Romeo is already dead. Penny has set her lines to a hip-hop beat and delivers them as a rapper while dancing and addressing the camera directly. Yet the lines are accurately quoted rather than modernized. When she finishes, the camera pulls away to reveal that the theatre is now empty except for the teacher, who applauds and shouts 'Brave-O, Brave-O'. Although the episode separates out two versions of the performance, it does not oppose a modernized, new school Shakespeare to a traditional, old school Shakespeare. The separation, rather, both advances and retards Penny's star turn, an asymmetry which serves the show and which also reinforces an earlier asymmetry between Penny's Aunt Diane, an actress, and the teacher/director who salivates over her when she offers to help direct the performance. The asymmetry continues in the tomb scene, but here Penny triumphs dramatically performs for an audience of one. She wins by defaulting into another loser, allegorizing again the failure of Shakespeare's crossover from one medium to another, from one relatively meaningless derivation of Shakespeare to another.

Of all those discussed here, the show most explicitly aimed at tweens is Disney's *Lizzie McGuire*. In the 'Lizzie in the Middle' episode, Lizzie (played by Hilary Duff) wins a Scrabble game by putting down the word 'tween', which she points out does not need an apostrophe because it refers to a group of children between the ages of eight and twelve. The episode makes a rather bizarre use of a guest star Frankie Muniz, who plays a similar loser character as the star of the family television sitcom *Malcolm in the Middle*. As Malcolm, (Muniz) played Puck in an episode of *Malcolm in the Middle* about a school production of *A Midsummer Night's Dream* entitled 'High School Play'. During the performance, Malcolm forgets his lines and is literally left hanging in the air as everyone leaves the auditorium, including his own family. At this point he remembers his lines and recites them. The use of guest stars in situation comedies has a long history. At the beginning of the Lizzie McGuire episode, Mr Dig, an African-American substitute teacher, casts Ethan and Lizzie as Romeo and Juliet. In an animated aside Lizzie appears on a balcony gushing about her good luck in playing opposite Ethan. But when Muniz turns up, Lizzie and Ethan are both wowed and dumbstruck. The camera cuts to Muniz, who because of his celebrity naturally replaces Ethan as Romeo. Muniz recites Romeo's 'But soft, what light from yonder window breaks?' speech. *Romeo and Juliet* is used to code a (non)difference (')tween tween star and loser character. Muniz and Lizzie are divided not by a family feud but by their stardom and lack of stardom. Muniz asks Lizzie out and she accepts, but their dates are disrupted by his swarming fans. By the end of the episode, Lizzie decides that Muniz's fame is too much, and they decide not to see each other any more. But the episode ends happily as Lizzie and two of her friends show up on the set of Muniz's forthcoming action/spy James Bond tribute film, *Agent Cody Banks* (dir. Harald Zwart, USA 2003) and Lizzie is cast as the co-star.

The episode fulfils the tween loser's fantasy of achieving stardom, while doing double-time as a promotion spot for Duff's and Muniz's television shows. *Romeo and Juliet* gradually disappears from the episode. After the opening sequence, the play comes back only in mediated form as a boy band's pop song addressed to 'Juliet' plays over a montage sequence with Lizzie and Frankie on a date. The displacement of *Romeo and Juliet* from Ethan and Lizzie on to Muniz and Lizzie by virtue of Muniz's stardom effectively squeezes Shakespeare out.

I began this chapter by suggesting that Shakespeare studies might do better to put a cultural studies approach to Shakespeare on hold and follow the lead of psychoanalysis and media theory instead, adopting a transmedia approach to tween 'Shakespeares' that attends to placing the fragments of Shakespeare within a narrative frame and accounts for their crossover from the symbolic and meaningful into the imaginary and meaningless. Avowedly political readings of Shakespeare, whether from academic cultural materialists or right-wing politicians and federally funded Shakespeare programmes, repress, in my view, questions of loss of meaning, (de)valuation, stupidity and trash entailed by Shakespeare's transmediation, instead equating Shakespeare's cultural capital with Shakespeare's meaningfulness.

Let me close by suggesting that a political reading both of Shakespeare and of childhood might profitably engage the media or mediatic by tuning in on the pre-Oedipal and post-Oedipal Shakespeare frequency to which Avital Ronell and Laurence Rickels are already listening. References to *Hamlet* course through Ronell's *The Telephone Book* (1989), for example. Noting that Alexander Graham Bell and Thomas Watson's first public demonstration of the telephone was a compressed citation from *Hamlet*, 'To be, or not to be . . . there's the rub', Ronell writes that 'Hamlet was swallowed by telephonics – the father's umbilical couldn't cease naming itself and its ghostly partner. This perhaps explains why the telephone's most sacredly repeated declamation before an audience was "to be or not to be", marking the interstice between ghostly conjuration and the voice of the other.'[20] Ronell's Freudian analogy between the telephone cord and the (father's) umbilical cord may help us to extend the multiple connections (')tween Shakespeare, media, and markets noted in this chapter; that is, focusing primarily on television through the lines of childhood and infancy lets us take into consideration the impact of digitalization on both electronic media and Shakespeare's entry as well into new media such as the mobile phone and Ipod, both associated with short 'a-teen-tion' spans.[21] Shakespeare's circulation in a culture of cool involves uncanny hauntings of capital that cannot be exorcized and redeemed either by conservatives or cultural critics. (')Tween Shakespeare is worth attending to because it puts into question an equation of political Shakespeare as openly partisan, as is the case with the right-wing agenda in the United States, where the (very) young are on the frontline in the Shakespeare culture wars, and the cool as somehow nonpolitical, as fantasies of stardom and loserdom were non-political. Rather, the matter of the political and the symbolic, both for the right and the left, is a matter of remainders and residues that put Shakespeare's significance into question and make his transvaluation always a matter of resistances, and more or less acute reception.

NOTES

1 For a recent account, see Jumana Farouky, 'Shakespeare, Inc.', *Time Magazine* (international edition), 27 March 2006, 53–7.

2 See Don Hedrick, 'Bardguides of the New Universe: Niche Marketing and the Cultural Logic of Late Shakespeareanism', in Richard Burt, ed., *Shakespeare After Mass Media* (Basingstoke: Palgrave, 2002), pp. 35–58.

3 For more examples, see Richard Burt, ed. *Shakespeares After Shakespeare: An Encyclopedia of the Bard in Mass Media and Popular Culture* (Westport, CT: Greenwood Press, 2006).

4 On these public relations developments, see Richard Burt, 'Civic ShakesPR: Middlebrow Multiculturalism, White Television, and the Color Bind', in Ayanna Thompson, ed., *Colorblind Shakespeare: New Perspectives on Race and Performance* (New York: Routledge, 2006), pp. 157–85.

5 See Graham Holderness, ed., *The Shakespeare Myth* (Manchester: Manchester University Press, 1988), and Barbara Hodgdon, *The Shakespeare Trade: Performances and Appropriations* (Philadelphia: University of Pennsylvania Press, 1998).

6 See Richard Burt, *Unspeakable ShaXXXspeares: Queer Theory and American Kiddie Culture* (Basingstoke: Macmillan, 1999), pp. xxvii–xxxiii.

7 Friedrich A. Kittler, *Gramophone, Film, Typewriter*, trans. Geoffrey Winthrop-Young and Michael Wutz (Stanford: Stanford University Press, 1999); Laurence A. Rickels, *The Case of California* (Baltimore: Johns Hopkins University Press, 1991) and *Nazi Psychoanalysis*, 3 vols. (Minneapolis: University of Minnesota Press, 2003); Avital Ronell, *The Telephone Book: Technology, Schizophrenia, Electric Speech* (Lincoln and London: University of Nebraska Press, 1989) and *Stupidity* (Champaign, IL: University of Illinois

Press, 2003). See also Catherine Liu's excellent article on Lacan and television, 'Lacanian Reception', in Jean-Michel Rabaté, ed., *Lacan in America* (New York: Other Press, 2000), pp. 107–38.

8 I explore other aspects of Shakespeare ad media technologies in two articles: Richard Burt, 'What the Puck?: Screening the (Ob)Scene in Bardcore *Midsummer Night's Dreams* and the Transmediatic Technologies of Tactility', in Sarah Hatchuel and Nathalie Vienne-Guérin, eds., *Shakespeare on Screen: A Midsummer Night's Dream* (Rouen: Publications de l'Université de Rouen, 2004), pp. 57–86 and Burt, 'SShockspeare: (Nazi) Shakespeare Goes Heil-lywood', in Barbara Hodgdon and W. B. Worthen, eds., *A Companion to Shakespeare in Performance* (Oxford: Blackwell Press, 2005), pp. 437–56.

9 Alan Liu, 'The Future Literary: Literature and the Culture of Information', in Karen Newman, Jay Clayton and Marianne Hirsch, eds., *Time and the Literary* (London: Routledge, 2002), p. 63.

10 John Kiesewetter, '"Lions" Introduces The Bard to Kids', www.enquirer.com/editions/2001/01/23/tem_kiesewetter_lions.html.

11 *Ibid.*

12 On adaptation from novels and comics into film and vice versa, see Deborah Cartmell and Imelda Whelehan, eds., *Adaptations: From Text to Screen, Screen to Text* (London: Routledge, 1999), pp. 3–4 and 28.

13 Fredric Jameson, *The Geopolitical Aesthetic: Cinema and Space in the World System* (Bloomington: Indiana University Press, 1992), pp. 62 and 84 (note 19).

14 Lawrence Levine, *Highbrow/Lowbrow: The Emergence of Cultural Hierarchy in America* (Cambridge, MA: Harvard University Press, 1988).

15 The other tales in *The Simpsons* episode are Homer's *Odyssey* and the story of Joan of Arc.

16 To Larry's disapproval, Buck also cites Arnold Schwarzenegger's *Terminator* tagline, 'Hasta la vista, baby' as he sits atop a trash heap of tuna cans.

17 See also the UK film *Time Flies* (dir. Walter Forde, 1944).

18 *The Lizzie McGuire Movie* (dir. Jim Fall, USA 2003), which includes a line from *Twelfth Night*, makes use of them, as do the Shakespeare episodes of *Jett Jackson. The Proud Family* and *Lizzie McGuire* connect Shakespeare performance to stardom. Space does not permit consideration of the 'Terence and Philip: Behind the Blow' episode of the late-night Canadian animated cartoon series *South Park* (addressed to adults, but about children). In this episode Terence performs in *Hamlet* in Toronto. See also the films *Porky's 2* (dir. Bob Clark, USA 1983) and *Get Over It* (dir. Tom O'Haver, USA 2001) for a similar contrast in the teen versions of Shakespeare and the variety/talent show.

19 Most of Anger's films begin with a Puck Productions opening credit, and Anger maintains that he played the changeling boy in Reinhardt's film; but, in true loser fashion, Anger is not credited, the opposite of a child star like Rooney.

20 Ronell, *The Telephone Book*, p. 283.

21 See, for example, a mobile phone advertisement by Nextel using a modernized language *Romeo and Juliet* (dir. Joe Pytka, USA 2003). For details, see Burt, *Shakespeares After Shakespeare*. On teen Shakespeare films, see Burt, ed., *Shakespeare After Mass Media*. More recent examples are *The Prince and Me* (dir. Martha Coolidge, USA 2004), *Confessions of a Teenage Drama Queen* (dir. Sara Sugarman, USA 2004), *Mean Girls* (dir. Mark Waters, USA 2004), *Undiscovered* (dir. Meiert Avis, 2005) and *She's the Man* (dir. Andy Fickman, 2006).

APPENDIX 1

Children in Shakespeare's plays: an annotated checklist

Mark Lawhorn

Children appear frequently in Shakespeare's plays. When one looks at efforts to account for the number of children in the plays, however, one immediately encounters disagreement. Thomas Pendleton asserts that 'by the most liberal definition, there are only about thirty child characters in the . . . canon'.[1] Mark Heberle's larger count finds 'altogether thirty-nine child characters in the canon'[2] and my own reckoning comes in at about forty-five, not counting the choristers mentioned in *Henry VIII*. It is telling, I believe, that Pendleton, who claims that 'Shakespeare's insight into the child's experience occurs only randomly',[3] sees fewer child figures than Heberle, who reminds us that 'the appearance of *any* children on the stage is unusual' and suggests that the popularity of the boy actors in Elizabethan England reflected 'a striking new interest in childhood and children within Elizabethan society' and that a number of plays 'posit a direct relation between social health and the welfare of children'.[4]

Children in plays may evoke concerns about political stability, threats to authority, the continuity of community values, pregnancy and birth, processes of maturation, education, moral training, and employment experiences away from home. Because age-marked social boundaries, being in large measure culturally defined, are often in practice quite flexible, a child character represents a rather wide range of possibilities. Furthermore, in the world of the early modern theatre, dramatic considerations of age, size and sound were frequently shaped by practicalities which governed and continue to govern casting decisions.

The account of child characters that follows, therefore, is meant to suggest a generous range of performance possibilities. This effort has meant placing on the list a number of page figures whose years may seem especially indeterminate since their dramatic enactment depends almost wholly on directorial imagination and choice. Having exact numbers may not be exceptionally important – not the number of children, not their line counts, not even necessarily their time on stage. Surely one engages more profitably in examining these figures by asking why they are there and what effect they may be having while they are present for whatever length of time. In fact, while parts for children in the plays are routinely subjected to severe cuts in performance, a curious expansion of some parts also takes place fairly regularly. Audience members frequently may not get to hear from Clarence's children in *Richard III* (United Artists 1995; RSC 1998) or from Falstaff's former page in *Henry V* (Renaissance Films 1989) because their roles have been cut, but suddenly they see Benedick's boy popping up all over the place in *Much Ado About Nothing* (RSC 1998). To add to the confusion, Mamillius has been acted by a grown woman tooling around the Sicilian stage in a wheelchair (RSC 1999) and the diminutively monikered Moth in *Love's Labour's Lost* has been played by a grown man (RSC 1993; Miramax 2000) or woman (RSC 1984). The soothsayer in *Julius Caesar* has appeared as a boy (English Shakespeare Company 1993) and *Hamlet* has opened with a short film prologue depicting Hamlet as a boy playing in the snow with his youthful father (RSC 1997). Can anyone who has seen it forget the transgendering imposed on the infant Hamlet in Svend Gade's silent film (1920)? Who has not observed the changeling child in *A Midsummer Night's Dream* making yet another 'unscripted' appearance? Occasionally, Juliet has appeared with her child in performances of *Measure for Measure* (RSC 1999) despite the failure of Shakespeare's text to apprise anyone of the birth. Shakespeare himself, of course, saw no harm in changing source materials to make thematic or dramatic capital. By having Helena, for example, confront Bertram at the end of *All's Well That Ends Well* with her pregnant body rather than with twin sons that closely resemble their father, Shakespeare deviated significantly from his source material in order to highlight the contrast between the new ground of trust on to which the marriage is being impelled to move and the duplicities of Bertram's faithlessness and Helena's bedtrick.

The children of early modern English drama evoked cultural concerns that ran deeply through the society of the period. They continue to provide linguistic and situational variety, often contributing to dramatic tensions. They are not overly precocious within the boundaries of the dramatic work that they do. Besides being entertaining, the cleverness of youth can evoke the tensions between the young and the old, who may see them as a societal threat. Youthful savvy can also reflect the ability of children to resist corrupting adult influences. Portraying clever children with independent moral compasses could have been one way of countering antitheatrical criticism that claimed that the theatrical environment put children in spiritual peril. In short, these children are due some careful attention and consideration.

The organization of the list that follows has been guided mostly by my own explorations into how child figures are employed in the plays. Partly in recognition of space limitations and partly as a reflection of ideas and information that I have found most useful in my own work, notes are included selectively for some characters. Someone more interested in the composition of the Shakespearean playing company, for example, might prefer a list sorted *in toto* by play chronology, a scheme that has been employed instead within the discrete groupings I have preferred. In this instance the chronology suggested by A. R. Braunmuller and Michael Hattaway in *The Cambridge Companion to English Renaissance Drama* (1990) has been employed. The overarching pattern used to group child figures reflects the way that a range of concerns may be found to cluster around each of the major groupings, the first three of which are infants, pages (children in service), and children of noble birth. Shakespearean drama particularly chose images of infancy that are evocative of a number of specific societal concerns such as legitimacy, inheritance, deformity, abandonment and infanticide. Many of the plays also depict figures about whom comparably little has been written, such as those young individuals whose duty it was to serve a noble household. How might a play's focus on the young body as a valued and serviceable commodity within the royal domestic sphere resonate with the development in early modern English theatre of a youthful labour force that was subject to economic and sexual exploitation?

The treatments of noble children in this volume (particularly the chapters by Catherine Belsey and A. J. Piesse) go a long way towards countering the historical tendency of Shakespearean critics generally to lump these figures together as victims and as shallow roles of little interest. The emergence in recent years of criticism that attends directly to children has led to the recognition that not only are not all the children victims, but some are resilient survivors who signal the return of political stability and peace. The roles themselves may only seem shallow when they have been diminished by cuts in performance and are effectively prevented from contributing to the rich texture and diverse characterization that enhance the plays' structural and thematic concerns involving children, the future political landscape and the human community. Children and family are essential parts of the social fabric that both appeal to desires for domestic, societal and cosmic order and invoke the bonds of human compassion. As significant parts of Shakespeare's dramatic substance, the noble children that are grouped together here reflect a good deal of diversity.

The fourth category, 'Children who are silent or say very little', arose from my questions about what effects the mere presence of a child on stage might evoke or produce; the possible meanings of a child's silent physical presence are many and varied, as this section shows.

The penultimate category entitled 'Pregnant women on stage' is meant to highlight the potential power of the anxieties or expectations preceding a child's entrance into domestic and political spheres. Gower's description in *Pericles* of Thaisa's pregnancy is rather blunt and matter of fact: 'Hymen hath brought the bride to bed, / Where, by the loss of maidenhead, / A babe is moulded' (10.9–11). Oberon's final speech in *A Midsummer Night's Dream* (5.2. 31–52), however, begins by linking the concept of nativity with the idea of Fortune and goes on to associate spousal fidelity with good fortune in conception and birth. Astrologers looked to the stars even before a child was born for providential signs that indicated gender and health, and midwives closely examined even aborted foetuses for malformations that might suggest the workings of divine justice to punish parents for sexual sins. In *3 Henry VI* Queen Elizabeth (Woodville) expresses a concern that her emotions may have a negative effect on the child in her womb:

> And I the rather wean me from despair
> For love of Edward's offspring in my womb.
> This is it that makes me bridle passion
> And bear with mildness my misfortune's cross.
> Ay, ay, for this I draw in many a tear
> And stop the rising of blood-sucking sighs,
> Lest with my sighs or tears I blast or drown
> King Edward's fruit, true heir to th' English crown. (4.4.17–24)

While having children within marriage was virtually always couched in favourable terms in period documents, the idea that all women wanted children ought to be tempered with some consideration of individual desire and of biological risks. Parents feared not only birth defects, as Oberon's blessing suggests, but also the deaths of mother and child. Childbirth was fraught with such danger for mothers and children of all classes that one cannot help but suspect that the primacy placed on the bearing of children was largely a result of traditional religious structures that defined a woman's social role in a very restrictive way. The constraining domestic role of women, on the other hand, had the effect of authorizing childbirth and motherhood as areas of 'power and autonomy' for married women, whose association with and reliance on other women in the culture of childbirth and whose duties in establishing a child's moral foundation created a more empowered subject position from which wives who were also mothers could speak and write.

The final category 'Miscellaneous' reflects the limits to the listmaker's hope to fit every child tidily into a group. Still, the figures mentioned there are not without theatrical significance, as my comments on these diverse characters make plain.

INFANTS/BABES IN ARMS

Shakespearean drama particularly chose to foreground images of infancy that are evocative of a number of specific societal concerns such as legitimacy, inheritance, deformity, abandonment and infanticide. The many references to childhood and infancy made by adult characters in Shakespearean drama, by evoking a range of societal affections and anxieties, may also contribute in subtle ways to the audience's reception of child figures when they appear. The witches' reference in *Macbeth*, for example, to 'Finger of birth-strangled babe, / Ditch-delivered by a drab' evokes what Fran Dolan has called 'the gender- and class-inflected' representation of the crime of parental child murder in the early modern period.[5] Rather than make the mistake of thinking of these infants as mere stage props with little dramatic effect, it is important to see them in a larger context that includes the ideas and concerns that their silent presences may evoke and which are often woven throughout the texts surrounding them.

Edward V in *3 Henry VI*
son and heir of King Edward IV and Elizabeth Woodville
historically, b. 1470, d. 1483

Appears in play's final scene to be kissed by his uncles, including Richard, who, comparing himself to Judas in an aside, reveals the threat that his ambitions pose to the child.

Aaron's child in *Titus Andronicus*
son of Aaron the Moor and Tamora, Queen of the Goths
appears in 4.2; 5.1; 5.3

Aaron's child is threatened twice with infanticide, once when the nurse delivers the child to its father to be disposed of at the behest of Tamora and later as a point of leverage between Aaron and his inquisitors. The ultimate fate of Aaron's child in *Titus Andronicus* is somewhat ambiguous, although there is no mistaking the precarious nature of his life. In Jane Howell's 1985 BBC production of *Titus Andronicus*, in which she used close shots of the troubled face of Titus's grandson Young Lucius as a means to focus response to the 'violent male public rituals'[6] taking place in front of a child, the director chose to have the boy's bespectacled gaze turn upon the corpse of Aaron's baby lying in a small coffin. Julie Taymor's *Titus* (USA 1999), however, ends on a more hopeful note.

Marina in *Pericles*
daughter of Pericles and Thaisa
appears in scenes 10 and 11

The affection expressed by Pericles towards his new born daughter and the resolve inspired by the sight of her (along with the urgings of the nurse) resonate with similar expressions by Prospero as he recalls how the sight and presence of the infant Miranda strengthened his resolve in a desperate situation at sea. In the context of the post-Romantic flourishing of interest in Shakespearean children, the Wordsworthian affection towards infancy revealed in Prospero's language is striking:

> O, a cherubin
> Thou wast that did preserve me. Thou didst smile,
> Infused with a fortitude from heaven,
> When I have deck'd the sea with drops full salt.
> Under my burthen groan'd, which rais'd in me
> An undergoing stomach, to bear up
> Against what should ensue. (1.2.152–8)

Leontes, on the other hand, scrupulously tries to avoid looking on the newborn Perdita.

Perdita in *The Winter's Tale*
daughter of Leontes and Hermione
appears in 2.3; 3.3 (where her abandonment signals a structural shift in the play)

One might consider the narrative of Perdita's abandonment and recovery in the light of Dolan's account of 'gender- and class-inflected' representations of parental child murder in the early modern period. While the lower-class child's death alluded to by the witches in *Macbeth* has no place in a narrative that highlights the kindness of strangers as much as parental cruelty, upper-class status is not enough to settle all the dramatic and societal disturbances wrought by the abandonment of an infant and the death of her innocent brother Mamillius.

Elizabeth in *Henry VIII*
daughter of King Henry VIII and Anne Boleyn
appears in 5.4
historically, b. 1533, d. 1603

Of the five infants that appear in Shakespeare's plays, only the infant Elizabeth in *Henry VIII* does not face some kind of immediate peril, although the dangers that accompany Marina's birth at sea in *Pericles* are effects of the natural world and the political and human threat against Edward V that Richard manifests in *3 Henry VI* becomes truly potent only in *Richard III*. Cranmer's prophetic speech near the end of the play is designed to appeal to the dynastic ambitions of the playwright's patron James I, who is expected to lend his royal ears to Cranmer's words just as the stage King Henry must. Because the power to rule comes from God, it is not surprising that Shakespeare crafts a careful poetic link for James I as heir to Elizabeth. Presenting to his listeners the infant who is not only the natural embodiment of her parents' generative power and human fallibility but also the select agent of God's mysterious providence, Cranmer looks ahead to a time when 'The bird of wonder dies – the maiden phoenix – / Her ashes new create another heir' (5.4.40–1).

CHILDREN IN SERVICE: PAGES AND MESSENGERS, SINGERS AND PERFORMERS

Page in *Taming of the Shrew* – 16 lines
appears in Induction 2; 1.1 (Christopher Sly's boy bride)

Page in *Richard III* – 6 lines
appears in 4.2

The go-between who brings Richard and Tyrell together is a boy page figure to whom Richard turns to seek recommendation for an assassin. This troubling moment is worth examining, not merely because it seems to qualify assertions about children in Shakespeare's plays such as Ann Blake's observation that 'they are free from adult vices, and emphatically innocent',[7] but also because it raises the vexing question of what structurally, thematically or culturally significant purpose the boy figure might be serving. While the page is often cut in performance or replaced with an adult servant, Jane Howell chose in her BBC/Time-Life production to cast a child in the role, a young-looking actor whose voice and facial expression reflected a sweetness and innocence at odds with the content of his character's speech.

Moth in *Love's Labour's Lost* – 159 lines
appears in 1.2; 3.1; 5.1; 5.2

The lengthiest child's part in the Shakespeare canon belongs to Moth in *Love's Labour's Lost.* The only such character in the play, he furnishes a stellar example of the structural and thematic importance of children in early modern English drama. His lively presence flutters over the many cultural concerns regarding heirship, procreation, pregnancy, cuckoldry, paternity, service, education and performance that the play's classical allusions, rhetorical figures and dramatic situations evoke.

Despite the centrality of Moth to the themes and structural integrity of *Love's Labour's Lost*, the complexity of his language has often been viewed as placing too many demands on young actors. Before 1936, when 'Tyrone Guthrie cast a boy, Gordon Miller, in the role so obviously meant for a boy-actor . . . grown-up (though small) actresses and actors had taken the part.'[8] Peter Brook used the fifteen-year-old David O'Brien in his 1946 RSC production, and as Miriam Gilbert notes, 'recent productions have swung back and forth between petite actresses (such as Amanda Root, Stratford-upon-Avon 1984) and boys (such as Jo James, Stratford-upon-Avon 1978)'.[9] While the role has been subjected to cuts of various dimensions over the years, none of these prunings is more surprising than Elijah Moshinsky's extensive cuts in the 1984 BBC version in which an adult John Kane was cast in the role against the advice of series adviser John Wilders.[10] It should be clear that changing Moth into an adult character would destroy a significant part of the thematic and structural design of *Love's Labour's Lost.*

Page in *Romeo and Juliet* – silent
appears in 3.1 (sent by mortally wounded Mercutio to seek a surgeon)

Page in *Romeo and Juliet* – 2 lines
appears in 5.3

Traveller's boy in *1 Henry IV* – silent
appears in 2.1

Falstaff's page in *2 Henry IV* – 29 lines
appears 1.2; 2.1; 2.2; 2.4; 5.1; 5.3; 5.5. Reappears as Boy in *Henry V*

The page boy's history of dramatic treatment as a character of little importance may be partly based on a general impression of his line count. In *2 Henry IV*, for example, the character has only twenty-nine lines. Nevertheless, the page 'appears' in seven out of the play's seventeen scenes. A third of the play's lines are spoken while the boy is on stage. The boy's presence for such a large portion of the play certainly presents the possibility of a greater significance than modern productions or analyses of the play would suggest. A page serving in the royal household could look forward to social advancement of the sort that Geoffrey Chaucer enjoyed. But Falstaff's page has been placed among rogues. The question of whether the boy will survive the corrupting influences of the adult rogues with whom he appears is expressed in Bardolph's dark-humoured jest to Falstaff and his companions: 'An you do not make him hanged among you, the gallows shall be wronged' (*2 Henry IV* 2.2.81–2). The sight of the boy associating with scoundrels and knaves for much of *2 Henry IV* does not suggest a future of physical security or social advancement for him.[11]

King's page in *2 Henry IV* – silent
appears in 3.1

The King's page in *2 Henry IV* makes a speedy exit at the beginning of Act 3, scene 1 after the King utters a three-line command for the boy to depart in haste with letters for the Earls of Warwick and Surrey. Mirroring a similar order to deliver letters given by Falstaff to his page in the previous act, this brief appearance of an obedient, quiet royal page is arguably an important counterpoint to the role of Falstaff's page.

Page in *The Merry Wives of Windsor* – 3 lines
appears in 1.1

Robin in *The Merry Wives of Windsor* – 16 lines
appears in 1.3; 2.2; 3.2; 3.3 (perhaps doubled William Page or other role)

Children playing fairies in *The Merry Wives of Windsor*

Benedick's boy in *Much Ado About Nothing* – 3 lines
appears in 2.3

Boy in *Henry V* – 60 lines
appears 2.1; 2.3; 3.2; 4.4

Continuing his contribution to dramatic tension associated with societal concerns regarding youth and vagrancy, Falstaff's former page also becomes a focal point for considering brutality in war, as Kate Chedgzoy's Introduction to Part 1 of this volume notes (pp. 19–20).

Because Falstaff's page rejects in *Henry V* many of the lessons provided to him by his unseemly companions and because Robin's activities in *The Merry Wives of Windsor* are directed to subverting the ignoble efforts of his master, the page figure may represent an impulse to resist the cycle of child-related anxiety that permeates male society. By reflecting the ability of the youth's conscience to discern and resist the morally compromising nature of his surroundings and teachers, the character of Robin operates against the inculcation of cultural anxieties related to cuckoldry. The positive nature of this child's role also effectively works against the antitheatrical criticism of the dramatic enterprise as a destroyer of children. The page in *2 Henry IV*, *Henry V*, and *The Merry Wives of Windsor* is a portrait of childhood resistance to, and ultimate wisdom in the face of, adult weaknesses, fears and follies. While his role in the histories quite clearly evokes anxieties about adult responsibilities towards the young and may glance at this anxiety in more subtle ways in *Merry Wives*, the page's collusion with Mistresses Page and Ford would seem to inoculate against anxiety about cuckoldry rather than inculcate it.

Lucius in *Julius Caesar* – 32 lines
appears 2.1; 2.4; 4.2 (sings in last appearance)

The appeal or anxiety produced by a combined awareness of the age of a speaker/singer and his vocal range would have been a result of a playgoer's participation with a variety of discursive fields regarding youth and service on and off the stage. A director who chooses not to make use of a boy with a well-trained singing voice for Lucius in *Julius Caesar* or the boy singer in *Antony and Cleopatra* may be muffling the power of a young voice to resonate in complex ways with structural and thematic elements of the drama and with audience desires. Considerations of age, voice and desire can profoundly shape casting choices, textual interpretation and script editing for performance. Cultural and performance concerns related to age, maturity, eroticism and service that may be elicited by the brief vocal performance of a singing page are worthy of our careful attention, especially when one considers what needs a voice may serve and questions the ways in which that service may be rendered.

Pages (2) in *As You Like It* Page one – 6 spoken lines; Page two – 3 spoken lines
appear in 5.3 (also sing 'A lover and his lass')

Boy in *Troilus and Cressida* – 2 lines
appears in 1.2

Marianna's page in *Measure for Measure* – 8 lines
appears in 4.1 (sings)

Page in *All's Well That Ends Well* – 1 line
appears in 1.1

Messenger in *All's Well That Ends Well* – 4 lines
appears in 4.3 (perhaps not a child)

Most of the more than thirty further messenger figures in the plays do not appear to be children.

'Cupid' in *Timon of Athens* – 6 lines
appears in 1.2 (presenter of masque at Timon's banquet)

Page in *Timon of Athens* – 8 lines
appears in 2.2

Messenger in *Macbeth*
Several scenes include servants rendering messages, but the messenger who announces to Macbeth in Act 5 that 10,000 soldiers are approaching has been occasionally cast as a boy, perhaps because Macbeth calls him a 'lily-liver'd boy' (5.3.16) or perhaps to accentuate the play's preoccupation with children. Ian McKellen as Macbeth cuts the boy's face in the RSC version filmed for television in 1978.

Boy in *Antony and Cleopatra* – 6 lines (singing)
appears in 2.7 (not in Folio text)

A company of Quiristers (choristers) march across the stage singing in *Henry VIII* at 4.1 during the coronation procession.

Gardiner's page (and others) in *Henry VIII*
appears in 5.1

Boy in *Two Noble Kinsmen* – 24 singing lines
appears in 1.1

INNOCENT AND NOBLE VICTIMS

While it is not surprising that innocence is a quality that Shakespeare almost uniformly associates with his child characters, the figures who might be categorized under a tidy heading such as 'innocent victims' are placed in a wide variety of situations by Shakespeare and can contribute to dramatic goals in significantly different ways. From the doomed young Arthur in *King John* to Mamillius in *The Winter's Tale*, child victims emerge as a multifaceted throng of dramatic shapes and effects. Distinguished by the fashioning of dramatic situation and language, these young figures connect in various ways with oscillating cultural concerns such as class, gender, ethnicity, legitimacy and power.

Children and family are essential parts of the social fabric that both appeal to desires for domestic, societal and cosmic order and invoke the bonds of human compassion. As significant parts of Shakespeare's dramatic substance, the children discussed in this volume emerge as compelling characters who reflect a good deal of diversity. Clarence's children differ from their princely cousins. The young page who tells Richard about Tyrell is different again and he evokes other social concerns. Young Macduff's defiant response to his killers contrasts with the fainting spell of the young Rutland, whose unsuccessful pleas to Clifford for mercy diverge from Arthur's successful pleading with Hubert. More importantly, the crucial roles that these children may play in contributing to the development of central themes and to the evocation of cultural concerns suggests that cutting them in performance may do serious violence to the structure of a play.

Rutland in *3 Henry VI* – 24 lines
son of Richard, Duke of York and Cicely Neville, Duchess of York
appears 1.3 (perhaps doubled with Richmond)
historically, b. 1443, d. 1460

Margaret Plantagenet, Clarence's daughter in *Richard III* – 9 lines
appears 2.2; 4.1 (perhaps doubled with Richard of York)
historically, b. 1473, d. 1541

Edward Plantagenet, Clarence's son in *Richard III* – 22 lines
appears 2.3 (perhaps doubled with Prince Edward)
historically, Earl of Warwick, b. 1475, d. 1499

Richard, Duke of York in *Richard III* – 39 lines in addition to 9 lines doubled with his brother as ghosts addressing King Richard in Act 5
appears in 2.4; 3.1 (perhaps doubled with Clarence's daughter)
historically, b. 1472, d. 1483

Edward V (Prince of Wales) in *Richard III* – 36 lines
appears in 3.1 (perhaps doubled with Clarence's son)
historically, b. 1470, d. 1483

Perhaps to highlight the horror of war and cycles of vengeance, Shakespeare adhered to Edward Hall's 1548 historical account, *The Union of the Noble and illustre Famelies of Lancastre and Yorke*, which placed Rutland's age of death at twelve years, heavily emphasizing Rutland's youth and innocence in *3 Henry VI* and *Richard III* and making Rutland a child who is murdered rather than a young man slain in battle.

Arthur in *King John* – 121 lines
appears in 2.1; 3.1; 3.3; 4.1; 4.3 (has been doubled with Henry, King John's son)
historically, b. 1187, d. 1203

Arthur has the largest speaking scene (100 lines in 4.1) of any Shakespearean child figure. The structure of the play 'centers about the treatment of Arthur from beginning to end'.[12] It is not unusual to see the same young actor doubling the roles of Arthur and Prince Henry, John's son.

As though Arthur has achieved some kind of miraculous rebirth, the image of childhood presented by Prince Henry standing tearfully before his father's body and commenting on his father's 'swan song' seems designed as another forceful reminder of adult duty to the young. Childhood and political power coalesce in the young figure of Henry III, whose reign of fifty-six years presents a historical lesson to counter the fears of political instability brought on by a child ruler – societal anxiety with which Shakespeare deals in other history plays. The rare possibility that the adult world, by living up to its responsibilities towards the young, can reap long-lasting political advantages is figured dramatically in the final scene of *King John* as the boy king is surrounded by kneeling adults.

Mamillius in *The Winter's Tale* – 21 lines
appears 1.2; 2.1 (perhaps doubled with Perdita)

In Act 1, scene 2 of *The Winter's Tale*, Mamillius is forced to attend his tortured father's expressions of anxiety about cuckoldry. 'Thou want'st a rough pash and the shoots that I have / To be full like me,' Leontes says in reference to his sense that he is growing horns. 'Yet, they say we are / Almost as like as eggs', he adds, coming briefly to a full stop at the word 'eggs', the female associations of which seem to propel him back in the direction of the fears reflected in his subsequent pronouncement that 'women say so, / That will say anything' (ll. 131–3). What Mamillius is depicted as absorbing during his exchange with his father can be illustrated by a simple comparison of his response at the beginning of the scene with one at the end. 'Ay, my good lord,' says Mamillius, in phrasing that suggests some measure of confidence, when Leontes first asks, 'Art thou my boy?' (l. 122). More than eighty-five lines later, Mamillius mimics the paranoid pattern of his father's words when he says, 'I am like you, *they say*' (l. 209; italics mine).

Young Macduff in *Macbeth* – 20 lines
appears 4.2 (perhaps doubled with Fleance)

While the symbolism of childhood innocence is of central importance in *Macbeth*, it is all too easy to overlook the liveliness and variety of the lines that young Macduff speaks in his exchange with his mother before the arrival of the killers. The boy's witty attempts to get a smile from his mother, who remains put out with her absent husband, can make for a dynamic portrait of a child's astute sensitivity to a mother's moods and to her sense of humour.

CHILDREN WHO ARE SILENT OR SAY VERY LITTLE

Richmond in *3 Henry VI* (Henry Tudor, later Henry VII) – silent
appears 4.6 (where Henry VI predicts that the boy will grow up to save England)
historically, b. 1457, d. 1509

Young Lucius in *Titus Andronicus* – 44 lines
In the last three acts of the play, Young Lucius is present during four of nine scenes (3.2, 2 lines; 4.1, 25 lines; 4.2, 13 lines; 5.3, 4 lines). His significance for the drama is made plain in A. J. Piesse's chapter in this volume, and he has become an important figure in recent productions.

Boy in *1 Henry VI* – 4 lines
appears 1.5; 1.6 (son of Master Gunner of Orleans; shoots and kills Duke of Salisbury; account given in Hall[13])

William Page in *The Merry Wives of Windsor* – 13 lines
appears 4.1

His initial appearance offers a parodic portrait of a young student of Latin grammar. Later, he appears as one of the children dressed as fairies who torment Falstaff.

'great lubberly boy' in *The Merry Wives of Windsor* – silent
appears 5.5 (Slender's boy bride, the fairy in white)

'un Garçon' in *The Merry Wives of Windsor* – silent
appears 5.5 (Caius's boy bride, the fairy in green)

Fleance in *Macbeth* – silent
Son of Banquo
appears 3.3

Anxiety over heirship is evoked repeatedly in *Macbeth*, beginning with Macbeth's fixation on the witches' prediction about 'Banquo's issue' and 'the seeds of Banquo' (3.1.60–71). The Royal Shakespeare Company's 1996 production of *Macbeth*, directed by Tim Albery, drew deeply on this obsession by having the witches force Macbeth, who had put his arm around Fleance in Act 2, scene 1, to confront 'seven look-alike Fleances, each with a little blond beard . . . torturing him with their boyishness'.[14]

Young Martius in *Coriolanus* – 2 lines
appears 5.3

PREGNANT WOMEN ON STAGE

What Jacobean playgoer could look upon the figure of a pregnant Anne Boleyn without contemplating the historical details of her demise, including accusations of incest with her brother? What more powerful evocation of paternal anxiety can one point to than Leontes's rage towards Hermione? As a site that provoked considerable societal anxiety, the pregnant body had the potential to bring a good deal of dramatic energy into a scene. What to do, for example, with the knowledge that Tamora gives birth in the fourth act of a five-act play is a performance issue, not merely a textual one, as the 'Peacham drawing' so tantalizingly suggests. Chiron's comment to Lavinia, 'What, wouldst thou have me prove myself a bastard?' (2.3.148) probably foreshadows the arrival of his bastard half-brother and the problems that will swirl around the child. Because their respective dramas conclude before their births, the children of Helena, Jaquenetta and Julietta never make an appearance. Instead, they lie in the womb as in the minds of the audience, unresolved issues that contribute to the other lingering questions of *All's Well That Ends Well*, *Love's Labour's Lost*, and *Measure for Measure*. Just as the children of Shakespearean drama evoke a range of societal concerns, the pregnant women in the plays function dramatically in diverse ways.

Queen Elizabeth (Woodville) in *3 Henry VI*

Tamora in *Titus Andronicus* (child is son of Aaron the Moor)

Jaquenetta in *Love's Labour's Lost*

Julietta in *Measure for Measure* (child not yet born at end of play, though sometimes appears in performances)

Helena (alleged) in *All's Well That Ends Well* (child not yet born at end of play)

Thaisa in *Pericles* (appears in dumbshow narrated by Gower in scene 10)

Hermione in *The Winter's Tale* (child in womb is Perdita)

Anne Boleyn in *Henry VIII* (compare with Jane Seymour in Samuel Rowley's *When You See Me, You Know Me*, 1605)

MISCELLANEOUS

Fairies in *A Midsummer Night's Dream*[15]

Changeling child in *A Midsummer Night's Dream* (whom the text does not place on stage)

George Stanley in *Richard III* (whom the text does not place on stage)

In Shakespeare's play the boy never appears, and when Lord Stanley refuses to bring his forces to Richard's aid, the King cries, 'Off with young

George's head!' (5.6.74). The dramatic tension over the fate of young Stanley is immediately relieved as Norfolk points out the nearness of the enemy forces and urges, 'After the battle let George Stanley die' (5.6.76). Norfolk's words and the lack of argument from Richard suggest that the boy may survive. Immediately after he has slain Richard, Richmond asks Lord Stanley, 'But tell me – young George Stanley, is he living?' (5.8.9). In Richard Loncraine's film (UK/USA 1995) we glimpse the shadow of young George (the child cast in role appears nine years old or so at most) escaping under a train carriage through the haze of exploded ordnance, but we get no confirmation of his reaching safety. Loncraine uses the pathetic appeal of the threatened child, but, in truncating the play so that it ends with Richard's death, discards the significantly placed weight given to the preservation of Lord Stanley's hostage son. In the text it is clearly important that Richard's final order for an individual execution proves ineffective; a child-killer has been thwarted. Because Shakespeare's *Richard III* deals directly with the disturbing murder of children, the decision to offer at the play's conclusion the deliverance of another imperilled young life seems an astute dramatic choice calculated to link Richmond with the safeguarding of innocence and England's hopes for a future unlike its recent past full of instances of murdered children. Such a linkage seems especially appropriate when one remembers how young Henry, Earl of Richmond's life was preserved in *3 Henry VI* from the murderous aims of Edward IV and how a prophetic Henry VI laid blessings on the 'pretty lad' and called him 'England's hope' (4.7.68).

As I have written elsewhere, 'Shakespeare's children are purposefully written and may have a penetrating impact on a play's dramatic realization. Attending to their potential in performance can be a crucial way to capture a play's richness and raise important questions about the place of children in Shakespeare's world and our own.'[16] Good luck to all who seek the answers to those questions.

NOTES

1 Thomas A. Pendleton, 'Shakespeare's Children', *Mid-Hudson Language Studies* 3 (1980), 39–55 (40).

2 Mark A. Heberle, '"Innocent Prate": *King John* and Shakespeare's Children', in Elizabeth Goodenough, Mark A. Heberle and Naomi Sokoloff, eds., *Infant Tongues: The Voice of the Child in Literature*, (Detroit: Wayne State University Press, 1994), pp. 28–43 (p. 30).

3 Pendleton, 'Shakespeare's Children', 40.

4 Heberle, '"Innocent Prate"', pp. 30–1.
5 Frances E. Dolan, *Dangerous Familiars: Representations of Domestic Crime in England, 1550–1700* (Ithaca and London: Cornell University Press, 1994), p. 142.
6 Jonathan Bate, ed., *Titus Andronicus* (London: Routledge, 1995), p. 63.
7 Ann Blake, 'Children and Suffering in Shakespeare's Plays', *Yearbook of English Studies* 23 (1993), 293–304 (293).
8 Miriam Gilbert, *Love's Labour's Lost*, Shakespeare in Performance series (Manchester: Manchester University Press, 1997), p. 59.
9 *Ibid.*
10 *Ibid.*, pp. 59–60.
11 For a fuller treatment of Falstaff's page, see Mark Lawhorn, 'Falstaff's Page as Early Modern Youth at Risk', in Edward Esche, ed., *Shakespeare and His Contemporaries in Performance* (Aldershot, Burlington, Singapore and Sydney: Ashgate, 2000), pp. 149–59.
12 Heberle, '"Innocent Prate"', p. 38
13 Geoffrey Bullough, *Narrative and Dramatic Sources of Shakespeare*, 8 vols. (New York: Columbia University Press, 1960), vol. 3, p. 55.
14 Robert Smallwood, ed., 'Shakespeare Performances in England', *Shakespeare Survey* 50 (1997), 201–24 (209).
15 On the casting of children as fairies, see Robert Shaughnessy, 'Introduction', ch. 1 of this volume, pp. 1–2.
16 Mark Lawhorn, 'Staging Shakespeare's Children', in Naomi J. Miller, ed., *Reimagining Shakespeare for Children and Young Adults* (New York and London: Routledge, 2003), p. 96.

APPENDIX 2

Bibliography of Shakespeare and childhood in English

Kate Chedgzoy and Susanne Greenhalgh, with Edel Lamb

I EDITIONS AND ADAPTATIONS FOR CHILDREN

(a) Selections and extracts

Alias, C. *Scenes from Shakespeare for the Young*, illus. H. Sydney. London: Alfred Hays, 1885

Anon. *The Beauties of Shakespeare, Selected from his Plays and Poems*. London: G. Kearsley, 1783

Anon. [Henrietta Bowdler, ed.] *The Family Shakespeare*, 10 vols. London: Longman, 1807

Austen, J., illus. *As You Like It*. London: William Jackson, 1930

Bansavage, L. et al., eds. *Sixty Shakespeare Scenes*. Hanover, NH: Smith and Kraus, 2003

Baughan, R. *Shakespeare's Plays Abridged and Revised for the Use of Girls*, Book I. London: T. Allman, 1863

Bellamy, D. *The Young Ladies Miscellany; or, Youth's Innocent and Rational Amusement.* London: E. Say, 1723

Bowdler, T. and H., eds. *The Family Shakespeare*, 10 vols. London: Longman, 1818

Bowen, H. C. *The Shakspere Reading Book; Being a Selection of Plays Abridged for the Use of Schools and Public Readings.* London: Cassell and Co., 1881

Brandram, S. *Shakespeare: Certain Selected Plays Abridged for the Use of the Young.* London: Smith, Elder and Co., 1881

Brandram, S. *Selections from Shakespeare Suitable for Recitation.* London: Routledge, 1893

Burson, L. *Play with Shakespeare.* Charlottesville, VA: New Plays Books, 1992

Chenery, J. and M. Gimblett. *Shakespeare 4 Kidz* series. London: Shakespeare 4 Kidz Publishing, 1996–

Chenery, J. and M. Gimblett. *Shakespeare's Greatest Italian Hits.* London: Shakespeare 4 Kidz Publishing, 2004

Crowther, J. *No Fear Shakespeare Sonnets: Plus a Translation Anyone Can Understand.* New York: Spark Publishing, 2004

Cullum, A. *Shake Hands with Shakespeare: Six Plays for Elementary Schools.* New York: Citation Press, 1968

Davies, R. *Shakespeare for Young Players*, illus. G. Macdonald. Toronto: Clarke, Irwin & Co., 1947

De Witt, R. *Under the Greenwood Tree: Shakespeare for Young People*, illus. P. de Witt. Owings Mills, MD: Stemmer House Publishers, 1986

Dodd, W. *The Beauties of Shakespeare, Regularly Selected from Each Play*, 2 vols. London: T. Waller, 1752

Durband, A. *Shakespeare Made Easy* series. Woodbury, NY: Barron's, 1985–6

Elis, A. J. *Macbeth: A Trajedi: Fonetic Famili Edisun, Wid Nots.* London: 1849

Elis, A. J. *The Tempest: A Play: Fonetic Famili Edisun, Wid Nots.* London: 1849

Evans, J. *Shakspere's Seven Ages of Man; or, The Progress of Human Life, Illustrated by a Series of Extracts in Poetry and Prose, for the Use of Schools and Families.* Chiswick: Charles Whittingham, 1823

Fogerty, E. *Standard Plays for Amateur Performance in Girls' Schools* series. London: Swan Sonnenschein and Co., G. Allen and Unwin, 1900–12

Foster, C. *The Sixty-Minute Shakespeare* series. Chandler, AZ: Five Star Publications, 1997–

Gent, L. C. *Choice Thoughts from Shakespere.* London: Whittaker & Co., 1861

Greaves, S. *Comic Book Shakespeare* series. Wem, Shropshire: Timber Frame Publications, 2001–04

Greet, B. *The Ben Greet Shakespeare for Young Readers and Amateur Players.* Garden City, NY: Doubleday, 1912

Griffith, E. *The Morality of Shakespeare's Drama Illustrated.* London: T. Cadell, 1775

Grosz, T. and L. Wendler. *Shakespeare Made Easy* series, Portland, ME: Walch Publishing, 2003–4

Guthrie, T., intr. *Ten Great Plays*, illus. M. and A. Provensen. New York: Golden Press, *c.*1962

Hall-Schor, C. *Young People's Shakespeare* series. Shaftsbury, VT: Mountainside Press, 2003

Hudson, H. N. *Plays of Shakespeare Selected and Prepared for Use in Schools, Clubs, Classes, and Families*, 3 vols. Boston: Ginn Brothers, 1870–3

Kasten, D. S. and M. M. *Poetry for Young People: William Shakespeare*, illus. G. Harrington. New York: Sterling Publishing, 2000

Kerman, G. L. *Shakespeare for Young Players: From Tens to Teens*, illus. A. Lewis. New York: Harvey, 1964

Kroll, J. L., ed. *Simply Shakespeare: Reader's Theatre for Young People*. Portsmouth, NH: Teacher's Ideas Press, 2003

Marshall, J. *Mother Goose's Melody, or Sonnets for the Cradle: Part Two ... Containing the Lullabies of Shakespeare*. London: J. Newbery, 1781

Mathias, D. *The Prince's Shakespere: A Selection of the Plays of Shakespere Carefully Expurgated and Annotated for the Use of Families and School*. London: Richard Bentley, 1867

[Maurice, M. A.] *Readings from the Plays of Shakspeare: An Illustration of his Characters*. London: J. W. Parker, 1848

Maxwell, C. *The Juvenile Edition of Shakspeare: Adapted to the Capacities of Youth*. London: Chapple Hailes, Wells, 1828

Mayhew, J. *To Sleep, Perchance to Dream: A Child's Book of Rhymes*. Frome: Chicken House Ltd., 2001

Mee, A., ed. *The Children's Shakespeare, In Shakespeare's Own Words*, 2 vols. London: Hodder and Stoughton, 1926, 1928

Miles, A. F. *The Shakespeare Reciter*. London: Aldine, 1886

Millard, J. *Shakespeare for Recitation ... for the Use of Schools*, ed. E. Millard. London: Sonnenschein and Co., 1894

Newbolt, F., ed. *Shakespeare's Plays for Community Players*. London: T. Nelson, 1927

Pearls of Shakespeare, A Collection of the Most Brilliant Passages Found in his Plays, illus. K. Meadows. London: Cassell, Petter and Galpin, 1860

Pitman, J. R. *The School Shakspeare*. London: C. Rice, 1822

Pollinger, G. *Something Rich and Strange: A Treasury of Shakespeare's Verse*, illus. E. Chichester Clark. London: Kingfisher, 1995 (rpt. 2005)

Raymond, R. R. *Shakespeare for the Young Folk*. New York: Fords, Howard, and Hulbert, 1881

Shorter, T., ed. *Shakespeare for Schools and Families*. London: T. J. Allman, 1865

Smart, B. H. *Shakespearian Readings. Selected and Adapted for Young Persons and Others*, first series. London: J. Richardson, J. G. & F. Rivington, 1839

The Twelfth-Day-Gift: or, the Grand Exhibition. London: John Newbery, 1867

Walker, R. *Macbeth on the Loose*, Heinemann Plays series. London: Heinemann Education Publishers, 2002

Wilson, J. D. *First Steps in Shakespeare*. Cambridge: Cambridge University Press, 1931

Wilson, M. *Scenes from Shakespeare*. Colorado Springs: Meriweather, 1993

Wilson, M. *More Scenes from Shakespeare*. Colorado Springs: Meriweather, 1999

Woods, M. *Scenes from Shakespeare for Use in Schools*. London: Macmillan and Co., 1898

Wykes, C. H. *The Shakespeare Reader, being Extracts from the Plays of Shakespeare*. London: Blackie and Son, 1879

Wykes, C. H. *Scenes from Shakespeare, Arranged for School Reading*. London: Blackie and Son, 1909

Yonge, C. M. *Shakespeare's Plays for Schools*, 5 parts. London: National Society's Depository, 1883–5

(b) *Retellings*

Anon. *The History of Shylock the Jew, and Anthonio The Merchant, with that of Portia and the Three Caskets ... Adapted to the Minds of Young Children*, n.p., 1794

Anon. *The History of King Lear, and his Three Daughters*. London : W. Moore, 1794

Aronson, B. *Wishbone Classics: Romeo and Juliet*, illus. Hokanson, Cichetti and K. Yingling. New York: Scholastic Press, 1998

Barr, A. E. *The Young People of Shakespeare's Dramas; for Youthful Readers*. New York: D. Appleton and Company, 1882

Bayne, L. *Fidelity, as Exemplified by the Heroes and Heroines of Shakespeare*. London: Rose and Dragon Books, *c.*1921

Beneduce, A. *The Tempest*, illus. G. Spirin. New York: Wing Books, 1993

Bentley, N. *Nicholas Bentley's Tales from Shakespeare*. London: Mitchell Beazeley, 1972

Bevan, C. *A Midsummer Night's Dream*, illus. R. Collins. New York: Oxford University Press, 2000

Birch, B. *Shakespeare Stories*, 3 vols. New York: Wing Books, 1993

Birch, B. *Shakespeare's Stories*, illus. J. Mayhew. Hove: McDonald Young Books, 1997

Birch, B. *Shakespeare's Tales*, illus. S. Lambert. London: Hodder and Stoughton, 2002

Brett, E. J. 'Stories of Shakespeare', in *Boys of England*, Complete Numbers 1–12. London: 1881

Britton, F. A. *Fairy Tales from Shakespeare*, First Steps in Shakespeare for Little Folks, illus. C. P. Wilson, 2 vols. Chicago: Werner Company, *c.*1896

Buckman, I. *Twenty Tales from Shakespeare*. London: Methuen, 1963

Burdett, L. *Shakespeare Can be Fun* series. Willowdale: Firefly Books, 1994–2002

Burningham, H. *The Graphic Shakespeare* series, illus. N. Deans. London: Evans Brothers, 1997–2005

Carpenter, H. *Shakespeare Without the Boring Bits*. New York: Viking Children's Books, 1994

Carpenter, H. *More Shakespeare Without the Boring Bits*. New York: Viking Children's Books, 1997

Carter, T. *Stories from Shakespeare Retold*, illus. G. D. Hammond. London: George Harrap & Co., 1910

Carter, T. *Four Stories from Shakespeare (The Merchant of Venice, The Winter's Tale, Macbeth, Julius Caesar) Adapted and Rewritten within the Thousand-Word Vocabulary by Harold E. Palmer*, illus. T. Robinson. London: G. G. Harrap, 1937

The Children's Shakespeare: Stories from As You Like It, The Merchant of Venice, A Midsummer Night's Dream, The Tempest. London: Henry Frowde, Hodder and Stoughton, 1909

The Children's Shakespeare: Scenes from the Play, with Introductory Readings from Charles and Mary Lamb's 'Tales from Shakespeare', Arranged as a Continuous Reader with Exercises in Composition, 16 vols. London: Macmillan, 1910–32

Chute, M. *Stories from Shakespeare*. New York: New American Library of World Literature, 1959

Clarke, M. C. *The Girlhood of Shakespeare's Heroines*, 5 vols. London: W. H. Smith & Son, 1850

A Classic in Pictures, 3, 9, 12, New York: Amex, 1949–51 (*Macbeth, Henry V, Julius Caesar*); rpt. as *Famous Stories in Pictures*. New York: Barins Books, 1955

Claybourne, A. *Stories from Shakespeare*, illus. E. Temporin. London: Usborne, 2004

Collins, A. *Stories from Shakespeare*. Harlow: Pearson Education in Association with Penguin, 2000 (with audio cassette)

Cover, A. B. *Macbeth*, Puffin Graphics series, illus. L. T. Tamai. Harmondsworth: Puffin, 2005

Coville, B. *William Shakespeare's The Tempest*, illus. R. Sanderson. New York: Doubleday, 1994

Coville, B. *William Shakespeare's Macbeth*, illus. G. Kelley. New York: Doubleday, 1996

Coville, B. *William Shakespeare's A Midsummer Night's Dream*, illus. D. Nolan. New York: Doubleday, 1996

Coville, B. *William Shakespeare's Romeo and Juliet*, illus. D. Nolan. New York: Doubleday, 1999

Coville, B. *William Shakespeare's Twelfth Night*, illus. L. Gore. New York: Doubleday, 2003

Coville, B. *William Shakespeare's Hamlet*, illus. T. Raglin. New York: Doubleday, 2004

Davidson, D. *Shakespeare for Young People* series. Fair Oaks, CA: Swan, 1985–93

Davis, S. *Shakespeare Retold for Little People*, 13 parts, illus. A. Woodward. London: G. Bell and Sons, 1928–35

Dean, J. *Twelfth Night*, illus. C. Mould. New York: Oxford University Press, 2000

Dean, J. *Much Ado About Nothing*, illus. C. Mould. New York: Oxford University Press, 2002

Deary, T. *Top Ten Shakespeare Stories*, illus. M. Tickner. London: Hippo, 1998

Dodd, E. F., ed. *Six Stories from Shakespeare.* London: Macmillan Education, 1953

Dutch, D. E., adapt. *Hamlet: Famous Authors Illustrated 8*, illus. H. Kiefer. Bridgeport, CT: Seaboard Press, 1950

Early, M. *The Most Excellent and Lamentable Tragedy of Romeo and Juliet.* New York: Harry M. Abrams, 1998

Elgin, K. *Antony and Cleopatra*, illus. C. Molan. New York: Oxford University Press, 2000

[Elliott, M. L.] *Shakespeare's Garden of Girls.* London: Remington and Co., 1885

Farr, N., adapt. *Hamlet*, illus. E. R. Cruz; *Othello*, illus. Fred Carillo; *The Taming of the Shrew.* Pendulum Classics. 1980. Rpt. Belmont, CA, Lake Illustrated Classics, 1994

Flather, J. H., ed. *Selection of Tales from Shakspeare.* Cambridge: Cambridge University Press, 1875

Foster, C. *Shakespeare for Children: The Story of Romeo and Juliet*, illus. L. G. Johnston, Chandler, AZ, Five Star Publications, 2000

Foulds, D., ed. *A Midsummer Night's Dream and Other Stories from Shakespeare's Plays.* Hong Kong and Oxford: Oxford University Press, *c.*1992

Foulds, D., ed. *The Merchant of Venice and Other Stories from Shakespeare's Plays.* Hong Kong and Oxford: Oxford University Press, 1993

Foulds, D., ed., *Othello and Other Stories from Shakespeare's Plays.* Hong Kong and Oxford: Oxford University Press, 1993

Garfield, L. *Shakespeare Stories.* London: Gollancz, 1974

Garfield, L. *Shakespeare Stories*, illus. M. Foreman. London: Victor Gollancz, 1985

Garfield, L. *Six Shakespeare Stories*, New Windmill series. London: Heinemann Educational Secondary Division, 1994

Garfield, L. *Six More Shakespeare Stories*, New Windmill series. London: Heinemann Educational Secondary Division, 1996

Gollancz, I., ed. *The Lamb Shakespeare for the Young: The Merchant of Venice*, London, Chatto & Windus, 1908

Gordon, G., ed. *Shakespeare Stories*, illus. R. Jacques. London: Hamish Hamilton, 1982

Grant, S., adapt. *Hamlet: Classics Illustrated 5*, illus. T. Mandrake. New York: Berkley/First, 1990

Graves, J. *Dramatic Tales Founded on Shakespeare's Plays. To Which is Added, the Life of this Eminent Poet*, 3 vols. London, 1840

Green, R. L. *Tales from Shakespeare: The Tragedies and Romances*, 2 vols. London: Gollancz, 1964, 1965

Hardy, T. M. *The Lamb Shakespeare for the Young. Based on Lambs' Tales; with Passages and Scenes Inserted and Songs Set to Music.* London: Chatto & Windus, 1908

Harrison, G. B. *New Tales from Shakespeare*, illus. C. W. Hodges. London: Nelson, 1938

Heaton, A. B. and M. West. *Stories from Shakespeare. Written within the Vocabulary of New Reader 3*, illus. Whitear. London: Longmans, 1966
Hoffman, A. S. *Stories from Shakespeare for Children*. London: Dent, 1904
Hoffman, A. S. *The Story of the Merchant of Venice: Retold from Shakespeare's Play*. London: Dent, 1904
Hoffman, A. S. *The Children's Shakespeare: Being Stories from the Plays with Illustrative Passages*, illus. C. Folkard. London: J. M. Dent, 1911
Howard, J. H., illus. *Twelfth Night*. London: Oval Projects Ltd., 1985
Hudson, R. *Tales from Shakespeare*, Tales for the Children 6. London: Collins Clear Type Press, 1907
Hufford, L. G. *Shakespeare in Tale and Verse*. London: Macmillan, 1902
Jameson, A. *Shakespeare's Heroines: Characteristics of Women, Moral, Poetical, and Historical*. London: George Bell & Sons, 1832
Johnson, M., illus. *Children's Macbeth*. Santa Barbara: Bellerophon, 1997
Jones, J. *Stories from Shakespeare's Plays*. Oxford: Oxford University Press, *c*.1980
Kennedy, M. L. *Bill S.: Shakespeare for Kids*. Tryon: Gallopade, 1983
Kincaid, E., illus. *Tales from Shakespeare: A Midsummer Night's Dream*. Newmarket: Brimax Books, 1996
Kincaid, E., illus. *Tales from Shakespeare: The Tempest*. Newmarket: Brimax Books, 1996
Kincaid, E., illus. *Tales from Shakespeare: Macbeth*. Newmarket: Brimax Books, 1997
Lacie, C. *Picture This! Shakespeare* series. Hauppauge, NY: Barron's, 2005–6
Lamb, C. and M. *Tales from Shakespear. Designed for the Use of Young Persons*, 2 vols. London: Thomas Hodgkins at the Godwin Juvenile Library, 1807
Lamb, C. and M. *Tales from Shakespear. Designed for the Use of Young Persons*, 2 vols. London: Printed for M. Godwin at the Juvenile Library, Second edn 1809, rpt. 1810
Lamb, C. and M. *Tales from Shakespear. Designed for the Use of Young Persons*, illus. W. Mulready, 2 vols. London: M. J. Godwin & Co., 1816. Rpt. 1822, 1831, 1837, 1838
Lamb, C. and M. *Tales from Shakespeare*. New York: Harper and Bros., 1877
Lamb, C. and M. *Tales from Shakespeare*, intr. A. Ainger. London: Macmillan, 1879
Lamb, C. and M. *Tales from Shakspeare*, ed. A. Gardiner. Manchester: John Heywood, 1888
Lamb, C. and M. *Tales from Shakespeare*. Philadelphia: H. Altemus, 1895
Lamb, C. and M. *Tales from Shakespeare*, intr. F. J. Furnivall, illus. A. Copping, 2 vols. London: Raphael Tuck & Sons, 1901
Lamb, C. and M. *Tales from Shakespeare*, illus. W. H. Robinson. London: Sands and Company, 1901
Lamb, C. and M. *Tales from Shakespeare*. Boston: D. C. Heath, 1901
Lamb, C. and M. *The Lamb Shakespeare for the Young*, intr. I. Gollancz, illus. E. Stratton, L. E. Wright. London: Alexander Moring, 1904–8
Lamb, C. and M. *Tales from Shakspeare*, illus. A. Rackham. London: Dent, 1906

Lamb, C. and M. *Tales from Shakespeare. The Works in Prose and Verse of Charles and Mary Lamb*, 2 vols., vol. 2., ed. T. Hutchinson. London: Oxford University Press, 1908

Lamb, C. and M. *Tales from Shakspeare*, intr. A. Lang. London: S.T. Freemantle, 1909

Lamb, C. and M. *Tales from Shakespeare*, illus. M. Lavars Harry. London: George G. Harrap, 1910

Lamb, C. and M. *All Shakespeare's Tales*. New York: Frederick A. Stokes, 1911

Lamb, C. and M. *Tales from Shakspeare, Edited for the Use of Schools*, ed. E. Ginn. Boston: Ginn and Co., 1915

Lamb, C. and M. *Tales from Shakespeare*, adapt. and illus. M. Mulliner. London: Robert Scott, 1915

Lamb, C. and M. *Tales from Shakespeare*, illus. L. Rhead. New York and London: Harper Brothers, 1918

Lamb, C. and M. *Great Tales from Shakespeare*, illus. A. Rackham. London: Daily Sketch, *c.*1920

Lamb, C. and M. *Tales from Shakespeare*, illus. E. S. Green. Philadelphia: Mackay, 1922

Lamb, C. and M. *Tales from Shakespeare*, illus. G. Soper. London: Allen & Unwin, 1923

Lamb, C. and M. *Tales from Shakespeare*, illus. R. F. Elwell. New York: Houghton Mifflin, 1925

Lamb, C. and M. *Tales from Shakespeare*, illus. N. Price. New York: T. Nelson, *c.*1926

Lamb, C. and M. *Tales from Shakespeare*. New York: E. P. Dutton and Co., 1930

Lamb, C. and M. *Lambs' Tales from Shakespeare*, illus. F. Kredel. New York: Garden City Publishing, 1932

Lamb, C. and M. *Tales from Shakespeare*, illus. E. Blaisdell. New York: Thomas Y. Crowell, 1942

Lamb, C. and M. *Tales from Shakespeare*, illus. L. Weisgard. Garden City, NY: Junior Deluxe Editions, *c.*1955

Lamb, C. and M. *Ten Tales from Shakespeare*, illus. M. Powers. New York: Macmillan, 1963

Lamb, C. and M. *The Complete Tales from Shakespeare, All Those Told by Charles and Mary Lamb, with Twelve Others Newly Told by J. C. Trewin.* New York: F. Watts, 1964

Lamb, C. and M. *Tales from Shakespeare*, illus. W. Paget. New York: Hart Publishing, 1976

Lamb, C. and M. *Shakespear: Three Stories*, illus. J. Mastrangelo. New Jersey: Unicorn Publishing, 1989

Lamb, C. and M. *Tales from Shakespeare*, ed. J. Briggs, illus. A. Rackham. London: Everyman, 1995

Lamb, C. and M. *Tales from Shakespeare*, rev. edn. in modern idiom, illus. G. Andrews. Edinburgh: Capercaillie, 2002

Lamb, C. and M. *Tales from Shakespeare*, intr. K. Duncan-Jones. London: Folio, 2003

Lamb, C. and M. *Ten Tales from Shakespeare*. Mineola, NY: Dover, 2003

The Gateway to Shakespeare for Children: Containing a Life of Shakespeare by Mrs Andrew Lang, a Selection from the Plays and from Lambs' Tales. London: Thomas Nelson, 1908

Lang, J. *Stories from Shakespeare Told to the Children*, illus. N. M. Price et al. London: T. C. and E. C. Jack, 1905

Lang, J. *More Stories from Shakespeare Told to the Children*, illus. N. M. Price et al. London: T. C. and E. C. Jack, 1910

Leigh-Noel, M. *Shakespeare's Garden of Girls*. London: Remington and Co., 1805

Lewis, N. *A Midsummer Night's Dream*, illus. S. Monti. London: Hutchinsons Children's Books, 1988

Lisle, R. *Romeo and Juliet*, illus. L. Su. New York: Oxford University Press, 2002

Macauley, E. W. *Tales of the Drama*. London: Sherwood, Neely and Jones, 1822

Macfarland, A. S. and A. Sage. *Stories from Shakespeare*. London: Blackie and Son, 1882

Macleod, M. *The Shakespeare Story Book*, intr. S. Lee, illus. G. Browne. London: Wells Gardner, Darton and Co., 1902

Manton, J. *The Story of Titania and Oberon: From A Midsummer Night's Dream by Shakespeare*, illus. P. Bray. London: Peter Lunn, 1945

Marshall, H. E. *The Child's English Literature*. London: T. C. & E. C. Jack, 1909

Martin, C. M. *Stories from Shakespeare*, illus. M. Gordon. London: Philip & Tacey, 1935

Masters, A. *Macbeth Retold*, illus. S. Player. New York: Oxford University Press, 2001

Masters, A. *Hamlet Retold*, illus. S. Player. New York: Oxford University Press, 2001

Matthews, A. *The Orchard Book of Shakespeare Stories*, illus. A. Barrett. London: Orchard Press, 1997

Matthews, A. *The Orchard Classics* series, illus. T. Ross. London: Orchard Books, 2003

Matthews, A. *The Random House Book of Shakespeare Stories*, illus. A. Barrett. New York: Random House, 2003

Mattock, K. *Stories from Shakespeare's Comedies*, Hong Kong and Oxford: Oxford University Press, 1994

Maud, C. and M. Maud. *Shakespeare's Stories*. London: Edward Arnold, 1913

Mayer, M., ed. *William Shakespeare's The Tempest*, illus. L. Bywaters. San Francisco: Chronicle Books, 2005

McCaughrean, G. *Stories from Shakespeare*, illus. A. Maitland. London: Orion, 2004

McKeown, A. *The Young Reader's Shakespeare* series. New York: Sterling Juvenile, 2003

Miles, B. *Favourite Tales from Shakespeare*, illus. V. Ambrus. Twickenham: Hamlyn, 1976

Miles, B. *Well-Loved Tales from Shakespeare*, illus. V. Ambrus. Twickenham: Hamlyn Young Books, 1986

Milford, H. *A Gateway to Shakespeare*. Oxford: Oxford University Press, 1934

Miller, D. *Stories from Shakespeare*. Oxford: Oxford University Press, 1934

Morris, H. S. *Tales from Shakespeare, Including Those by Charles and Mary Lamb, With a Continuation by Harrison S. Morris*, 4 vols. Philadelphia: L. P. Lippincott, 1893

Morris, M. *Two Roman Stories from Shakespeare*, illus. C. Kennedy. London: Collins, 1979

Mulherin, P. *Shakespeare for Everyone* Series, illus. A. Frost. London: Evans, 1988–2001

Mulherin, P. *Shakespeare for Everyone* Series, rev. edn. London: Evans, 2001

Mulherin, P. *The Best-Loved Plays of Shakespeare*, illus. A. Frost. London: Evans, 2003

Murray, G. *Let's Discover More Shakespeare*. London: Hamish Hamilton, 1960

Nesbit, E. and C. Chesson *Cymbeline and Other Stories: Children's Stories from Shakespeare*, illus. F. Brundage, M. Bowly. London: Raphael Tuck & Sons, *c.*1897

Nesbit, E. *The Children's Shakespeare*, illus. F. Brundage, M. Bowly, J. W. Grey. London: Raphael Tuck and Sons, 1895

Nesbit, E. *A Midsummer Night's Dream and Other Stories: Children's Stories from Shakespeare*, illus. F. Brundage, J. W. Grey. London: Raphael Tuck & Sons, *c.*1897

Nesbit, E. *Romeo and Juliet and Other Stories: Children's Stories from Shakespeare*, illus. F. Brundage, J. W. Grey. London: Raphael Tuck & Sons, *c.*1897

Nesbit, E. *Twenty Beautiful Tales from Shakespeare*. London: D. E. Cunningham and Co., 1907

Nesbit, E. *Shakespeare Stories for Children*, illus. J. H. Bacon, H. Copping, A. A. Dixon. London, Paris and New York: Raphael Tuck and Sons, *c.*1912

Nesbit, E. *The Best of Shakespeare: Retellings of 10 Classic Plays*, intr. I. Opie. New York: Oxford University Press, 1997

Owens, L. L. *Tales of William Shakespeare: Retold Timeless Classics*, illus. S. Cornelison. Logan, IA: Perfection Learning, Inc., *c.*2000

Packer, T. *Tales From Shakespeare: An Introduction to the Bard*, illus. G. de Marcken et al. New York: Scholastic, 2004

Perkins, L. F., illus. *A Midsummer Night's Dream for Young People*. New York: F. A. Stokes, 1907

Pollock, I., illus. *King Lear*. London: Oval Book Projects, 1984.

Powling, C. *The Tempest*, illus. T. Morris. New York: Oxford University Press, 2001

Quiller-Couch, A. T. *Historical Tales from Shakespeare*. London: Edward Arnold, 1899

Rao, A. R. *Four Stories from Shakespeare*, illus. U. Krishnaswamy. Hyderabad: Longman Orient, 1979. Rpt. London: Sangam, 1993

Riordan, J. *Richard III*, Shakespeare Collection series, illus. S. Player. London: Hodder Wayland, 2002

Rosen, M. *Romeo and Juliet*, illus. J. Ray. London: Walker Books, 2004

Roslyn, G. [J. Hatton] 'Nursery Tales from Shakespeare', *New Monthly Magazine* 116 (Jul.–Dec. 1879), 717, 920, 961, 1189

Rubie, E. *The Merchant of Venice*, Little Books for Africa series. London: Sheldon Press, 1928

Ryan, P. *Shakespeare's Storybook: Folk Stories That Inspired the Bard*, illus. J. Mayhew. New York: Barefoot Books, 2001

Sanderson, J. *Shakespeare Mini-Books* series. Teaching Resources, 2003

Schreiber, M. *Favorite Tales from Shakespeare*, illus. D. Lynch. New York: Grosset & Dunlap, *c*.1956

Serraillier, I. *The Enchanted Island: Stories from Shakespeare*, illus. P. Farmer. London: Oxford University Press, 1964

Seymour, M. *Shakespeare's Stories Simply Told: Comedies*. London: T. Nelson, 1883

Sim, A. C. G. *Phoebe's Shakespeare, Arranged for Children*. London: Bickers and Son, 1894

Six Stories from Shakespeare, illus. F. Matania. London: George Newnes, 1934, rpt. from *The Children's Shakespeare*, 1909 (J. Buchan, *Coriolanus*; W. Churchill, *Julius Caesar*; C. Dane, *The Taming of the Shrew*; P. Snowden, *The Merchant of Venice*; H. Walpole, *King Lear*; F. B. Young, *Hamlet*)

Stewart, D. *Romeo and Juliet*, illus. C. Shaw. Milwaukee: Raintree Publishers, *c*.1980

Stidolph, A. B. *The Children's Shakespeare*. London: Allman and Sons, 1902

Stories from Great Writers: The Children's Shakespeare. Oxford: Oxford University Press, 1935

Takata, T. *Lamb's Stories from Shakespeare. Put into Basic English*. London: Kegan Paul and Co., 1932

Tilney, E. F., ed. *Tales from Shakespeare: Tales for Children from Many Lands*, illus. C. J. Folkard. London: J. M. Dent and Co., 1933

Townsend, M. S. *Stories from Shakspeare*. London: Frederick Warne & Co., 1889

Von, illus. *Macbeth*. London: Oval Projects Ltd., 1985

Ward, R. S. *The Picture Shakespeare*, illus. B. Le Fanu. London: Blackie and Son, 1901

Weil, L. *Donkey Head*. New York: Atheneum, 1977

Welles, O. and R. Hill. *Everyone's Shakespeare, Three Plays Edited for Reading and Arranged for Staging*. Woodstock: Todd Press, 1934

Williams, M. *Mr William Shakespeare's Plays*. London: Walker Books, 1998

Williams, M. *Bravo, Mr William Shakespeare!* London: Walker Books, 2001

Williams, M. H. *Five Tales from Shakespeare*. Strathtay: Clunie, 1996

Willinsky, S., adapt. *A Midsummer Night's Dream: Classics Illustrated 87*, illus. A. A. Blum. New York: Gilberton, 1951

Willinsky, S., adapt. *Hamlet: Classics Illustrated 99*, illus. A. A. Blum. New York: Gilberton, 1952
Willis, J. *Capulet and Montague; or, The Tragical Loves of Romeo and Juliet*. London: Hodgson, 1823
Willis, J. *The Lives and Tragical Deaths of Hamlet, Prince of Denmark, and the Lovely Ophelia*. London: Hodgson, 1823
Wright, H. C. *Children's Stories from English Literature, from Taliesin to Shakespeare*. London: Ward and Downey, 1889
Wright, H. C. *Children's Stories from English Literature from Shakespeare to Tennyson*. London: T. Fisher Unwin, 1892
Wyatt, H. G. *More Stories from Shakespeare*. Oxford: Oxford University Press, 1935
Zarate, O., illus. *Othello*. London: Oval Projects Ltd., 1983

II SHAKESPEARE IN CHILDREN'S BOOKS

(a) Fiction

Anderson, H. M. *Golden Lads: A Tale*. London: William Blackwood, 1928
Apps, R. *The Hunt for Shakespeare*, illus. G. Wade. Hove: McDonald Young, 1999
Avi. *Romeo and Juliet Together (And Alive) At Last*. New York: Avon Camelot, 1987
Barlow, S. and S. Skidmore. *The Lost Diary of Shakespeare's Ghost Writer*. London: Collins, 1999
Belbin, D. *Love Lessons*. New York: Scholastic Press, 1998
Bennett, J. *Master Skylark: A Story of Shakespeare's Time*. New York: The Century Company, 1898; rpt. Amsterdam: Fredonia Books, 2004
Blackwood, G. *Shakespeare's Stealer*. New York: Dutton's Children's Books, 1998
Blackwood, G. *Shakespeare's Scribe*. New York: Dutton's Children's Books, 2000
Blackwood, G. *Shakespeare's Spy*. New York: Dutton's Children's Books, 2003
Boock, P. *Dare Truth or Promise*. Boston: Houghton Mifflin, 1999
Broach, E. *Shakespeare's Secret*. New York: Henry Holt and Company, 2005
Brown, P. *The Swish of the Curtain*. Leicester: Brockhampton Press, 1968
Cheaney, J. B. *The Playmaker*. New York: Knopf, 2000
Cheaney, J. B. *The True Prince*. New York: Knopf, 2002
Childs, R. *A Sting in the Tail*, Time Rangers series. New York: Scholastic, 1998
Chute, M. *The Wonderful Winter: A Boy's Adventures in Shakespeare's London*, illus. G. Golden. New York: E. P. Dutton, 1954
Clark, I. *Will Shakespeare's Little Lad*. New York: Charles Scribner, 1897
Cooney, C. B. *Forbidden*. New York: Scholastic, 1993
Cooper, S. *King of Shadows*. London: Bodley Head, 1999
Covington, D. *Lizard*. New York: Bantam Doubleday Dell, 1991
Curry, J. *Poor Tom's Ghost*. New York: Atheneum, 1977
Dalton, A. *Losing the Plot*. London: HarperCollins, 2001

Davidson, R. P. *All the World's a Stage*, illus. A. Lobel. New York: Greenwillow Books, 2003
Deary, T. *The Lord of the Dreaming Globe*, illus. H. Alles. London: Dolphin, 1998
Deary, T. *The Actor, the Rebel and the Wrinkled Queen*. London: A. & C. Black, 2003
Dhondy, F. *Black Swan*. London: Victor Gollancz, 1992
Draper, S. M. *Romiette and Julio*. New York: Simon and Schuster, 1999
Duncan, L. *Killing Mr. Griffin*. Boston: Little, Brown, 1978
Fiedler, L. *Dating Hamlet: Ophelia's Story*. New York: Holt, 2002
Forest, A. *The Player's Boy*. London: Faber and Faber, 1970
Forest, A. *The Players and the Rebels*. London: Faber and Faber, 1971
Forest, A. *Cricket Term*. London: Faber and Faber, 1974
Forest, A. *The Attic Term*. London: Faber, 1976
Francis, P. *Sam Stars at Shakespeare's Globe*, illus. J. Tattersfield. London: Frances Lincoln, 2006
Freeman, D. *Will's Quill, or How a Goose Saved Shakespeare*. New York: Viking, 1975
Gandolphi, S. *Aldabra, or the Tortoise who Loved Shakespeare*, trans. L. S. Schwartz. New York: Arthur A. Levine Books, 2004
Gibbons, M. *The Story of Ophelia*, illus. E. Ness. New York: Doubleday, 1954
Gilmore, K. *Enter Three Witches*. New York: Scholastic, 1990
Gilmore, K. *Jason and the Bard*. Boston: Houghton Mifflin, 1993
Goffstein, B. *Lead: An Actor*. New York: Harper & Row, 1987
Golding, J. *The Diamond of Drury Lane*. London: Egmont, 2006
Golding, J. *Cat Among the Pigeons*. London, Egmont, 2006
Gorman, C. *A Midsummer Night's Dork*. New York: HarperCollins, 2004
Gwaltney, D. *Shakespeare's Sister*. Charlottesville, VA: Cypress Creek Press, 1996
Harris, R. J. *Will Shakespeare and the Pirate's Fire*. New York: HarperCollins Children's Books, 2006
Hassinger, P. W. *Shakespeare's Daughter*. New York: Laura Geringer Books, 2004
Holmes, B. *Charlotte Shakespeare and Annie the Great*, illus. J. Himmelman. New York: HarperCollins, 1989
Horowitz, A. *The Devil and his Boy*. London: Walker Books, 1998
Howe, N. *Blue Avenger Cracks the Code*. New York: Henry Holt and Company, 2000
Karlinsky, H. *All the World's a Stage, a Special Board Book for Very Young Children*, illus. B. Irwin. Toronto: Davis Press, 1991
Katz, W. W. *Come Like Shadows*. New York: Viking Penguin, 1993
Kipling, R. *Puck of Pook's Hill*. London: Macmillan, 1906
Klein, L. *Ophelia*. London: Bloomsbury, 2006
Koscielniak, Bruce, *Hear, Hear, Mr Shakespeare*. Boston: Houghton Mifflin, 1998
Kositsky, L. *A Question of Will*. Montreal: Roussan Publishers, 2000
Lawlor, L. *The Two Loves of Will Shakespeare*. New York: Holiday House, 2006

Lawrence, M. *Mystery at the Globe: A Tale of Shakespeare's Theatre*. London: Franklin Watts, 1998

L'Engle, M. *A Wrinkle in Time*. New York: Farrar, Straus, and Giroux, 1962

Lepscky, I. *William Shakespeare*, illus. P. Cardoni. New York: Barron's Educational, 1989

Lester, J. *Othello: A Novel*. New York: Scholastic, 1995

Lilly, G. *On a Scaffold High*. London: Pont Books, 1993

Linnell, R. *Robin Babb, Actor's Apprentice*. London: Book Guild, 2003

Mark, J. *Stratford Boys*. London: Hodder and Stoughton, 2003

Masson, S. *Malkin*. Winona, MN: St Mary's Press, 1998

Masson, S. *The Tempestuous Voyage of Hopewell Shakespeare*. London: Hodder Children's Books, 2003

Masson, S. *Malvolio's Revenge*. London: Hodder Children's Books, 2005

Matthews, A. *The Flip Side*. New York: Random House, 2003

Mayfield, S. *Voices*. London: Hodder Children's Books, 2003

McCaughrean, G. *A Little Lower Than the Angels*. New York: Oxford University Press, 1987

Melnikoff, P. *Plots and Players*. Philadelphia: Jewish Publication Society of America, 1988

Mercati, C. *Shakespeare and Me*, illus. M. Sanfilippo. Logan, IA: Perfection Learning, 2001

Meyer, C. *Loving Will Shakespeare*. New York: Harcourt Children's Books, 2006

O'Dwyer, B. *Celtic Night: A Fifteen Year-old Girl's Modern Retelling of Shakespeare's A Midsummer Night's Dream*. Uniontown: Holy Macro! Books, 2006

O'Neal, Z. *In Summer Light*. New York: Bantam Books, 1985

Ortiz, M. J. *Swan Town: The Secret Journal of Susannah Shakespeare*. New York: HarperCollins, 2006

Paterson, K. *Bridge to Terabithia*. New York: Harper Trophy, 1977

Pearson, M. *Scribbler of Dreams*. Orlando: Harcourt, 2001

Plummer, L. *The Unlikely Romance of Kate Bjorkman*. New York: Bantam Doubleday Dell, 1995

Porter, T. H. *The Maid of the Malverns: A Romance of the Blackfriars Theatre*. London: Lynwood, 1912

Pratchett, T. *Wyrd Sisters*. London: Victor Gollancz, 1988

Pratchett, T. *Lords and Ladies*. London: Victor Gollancz, 1992

Pressler, M. *Shylock's Daughter*. London: Macmillan, 2001

Quiller-Couch, A. T. *True Tilda*. Bristol: J. W. Arrowsmith, 1909

Rowlands, A. *The Shakespeare Connection*. Harmondsworth: Penguin, 1994

Singer, M. *The Course of True Love Never Did Run Smooth*. New York: Harper & Row, 1983

Sisson, R. A. *The Young Shakespeare*, illus. Denise Brown. London: Max Parrish, 1957

Sisson, R. A. *Stratford Story*, London: W. H. Allen 1975 (issued as *Will in Love*. New York: Morrow, 1977)

Slaughter, G. *Shakespeare and the Heart of a Child: A Story for Children*, illus. E. Pape. New York: Macmillan, 1922

Sonnenmark, L. *Something's Rotten in the State of Maryland*. New York: Scholastic, 1990

Sterling, S. H. *Shakespeare's Sweetheart*. Philadelphia: G. W. Jacobs and Co., 1905

Streatfeild, N. *Ballet Shoes*. London: J. M. Dent and Sons, 1936

Streatfeild, N. *Curtain Up!* London: J. M. Dent and Sons, 1944 (issued as *Theatre; or Other People's Shoes*. New York: Random House, 1945)

Sutherland, T. *This Must be Love: Or How I Made my Midsummer Dreams Come True*. London: Collins, 2005

Tiffany, G. *My Father Had a Daughter: Judith Shakespeare's Tale*. New York: Berkley, 2003

Tiffany, G. *Will*. New York: Berkley, 2004

Tiffany, G. *Ariel*. New York: HarperCollins, 2005

Tiffany, G. *The Turquoise Ring*. New York: Berkley, 2005

Tolan, S. S. *The Face in the Mirror*. New York: Morrow Junior Books, 1998

Trease, G. *Cue for Treason*. Oxford: Blackwell, 1940

Turk, R. *The Play's the Thing: A Story About William Shakespeare*. New York: Milbrook Press, 1998

Updike, J. *Bottom's Dream*. New York: Knopf, 1969

Vining, E. G. *I Will Adventure*. New York: Viking, 1962

Walsh, J. P. *A Parcel of Patterns*. New York: Farrar, Straus, and Giroux, 1983

White, A. T. *Three Children and Shakespeare*, illus. B. Tobias. New York: Harper, 1935

Williams, T. *Caliban's Hour*. New York: Harper Prism, 1994

Windling, T. *A Midsummer Night's Faery Tale*, illus. W. Froud. New York: Simon and Schuster, 2000

Wise, W. *Nell of Branford Hall*. New York: Dial Books, 1999

(b) Nonfiction and biography

Aagesen, C. and M. Blumberg. *Shakespeare for Kids: His Life and Times*. Chicago: Chicago Review Press, 1999

Aliki. *William Shakespeare and the Globe*. New York: HarperCollins, 1999

Bender, M. *All the World's A Stage: A Pop-Up Biography of William Shakespeare*. San Francisco: Chronicle, 1999

Birch, B. *Shakespeare, Man of the Theatre*. London: Macdonald Educational, 1977

Brassey, R. *Shakespeare*, Brilliant Brits series. London: Orion Children's Books, 2003

Burdett, L. *A Child's Portrait of Shakespeare*. Willowdale: Firefly Books, 1995

Chrisp, P. *Eyewitness Books: Shakespeare*. New York: Firefly, 1999

Christiansen, R. *William Shakespeare: The Mystery of the World's Greatest Playwright*, Who Was . . . ? series. London: Short Books, 2004

Chute, M. *Shakespeare of London*. New York: E. P. Dutton and Company, 1949

Chute, M. *An Introduction to Shakespeare*, illus. I. Smith. New York: Dutton Children's Books, 1951

Claybourne, A. et al. *The Usborne Internet-Linked World of Shakespeare*, rev. edn. Tulsa: E. D. C. Publishing, 2002

Doder, J. *The Time Traveller's Guide to Shakespeare's London*. London: Watling St Ltd., 2004

Donkin, A. *William Shakespeare and his Dramatic Acts*, Dead Famous series, illus. C. Goddard. London: Scholastic Hippo, 2004

Earle, G. *William Shakespeare*, illus. Roger Hall. London: Ladybird Books, 1981

Forward, T. *Shakespeare's Globe: An Interactive Pop-Up Theatre,* illus. J. Wijngaard. London: Walker Books, 2005

Fox, L. *Discovering Shakespeare's Country*. London: Ladybird Books, 1987

Furnivall F. J. 'When Shakespeare was a Boy', in *Shakespeare Stories for Children*, ed. E. Nesbit, illus. J. H. Bacon, H. Copping and A. A. Dixon. London: Raphael Tuck and Sons, *c.*1912

Ganieri, A. *What They Don't Tell You About Shakespeare*, illus. A. Rowe. London: Hodder Children's Books, 1996

Hamley, D. *Spilling the Beans on William Shakespeare,* illus. M. Mosedale. Great Bardfield: Miles Kelly Publishing Ltd., 2000

Hodges, C. W. *Shakespeare and the Players*. London: G. Bell, 1948

Hodges, C. W. *Shakespeare's Theatre*. Oxford: Oxford University Press, 1964

Hodges, C. W. *Playhouse Tales*. New York: Coward, McCann & Geoghegan, 1974

Lambert, H. M. *The Merry England Picture Book*. Birmingham: Allday, 1922

Langley, A. *Shakespeare's Theatre*, illus. J. Everett. Oxford: Oxford University Press, 1999

Martin, G. M. *A Warwickshire Lad: The Story of the Boyhood of William Shakespeare*. New York: Appleton, 1916

Middleton, H. *William Shakespeare: The Master Playwright*. Oxford: Oxford University Press, 1988

Nettleton, P. H. *William Shakespeare, Playwright and Poet*. Minneapolis, MN: Compass Point Books, 2005

Rolfe, W. J. *Shakespeare the Boy*. London: Chatto & Windus, 1897

Rosen, M. *Shakespeare: His Work and his World*. Cambridge, MA: Candlewick, 2001

Ross, S. *Shakespeare and Macbeth: The Story Behind the Play*, illus. T. Karpinski and V. Ambrus. New York: Viking Children's Books, 1994

Ross, S. *William's Words: The Story of William Shakespeare*, illus. S. Shields. London: Hodder Wayland, 2003

Sisson, R. A. *The Young Shakespeare*. New York: Roy Publishers, 1959

Stanley, D. *Bard of Avon: The Story of William Shakespeare*, illus. D. Stanley. New York: Morrow Junior Books, 1992

Stockdale, M. C. *William's Window: Introduction to Shakespeare's Plays for Young People*. Schulenberg, TX: I. E. Clark, 1983

Toporov, B. *Shakespeare for Beginners*, illus. J. Lee. New York: Writers and Readers Publishing, 1997

White, A. T. *Will Shakespeare and the Globe Theater*, illus. C. W. Hodges. New York: Random House *c.*1955

Whitehouse, J. H. *The Boys of Shakespeare*. Birmingham: Cornish Bros., 1953

III AUDIO-VISUAL

Baby Shakespeare World of Poetry, Baby Einstein Company, 2000 (video/DVD)

Carpenter, H. *Shakespeare Without the Boring Bits: Complete and Unabridged*, narr. C. Boyd. London: Chivers Children's Audio Books, 1998 (audio cassette)

Carpenter, H. *More Shakespeare Without the Boring Bits: Complete and Unabridged*, narr. C. Boyd. London: Chivers Children's Audio Books, 1999 (audio cassette)

The Children's Midsummer Night's Dream, dir. C. Edzard, Squirrel Films Distribution Ltd., 2000 (video/DVD)

Cocoluzzi, C. and M. Toner, *Shakespeare's Sports Canon*. Toronto: Upstart Crow Publishing, 2006

Coville, B. *Shakespeare's Greatest Hits*, narr. B. Coville and C. Bishop, Full Cast Audio, 2003 (audio cassette/CD)

A Fair Fantasy: Music and Verse of Fairyland, Classical Communications Ltd., 2005 (CD)

Garfield, L. *Shakespeare Stories: Merchant of Venice*, narr. S. R. Beale. London: Chivers Word for Word Audio Books, 1999 (audio cassette)

The Hobart Shakespeareans, dir. M. Stuart, PBS, 2005 (TV programme)

Lamb, C. *Shakespeare for Children*, narr. J. Bailey and S. Vance, Saybrook, Trantor Media, 2005 (CD)

McCaughrean, G. *Stories from Shakespeare*, narr. J. Wilby, Cover to Cover, 1991 (audio cassette)

McColloch, J. *Shakespeare's Stories*, narr. D. Jacobi and J. Lapotaire, Delos, 1999 (CD)

Nesbit, E. *The Children's Shakespeare*, narr. J. Balushi et al. London: Dove Kids 1998 (audio cassette/CD)

Rachlin, A. *Romeo and Juliet: The Story of the Ballet*. Icklesham: Fun with Music, 2000 (audio cassette)

Shakespeare: The Animated Tales (1992), dir. J. Carter et al., Metrodome Distribution Ltd., 2005 (video/DVD)

Shakespeare for Beginners: ArtWorks Scotland, dir. S. McCubbin, UK BBC2 Scotland, 2005 (TV programme)

Shakespeare for Children, narr. Jim Weiss. Charlottesville, VA: Greathall Productions, 2000 (CD)

Shakespeare's Children, dir. I. Saraf and A. Light, 1996 (film)

Shakespeare 4 Kidz: A Midsummer Night's Dream. London: S4KT Productions, 2003 (DVD)

Shakespeare 4 Kidz: Macbeth. London: S4KT Productions, 2004 (DVD)

'Shivering Shakespeare', in *Little Rascals Comedy Classics*, 4 vols., vol. 2, dir. R. A. McGowan, Republic Pictures, 1929 (film)

Timson, D. *Shakespeare Stories*, 2 vols., vol. 1, narr. J. Stevenson. London: Naxos Audiobooks, 2005 (CD)

Timson, D. *Stories from Shakespeare*, 2 vols., vol. 2, narr. J. Stevenson and A. Jennings. London: Naxos Audiobooks, 2006 (CD)

Under the Greenwood Tree: Shakespeare for Young People. Gilsum: Stemmer House Publishers Inc., 1997 (audio cassette)

IV MISCELLANEOUS

Barker, F. G. *Forty-Minute Plays from Shakespeare*. New York: Macmillan, 1924

Brownfoot, A. *High Fashion in Shakespeare's Time: A Study of Period Costume with Pull-up Scenes*. St Albans: Tarquin Publications, 1992

Brownfoot, A. *Shakespeare on Stage: Including Pop-up Theatre Scenes to Make Yourself*. St Albans: Tarquin Publications, 1998

'The Children of Shakespeare', in *The Will o' the Wisp: A Magazine of General Literature* (June 1866)

The Children's Newspaper. London: Fleetway, 1963–4 (occasional comic-strip versions)

Colson, P. 'The Boys in Shakespeare's Plays', *Good Housekeeping* (March 1936)

Cottrell, W. F. 'The Children of Shakespeare's Plays', *Manchester Literary Club Papers* 14 (1888)

Cullum, A. *Shake Hands with Shakespeare: Eight Plays for Elementary Schools*. New York: Scholastic, 1968

Diana. London: Fleetway, 1963 (occasional comic-strip versions)

Dunstan, R. *Music to Shakespeare's Plays, Selected and Arranged for the Use of Schools and Colleges*. London: Novello and Co., 1912

Hamlet, Romeo and Juliet, The Tempest, Othello, Macbeth, Richard III. London: Hodgson and Co., 1822–54 (play texts and sheets of characters)

Henry, J. E. *Beat the Bard: What's Your Shakespeare IQ?* New York: Citadel, 2003 (quiz book)

Langdon-Davies, J. (comp. and ed.). *Young Shakespeare: A Collection of Contemporary Documents*, Jackdaw 9. London: Jonathan Cape, 1963

Look and Learn. London: Fleetway, 1964–69 (occasional comic-strip versions)

Lord, K. 'The Day William Shakespeare went to Kenilworth: A Pageant Play', *The Little Playbook*. New York: Duffield and Company, 1920

Macbeth (1811), *Julius Caesar* (1812), *The Merry Wives of Windsor, Romeo and Juliet, A Midsummer Night's Dream* (1815), *Richard III* (1817), *Hamlet* (1819), *Henry IV* (1824) *Richard II* (n.d.). London: William West (theatrical prints for colouring)

A Midsummer Night's Dream, Play for Families, Shakespeare in Costume, www.shakespeareincostume.com/ (costumes and abbreviated script)

Munby, J. *Shakespeare's Merrie Meeting: A Juvenile Dramatic Cantata*, *c.*1892

Patmore, E. Y. *Shakespeare for Young Actors*. New York: Exposition University Press, 1957

Playing Shakespeare. Oxford: Finch and Scott, 1990 (boardgame)

Ranger. London: Fleetway, 1965–66 (occasional comic-strip versions)

Shakespeare Colouring Book. Santa Barbara: Bellerophon Books, 1985

Stone, M. *The Bankside Costume Book for Children*. Akron: Saalfield Publishing Company, 1919

Tierney, T. *Great Scenes from Shakespeare*. New York: Dover Publications, 2000 (colouring book)

Tierney, T. *Great Characters from Shakespeare*. New York: Dover Publications, 2001 (paper dolls)

The Twelfth-Day-Gift: or, the Grand Exhibition. London: John Newbery, 1867 (folder with games and activities)

Young Albert, the Roscius. London: S. and J. Fuller, 1811 (storybook with paper dolls and costumes of Richard III, Hamlet, Othello, Orlando, Falstaff)

V CRITICAL WORKS

A. I. S., 'Some of Shakespeare's "Children"', *The Institute Magazine* 5 (1890), 17–19

Aers, L. and N. Wheale. *Shakespeare in the Changing Curriculum*. London: Routledge, 1991

Amussen, S. D. 'The Family and the Household', in D. S. Kastan, ed., *A Companion to Shakespeare*. Oxford: Blackwell, 1999, pp. 85–99

Andrews, M. C. 'He Has No Children', *Notes and Queries* 31 (June 1984), 210–11

Armstrong, A. 'Arthur's Fall', *Shakespeare Bulletin* 24:1 (2006), 1–10

Austen, P. and C. Woltering. 'Such Stuff as Dreams are Made On: Connecting Children with Shakespeare', *BookLinks* (October 2001)

Barber, C. L. 'The Family in Shakespeare's Development: Tragedy and Sacredness', in C. Kahn and M. Schwartz, eds., *Representing Shakespeare: New Psychoanalytic Essays*. Baltimore: Johns Hopkins University Press, 1980, pp. 188–202

Barbour, R. '"When I Acted Young Antinous": Boy Actors and the Erotics of Jonsonian Theater', *PMLA* 110:5 (October 1995), 1006–22

Bate, J. 'Lamb on Shakespeare', *Charles Lamb Bulletin* 51 (July 1985), pp. 76–85

Beehler, S. A. '"Such Impossible Passages of Grossness": Education and the Censoring of Shakespeare', *Nebraska English Journal*, 35 (Spring–Summer 1990), 16–31

Belsey, C. *Shakespeare and the Loss of Eden: The Construction of Family Values in Early Modern Culture*. Basingstoke: Palgrave, 1999

Belsey, C. 'Shakespeare's Little Boys: Theatrical Apprenticeship and the Construction of Childhood', in B. Reynolds and W. West, eds.,

Rematerializing Shakespeare: Authority and Representation on the Early Modern English Stage. Basingstoke: Palgrave 2005, pp. 53–72

Blake, A. 'Children and Suffering in Shakespeare's Plays', *The Yearbook of English Studies* 23 (1993), 293–304

Blake, A. 'Shakespeare's Roles for Children: A Stage History', *Theatre Notebook* 48 (1994), 122–37

Bloom, G. '"Thy Voice Squeaks": Listening for Masculinity on the Early Modern Stage', *Renaissance Drama* 29 (1998), 39–71

Boas, G. *Shakespeare and the Young Actor: A Guide to Production*. London: Rockliff, 1955

Bottoms, J. 'Representing Shakespeare: Critical Theory and Classroom Practice', *Cambridge Journal of Education* 25:3 (1995), 361–75

Bottoms, J. 'Of Tales and Tempests: The Problematic Nature of Prose Retellings of Shakespeare's Plays', *Children's Literature in Education* 27:2 (1996), 73–87

Bottoms, J. '"What's a Cultural Heritage When it's at Home?": Playing with Shakespeare in the Primary School', in M. Styles, E. Bearne and V. Watson, eds., *Voices Off: Texts, Contexts and Readers*. London: Cassell, 1996, pp. 128–38

Bottoms, J. 'In the Absence of Mrs Leicester: Mary Lamb's Place in the Development of a Literature of Childhood', in M. Hilton, M. Styles and V. Watson, eds., *Opening the Nursery Door: Reading, Writing and Childhood, 1600–1900*. London: Cassell, 1997, pp. 117–32

Bottoms, J. 'Familiar Shakespeare', in E. Bearne and V. Watson, eds., *Where Texts and Children Meet*. London: Routledge, 2000, pp. 11–25

Bottoms, J. 'Speech, Image, Action: Animating Tales from Shakespeare', *Children's Literature in Education* 32:1 (2001), 3–15

Bottoms, J. 'To Read Aright: Representations of Shakespeare for Children', *Children's Literature: Annual of The Modern Language Association Division on Children's Literature and The Children's Literature Association*, 32 (2004), 1–14

Bristol, M. D. 'How Many Children Did She Have?', in J. J. Joughin, ed., *Philosophical Shakespeares*. London: Routledge, 2000, pp. 18–33

Britton, J. 'A. C. Bradley and Those Children of Lady Macbeth', *Shakespeare Quarterly* 12.3 (Summer 1961), 349–51

Burnett, M. T. 'Impressions of Fantasy: Adrian Noble's *A Midsummer Night's Dream*', in M. T. Burnett and R. Wray, eds., *Shakespeare, Film, Fin de Siècle*. Basingstoke: Macmillan, 2000, pp. 89–101.

Burt, R. *Unspeakable ShaXXXspeares: Queer Theory and American Kiddie Culture*. Basingstoke: Macmillan, 1998

Butler, F. 'The Child in Shakespeare: Letters and Comments to the Editor by Shakespearians', in F. Butler, ed., *Children's Literature: The Great Excluded*. Storrs, CT: Children's Literature Association, 1973, pp. 209–12

Cecil, L. A. 'Lois Burdett', *Canadian Children's Literature/Littérature Canadienne pour la Jeunesse* 23:1 (Spring 1997), 41–4

Chedgzoy, K. *Shakespeare's Queer Children: Sexual Politics and Contemporary Culture*. Manchester: Manchester University Press, 1996

Chedgzoy, K. 'Playing with Cupid: Gender, Sexuality, and Adolescence', in Diana Henderson, ed., *Alternative Shakespeares 3*. New York: Routledge, 2007

Chedgzoy, K. and S. Greenhalgh, eds., *Shakespeare and the Cultures of Childhood, 1807–2007*, special issue of *Shakespeare* 2:2 (2006)

Ciraulo, D. 'Fairy Magic and the Female Imagination: Mary Lamb's *A Midsummer Night's Dream*', *Philological Quarterly* 78:4 (1999), 439–53

Clark, C. *Shakespeare and Home Life*. London: Williams & Norgate, 1935

Clarke, M. C. 'Shakespeare as the Girl's Friend', *The Girl's Own Paper* 7 (June 1887), 562–4

Clayton, T. 'Who "Has No Children" in *Macbeth*?', in J. L. Halio and H. Richmond, eds., *Shakespearean Illuminations: Essays in Honor of Marvin Rosenberg*. Newark: University of Delaware Press, 1998, pp. 164–79

Coursen, H. R. 'Washing the Mouth with Soap: Shakespeare's Texts in American Secondary Schools', *Nebraska English Journal* 35 (Spring–Summer 1990), 11–15

Courtney, A. 'The Boy Genius and the Bard: Orson Welles, Childhood, and *Everybody's Shakespeare*', *Shakespeare* 2:2 (2006), 193–207

Davies, J. A. 'Charles Lamb, John Forster, and a Victorian Shakespeare', *Review of English Studies* 26 (1975), 442–50

Davies, W. R. *Shakespeare's Boy Actors*. London: J. M. Dent and Sons, 1939

Davis, D. M. 'The Lesson of Shakespeare Complete', *English Journal* 13:10 (December 1924), 743–4

Davis, J. 'Freaks, Prodigies and Marvellous Mimicry: Child Actors of Shakespeare on the Nineteenth Century Stage', *Shakespeare* 2:2 (2006), 179–93

De Grazia, M. 'Imprints: Shakespeare, Gutenberg, and Descartes', in Terence Hawkes, ed., *Alternative Shakespeares 2*. London: Routledge, 1996, pp. 63–94

Dobson, M. 'Bowdler and Britannia: Shakespeare and the National Libido', *Shakespeare Survey* 46 (1994), 137–44; rpt. in C. M. S. Alexander and S. Wells, eds., *Shakespeare and Race*. Cambridge: Cambridge University Press, 2000, pp. 112–23.

Dreher, D. E. *Domination and Defiance: Fathers and Daughters in Shakespeare*. Lexington: University Press of Kentucky, 1986

Dubrow, H. *Shakespeare and Domestic Loss: Forms of Deprivation, Mourning, and Recuperation*. Cambridge: Cambridge University Press, 1999

Dubrow, H. '"The Infant of Your Care": Guardianship in Shakespeare's *Richard III* and Early Modern England', in K. B. McBride, ed., *Domestic Arrangements in Early Modern England*. Pittsburgh: Duquesne University Press, 2002

Duncan-Jones, K. 'Did the Boy Shakespeare Kill Calves?', *Review of English Studies* 55 (2004), 183–95

Eidenier, E. 'Bottom's Song: Shakespeare in Junior High', *English Journal* 60:2 (February 1971), 208–11

Ellis, C. B. 'Shakespeare's Child Characters', *The Holborn Review* (1930), 4

Estrin, B. L. *The Raven and the Lark: Lost Children in Literature of the English Renaissance*. Lewisburg: Bucknell University Press, 1985

Findlay, A. *Illegitimate Power: Bastards in Renaissance Drama*. Manchester: Manchester University Press, 1994

Finkelstein, R. 'Disney Cites Shakespeare: The Limits of Appropriation', in C. Desmet and R. Sawyer, eds., *Shakespeare and Appropriation*. London: Routledge, 1999, pp. 179–96

Fortier, M. 'Married with Children: The Winter's Tale and Social History; Or Infanticide in Earlier Seventeenth-Century England', *Modern Language Quarterly* 57:4 (December 1996), 579–603

Foxon, D. 'The Chapbook Editions of the Lambs' *Tales From Shakespear*', *Book Collector* 6 (1957), 40–53

Franklin, C. 'The Bowdlers and their Family Shakespeare', *Book Collector* 49:2 (Summer 2000), 227–43

Frey, C. H. 'A Short History of Shakespeare as Children's Literature', *New Review of Children's Literature and Librarianship* 7 (2001), 147–56

Gair, W. R. *The Children of Paul's: The Story of a Theatre Company, 1553–1608*. Cambridge: Cambridge University Press, 1982

Garber, M. *Coming of Age in Shakespeare*. London: Routledge, 1980

Garfield, L. 'The Penny Whistle: The Problem of Writing *Stories from Shakespeare*', *Essays by Divers Hands* 46 (1990), 92–108

Gibson, R. *Teaching Shakespeare*. Cambridge: Cambridge University Press, 1998

Gibson, R. *Stepping into Shakespeare: Practical Ways of Teaching Shakespeare to Young Learners*. Cambridge: Cambridge University Press, 2000

Gilmour, M. *Shakespeare for All in Primary Schools*. London: Cassell, 1997

Godfrey, E. 'Children in Shakespeare's Plays', in Godfrey, *Children of the Olden Times*. London: Methuen & Co., 1907, pp. 99–114

Greenhalgh, S. 'The Eye of Childhood: Shakespeare, Performance and the Child Subject', in F. Collins and J. Ridgman, eds., *Turning the Page: Children's Literature in Performance and the Media*. Berne: Peter Lang 2006

Gross, G. C. 'Mary Cowden Clarke, *The Girlhood of Shakespeare's Heroines*, and the Sex Education of Victorian Women', *Victorian Studies* 16 (1972), 37–58

Hadley, E. 'Bill Shakespeare's Blind Date', *Reading Literacy and Language* 36:2 (July 2002), 75–9

Hale, D. G. '"Her Indian Boy": Postcolonial Criticism and Performance on Film and Television', *Shakespeare in Southern Africa* 16 (2004), 53–7

Harrington, L. '"And Children Should Be Given Excellent Literature": Adapting Shakespeare for Children', *Journal of Children's Literature Studies* 1:3 (November 2004), 17–33

Hateley, E. 'Shakespeare as National Discourse in Contemporary Children's Literature', *Papers: Explorations into Children's Literature* 13:1 (Spring 2003), 11–24

Heberle, M. A. '"Innocent Prate": *King John* and Shakespeare's Children', in E. Goodenough, M. A. Heberle, and N. Sokoloff, eds., *Infant Tongues: The*

Voice of the Child in Literature. Detroit: Wayne State University Press, 1994, pp. 28–43

Helson, P. and T. Daubert. *Starting with Shakespeare: Sucessfully Introducing Shakespeare to Children*. Portsmouth, NH: Teachers Ideas Press, 2000

Hiken, A. J. 'Shakespeare's Use of Children', *Educational Theatre Journal* 15:3 (October 1963), 241–54

Hill, J. L. '"What, are they Children?": Shakespeare's Tragic Women and the Boy Actors', *Studies in English Literature, 1500–1900* 26:2 (1986), 235–58

Hillebrand, H. N. *The Child Actors: A Chapter in Elizabethan Stage History*. Urbana: University of Illinois Press, 1926

Hosley, R. 'How Many Children Had Lady Capulet?', *Shakespeare Quarterly* 18:1 (Winter 1967), 3–6

Isaac, M. L. *Heirs to Shakespeare: Reinventing the Bard in Young Adult Literature*. London: Heinemann, 2000

James, F. '"Wild Tales": Readings of Charles and Mary Lamb', *Shakespeare* 2:2 (2006), 152–67

Jeffcoate, R. 'Introducing Children to Shakespeare: Some Conclusions', *Use of English* 48:2 (Spring 1997), 122–33

Jeffcoate, R. 'Introducing Children to Shakespeare (2): *Twelfth Night* in Years 5 and 6', *Use of English* 48:3 (Summer 1997), 216–26

Johnson-Haddad, M. 'Childhood Dreams and Nightmares: Children in Productions of *A Midsummer Night's Dream*', in P. Nelsen and J. Schlueter, eds., *Acts of Criticism: Performance Matters in Shakespeare and his Contemporaries: Essays in Honor of James P. Lusardi*. Cranbury, NJ: Associated University Presses, 2006, pp. 232–44

Kathman, D. 'How Old Were Shakespeare's Boy Actors?', *Shakespeare Survey* 58 (2005), 220–46

Kehler, D. 'Shakespeare, Okada, Kingston: The First Generation', *Comparatist: Journal of the Southern Comparative Literature Association* 22 (May 1998), 110–22

Kellett, E. E. 'Shakespeare's Amazons, Shakespeare's Children', in Kellett, *Suggestions: Literary Essays*. Cambridge: Cambridge University Press, 1923

Kempton, E. 'Children in Shakespeare's Plays', in *Book-ways* (1914), 56–62

Knox, K. 'On the Study of Shakespeare for Girls. A Letter to a Girl-Friend', *The Journal of Education* 17 (1895), 223

Koscielniak, B. and J. Field-Pickering. *Discovering Shakespeare's Language*. Cambridge: Cambridge University Press, 1998

Kott, J. 'Bottom and the Boys', *New Theatre Quarterly* 36 (November 1993), 307–15

Lamb, M. E. 'Engendering the Narrative Act: Old Wives' Tales in *The Winter's Tale, Macbeth*, and *The Tempest*', *Criticism* 40:4 (1998), 529–53

Lawhorn, M. H. 'Falstaff's Page as Early Modern Youth at Risk', in E. Esche, ed., *Shakespeare and His Contemporaries in Performance*. Aldershot: Ashgate, 2000, pp. 149–59

Lawhorn, M. H. 'Staging Shakespeare's Children', in N. J. Miller, ed., *Reimagining Shakespeare for Children and Young Adults*. London: Routledge, 2003, pp. 89–97

Leach, S. *Shakespeare in the Classroom: What's the Matter?* Buckingham: Open University Press, 1992

Levinson, N. B. 'Bowdler Revisited', *Index on Censorship* 19:3 (March 1990), 20–1

Lin, S. 'How Old were the Children of Paul's?', *Theatre Notebook* 45 (1991), 121–31

Lindblad, I. 'In the Company of Shakespeare', *Signal: Approaches to Children's Books* 34:100 (Winter 2003), 127–34

Lloyd, Jr., F. V. 'Shakespeare in Junior High', *English Journal* 32:6 (June 1943), 337–8

Loveall, J. 'Shakespeare is for Adults', *English Journal* 36:7 (September 1947), 363–6

Luscombe, C. 'Launcelot Gobbo in *The Merchant of Venice* and Moth in *Love's Labour's Lost*', in Robert Smallwood, ed., *Players of Shakespeare 4*. Cambridge: Cambridge University Press, 1998, pp. 18–29

Lydon, L. M. 'Shakespeare for Children', *The Shakespeare Newsletter* 43:1 (1993), 15

Magarey, K. 'Lady Macbeth's Children at School: Character, Verse, and Theme', in *Teaching Shakespeare, Proceedings of the Ninth Congress of the Australasian Universities' Languages and Literature Association*, ed. M. Adams. Melbourne: University of Melbourne, 1964, pp. 51–3

Marsden, J. I. 'Shakespeare for Girls: Mary Lamb and *Tales from Shakespeare*', *Children's Literature* 17 (1989), 47–63

McBride, O. 'Progressive Shakespeare in the High School', *Peabody Journal of Education* 15:1 (July 1937), 23–4

McDonald, S. 'Starting Shakespeare: Successfully Introducing Shakespeare to Children', *Education Libraries* 24:1 (1999)

McEwan, N. 'The Lost Childhood of Lear's Fool', *Essays in Criticism* 26 (1976), 209–17

Miller, N. J., ed. *Reimagining Shakespeare for Children and Young Adults*. London: Routledge, 2003

Misenheimer, C. 'The Pleasures of Early Enlightenment: The Lambs' *Tales from Shakespeare*', *Charles Lamb Bulletin* 67 (1989), 69–82

Moesbergen, G. 'Dutch Shakespeare Productions for Children: A Bibliography (1984–1996)', *Folio: Shakespeare-Genootschap van Nederland en Vlaanderen* 4:2 (1997), 56–60

Moore, O. 'Othello, Othello, Wherefore Art Thou?', *The Lion and the Unicorn* 25 (2001), 375–90

Moore, J. N. 'Intertextualities: *The Tempest* in *Morning Girl*, *Lizard*, and *In Summer Light*', in J. F. Kaywell, ed., *Adolescent Literature as a Complement to the Classics*, 4 vols., vol. 3. Norwood, MA: Christopher-Gordon, 1997

More, H. 'Shakespeare', *Hints Towards Forming the Character of a Young Princess*. London: T. Cadell & W. Davies, 1805, pp. 176–90

Muir, P. *English Children's Books 1600 to 1900*. London: B. T. Batsford, 1954

Munro, L. *Children of the Queen's Revels: A Jacobean Theatre Repertory*. Cambridge: Cambridge University Press, 2005

Murphy, A. 'Shakespeare Goes to School: Educational Stationers', *Analytical and Enumerative Bibliography* 12 (2001), 241–63

Novy, M. 'Multiple Parenting in Shakespeare's Romances', in K. B. McBride, ed., *Domestic Arrangements in Early Modern England*. Pittsburgh: Duquesne University Press, 2002

Novy, M. *Reading Adoption: Family and Difference in Fiction and Drama*. Ann Arbor: University of Michigan Press, 2005

Novy, M. 'Adopted Children and Constructions of Heredity, Nurture, and Parenthood in Shakespeare's Romances', in A. Immel and M. Witmore, eds., *Childhood and Children's Books in Early Modern Europe, 1550–1800* New York: Routledge, 2006, pp. 55–74

O'Brien, P., ed. *Shakespeare Set Free: Teaching 'Hamlet' and 'Henry IV Part 1'*, Washington, DC: Washington Square Press, 1993

O'Brien, P., ed. *Shakespeare Set Free: Teaching 'Romeo and Juliet', 'Macbeth' and 'A Midsummer Night's Dream'*. Washington, DC: Washington Square Press, 1993

O'Brien, P., ed., *Shakespeare Set Free: Teaching 'Twelfth Night' and 'Othello'*, Washington, DC: Washington Square Press, 1993

Omberg, M. 'Macbeth's Barren Sceptre', *Studia Neophilologica: A Journal of Germanic and Romance Languages and Literature* 68:1 (1996), 39–47

Orgel, S. *Impersonations: The Performance of Gender in Shakespeare's England*. Cambridge: Cambridge University Press, 1996

Osborne, L. E. 'Poetry in Motion: Animating Shakespeare', in L. E. Boose and R. Burt, eds., *Shakespeare the Movie: Popularizing the Plays on Film, TV and Video*. London: Routledge, 1997, pp. 103–20

Osborne, L. E. 'Mixing Media and Animating Shakespeare Tales', in R. Burt and L. E. Boose, eds., *Shakespeare the Movie II: Popularizing the Plays on Film, TV, Video, and DVD*. London: Routledge, 2003, pp. 140–53

Parry, P. H. 'The Boyhood of Shakespeare's Heroines', *Shakespeare Survey* 42 (1990), 99–109

Partee, M. H. 'Shakespeare and the Aggression of Children', *University of Mississippi Studies in English* 10 (1992), 122–33

Partee, M. H. *Childhood in Shakespeare's Plays*. Berne: Peter Lang, 2007

Pattison, R. *The Child Figure in English Literature*. Athens: University of Georgia Press, 1978

Pendleton, T. A. 'Shakespeare's Children', *Mid-Hudson Language Studies* 3 (1980), 39–55

Perret, M. D. 'More than Child's Play: Approaching *Hamlet* through Comic Books', in B. W. Kliman, ed., *Approaches to Teaching Shakespeare's 'Hamlet'*. New York: The Modern Language Association of America, 2001, pp. 161–4

Perret, M. D. 'Not Just Condensation: How Comic Books Interpret Shakespeare', *College Literature* 31:4 (Fall 2004), 72–93

Perrin, N. *Dr. Bowdler's Legacy*. Boston: David R. Godine, 1992

Pinsent, P. '"Not for an Age but for All Time": The Depiction of Shakespeare in Selected Children's Fiction', *New Review of Children's Literature and Librarianship* 10:2 (2004), 115–26

Potter, U. 'Performing Arts in the Tudor Classroom', in L. E. Kermode, J. Scott-Warren and M. Van Elk, eds., *Tudor Drama Before Shakespeare, 1485–1590*. Basingstoke: Palgrave, 2004, pp. 143–66

Price, L. 'The Poetics of Pedantry from Thomas Bowdler to Susan Ferrier', *Women's Writing* 7:1 (2000), 75–88

Rich, J. *Charles Lamb's Children's Literature*. Salzburg: Salzburg Studies in English Literature, 1980

Rossky, W. 'An Elizabethan Perspective on *Richard II*: The King as Child', *Hebrew University Studies in Literature and the Arts* 15 (1987), 55–77

Rutter, C. C. 'Looking Like a Child; Or, Titus: The Comedy', *Shakespeare Survey* 56 (2003), 1–26

Rutter, C. C. 'Remind Me: How Many Children had Lady Macbeth?', *Shakespeare Survey* 57 (2004), 38–53

Rutter, C. C. *Shakespeare and Child's Play*. London: Routledge, forthcoming 2007

Rygiel, M. A. *Shakespeare Among Schoolchildren: Approaches for the Secondary Classroom*. Urbana, IL: National Council of Teachers, 1992

Sanders, J. *Novel Shakespeares: Twentieth-Century Women Novelists and Appropriation*. Manchester: Manchester University Press, 2001

Schumacher, A. W. *Shaking Hands with Shakespeare: A Teenager's Guide to Reading and Performing the Bard*. New York: Simon and Schuster, 2004

Sedgwick, F. 'Shakespeare and Children', *Montessori International Magazine* 9:2 (1999), 21–2

Sedgwick, F. *Shakespeare and the Young Writer*. London: Routledge, 1999

Shapiro, M. *Children of the Revels: The Boy Companies of Shakespeare's Time and Their Plays*. New York: Columbia University Press, 1977

Shapiro, M. *Gender in Play on the Shakespearean Stage: Boy Heroines and Female Pages*. Ann Arbor: University of Michigan Press, 1994

Shaughnessy, R. 'Dreams of England', in S. Massai, ed., *Worldwide Shakespeares: Local and Global Appropriations in Film and Performance*. London: Routledge, 2005, pp. 112–22

Simon, H. W. *The Reading of Shakespeare in American Schools and Colleges*. New York: Simon and Schuster, 1932

Sokolova, B. '"If to Have a Lot is Not Possible": The Bulgarian Journey of Mary and Charles Lamb's *Tales from Shakespear* and Other Shakespeare Adaptations for Children', *Shakespeare* 2:2 (2006), 169–78

Stabler, J. 'Women and Children First: Charles Lamb, Lord Byron and the Nineteenth-Century Readership', *Charles Lamb Bulletin* 105 (January 1999), 2–15

Stallybrass, P. 'Transvestism and the Body Beneath: Speculating on the Boy Actor', in S. Zimmerman, ed., *Erotic Politics: Desire on the Renaissance Stage*. New York: Routledge, 1992, pp. 64–83

Stephens, J. and R. McCallum. 'Reversions of Early Modern Classics', in Stephens and McCallum, *Retelling Stories. Framing Cultures: Traditional Stories and Metanarratives in Children's Literature*. New York: Garland, 1998, pp. 253–92

Sugarman, R. *Performing Shakespeare: A Way to Learn*. Shaftsbury, VT: Mountainside Press, 2005

Taylor, G. *Reinventing Shakespeare: A Cultural History from the Restoration to the Present*. London: The Hogarth Press, 1990, pp. 206–10

Tiner, E. C. 'The Queen's "Unfledg'd Minions": An Alternate Account of the Origins of Blackfriars and of the Boys' Company Phenomenon', in P. Menzer, ed., *Inside Shakespeare: Essays on the Blackfriars Stage*. Selinsgrove: Susquehanna University Press, 2006

Wallace, C. W. *The Children of the Chapel at Blackfriars, 1597–1603*. New York: AMS Press, 1908

Wells, P. '"Thou Art Translated": Analysing Animated Adaptation', in D. Cartmell and I. Whelehan, eds., *Adaptations: From Text to Screen, Screen to Text*. London: Routledge, 1999, pp. 199–213

Wells, S. 'Tales from Shakespeare', *Proceedings of the British Academy* 73 (1987), pp.125–52

Wells, S. 'Making Shakespeare Decent', *Around the Globe* 15 (Autumn 2000), 32–3

Welsh, A. 'The Loss of Men and Getting of Children: *All's Well That Ends Well* and *Measure for Measure*', *Modern Language Review* 73 (January 1978), 17–28

Wetmore, K., J. Hulbert and R. York, eds., *Shakespeare and Youth Culture*. Basingstoke: Palgrave, 2006

White, R. S. *Innocent Victims: Poetic Injustice in Shakespearean Tragedy*. London: Athlone Press, 1986

Wilson, D. G. 'Lamb's *Tales from Shakespear*', *Charles Lamb Bulletin* 49 (Winter 1985), 14–17

Wolfson, S. J. 'Explaining to her Sisters: Mary Lamb's *Tales from Shakespeare*', in M. Novy, ed., *Women's Re-Visions of Shakespeare*. Urbana: University of Illinois Press, 1990, pp. 16–40

Wooden, W. W. 'A Child's Garden of Sprites: English Renaissance Fairy Poetry', in Wooden, *Children's Literature of the English Renaissance*. Lexington, KY: University of Kentucky Press, pp. 97–120

Yin, W. *The Annotated Bibliography of Prose Narratives Adapted for Children from Shakespeare's Plays, 1807–1998*, http://mail.thu.edu.tw/~yinwf/

Yin, W. 'Textual Basis of Lambs' *Tales from Shakespear*', *Charles Lamb Bulletin* 120 (2002), 124–33

Ziegler, G. 'Alice Reads Shakespeare: Charles Dodgson and the Girl's Shakespeare Project', in N. J. Miller, ed., *Reimagining Shakespeare for Children and Young Adults*. London: Routledge, 2003, pp. 107–19

Ziegler, G. 'Introducing Shakespeare: The Earliest Versions for Children', *Shakespeare* 2:2 (2006), 132–51

Index